THOMAS
JEFFERSON

AS AN ARCHITECT AND DESIGNER OF LANDSCAPES

WILLIAM ALEXANDER LAMBETH, M.D.
& WARREN H. MANNING

APPLEWOOD BOOKS

Bedford, Massachusetts

*Thomas Jefferson as an Architect
and Designer of Landscapes*
was originally published in
1913

ISBN: 978-1-4290-1401-4

For a free copy of our current print catalog featuring our
bestselling books, write to:

APPLEWOOD BOOKS
P.O. Box 365
Bedford, MA 01730

For more complete listings, visit us on the web at:
awb.com

Prepared for publishing by HP

University of Virginia
From Lew

...ttsville and Monticello

...in in 1856

Thomas Jefferson

AS AN ARCHITECT AND A DESIGNER OF LANDSCAPES

THOMAS JEFFERSON

As an Architect and a Designer of Landscapes

BY

WILLIAM ALEXANDER LAMBETH, M.D.

AND

WARREN H. MANNING

BOSTON AND NEW YORK

HOUGHTON MIFFLIN COMPANY

MDCCCCXIII

FIVE HUNDRED THIRTY-FIVE NUMBERED COPIES PRINTED
AT THE RIVERSIDE PRESS CAMBRIDGE MASSACHUSETTS
NO. 244

CONTENTS

ILLUSTRATIONS

Illustrations

Illustrations

PLATES

Illustrations

Thomas Jefferson as an Architect

BY

WILLIAM ALEXANDER LAMBETH, M.D., Ph.D.

Professor of Hygiene and Superintendent of Buildings and Grounds,
University of Virginia

THOMAS JEFFERSON

As an Architect

THE revival of interest in Thomas Jefferson's versatility has stimulated anew a study of his work as an architect. This study has been accompanied by an increased appreciation of his very successful architectural achievements, and, as was natural, when one is told that a man without special training did accomplish so well what others with ample training so often have failed to accomplish, wonder and amazement have occasionally grown into skepticism.

During Jefferson's lifetime, and for a half-century thereafter, no question was raised as to who was the architect of Virginia's great seat of learning. Many were then living who had watched these buildings take their form under his hand. Many were then living whose own colonial homes were the offspring of his genius.

Aside from the successful character of the work itself, the only particular ground for doubting that Jefferson was the architect is based upon certain passages in his letters asking assistance in his undertaking.

On May 9, 1817, Jefferson wrote a letter to Dr. William Thornton, from which is taken the following oft-quoted passage, "We are commencing here the establishment of a college; will you set your imagination to work and sketch some designs for us?"

Unquestionably, Jefferson sought aid from Thornton, for a copy of the original letter from which this passage is taken is now preserved in the archives of the University. Not only did he seek help from Thornton, but doubtless from many others among his extensive list of able acquaintances. While there is no evidence to show that Thornton complied with Jefferson's request, it is fair to assume that he did.

If we, however, read the entire letter from which the extract is made, and understand the character of the aid sought, we can with some assurance decide upon the extent and nature of the help, if any, that was probably rendered. Here is the text in full:—

MONTICELLO, May 9, 17.

DEAR SIR:

Your favor of April 18th was duly received, and the two drawings were delivered by Mr. & Mrs. Madison in perfectly good order. With respect to Carrachi's bust, any artist whom you may dispose to do so shall be welcome to come and make a cast of plaister from it, we have always plaister at hand.

We are commencing here the establishment of a College and instead of building a magnificent house which would exhaust all our funds, we propose to lay off a square of 7. or 800 ft. on the outside of which we shall arrange separate pavilions, one for each professor and his scholars. Each pavilion will have a school room below and two rooms for the professor above, and between pavilion and pavilion a range of dormitories for the boys, one story high giving to each a room 10 ft. wide and 14 ft. deep. The pavilions about 36 ft. wide in front and 26 ft. in depth.

[Here follows sketch]

" With trees & Grass."

The whole of the pavilions and dormitories to be united by a colonnade in front, of the height of the lower story of the pavilions, under which they may go dry from school to school. The colonnade will be of square brick pilasters (at first) with a Tuscan entablature. Now what we wish is that these pavilions as they will show themselves above the dormitories shall be models of taste and good architecture, and of a variety of appearance, no two alike, so as to serve as specimens for the architectural lectures. Will you set your imagination to work and sketch some designs for us, no matter how loosely with the pen, without the trouble of referring to scale or rule. For we want nothing but the outline of the architecture as the internal must be arranged according to local convenience. A few sketches such as need not take you a moment, will greatly oblige us. The Visitors of the College are President Monroe, Mr. Madison, 3 others whom you do not know and myself. We have to struggle against two important wants, money, and men for professors capable of fulfilling our views. They may come in time for all Europe seems to be breaking up. In the meantime help us to provide snug and handsome lodges for them. I salute you with friendship and respect.   THOMAS JEFFERSON.

Assuming that Dr. Thornton complied with the request, — and it is hardly to be presumed that he did more than this, for reasons which will appear later, — examination of the request itself shows that the favor which Jefferson asked is warranted by the request of Thornton to be permitted to make a plaster cast of Carrachi's bust of Jefferson which was then at Monticello.

Dr. Thornton being an architect by profession whose talent was to be had for value received, Mr. Jefferson was hardly the man to ask of him a real professional service without giving *quid pro quo*. There is no doubt after reading the entire letter that Dr. Thornton was made to feel and did feel that Jefferson's request was no greater than his request for permission to make the cast.

The character of the request strengthens this belief, for he says, "Sketch for us some designs, no matter how loosely, with the pen, without the trouble of referring to rule or scale, for we want nothing but the outline" — "A few sketches such as need not take you a moment."

This request carries with it its own limiting qualifications, showing clearly that he only wanted "suggestions" as to the style of the pavilions, which he himself describes in the letter of request. He in no manner indicates that he proposes to employ or to use him as an architect; but, on the contrary, the letter itself negatives any such possibility by specifically limiting him in both the quality and quantity of his suggestions, and the limits are those which would no more than balance the request concerning the bust.

Monticello : View from entrance lawn, having the appearance of a one-story building

Jefferson as an Architect

The buildings and their grouping as they were actually produced are in accordance with the general scheme which Jefferson describes in the very letter of request; hence, whatever might have been Thornton's suggestions, they did not result in any change of Jefferson's original architectural conceptions. It was, perhaps, one of those requests so commonly made for advice, which is taken only if it harmonizes with one's own ideas. It must be seen, therefore, that if Thornton rendered any assistance of any kind it was of a very general character, pertaining to the style of the pavilions, and if used at all must have been in accordance with Jefferson's plan which he had outlined in the letter of request and according to which the buildings were actually constructed. This same plan, as will develop later, had been adopted by the Board of Visitors four days before the date of Jefferson's letter to Thornton.

As the internal evidence does not warrant the assumption that Jefferson was seeking or intending to use Dr. Thornton as his architect, neither does the external evidence.

There is no mention of Dr. Thornton's name in any of the official papers of the University, its records, its minutes, or its financial reports, yet these records mention names from all classes; his superintendent of construction, his carpenters, his brickmasons, his Italian stonecutters, his tinners, slaters, and painters. The relations existing between the two men

Jefferson as an Architect

subsequent to May 9, 1817, do not seem to have been of such a character as to permit us to suspect that Jefferson regarded himself as under any serious personal obligation. The following letter from Jefferson to Thornton answering a request of Thornton's for aid in securing a government appointment encourages this belief. Here is the letter in full : —

MONTICELLO, January 19. 1821.

DEAR SIR :

Your letter of the 9th was nineteen days in its passage to me, being received yesterday evening only ; and now that I have received it, I wish I could answer it more to your satisfaction. I must explain to you my situation. When I retired from office at Washington, my intimacy with my successor being well known, I became the center of application from all quarters by those who wished appointment, to use my interposition in their favor. I gave into it for a while until I found that I must keep myself forever prostrate and in the posture of a supplicant before the Government, or renounce altogether the office of intercession. I determined on the latter ; and the number of applicants obliged me to have a formal letter printed in blank, to which I had only to put the date, signature, and address. I inclose you one of these in proof of the necessity I was under of laying down such a law for myself, and of a rigorous adherence to it. I comfort myself, however, in your case with the unimportance of any interposition. You are so well known to the President and heads of departments that they need nobody's information as to your qualifications and means of service. Where they know the facts they will act on their own judgments, and in your case particularly with every disposition in your favor ; and whatever they shall do for you will give no one greater pleasure than myself. I am much indebted to you for the pamphlet of patents. It is a document which I have often occasion to consult. With my respectful souvenirs to the ladies of your family, I pray you to accept the assurance of my continued esteem and attachment   THOMAS. JEFFERSON.

This letter indicates Jefferson's appreciation of Thornton, but it also shows that Jefferson did not acknowledge any personal obligation. It suggests only such relations as might exist between two men conspicuous in public life and not such relation as would have existed if Thornton, without being retained in his professional capacity, had given gratuitously great aid in Jefferson's architectural undertaking.

The external evidence, then, so far as it pertains to the Thornton letter, indicates that Thornton was not retained by Jefferson, since the records do not mention him or show that he received compensation, and Jefferson's refusal personally to aid him in securing public office indicates that he had not rendered Jefferson any very great personal service. At this point it might be worth mentioning that when as President of the United States it became Jefferson's duty to appoint an architect for the Capitol, he did not appoint Thornton, but Latrobe, the latter holding the office until the War of 1812.

The firstborn of Jefferson's architectural children, the most ingenious, and, in many respects the most difficult, was his own home, Monticello. This was begun in 1769 and was essen-

tially fully conceived on that date, for, while it was not completed for thirty-one years (until 1801), the foundation plan
was modified during that time in only one important respect,
that of projecting as a segment of an octagon the west elevation of the main building into the west portico. A change
in the elevation of the main story consisted only of arching
over the north and south piazzas around which he returned the
cornice of the main building. Examination of the structural
work as it exists to-day quickly verifies these conclusions.

The tradition that he constantly changed his plans after
traveling abroad is true only in respect to the two features mentioned. Yet this tradition has been given great character by
a statement of the Duc de la Rochefoucauld-Liancourt in his
classic description of Monticello as he saw it while visiting Mr.
Jefferson in 1796. The statement which has been referred to
says: " He continues his original plan and even improves
on it by giving his building more elevation and extent"; and
further on, " — his travels in Europe have supplied him
with models; he has appropriated them to his design." This
entire letter is well worth repeating, not only because of its
splendid description, but in order to show that, after all, the
Duke did not mean that the original plan was changed but
that the decoration and the detail were constantly evolving
during the time of Mr. Jefferson's travels. Here is the
letter: —

Monticello : View from living lawn, no visible outbuildings, — no kitchen. Arrangement of window and doors so as to appear one-storied

Jefferson as an Architect

June, 1796.

The house stands on the summit of the mountain, and the taste and arts of Europe have been consulted in the formation of its plan. Mr. Jefferson had commenced its construction before the American Revolution; since that epoch his life has been constantly engaged in public affairs, and he has not been able to complete the execution of the whole extent of the project it seems he had at first conceived. That part of the building which was finished has suffered from the suspension of the work, and Mr. Jefferson, who two years since resumed the habits and leisure of private life, is now employed in repairing the damage occasioned by this interruption, and still more by his absence; he continues his original plan, and even improves on it by giving to his building more elevation and extent. He intends that they shall consist only of one story, crowned with balustrades; and a dome is to be constructed in the centre of the structure. The apartments will be large and convenient; the decoration both outside and inside, simple, yet regular and elegant. Monticello, according to its first plan, was infinitely superior to all other houses in America, in point of taste and convenience; but at that time Mr. Jefferson had studied taste and the fine arts in books only. His travels in Europe have supplied him with models; he has appropriated them to his design; and his new plan, the execution of which is already much advanced, will be accomplished before the end of next year, and then his house will certainly deserve to be ranked with the most pleasant mansion in France and England.

The Duke's prediction of the early completion of Monticello was in error, for in November, just as the walls for the dome were completed and ready for the roof, a blizzard came and the freezing weather arrested the progress for another season.

Jefferson as an Architect

The dream of erecting a house of noble distinction was taking possession of the mind of young Jefferson while he was a student in college, enjoying the pleasures of Virginia's polite society, the guest of Governor Fauquier and the protégé of Small and Wythe. During the vacation of 1762–63, when he was in his twentieth year, after spending his days in study, he would at sunset cross the Rivanna, in his own canoe, from Shadwell to Monticello Mountain, and leave new grades for the laborers who were even then, seven years before he began building, leveling its summit upon which he was to erect his grand edifice. After the fire in 1770 destroyed his birthplace at Shadwell, he moved his mother's family into Monticello, which was far enough advanced to house them comfortably, and in the winter of 1772 it was, although incomplete, ready to receive his bride.

Whence could young Jefferson import an architect? These were days before Thornton, Turner, Latrobe, and Hallet — days in Virginia when such services were not to be found for the seeking nor to be had for the asking. In fact the absence of such talent forced Jefferson to become his own architect, as many other Virginians had been up to that time. But on the completion of his Monticello, he became the arbiter, the critic, and instructor in this art, and his advice and his services were urgently sought by all the prominent planters of the day, as well as by the public, for the

Jefferson as an Architect

Virginia Capitol Building was in great part his creation. His fame as an architect was not confined to his own state or even country. Monticello was visited by many distinguished foreigners and written of in books of travel in foreign languages, one Frenchman remarking that Jefferson was the first American who had consulted the fine arts to know how he should shelter himself from the weather.

Jefferson's conception was a step forward in the art of home-building. The colonists had crowded about themselves offices and shops for the conduct of a planter's business: weaving, dyeing, distilling, shoemaking, tailoring, blacksmithing, and wagonmaking. Jefferson began by concealing all these handicrafts, removing the symbols which suggested service, veiling the materials of our lower activities, perfecting and minimizing the labor in them, while he prevented their overflow into, and their hard intrusion upon, the spirit of a home. Not only did Monticello do this, but it went farther by obscuring those that performed the labor. Dishwashers and cooks, butlers and maids came quietly through concealed passages; with wood, water, food, and ashes they ascended and descended stairs which had been cunningly tucked away in unobtrusive fashion. The old-time Virginian required for his own living, as well as for the entertainment of his guests, that troops of slaves be moving in all directions with wood for fires, cans for ashes, cold water for drinking, warm water for bathing, and hot water for shaving. Such was the life lived at "The Grove," at "Brandon," and at "Shirley," where too often the offices to be performed created confusion in the main hall, the seat of the house's soul where quiet dignity should prevail.

The ingenuous ignorance affected by those who assert that Jefferson forgot his stairways would be highly offensive were not its absurdity so great as to make us know that it is meant to be a pleasant little irregularity of speech. Jefferson did not forget to provide stairs; on the contrary, stairways were the subject always of his serious consideration. He looked upon them as a horrible necessity; to his artistic sense they were extremely offensive. His attempt to secure greater architectural dignity than was usual to a home required stateliness, high ceilings, one roof — required that the ceiling should not at once with a vulgar voice tell the tale of its being at the same time the floor of a hall above. The earth itself was degraded in the Greek mind when it conceived that the sky was only the floor of a heaven above where Zeus reigned amidst his court. (See Plate III.)

It has always been the architect's most difficult task to discover opportunity in a dwelling for the successful display of his talent; the requirements for a dwelling are too personal, too narrow, too inflexible, and smack too much of the organic necessities of living, for him to secure dignity

Monticello: Main Hall; stairway hidden, — nothing to suggest chambers above

and at the same time satisfy these requirements. 'Jefferson successfully conquered these difficulties by making the exterior of Monticello appear to be a one-storied building, and safeguarded this delusion, for, upon entering, no stairway stood sentinel to announce the deception. How well he conceived and executed a piece of residential architecture ; how perfectly he adapted it to the spirit of true art and responded to the demands of his time are attested by the fact that for more than half a century after its construction it was the most renowned private residence in America.

Whence came the preparation for such tasks ? Jefferson, a twenty-seven-year-old Virginian planter, conceiving a new architecture, or ingeniously adapting classic forms to the unfolding of a new country's demands ! Such talent could not have been altogether inherent. We learn that he graduated with a fair reading knowledge of Latin, French, and Greek; that he further improved these accomplishments under the instruction of Wyeth, his law tutor, whom he describes as the best classical scholar in Virginia, and that he mastered mathematics and Italian in private study. So far as evidence exists, these moments of delving into classic literature were the only sources of his architectural inspiration up to the time he built Monticello. This home, which is still the shrine — the mecca — of the tourist-student of American architecture, to have been built by a twenty-seven-year-old

Jefferson as an Architect

Virginian will throughout time be the source of skeptical researchers in the architecture of the Colonial period. We may expect, therefore, to continue to hear the perennial voice of the doubting Thomas. And yet, whatever doubt exists as to the architectural authorship of the University of Virginia, there seems never to have been any question about Jefferson having been the real and only architect of Monticello.

The genius and versatility required and displayed in the production of a Monticello far surpass those which are demanded of the creator of a temple, a church, or public building, where the adaptations are never " personalized " ; and since, when an untraveled Virginia planter with only such preparation as could be gotten from the reading of books, he was able to produce a Monticello, surely no effort of the imagination is required to believe that he, after having been a world-character, a Governor of Virginia, a Minister to France, a traveler in Italy, and twice a President of the United States, could successfully undertake the buildings of the University of Virginia.

Monticello was the only complete piece of domestic architecture by Jefferson, but all of the most pretentious homes in the neighborhood, either in plan or decoration, embodied some of the Jeffersonian principle.

In a large package of Jefferson's drawings, which has come into the University's possession, was found a plan and

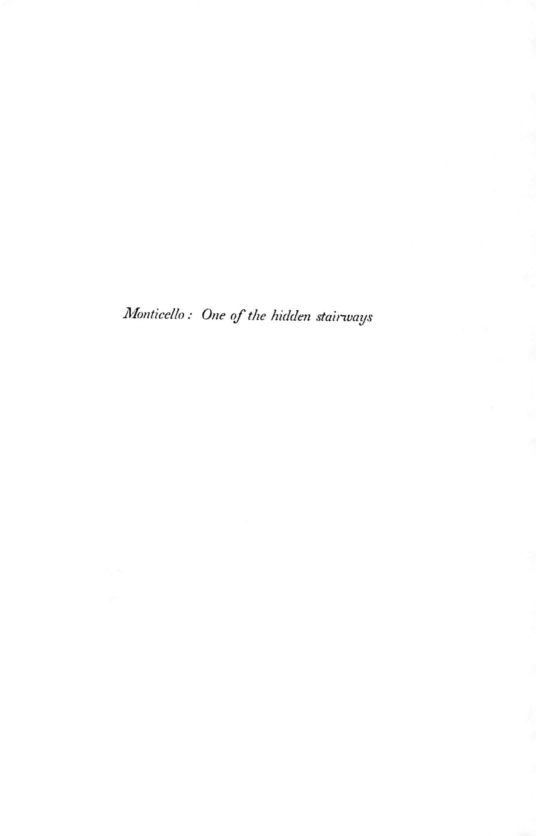

Monticello : One of the hidden stairways

front elevation of a typical Jeffersonian colonial residence. The drawing is undoubtedly Jefferson's, and on the back of it in Jefferson's hand is written "Jno. H. Cocke, Bremo." The plan, while not identically that upon which Bremo was constructed, is unquestionably its inspiration. The building is on a bluff which commands a view of the James River at its foot and a splendid western mountain view. Like Monticello it has two porticoes — one overlooking the fertile river-farm with the river in the background, the other commanding the western hill-view. The building is square, with a hip-roof with balustraded cornice and deck. The river portico is recessed and without approach from the grounds, which were formal and exacting in the foreground, but gradually in grading and planting blended with the pastoral view beyond. The west portico was more pretentious, and entrance was here effected. There were no underground passages from side to side; but, in place of these, there were two means of communication between front and rear and between one side and the other by which servants could perform their offices without appearing on the landscape. The front lawn is semi-circular in plan and bounded by a redoubt, a moat — an open ditch seven feet deep which is crossed directly opposite the portico by a bridge. There is no embankment raised on the margins of the ditch, or "ha-ha."

Jefferson as an Architect

The front elevation shows two and one quarter stories above the ground, and greater breadth and dignity to this elevation are gained by a parapet wall extending laterally to the two pavilions; a slate roof over the parapet wall projects toward the river from the top of this wall covering the lower walk-way from the mansion to the end pavilions. The walk-way grade is on the basement-floor level so that, if the wall were removed, a pedestrian would scarcely be visible to one standing on the front lawn. In other words, the rear lawn is five feet lower than the front lawn. Owing to this difference in grade the rear elevation shows three full stories instead of two and one quarter, as does the front. The west portico is strikingly Jeffersonian Doric, and if it were not made from the drawing left by Jefferson it was from an exact reproduction of that drawing.

The interior of Bremo does not exactly correspond with Jefferson's drawing, but the changes are too slight to obscure the identity of the architect. There are three features that show the Jefferson influence; the main entrance hall, the cross-halls or passages and the stairways. The entrance hall is the full building-height, from main floor to roof trusses, of pleasing proportions, with a hard-wood floor laid in squares of nine-inch blocks, dark and light wood alternating, without borders. The cornice is a reduced reproduction of that seen in Leoni's edition of Palladio from the

Monticello : Reception Hall connecting with Main Hall, and having also an entrance through the South Portico. Floor of walnut, beech, and wild cherry

Jefferson as an Architect

Baths of Caracalla, and exactly the same as that used in the first pavilion on West Lawn at the University of Virginia. This cornice came from Palladio, and Jefferson was the only Virginian at that time in possession of Palladio — a copy which he imported after many unsuccessful efforts to get it in America.

The cross-hall, or passages as Jefferson calls them, are essentially like those at Monticello in that they afford communication with the lateral rooms of the building from the sides of the main hall, and continue, with the walk on the roof of the covered way, onward to connect with the main floor of the lateral pavilions, or bachelors' quarters as they were called.

The two stairways — one in the right and one in the left passage — to reach the chambers above are obscurely placed in a well which continues to a skylight in the roof, so that they do not appear in the line of vision when all the doors are opened and a vista is secured from one end pavilion through the main hall, the two cross-passages to the other pavilion two hundred feet away.

The south hall is only one and one half stories high, much smaller, but with a Palladian cornice with soffits paneled between the modillions, and all the members in pleasing proportions.

Aside from evidences here offered confirming the assumption that Jefferson put his imprint upon Bremo, there was a personal relation between these two men extending through many years, ending only with Mr. Jefferson's death. Mr. Cocke was regarded as a disciple of Mr. Jefferson, and was finally associated with the great statesman as a member of the Governing Board of the University of Virginia. During this latter relationship, Cocke used frequently to submit his building plans at Bremo to Mr. Jefferson's criticism and seek aid. Letters are now extant attesting this fact. General Cocke succeeded Jefferson at the University as the practical builder and also as the architect for the community. He followed Mr. Jefferson's plan in training his own slaves as carpenters and stonecutters. (Refer to plan of Bremo, Plate I.)

During the progress of work at the University of Virginia, Jefferson was aiding his friend, George Divers, in planning a mansion-house at Farmington, three miles west of the University. In this structure the Jeffersonian hand is very apparent. A large octagonal structure, in front of an old-fashioned square house, with circular upper windows, a full-height hall behind a Doric portico with Jefferson's proportions, but certainly lacking in Jeffersonian detail. He embodied here the same principle of hidden passages leading through tunnels below grade, under colonnade and arcades above grade, past the doors of servants' quarters, behind area walls supported by flying buttresses to the stable three hundred feet away. A subsequent owner has desecrated the main hall and robbed it of its grandeur by putting in a floor just beneath the circular windows in order to make an upper room over the hall. Fortunately this splendid old estate is now in the possession of those having a reverence for history and a love of art, and we may hope to see the hall restored.

Monticello, Bremo, and Farmington are typical examples of Jefferson's ideals in domestic architecture and the University of Virginia illustrates his powers in relation to public buildings of a monumental character. It is certain that George Washington and his commissioners consulted Jefferson on the plans of the White House and the Capitol Building — that his knowledge and tastes were influential in the making of Virginia's State House. But it was in the University buildings that Jefferson's own mind ran free, untrammelled, and unrestrained in the field of monument.

The plan of the University did not, full panoplied, leap forth from the brain of Jefferson, but was an evolution out of the meditations of an intellect made fertile by a long life crowded with accurate observations and exceptional experiences.

By examination of the records, which are both verbal and graphic, it is possible to trace the growth and maturation of his architectural composition. As early as 1817, he had fixed

Jefferson as an Architect

certain fundamental principles from which he never deviated. (1) That the creation was not to be a single grand edifice, but was to consist of distinct yet blended, separate yet united, independent yet affiliated units; that it should be an architectural democracy. (2) That these units, despite the use of modest materials which the extent of his funds might prescribe, should in their lines and in their proportions conform with the laws of art. In this he was not flattering a vanity: he was complying with what he recognized as an obligation; for, as he explained to Madison, he conceived it a duty resting upon those responsible for the construction of public buildings, that they be so designed as to furnish models both for study and for imitation, in order that the public taste might be educated. (3) That in the arrangement of this artistic democracy—this academic village—there should be a central "square," an open court, a commons for both teacher and taught, professor, proctor, and student, who, having discarded their robes of rank in the environing pavilion and dormitory, as mere men might mingle here together. Never swerving from these principles, but, with irresistible energy, struggling against the indisposition of his time to provide for higher education, he labored relentlessly.

His first draft of a lay-out which he presented to the Trustees May 5, 1817, on which day Albemarle Academy

Farmington : Jefferson's portico and octagonal addition to the front of an old square Virginia farm dwelling

became Central College, was the same lay-out which five days later he sent to Thornton. It provided for nine two-storied pavilions or separate schools, arranged three on each of three sides of an open square, all connected by a range of single-story dormitories. The dormitories were each designed for two students. The main floor of each pavilion was to be used as the lecture-room and workshop, while the chambers above were for the use of the family of the professor in charge of that school. (See Plates IV, V.) The width of the square was 771 feet, but since the fourth boundary was undefined the space permitted of being indefinitely extended as a parallelogram. Each pavilion was provided with a garden in the rear. So far he had not even acknowledged the expediency of a structure to house functions common to, yet different from, those of all the schools. The time had not yet come when a mind of Jefferson's democratic temper could accept the necessity for a central edifice without coquetting with centralization and endangering the independence of the schools. To him the states were sovereign still, despite the fact that he had already presided over a United States. (See Plate IV.)

The study of the plans, with their notations, corrections, and amendments all in his own hand, makes it possible not only to read their growth, but the very order of their growth. The original plan which he presented and which was adopted

Jefferson as an Architect

by the Trustees was greatly modified within six months, and by the time the basement walls of his first building had reached the main-floor level, he was ready with his amended plan. A distinctive feature of his original plan was the provision for a side entrance to each pavilion, in order that the professor's household might reach their apartments above without being required to pass through the front or lecture-room. This feature was further emphasized in the more detailed plan drawn on a larger scale for the use of the builders. (See Plate v.)

Moreover, examination of this building as it stands to-day verifies the fact that it was actually proceeded with upon this plan until it had risen to the principal floor level. The rear wall of the adjoining dormitory on the north still bears the remains of the junction of the area wall of the side passage-way, and, further, the main north foundation wall extends twenty-four feet farther backward than the south wall which corresponds with the area wall plan. These facts enable us to locate the change in point of construction, and, by the fortunate preservation of a letter from Jefferson to Samuel Harrison, we are enabled to locate the change in point of time: —

Octo. 5th 1817

Mr. Sam'l Harrison, Dear Sir:

We have got one building up to the surface of the ground; and tomorrow being the periodical meeting of the Visitors and also that of our county and district courts, the ceremony of laying the 1st stone will take place. . . .

THOS. JEFFERSON.

During the two months that his builders were getting the pavilion up to the surface of the ground, Jefferson must have been busy with the extension of his plans as well as with modifications of his old ones, for at the meeting of the Visitors held the next day after laying the corner-stone, he presented his plans for two other pavilions with their attached dormitories. The two now proposed were far more pretentious than the one under construction, and no doubt the Visitors regarded them as needlessly extravagant and beyond the local builders' craftsmanship. But the Sage had anticipated this at a previous meeting held at Mr. Madison's home in Orange, July 28, and had then caused to be passed the following resolution : —

It is further agreed that it be expedient to import a stonecutter from Italy and that Mr. Jefferson be authorized and requested to take the requisite measure to effect that object.

The first University building, which was now under way was one of Palladio's lighter Dorics, which Jefferson felt could be successfully undertaken by the local artisans, but the two proposed at this meeting — one a Corinthian and one an Ionic — were of the heavier Roman type; he, therefore, felt that he would be on safer ground in possessing talent better trained.

Jefferson as an Architect

It was an ambition of Jefferson also to construct his University out of native materials. It cost him $1390 to demonstrate the unfitness of native stone, a mica schist, to be wrought into ornamental parts; he reports to the Literary Fund as follows: —

On trial the stone we had counted on in the neighborhood of the University was found totally unsusceptible of delicate work; and some from a very distant but nearest other quarry known, besides a heavy expense attending its transportation, was extremely tedious to work and believed not proof against the influences of the weather. We arrested the work here, therefore, and compromised with the artist at the expense of his past wages, his board and passage hither, amounting to $1390.86. (See Plate VII.)

These capitals which he endeavored to have cut from native stone are now, in various stages of completion, standing in the gardens of East Range.

His attempt to use local slate was more successful, for he covered his pavilions and hotels with a product that he had searched out. Here is his letter on this subject to Captain Peyton, of Richmond: —

MONTICELLO, June 12, 18

DEAR SIR:

You know we are engaged in the establishment of a Central College near Charlottesville and we are sure you will have your children educated at it. On that ground we claim a right to give you occasional trouble with its concerns. We wish to cover our buildings with slate and we believe all our lands on Henderson's and B.

University of Virginia : Jefferson's Palladian Doric on Tuscan. The first building constructed. Now occupied by the Faculty Club (Pavilion VIII)

island creeks to be full of what is excellent. We wish, therefore, to get a workman, a slater, to come and examine it and if found good, to undertake our work. There is a Mr. Jones, a Welshman who did some excellent work in Charlottesville, and who is supposed to be now in Richmond. If you can prevail on him to come, we would prefer him because we know him. If not to be had, then we request you to search out some other good slater and send him on to us, to examine our quarries and say whether the slate is good. I inclose a specimen of our slate from which he may form some judgment of the probability of finding what will answer.

THOS. JEFFERSON.

On the date of the adoption of the plans for the "two other pavilions" the lawn had not been contracted, for the resolution says "each pavilion with its *twenty dormitories*"; but before the second building was laid off in the spring of 1818 he had reduced the lawn to its present size, for this second building and all subsequent ones were laid out with ten or less dormitories instead of twenty. Here, then, in the spring of 1818 occurred his *second* serious modification.

These two buildings, making three in all, were well advanced when on January 25, 1819, the act passed the legislature converting Central College into the University of Virginia. The first meeting of the Board of Visitors of the new institution, held March 29, 1819, found Jefferson ready with plans for two other pavilions and one hotel. It was the location of this hotel which brought about the *third* change of plan.

Jefferson as an Architect

He had already constructed four buildings on West Lawn, and, in order to locate the first hotel (which was not located until April 3, 1820), he was forced to decide whether or not he should align it with his buildings for instruction or whether he should establish a new order. He decided on the latter, and on this date (April 3) we find the first record of a Western Back Street (now West Range) upon which he located Hotel "A," the building now used as a physiological laboratory. This was more in the nature of growth than change of plan, for in the beginning his scheme only comprehended feeding the mind; now, however, he must attend to the wants of the body. (See Plates VIII, IX.)

This enlargement of plan from ten to sixteen buildings, and from two to four parallel ranges of buildings gives him an opportunity to revert to his original size of space, so that the entire system of buildings from outside range to outside range measures seven hundred and seventy-one feet, exactly that which appears on his first draft. This could not have been an accident, for, as will be observed, his superintendent wanted to change this in order to avoid a deep excavation at hotel " A." Since he was not permitted to make this change, we can conclude that it is a matter upon which Jefferson was insistent.

Having decided upon two double ranges of buildings, he proceeded to draft his enlarged plan. His first new lay-out shows that he intended to have his two outer ranges also face toward his commons or lawn, for the plan is still in existence showing by dotted lines how he proposed to treat the rears of the buildings already constructed in order to prevent one row of buildings from looking into the back yards of another. (See Plates VIII, IX.) Finding, however, that the legislature, the source of his funds, was more interested in getting new buildings erected than in remodelling old ones, he regarded it as expedient to reverse his plans for the Western Back Street Range and face them away from the Lawn Range. Not possessing the luxury of a drafting department at Monticello, he resorted to the ingenious expediency of cutting out with a penknife the part to be changed and replacing it in the same drawing with a piece containing the revision. It is due to this fact that we are enabled to trace his order of change, for the original plan with the original dissected piece and the new piece supplied are still preserved. (See Plates VIII, IX.)

This change of plan in point of construction is certain to have been just at the completion of the first four pavilions on the West Lawn, and it is located in time by a minute of the Board April 3, 1820, as follows : —

Resolved, that [certain funds] be applied to the erection of buildings of accommodation on the Western Back Street.

Jefferson as an Architect

Although he does not seem to have announced it, this drawing which he presented to the Board had upon it the plan of the rotunda. It was, however, standing isolated in the middle of the north end of the commons or lawn. And at that time he clearly intended it to be so, for, in giving distances of the various buildings from this point, he says, "from a line drawn *across the lawn* through the middle of the library," indicating that there was a lawn on each *side* of the rotunda across which a line drawn through its middle must pass. The first official mention of the library was in such words as to leave no doubt but that the Board were already cognizant of the progress of the plan: —

Resolved, that it is expedient to proceed with the building of the library on the plan submitted to the Board, provided the funds of the University be adequate to the completion of the buildings already begun (April 2, 1821).

On October 7, 1822, Jefferson's annual report states that "ten pavilions with their gardens, six hotels, and 109 dormitories are completed except for some garden walls, a little plaistering, some of the capitals and part of the grounds."

On December 23, 1822, he first mentions the rotunda terraces. He says: —

An estimate made by the Proctor at an early period supposed that the last building called for by the report of 1818 and not yet executed

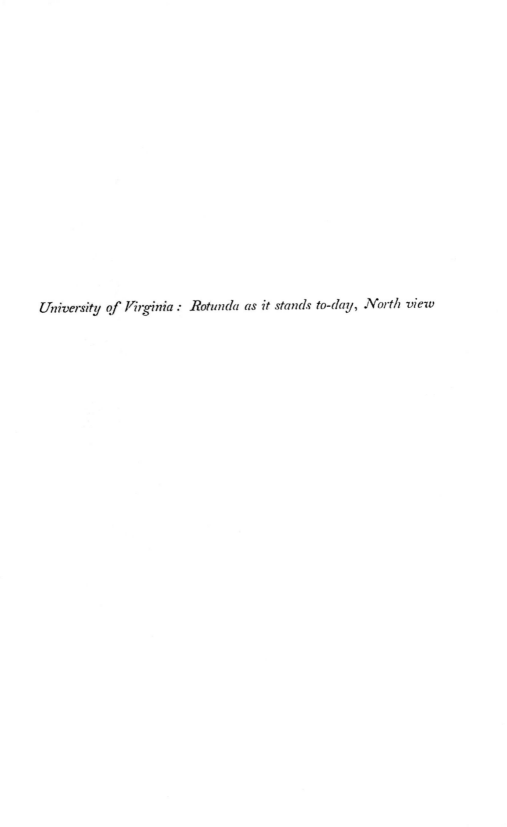

University of Virginia : Rotunda as it stands to-day, North view

Jefferson as an Architect

would cost $46,847.00, but this did not include two considerable appendages necessary to connect it with the other buildings.

On October 6, 1823, Jefferson tells us that the walls of the rotunda are ready for the roof, and that the missing capitals are now in place, that the garden walls are finished, that the plastering in the pavilions is completed, and that the lawn is graded. One year later, October 5, 1824, the roof is on the rotunda!

From February to October, 1819, must have been a busy time, for although Jefferson was in his seventy-seventh year he had in those eight months drawn the plans and written the specifications for five pavilions and five hotels; this task out of the way, he during the next year (April 2, 1821) submitted his completed plans for the rotunda. With the completion of this building his unified composition was rounded out, and while he did later furnish plans for an observatory and an anatomical theatre, they were not undertaken until after his death and then only partially executed.

Monticello, while overlooking the University, is on a mountain four miles away, and, although Mr. Jefferson was a frequent visitor, he did not come down every day, so that a running correspondence between himself and his superintendent of construction took the place of many personal interviews. A few scraps of this correspondence have been preserved.

Jefferson as an Architect

Here is a note in full:—

UNIVERSITY OF VIRGINIA, May 1st, 1820.

DEAR SIR:

I have procured you a pint of oil of our painters. If you have any of the other plans of the Hotels drawn you will oblige by sending them as it is important that the timber should be cut for them as soon as possible. Hotel A on account of the flat roof being so large, will be difficult. For that reason I believe I shall give it to Oldham. The others being smaller and consequently less difficult in the management of the roof I intend for Spooner & Perry. Hotel A if placed in a line with the north flank wall of Pav. No. 1 will have no dormitory attached to it as there is only 56 ft. from the north flank to the alley or cross street running up to the back of the dormitories. I wish to see you also before we begin the foundations of the hotels, as I find if we cut in the bank the depth of Hotel A we shall have a bank 7 feet high and then the cellar to dig out; in order to save some labor I propose advancing the buildings a few feet in the street and then throwing the street more to the East.

I am Sir your obt Ser.

A. S. BROCKENBROUGH.

To whom but the architect could this letter have been written? Every architect is receiving just such letters to-day. The problems he mentions are just the ones that every superintendent is confronted with and the answers to them are just such as only the architect is authorized to give.

A wealth of original plans, elevations, and specifications existing, some may ask what has become of the detail drawings? Detail drawings are for the use of builders. Jefferson probably furnished few full-size details; and, if he did, they were destroyed then, as they are now, by the rough handling of the artisans. There are, however, some of these preserved: One of his Chinese balustrade (see Plate x), one of a Doric cap for Pavilion IV, and one for the architrave of the dining-hall in Hotel A. There is also a three-quarter scale drawing of his column for the Tuscan colonnade.

Regardless of any aid Dr. Thornton or any other furnished, the real source of his rotunda and pavilions was Palladio. There is no difficulty in determining this fact by an examination of the buildings and comparing them with those represented by Palladio, but besides this, we have Jefferson's constant acknowledgment of this authority. His correspondence during the constructive period makes repeated reference to Palladio, or to his editors, Chambray and Leoni, in order to convey to his workmen his ideas without needless drawing. Here is a photograph of his specifications for capitals for four pavilions. (See Plates xi, xii, xiii.)

That Jefferson turned to Palladio was the natural result of his experience. He had seen the work of the few architects then working in America. He was familiar with their limitations, their untrained, inefficient, jealous, and quarrelsome dispositions. He knew personally Hallet, Hoban, Turner, Thornton, and Latrobe.

Palladio was his only source of accurate information concerning Roman classical architecture, and, while Palladio may have been undiscriminating enough to have admired most the Colosseum and the Triumphal Arches, the so-called degenerate forms of Rome's Antiquities, he nevertheless recorded and made accessible the plans and exact measurements of her purer forms as found in the Temple of Fortuna Virilis and the Pantheon.

Palladio had been the inspiration of Inigo Jones, who began an architecture which latter culminated in the so-called Georgian, a type which, although represented by some splendid monuments, is nevertheless the outgrowth of the worst that was in Palladio, a type characterized by order supporting order, clustering of columns, multiplication of pilasters crowned with broken entablatures, and frequently indulging inelegant, if not vulgar, ornament. The Georgian architecture of England was rooted in the depraved forms of Palladio — it was a leaning toward the Vitruvian, and while Jefferson also found his starting-point in Palladio, his development was in precisely the opposite direction. He refused to be led away from such types as the Pantheon, but used Palladio to work back into them; hence, while every type created by the Georgians became increasingly mongrel and depraved, every form by Jefferson became increasingly refined and classical. Jefferson rarely indulges a pilaster, only once superimposed an order, and never broke an entablature. The only excuse for care-

University of Virginia : Jefferson's Temple of Fortuna Virilis as it rises above the Rotunda Terraces (Pavilion II)

Jefferson as an Architect

lessly designating Jefferson's work as Georgian is found in the accident that during its construction a George was on the throne of England. Vitruvius describes the Roman architecture as it was under the Cæsars, including its beauties and its blemishes, its purity and its degradation. Palladio, while he saw these through the eyes of Vitruvius, did not use Vitruvius's discriminating brain. Inigo Jones, the "English Palladio," saw and comprehended only as Palladio did, while Jefferson, on the other hand, used Palladio's eyes, but his own powerful discrimination. To this is due, perhaps, the fact that the ponderous and sometimes impressive piles of the Georgian period fail to produce in the beholder that reverential satisfaction which Jefferson's simpler and purer work has invariably inspired. Jefferson's monumental architecture should have resulted in the organization and definition of those wandering and diffusive types which have characterized American architecture. The principles which are equally binding upon the designer, no matter what the style in which he chose to express himself, would have been more clearly understood. We should then have been spared offensive anachronism, ineffective contrasts, harmonies which do not harmonize, conformity non-conforming. Jefferson dug deeply and removed from the classic forms of the Cæsars the architectural rubbish of the centuries. It is, then, hardly to be presumed that he could have been greatly aided by his contemporaries, all of whom were developing either in the opposite direction or on a different line. All others were Georgian, Italo-Vitruvian, Gothic, or Renaissance; Jefferson was Roman Classical.

His method in design can be traced in his plans for the library, which as he has decided shall be a reduced Pantheon after Palladio. He says : —

> The diameter to be 77 feet being 1/2 that of the Pantheon consequently 1/4 its area and 1/8 its volume. The circumference is 242 feet. (See Plate xiv.)

To adjust itself to his general composition he has decided that he wants his columns to have a basal diameter of three feet. This being his module, one minute of the module is equal to one-sixtieth of thirty-six inches or six-tenths of an inch. With this lesser unit of measure he proceeds to devise all the proportions demanded in his reductions : —

			Module	Min		Ft.	In.
Column	1. Height of base of col. =	0	30 =	1 −	6
	2. " " shaft =	7	50 =	23 −	6
	3. " " capital =	1	10 =	3 −	6
Entablature	4. " " architrave =	0	38 =	1 −	10.8
	5. " " frieze =		28.5 =	1 −	5.1
	6. " " cornice =		45.5 =	2 −	3.3
Total height of order					34 −	1.2

The reduced diameter of the column is to be 54′ (minutes), making the top of the shaft two feet, eight and four-tenths inches.

Jefferson as an Architect

In the same manner he derives the breadth of his portico, which is to be sixteen modules or forty-eight feet.

		Ft.	In.
1.	Intercollonations, 2 diameters =	6	–
2.	Projection of Cornice 47¾ min =	2	– 4.65
3.	Pediment span =	52	– 5.75
4.	Pediment height =	11	– 8.

Here, then, in his own words, we have his method of deriving his proportions in transverse and vertical lines. Right or wrong, he concluded that these are correct for an entrance to his principal building.

Now out of this space, as a master of design he sets about, first, to secure to his major purpose its requisite share, without omitting to provide in a most economical manner for his minor demands. The upper two-thirds with its vaulted dome he devotes to his library, the lower one-third he utilizes in two floors, each containing two elliptical rooms with ample passsage- and entrance-ways. For the use of his builders he gives transverse and vertical sections of the rotunda, just as he did for the portico. Hence, we must conclude that Jefferson possessed ability as a designer. (See Plates xv, xvi, xvii.)

The second requisite of an architect is his ability to construct. What did Jefferson know of the properties of materials, of the methods of combining them? What practical experience had he? Did he conform to the laws of scientific theory? Did he correctly estimate the cost of material and labor?

All these questions can be answered in the affirmative by examination of the same building. The roof of this building was a sufficient test of his practical ability in construction. This is the manner in which he accomplished his task. He first drew the plan of the roof giving the plates and ribs; the primary ribs extending from plate to crown, the secondary, three-quarters the way from plate to crown heading in on a secondary crown, the third running one-half way, and the fourth set running one-quarter way. Here are his own drawings and specifications. He says: —

The thickness of the wall at top, to wit, at the spring of the vault of the roof is 22. in. On the top of the wall lay a curbed plate, in Delorm's manner, consisting of 4 thicknesses of 3.in. each, 22. in wide pieces 12 ft. long, breaking joints every 3 ft. bolted through with bolts of iron, having a nut and screw at their ends. On this curbed plate the ribs of the roof are to rest. The ribs are to be 4 in. thicknesses of one inch plank in pieces 4 ft. long, breaking joints at every foot. They are to be 18 in. wide, which leaves 4 in. of the plate for the attic upright to rest on. The ribs are to be keyed together by cross boards at proper intervals for the ribs to head in as they shorten. The curb of the sky light to be made also in Delorm's way but vertically. (See Plate xvii.)

Here is found illustrated a knowledge and a practical application of his ability in construction: a peculiar roof

Monticello: One of the cornices, constructed of wood, metal, and composition

University of Virginia: Detail of cornice soffit in Jefferson's Theatre of Marcellus. The guttæ are truncated wooden cones and the foliated ornaments of beaten lead (Pavilion X)

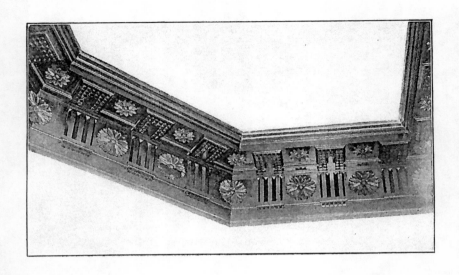

problem, which up to that time had not been solved with similar materials in America. His knowledge of the properties of materials was gained by a long life of very intelligent observation and very practical experience, to which he added scientific experiment. He exposed chestnut and hard pine to the weather in horizontal, vertical, and inclined positions for many years in order to measure their comparative durability. He personally examined brick construction in Lynchburg, Bedford, and elsewhere, and contrasted it with that of his own county, some of which he called barbarous. He directed that his brick walls should be laid throughout with alternate header and stretcher, not more than two bats to be used with every twelve brick, and that the joints should be solidly and evenly jointed throughout (not only on the surface). That mortar must be made of *one* third sand and *two* thirds lime.

His training in the management of mechanics, of laborers, and in the manufacture of building materials fitted him to calculate successfully the cost of construction. Further he had at hand Latrobe's estimate of the cost of Philadelphia building. On the back of each plan he enumerates the number of brick in each part of the building designed, even to the number in each column. From the number of brick he arrives at the total cost of construction, as is seen in the following example: —

Jefferson as an Architect

	Ft.		Height	Brick per ft.	Circumference		Brick
Foundation	3 – 0	3½ bricks thick	3	× 42 ×	242	=	30,492
Basement	7 – 6	3	7½	× 36 ×	242	=	65,340
Lower rooms	17 –	2½	17	× 30 ×	242	=	123,420
To spring of arch	18 – 4½	2	18.4½	× 24 ×	242	=	106,608
To top of wall	12 – 6	1½	12–6	× 18 ×	242	=	54,450

The whole circular external wall	380,310
Front and back buttresses 141 F area each..................	263,275
2 massive chimneys serving as buttresses....................	44,800
3 semi-elliptical partitions 2 bricks thick	108,450
Shafts of 12 columns 3 Ft. × 23 Ft...............	796,835
	315,840
	1,112,675

He says in Philadelphia they calculate roughly that: (1) The cost of brick walls as equal to the cost of carpenters' work. (2) The cost of carpenters' materials and iron-mongery as equal to the cost of brick walls. He points out that this is more expensive than in Virginia at that time. These calculations are copied from specifications written by his own hand. There can be no question, then, as to his being qualified to estimate the cost.

There remains the third test to be applied before con-clusion can be reached upon his architectural ability. It has been shown that he understood and appreciated the art of design and that he possessed the ability to construct. What ability did he have to decorate? What were his artistic powers?

Jefferson as an Architect

If it was assumed that the University group was his creation, no further answer would be required — they stand as an incontestable proof of some one's appreciative and highly developed artistic power. Such reverence for tradition, and such complete allegiance to the canons of good taste he has manifested in the detail of his ornament for the various units of his group and the various architectural members of his units, that no critic has yet pointed out a discordant note in the harmony of his theme. Always a *motif*, but never so often occurring as to appear monotonous nor so infrequent as to lose the air of continuity.

While he continuously had by him Palladio with his best types, he is never afraid to depart from the laws that authority works out; yet, when he has once departed, the end justifies the means. An example of one of his departures is preserved in his own words. What he says in his specifications for attic pilasters in his Theatre of Marcellus is highly interesting; he says : —

I have never seen an attic pilaster, with the measures of its parts minutely expressed except that of the Temple of Nerva Trajan. That temple is so overloaded with ornament, and its pilaster frittered away so minutely in its mouldings as to lose all effect. I have simplified these mouldings to suit our plainer style, still, however, retaining nearly their general outlines and proportions. (See Plate xviii.)

This is not the voice of one who dares not walk alone,

but that of one who, when once having weighed the matter, respectfully gives his reasons, to be sure, but acts.

Another example of his independent artistic judgment is seen in his Tuscan arcade, which, almost with effrontery, pursues its way along the boundaries of the lawn, leaping upward or diving downward, daringly raps at the doors of each of the three orders of his classic temples. An architectural unit in itself surmounted by an anachronistic Chinese balustrade, what more incongruous in thought? Yet what more satisfying in beholding? This is not the work of a mere copyist, but of one having within him a feeling of confidence.

Jefferson's distance compensation in the perspective of his *ensemble* was equally as ingenious and effective as was that of the Greeks who curved the lines of their temple eaves. Standing in the south rotunda portico, looking down the lawn each unit, while maintaining its relationship, is nevertheless possessed of its individuality. He secured this by geometrically varying the diverging lines in two directions — horizontal and vertical. Pavilions I and III and II and IV are spaced 89 feet, 8½ inches on centres; III and V and IV and VI are spaced 126 feet, 4½ inches on centres; V and VII and VI and VIII are spaced 143 feet, 6 inches on centres, and VII and IX and VIII and X are spaced 157 feet, 1 inch on centres. Thus he succeeds in holding apart

University of Virginia : Jefferson's Doric of the Theatre of Marcellus
(Pavilion X)

the visual lines as they tend to approach each other with increasing distance in a horizontal plane. While between Pavilions V and VII and VI and VIII there is a fall of 3 feet, 2 inches, and between Pavilions VII and IX and VIII and X the fall is 4 feet, 6 inches, increasing the drop with increasing distance overcoming the tendency of vertical visual lines to approach each other. In this manner he secured for a group of buildings the same pleasing deception that the Greeks provided in a single temple with convex or concave eaves or stylobate in plan and elevation. A section of the lawn cannot be resolved into an inclined plane nor the elevation of its units reduced to an equally spaced grouping.

Vitruvius, and Palladio after him, had endeavored to discover some mathematical principle or exact expression for the classic proportions manifest in the various orders. Columnar proportions, for example, were laid down as eight, nine, and nine and one-half diameters for Doric, Ionic, and Corinthian respectively. In like manner proportions were established for entablatures and inter-columniations. Palladio's effort was a successful revolt against the license then rampant in European architecture, but being founded only in a half-truth it inevitably led to errors in an opposite direction; The proportions of the human figure when enlarged into the lengths and girths of a giant serve only to magnify the errors and obscure its harmonies. Painters have less often made this mistake. Michael Angelo's David suffers from mathematical enlargement, although its proportions are mathematically correct, whereas the scale of his painted figures has escaped criticism. As the treatment of St. Peter's held to arbitrary rules of proportion instead of multiplying its detail to give grandeur, the units were proportionately enlarged and extended, thus forcing upon the composition such monstrous treatment as is seen even in the vulgar and exaggerated scale of its Cupids, which, like great masses of putty, have been slammed against the bases of its columns. The result has dwarfed rather than glorified the scale of the composition. St. Paul's, while more successful, endeavored to escape this fault by the superposition one upon the other of its Corinthian orders. Jefferson, as an architect, discovered that beauty and dignity in art refused to be forced into arbitrary and inflexible moulds; that it demanded ease and freedom of movement; that while it had a measurable body, its spirit is not measurable by rule or square.

Vitruvius and Palladio failed to discover a mathematical rule because none existed. The better Roman architects must have worked out for each composition their proportions in design, modelling in plan and in elevation until their critical eye could discover no offense and until their artistic spirit found peace and satisfaction. It was then, and not until then, that any place was found for measuring and for mathematical proportion. The Temple of Vesta and the columns of Jupiter Stator are the two preëminent and faultless examples of the Corinthian order, yet neither of them conforms with Vitruvius's dicta and neither has a single proportion in common with the other. Were there a mathematical principle, architecture would be nothing more than mimicry and the disciple only a copyist. There would be no place for genius and the calling would cease to be an art.

Some laws there were (and are, to be sure) which bound the Roman architect, laws with a penalty more unescapable than any mathematical laws enunciated by Vitruvius, Palladio, or any archæological student. They were laws of art and not of mathematics. Therefore while Jefferson drew his types from Palladio, he did not copy him, as is seen in a few of his buildings : —

	Diameters	
	Palladio and Vitruvius	*Jefferson*
Diocletian Doric	8.	9.2
Fortuna Virilis Ionic	9.	8.8
Albano Doric	8.	8.5
Theatre Marcellus Doric	8.	7.5
Diocletian Corinthian	9.5	9.5

Thus it is seen that only in one instance did he follow the mathematical maxims of Palladio and that in his Corinthian, whereas in the Doric of the Bath of Diocletian he diverged more than one diameter. These variations were requisite for what Jefferson conceived to be perfect proportions for his Tetra-style porticoes, which were of various dimensions. Examples of his artistic genius and of his artistic execution could be multiplied beyond number. Those given suffice the purpose of establishing his third or artistic qualification.

Moreover, remembering that this work was executed nearly a century ago, we could supply evidence of his fourth qualification — that of surveyor and engineer. The lawn itself, with its boundaries and its buildings, was laid out with transit and level manipulated by the hand of Jefferson. Architects of to-day are saved from this by later subdivisions of the sciences.

Architecture was only one of the many human interests with which Jefferson was identified in a most distinguished manner, and, whatever the subject, his relation to it was that of a diligent and discriminating student.

His talent in drawing, although far inferior to the splendid technique characteristic of the modern architect's office, and certainly very meagre as compared with the yards upon yards of blue-prints, elevations, sections, and full-size detail, is, however, despite these deficiencies, which were the limitations of the time rather than the man, clear, expressive, and intelligible. Nor should it be forgotten that the hand guiding the pen was more than seventy-five years old.

University of Virginia : Jefferson's Doric of Albano ; Present
Administration Building (Pavilion IV)

Jefferson as an Architect

Without the assistance of trained draftsmen, a handicap which he often deplored, he was loath to copy work which was injured by error or rendered useless by modification, and, as has been mentioned, this fact enables the student of his drawings to determine his order of sequence.

His discriminating selection of types, his genius in combination, the pleasurable exhilaration he produces in his daring but successful contrasts, the tranquillity secured by his harmony earn for him an incontestable place among artistic architects.

That he was able to take such classic models as the Temple of Fortuna Virilis, the Temple of Cori, and the Pantheon, reduce them, modify them, adjust them to a new setting, adapt them to a new purpose and to a different time, yet preserving with extreme fidelity the art in their lines and proportions, will perpetuate his fame as an architect with the power of splendid critical judgment. His was not the quickly grasped and drunken conception of the tyro, who with a few modillions, triglyphs, and metopes, a supply of columns, an assortment of capitals, and a few hundred yards of egg and dart moulding, would undertake the building of an institution for all men for all time. Nowhere does he sacrifice principle, practice rule-of-thumb, or bend to the cheapness of expediency. It was, therefore, with more than his usual characteristic optimism that he could disregard the critical cant of his own generation and leave the final judgment concerning his buildings to future ages. He reports to the Literary Board: —

It is confidently believed that no considerable system of building within the U.S. has been done on cheaper terms, nor more correctly, faithfully or solidly executed according to the nature of the material used. That the style or scale of the buildings should have met the approbation of every individual judgment was impossible from the various structure of various minds. Whether it has satisfied the general judgment, is not known to us, no previous expression of that was manifested but in the injunctions of the law to provide for the accommodation of ten professors and a competent number of students; and by the subsequent enactments, implying an approbation of the plan reported by the original commissioners, on the requisition of the law constituting them; which plan was exactly that now carried into execution. We had, therefore, no supplementary guide but our own judgments, which we have exercised conscientiously, in adopting a scale and style of building believed to be proportioned to the respectability, the means and wants of our country and such as will be approved in any future condition it may attain. We owed to it to do, not what was to perish with ourselves, but what would remain, be respected and preserved thro other ages. And we fondly hope that the instruction which may flow from this institution, kindly cherished, by advancing the minds of our youth with the growing science of the times, and elevating the views of our citizens generally to the practice of social duties, and the functions of self government, may ensure to our country the reputation, the safety and prosperity, and all the other blessings which experience proves to result from the cultivation and improvement of the general mind. And without going into the monitory history

Jefferson as an Architect

of the ancient world, in all its quarters, and at all its periods, that of the soil in which we live, and of its occupants indigenous and immigrant, teaches us the awful lesson, that no nation is permitted to live in ignorance with impunity.

In these words, when his plans were completed, he uttered his prophetic hope; his buildings, having now reached the closing years of their first century, are only in their youth, and an appreciative posterity answers him in the affirmative.

Since writing the chapter on the University buildings, there has come into the possession of the author, through Dr. W. M. Randolph, a descendant of Jefferson, the notebook used on July 18, 1817, the day on which Jefferson staked out his plan on a virgin hill. The notes in this book bear further testimony: that Jefferson himself used the theodolite and staked out the plan; that he had at this time constructed his square or lawn; and that he modified the natural fall into grades which would accentuate his architectural perspective. The following is taken from the first page of this notebook: —

Operations at & for the College.

July 18, a. the place at which the theodolite was fixed being the center of the Northern square, and the point destined for some principal building in the level of the square l. m. n. o.

Jefferson as an Architect

the fall from a. to d. 18 f.

*from a. to d. the bearing magnetically S. 21° W

add for variation . . . . . $2\frac{1}{2}$

S. $23\frac{1}{2}$ W

? the true meridian was that day $2\frac{1}{2}°$ to left of magnetic.

b. is the center of the middle square, and at

g. we propose to erect our first pavilion.

c. is the center of the Southern square.

locust stakes were driven at l. a. f. | g. b. h. | i. c. k. and at d. is a pile of stones.

. each square is to be level within itself, with a pavilion at each end to wit at ef. gh. ik. and 10 dormitories on each side of each pavilion filling up the sides of the squares.

from a. to b. was measured 255. f. or 85. yds., b. c. the same, & c. d. the half.

from the points a. b. c. was measured 100. f. each way to ef. gh. ik. making thus each square 255 f. by 200.

f. = .8541 of an acre or nearly $\dfrac{17}{20.}$

* Dec. 7. 19. I took the bearing accurately of the range of pavilions, & found it magnetically S. 21. W. the variation of the needle being that day 4° E. of the true N. or to the right, it is probable that at the operation of July 18, the merid. of mount'n. was inadvertently consid'd. as the true one.

In the same notebook is found an ingenious and interesting scheme for adapting his rotunda dome to the study of astronomy. He knew that it was impossible to secure a mechanic with the mathematical and astronomical training or an astronomer with the mechanical training and understand-

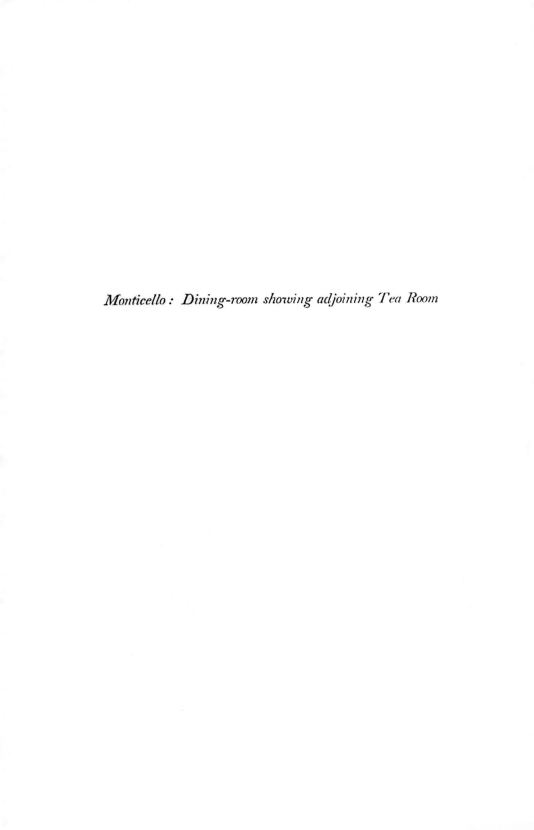

Monticello : Dining-room showing adjoining Tea Room

ing to appreciate his scheme, so he writes his directions so plainly that he insures the results desired whether the undertaker be either a mechanic or an astronomer. To do this he must have understood mechanics better than the best mechanic of his time, and astronomy as well as the best astronomer. To either proposition there are many subscribers. A photograph of the page of his notebook will be interesting in illustrating his ingenuity in adapting a building to astronomical study. We wonder how many architects of to-day are prepared to attack similar problems.

The concave ceiling of the Rotunda is proposed to be painted sky-blue and spangled with gilt stars in their position and magnitude copied exactly from any selected hemisphere of our latitude. A seat for the Operator movable and fixable at any point in the concave, will be necessary, and means of giving to every star it's exact position.

Machinery for moving the Operator.
a. b. c. d . e. f. g. is the inner surface of 90° of the dome.
o. p. is a boom, a white oak sapling of proper strength, it's heel working in the centre of the sphere, by a compound joint admitting motion in any direction, like a ball and socket.
p. q. r. is a rope suspending the small end of the boom, passing over a pully in the zenith at q. and hanging down to the floor, by which it may be raised or lowered to any altitude.
at p. a common saddle, with stirrups is fixed for the seat of the operator, and seated on that, he may by the rope be presented to any point of the concave.

Jefferson as an Architect

Machinery for locating the stars.

a. s. is the horizontal plane passing thro the centre of the sphere o. an annular ream of wood, of the radius of the sphere must be laid on this plane and graduated to degrees and minutes, the graduation beginning in the North rhomb of the place. Call this the circle of amplitude. a moveable meridian of 90° must then be provided, it's upper end moving on a pivot in the zenith, it's lower end resting on the circle of amplitude, this must be made of thin flexible white oak like the ream of a cotton spinning wheel, and fixed in it's curvature, in a true quadrant by a similar lath of white oak as it's chord a. n. their ends made fast together by clamps. This flexible meridian may be of 6 I. breadth, and graduated to degrees and minutes.

The zenith distance and amplitude of every star must then be obtained from the astronomical tables, place the foot of the moveable meridian in that of the North rhomb of the place, and the polar star at it's zenith distance, and so of every other star of that meridian; then move the foot to another meridian at a convenient interval, mark it's star by their zenith distance, and so go round the circle. bh. ci. dk. el. fm. are braces of window cord for keeping the meridian in it's true curve.

perhaps the rope had better be attached to the boom at s. instead of p. to be out of the way of the operator, perhaps also the chord board an. had better present it's edge to the meridian than it's side.

if the meridian ark and it's chord be 6 I. wide & 1/2 I. thick they will weigh about 135 lb. and consequently be easily manageable.

if the boom op. be 35 f. long, 6 I. at the but and 3. I. at the small end, it will weigh about 100 lb. and be manageable also.

While much of Mr. Jefferson's renown as an architect rests upon the success he attained in his monumental structures, he was not neglectful of obligation in those of less spectacular importance. As the President of the United States, before whom passed with the day's work a panorama of problems of national and absorbing interest, he found time to reflect upon the erection of chicken coops at his Pantops farm. He is unwilling to permit his granddaughter to erect a henhouse until the following summer when he shall have time to attend to its planning. In the construction of his own and his overseer's offices he bestows upon them the same absorbing attention as in the construction of Monticello. He is careful to force them into their proper spheres, by making the art of architecture proclaim and symbolize their function. They possess a dignity, but a dignity in harmony with their service. It was under such varied conditions that the brilliancy of his architectural genius shone. He used architecture for other purposes than shelter or gratification of the love of beauty. Always before him is the "eternal fitness of things." His structures announce their office with characteristic emphasis. A money-changer is a useful institution, but his vocation is not to be followed in the temple. He knew that the architecture of a church or chapel protected the structure and guaranteed its sanctity and that a barn on palatial lines cannot fail to jar the æsthetic sense.

Just before his death, but after he had completed all the

Jefferson as an Architect

plans for his democratic University, he began the consideration of plans for an astronomical observatory. As in all other problems he sought the experience of mankind. After consulting the plans of all the then existing similar structures, he commenced his rough draft (see Plate XX). On the back of the drawing he wrote his specifications. They are worthy of study, for they also give evidence of his knowledge of construction.

The 4 angular rooms of this drawing are 18 f. diam. in the clear & 18 f. high. This dimension determines all the others. For an Observatory the material attentions are 1. that it be so solid in it's construction, with a foundation and walls so massive as not to be liable to tremble with the wind, walking, etc. 2. That it have ample apertures in every direction. 3. That it have some one position perfectly solid which may command the whole horizon and heavens; with a cupola cover, moveable and high enough to protect long telescopes from the weather. As to height of the building, the less the solider. The Observatories in the considerable cities of Europe are high of necessity to overlook the buildings of the place. That of Paris is 80.f. high. but so much the worse, if avoidable. In the design on the other side, the body of the building is surrounded with a terras of 70.f. square, 4½ f. high, to be filled solidly with stone laid dry and compact, and paved. all the rooms of the building are to be filled compactly with stone, in like manner to the floors, which should be paved. the doors of the 4 passages to be arched in order to unite the 4 octagon rooms together, and to form them into one solid body, all the walls to be 2½ bricks thick. those of the middle rooms to be vaulted together at top, and the hollow between the hemisphere and the square of the walls to be honeycombed with

Monticello : The Dining-room

cross arches their crowns being made strait and level with the crown of the vault. this should rise a little above the top of the roof, so as to give a solid paved terras on the top which may command the whole horison. the Cupola cover should have a cylindrical body of thin light frame work moveable on pulley wheels at bottom in a circular groove, the top a hollow hemisphere, lightly ribbed and covered with tin, the two together high enough to cover a long refractor, of 15 f. for example. this moveable cover should be cut vertically into 2. halves from top to bottom, and the radius of one half should be less than that of the other, and move in an inner groove so that one may be shut into the other, leaving half of the vault of the heavens open to view, thus. over the wall of the mural quadrant must be a fissure in the roof closed with shutters water tight.

This building is proposed for the ordinary purposes of the Astronomical professor and his school, and should be placed on the nearest site proper for it, & convenient to the University. the hill on which the old buildings stand seems to be the best.

The mountain belonging to the University was purchased with a view to a permanent establishment of an Observatory, with an Astronomer resident at it, employed solely in the business of Observation. but I believe a site on the nearest mountain in the S. W. ridge, Montalto for example would be better, because of it's command of the fine horison to the East.

On the margin of this plan he portrays his sterling honesty. After having drawn them he found a scheme better adapted to the function, so he stamps upon his own scheme his emphatic condemnation in these words: —

See an infinitely better plan by Hassler in the Am. Philosoph.

Jefferson as an Architect

transaction, new series, vol II. Pl. X 1825. See Observatory of
Paris 2. Miliria. p.A; 187 Pl IX.c

The writer has had much practical experience with the
architects of to-day and has found them exceptionally sincere
in being willing to surrender the wrong and grasp the correct, quick to abandon their own error and follow another's
truth, but he is not sure that in making the transition they
would, all of them, tarry long enough to put the stamp of
their own condemnation upon their own work.

Jefferson's interest in art and monumental architecture is
clearly portrayed in his letter to the Comtesse de Tesse
while on a tour through Southern France. It also discloses in
words, as the University buildings proclaim in works, his slant
toward the Roman art.

NISMES, March 20th 1787.

Here I am, Madam, gazing whole hours at the Maison Quarree,
like a lover at his mistress. The stocking weavers and silk-spinners
around it consider me as a hypochondriac Englishman, about to
write with a pistol the last chapter of his history. This is the second
time I have been in love since I left Paris. The first was with a
Diana at the Chateau de Laye-Espinaye in Beaujolais, a delicious
morsel of sculpture, by M. A. Slodtz. This you will say, was in
rule, to fall in love with a female beauty; but with a house! It is
out of all precedent. No, madam, it is not without a precedent in
my own history. While in Paris, I was violently smitten with the
Hotel de Salm, and used to go to the Fisheries almost daily to
look at it. The *loueuse des chaises*—inattentive to my passion—

Monticello : Dining-room mantel showing concealed dumb-waiter for wine connected with basement

Jefferson as an Architect

never had the complaisance to place a chair there, so that sitting on
the parapet, and twisting my neck around to see the object of my
admiration, I generally left it with a *torti-coli.*

From Lyons to Nismes I have been nourished with the remains
of Roman grandeur. They have always brought you to my mind
because I know your affection for whatever is Roman and noble.
At Vienne I thought of you. But I am glad you were not there;
for you would have seen me more angry than, I hope, you will ever
see me. The Prætorian Palace as it is called — comparable, for its
fine proportions, to the Maison Quarree — defaced by the barbari-
ans who have converted it to its present purpose, its beautiful fluted
corinthian columns cut out, in part, to make space for Gothic windows, and hewed down, in the residue, to the plane of the building,
was enough, you must admit, to disturb my composure. At Orange,
too, I thought of you. I was sure you had seen with pleasure the
sublime triumphal arch of Marius at the entrance to the city. I went
then to the Arenæ. Would you believe, Madam, that in this eight-
eenth century, in France under the reign of Louis XVI., they are
at this moment pulling down the circular wall of this superb remain,
to pave a road? And that, too, from a hill which is itself an entire
mass of stone, just as fit, and more accessible !

An evidence of Jefferson's resourcefulness is seen in his
plan and specifications for a bell-clock which would work
automatically. This must be arranged so that the bell can be
struck by the operation of the clock machinery and yet it
must be possible for the bell-ringer voluntarily to ring it at
any hour. He secures this feature by fixing the bell so as to
prevent its motion from disturbing the hammers within it.

one of which is connected to the clock machinery by a wire and moves in one plane to make its stroke, the other is attached to a bell-rope to be voluntarily operated by the bell-ringer, and moves in a plane at right angles to the other. His rough sketch will make his mechanism plain. (See Plate XXI.) He calculates the spaces in its dial for hours and minutes, determines the length of the pendulum, improvises a ratchet key for its winding, specifies the weights for its momentum and details the mechanism for its escapement. The clock operated perfectly until it was destroyed in the fire of 1895. Will another survive so long?

It is not easy for those of our time to appreciate the many and the varied character of the difficulties that confronted Jefferson in his building operations.

The settlement at Charlottesville was too small to give aid in the way of mechanics' or of builders' supplies, consequently nearly every article for such purposes and even many of those things needed in everyday life must be made upon the farm. He taught some of the negroes to become good cabinetmakers, carpenters, stonecutters, bricklayers, and blacksmiths. He employed the pickaninnies in a miniature nail factory, which, beside supplying nails for his own use, furnished a surplus to be sold for profit in the neighboring village. In order to accomplish this he stimulated ambition by keeping in operation a system of rewards, distinctions, and promotions amongst those in the handicrafts. He sought out his own clay and made moulds for his brick after providing for shrinkage in burning. He personally investigated the native woods as to color, durability, and adaptability to the various building purposes. He experimented with mortar, seeking to produce one that would stand the dampness of underground tunnels and basement walls. He tried all manner of mixtures of lime, sand, and oils. He knew it could be done, for the Romans had left the Cloaca Maxima as evidence. His conclusions were, in his own words, "1 bushel each of lime, wood ashes and pulverized bricks brought to the proper consistence will harden in water," as he left them on the margin of a sheet of notes to his builders. That it did harden, all the plumbers and steam-fitters who have had to cut through his basement walls will testify. The oxide of lime with the potash which came from his burned wood ashes and his silica and alumina from his incinerated bricks gave the chemicals which the modern man has discovered are requisite for hydraulic cement, in which the following reaction is supposed to take place : —

$$CaO + H_2O = Ca(HO)_2$$
$$3Ca(HO)_2 + SiO_2 = Ca_3SiO_5 + 2H_2O.$$

He discovered that kiln-drying lumber injured its quality, made it brittle, and favored splintering; for this reason he specified that all flooring and finishing for cornices, windows, and inside trim should be air-dried for two years and followed by one year's seasoning under shelter. He directed the method by which his carpenter's glue was to be made from fresh hides in a pot which itself must rest in another pot of boiling water, in order, as he says, that the adhesiveness may not be lost by excessive heat, and that scorching may not destroy its light color. He made up his own mind about mixing paints and if nineteen and one-half pounds measured more than a gallon he insisted on further stirring.

Such as essayed to do the work of the architect during Jefferson's time were only amateurs, who with an itinerant habit migrated from place to place, to the seat of construction, because they were never able to communicate their ideas by either verbal or graphic instruction. They were in fact builder-architects who did not foresee difficulties, but attempted the solution of building problems only as they arose. Jefferson, on the other hand, while he never neglected personal super-vision, communicated his ideas in such exact terms, and in such order of succession, that if faithful adherence was observed the building in his mind would result and none other. No word was ever written which could be omitted, and none which was left out could be added without endangering the success-ful achievement of the conception.

In 1792, when the United States, a fledgling nation, found

Monticello : Wedgewood insets, one of the side pieces in dining-room mantel and the central piece

itself in need of governmental buildings, advertised for plans
for a national "Capitol," a great number were offered, prepared by those who were anxious to secure the prize of five
hundred dollars and a city lot, Hoban, Thornton, and "Judge
Turner" being among the contestants. The winner was William Thornton. We assume that the victor presented the best
plans of the best building, yet history records that the victo-
rious plans were not plans at all — only perspective sketches,
such as from which any one of forty different buildings might
have been constructed. There were neither ground plans,
elevation, nor sections, but only pictures which the Commissioners were forced to choose from. It would be as unfair
to contrast the work of the professed architect of that time
with the work of a powerfully trained mind like Jefferson's
as it would be to pit the pygmy against the giant.

The abiding integrity of Jefferson's building operations,
his honesty in construction, his resourcefulness in the combination of materials, his ingenuity in their adaptation, his
accurate observation, his scientific slant of mind, his versatility
in information, his powers of discrimination, his sense of
proportion, all combined with a bigness of mind and an artistic
temperament, lifted him at once as an architect from competition with all his contemporaries.

In his main hall at Monticello, Jefferson could face the embers
in his grand fireplace, watch the laborers on his Pantops farm,

observe the direction of the wind which by his ingenuity was registered in the ceiling of his portico, read the atmospheric pressure on a barometer constructed by his own hands, compare the external and internal temperature on a double thermometer from his own specifications, and observe the hour on the face of the great hall clock, whose pendulum, escapement, weights, and regulators were built under his personal directions.

To be sure it would be unfair to expect the specialized architect of our day to embody in his equipment such varied qualifications as the old statesman-architect possessed, just as it would be unfair to demand of Jefferson such splendid detail as the modern specialized architect offers. Yet out of the continuous stream of architects who pass his work in review, not one has departed without paying a graceful tribute to his supremacy. Stanford White, when asked why he did not locate his buildings nearer the old Jefferson group, replied in all sincerity that such temerity must be reserved for a more audacious architect.

It is a tribute to the profession of our own generation that, notwithstanding the development of their science and the specialization of their tasks, they maintain a reverence for those who labored under the limiting conditions of the past. And nowhere in their history have they found a figure standing for a higher truth or maintaining a nobler ideal. As future generations of architects, reviewing and in review, file past his work, they will bare their heads to his fidelity to their art, acknowledge him as the pioneer in an infant profession, and with one acclaim hail the Godfather of the American Architect.

Thomas Jefferson
As a Designer of Landscapes

BY

WARREN H. MANNING

THOMAS JEFFERSON

As a Designer of Landscapes

MR. JEFFERSON's writings, his University of Virginia, his Monticello, give unmistakable evidence of his appreciation of landscape, of the value of buildings as elements of landscape, and of the relation that they should bear to the topography and to the outlook of a site.

Had he not loved and appreciated landscape, he would not have said, " And our own dear Monticello, where Nature has spread such a rich mantle under the eye, mountains, forests, rocks, rivers. There is a mountain there in the opposite direction of the afternoon's sun, the valley between which and Monticello, is five hundred feet deep." "How sublime to look down upon the workhouse of Nature to see her clouds, hail, snow, rain, thunder, all fabricated at our feet."

In his outline of the University curriculum in the letter of September 7, 1814, to Peter Carr, President of the Board of Trustees, he designated as his third division, Professional Grades, stating that to the Professional School would come among others, the "agricultor"; to the Department of Rural Economy, the gentleman, the architect, the pleasure gardener, painter, and musician. In the School of Fine Arts he included

Jefferson as a Designer of Landscapes

Gardening, Painting, Sculpture, Civil Architecture, and the Theory of Music.

Thus in the educational forecast of his greatest monument, the University of Virginia, and in the design of his home as indicated elsewhere, does Jefferson recognize the broader phases of landscaping which at that time was no more clearly differentiated in the popular mind, from gardening, architecture, horticulture, or engineering, than it is to-day.

In Mr. Jefferson's day, the most important constructive work of his century, as well as the classics of the profession that deals with landscape, was being produced in England by such practitioners and writers as Repton, Kent, Price, Gilpin, Pope, and Addison. Of the books then produced, the late Frederick Law Olmsted, the master mind of this profession in America, first placed in the hands of his students Wheatley's "Observations on Modern Gardening." With this book in hand, Mr. Jefferson made "A tour to some of the English gardens" in March and April, 1776, made "chiefly," he states, "for such practical things as might enable me to estimate the expenses of making and maintaining a garden of that style." He says that Wheatley's descriptions "are, in point of style, models of perfect elegance and classical correctness; they are as remarkable for their exactness." Mr. Jefferson, in his own description of these gardens, intelligently and discriminatingly comments upon the merits and defects

Monticello : East elevation showing roof of underground passage (at left) leading to servants' quarters

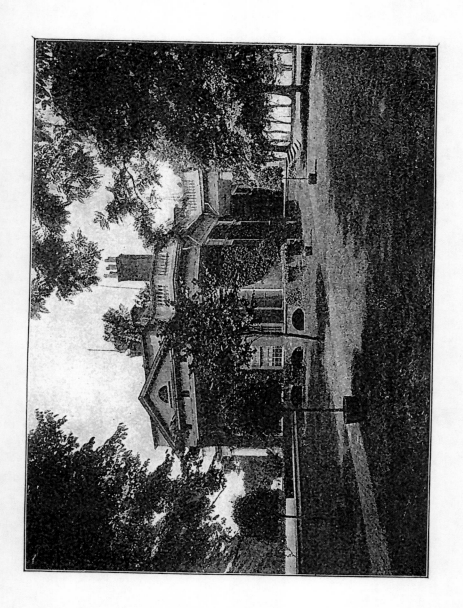

Jefferson as a Designer of Landscapes

of the English landscapes and the buildings therein, as he did in earlier notes on travels in France.

There was included with this knowledge and appreciation of the fine arts, a practical interest in and an intimate knowledge of the mechanical devices and methods, and the materials used in the construction of buildings and landscapes. The sketches in his notes of travel, his letters to friends, his minute instructions to his farm superintendent regarding the farming and manufacturing at his Monticello, and the plans and directions for the construction of the University made with his own hands, give abundant evidence of this. He was a skillful surveyor, too, for he in person surveyed and drew the plans of his own estates and the University site. His engineering knowledge enabled him to bring the University water-supply from basins fed with surface and spring water "in wooden pipes from the neighboring high lands," and also to seek for a contingent supply, as indicated by his inquiries "for a person acquainted with the art of boring for water to immense depths. We have occasion for such an artist at our University."

Mr. Jefferson's interest in city planning is also indicated in his letter of February 8, 1805, in which he refers to yellow fever as originating in low, ill-cleansed parts of the town and suggests a "checker-board plan" in which "black squares only to be building squares, and the white ones to be open in turf and trees." "I have accordingly proposed that

Jefferson as a Designer of Landscapes

the enlargement of New Orleans which must immediately take place shall be upon this plan."

That Mr. Jefferson's "garden" and "gardening" represented in his mind what we term "landscape," is indicated by the statement in his "traveling notes" of June 3, 1788, to young friends who were going abroad; "Gardens [are] peculiarly worth the attention of an American, because it is the country of all others where the noblest gardens may be made without expense. We have only to cut out the superabundant plants."

MONTICELLO

The most notable example of Jefferson's own cutting out of the super-abundant plants to make a landscape is to be observed on the road through his estate from Charlottesville to Monticello. This road, after leaving the village, crosses a tree-arched stream, then follows its shore for some distance before beginning its hillside climb. At a point a little more than halfway up to the saddle of the ridge which is terminated by Monticello is one spot which I conceive was sought out by Jefferson with much woods tramping and tree-climbing to establish viewpoints. Here the steep forested hillside towers uphill above you, and grassy fields fall steeply downhill away from you. To the right is the edge of the Monticello thirty-acre hilltop forest, from which Mr. Jefferson refused to allow the cutting of trees in his day, but which was cut, together with many of his lawn trees, before 1835 by Barkley before it was purchased by Lieutenant Uriah Levy. The edge of the forest touched just the right point on the horizon, and its height increased the depth of the valley below. To the left, a narrow strip of trees was left on the steep roadside bank. Well out and down the slope, and a little to the left of the picture centre, is a group of tall trees with branches sweeping up and out in a quick graceful curve that repeats the down sweeps of the grassy base of the knoll on which they stand. At the foot of the long slope winds the tree-fringed thread of the creek. Then come houses smothered in the trees of the valley. All this is the frame, the foreground, the middle distance with the range of the mountains against the sky. These mountains are made to appear very high by this view over the deep valley and its steep slopes, and between a flaring frame of tall trees, whereas over flat land from the same elevation they would have been rather unimpressive high hills.

The road from here soon passes into the woods, and to the entrance lodge that lies in the saddle of the ridge. From here there is a rather steep climb on a great curve through a wood with a Scotch broom undergrowth by Jefferson's monument to his home. Not far from the lodge the return branch road, recently constructed, is passed on the right, but

Jefferson as a Designer of Landscapes

its point of departure and angle are so skillfully taken off from the direct uphill road that one is not likely to notice it at all in going up. So, too, is the return road taken off from the inward approach soon after leaving the house and gardens. This down road winds around the slope and by the head of a small valley to the intersection point near the gate lodge. Both roads and the views therefrom lie wholly within the thirty-acre woods, for Jefferson reserved his next fine views for the house site. These views include three great valleys with the Blue Ridge twenty-five miles away, the course of which marks the horizon for eighty miles in view, as well as the Ragged Mountains on the south in the approach-road view.

The house is located just far enough back from the point of the ridge summit to make way for a sweep of gently sloping lawn where a large party of people and their vehicles could gather, turn, and move about. This was made distinctly the entrance side of the house. The house main floor elevation was fixed at a point where its occupants could look over a lawn one hundred and ten feet wide and one hundred and fifteen feet long. From near its floor level, platforms extend east and west to the edge of the retaining wall that holds a part of the south lawn quadrangle in place. This retaining wall extends back to office building terminals on each side, beyond which the lawn surface merges into the natural slope. Along the face of the west part of the retaining

Monticello : Tunnel connecting the basement of the main building with servants' quarters

wall was storage space. Along the face of the east part are the servants' quarters, and to each of these apartments went passages from the house basement under the platform. At the ends of these platforms were outlook points from which are magnificent views, west, north, and east, into valleys and on to distant hills.

From the point where the two roads through the woods meet near the south end of the lawn, the drive passed on a direct and level line, by the ivy-covered ruins of old buildings, then by the terraced kitchen garden on the steep easterly slope at the right, and then on to the farm. These kitchen gardens were constructed mostly during the period when Mr. Jefferson was President of the United States. His overseer states that there were grown here "vegetables of all kinds, figs, grapes, and the greatest variety of fruit." On the west of this entrance road as it passed the house, the terrace at the servants' quarter level was high enough up above the road so that activities thereon could be screened from visitors on foot or in vehicle by a low hedge.

The sunny south lawn was the home lawn where Jefferson and his family were completely protected from the intrusion of visitors who might come in by the only entrance road.

It is not necessary to go further in the description of Monticello to show this man's genius as a designer of a

Jefferson as a Designer of Landscapes

notable home estate plan, except to say that he gave as much attention to the tree and shrub planting as to other features. Captain Edmund Bacon, who for twenty years was the Monticello overseer, received such written instructions as these: Plant " four Purple Beeches in the clumps which are in the southwest and northwest angles of the houses. The places will be known by the sticks marked No. IV." There were similar notes regarding " Robinias, or Red Locust," " Prickly Ash," " Thorns for Hedges, Fruit Trees, Pecan Nuts," and " Some turfs of a particular grass." Bacon states that Mr. Jefferson always knew everything in every part of his grounds and garden, the name of every tree and just where one was dead or missing. He also states that the grounds about the house were most beautifully ornamented with flowers and shrubbery. There were walks and borders of flowers, some of them in bloom from early in the spring until late in the winter, and a good many were foreign.

The development of the home estate plan and the building of the house extended over a thirty-year period that followed 1764, yet I find no evidence of radical departures from his first conceptions. Study the topography of this section, and you will see that he selected the most commanding of its conveniently accessible sites, certainly the finest site on his father's thirty thousand acres. He clearly recognized in the beginning the big units in the natural beauty of the site, the

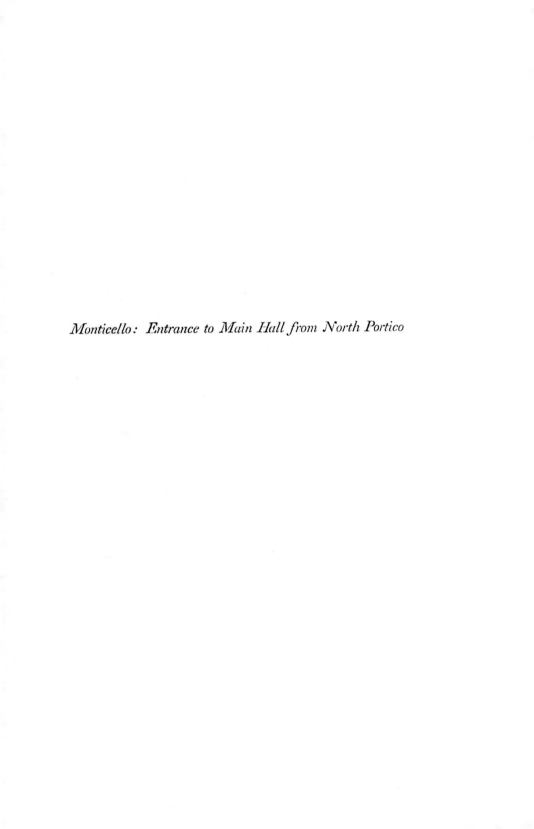

Monticello: Entrance to Main Hall from North Portico

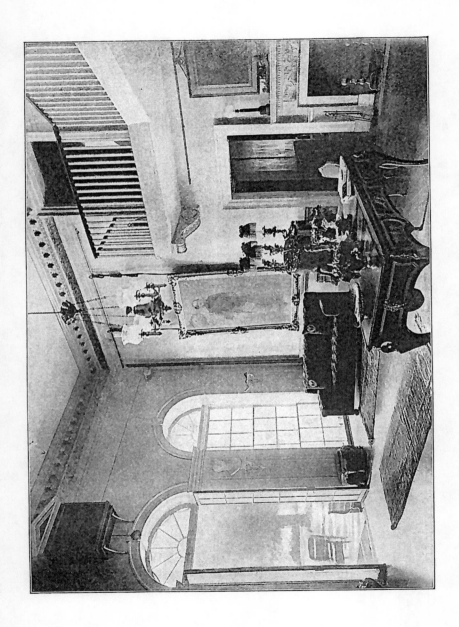

Jefferson as a Designer of Landscapes

relation that the house, its approaches, and the outdoor compartments about it should bear to this beauty, as well as to the convenience and comfort of his family and his visitors.

One of the most important of these landscape units was " the valley five hundred feet deep," the Charlottesville Valley, his " sublime workhouse of Nature." It was here that the site of the University of Virginia was officially located August 1, 1818, on a ridge, where the College Trustees had directed on May 5, 1817, that the first building should be erected. The beauty of this valley had so appealed to Mr. Jefferson, and his conception of the relation of building to landscape was so broad, that he must have had definitely in mind, during all these constructive years, the visual connection between his first love " Monticello " and the University, of which he expressed his desire to be called the father, in the epitaph which he wrote. At his home the westerly slope below the house and its south lawn were cleared of trees and laid in grass. This gave an unobstructed view of the University. On that side of the University ridge that faced Monticello, the outbuildings and the ranges were stepped down the slope to give views over their tops down into the valley and up to Monticello from the professors' quarters in the second story of the pavilion on the East Lawn, as well as from the students' quarters in the East Range. This arrangement pre-

Jefferson as a Designer of Landscapes

sented the most effective architectural grouping to Jefferson and his friends as they looked down into the valley and to the College group from the home.

THE UNIVERSITY

In the design of the College, Mr. Jefferson had the benefit of foreign travel and the intercourse with distinguished men and women that his position as Ambassador to France and as President of this United States gave him, advantages that had not come to him when he conceived Monticello's plan. This intercourse and his study of this plan gave rise to expressions that represented his appreciation of landscape and its place in design that I have referred to at the outset. While this intercourse aided him in the development of his University plan, it did not impair his originality of thought or independence of action, or his power of adapting the conceptions of others to his special problems without making servile copies. Not only was this true in the units of his plan, but also in his terms of identification, such as "The Lawns," "The Ranges," "The Pavilions."

In Mr. Jefferson's letter of September 7, 1814, to Peter Carr, he states that "In his acquaintance with the organization of the seminaries of other countries and with the opinions of the most enlightened individuals he found no two alike, each being adapted to the condition of the section or society for which they have been framed. No one could be adopted without change in our country."

His statement of April 2, 1821, with many reasons why a "Village form is preferable to a single great building," forecasts a plan which Mr. Herbert B. Adams refers to as the "modern adaptation of the mediæval idea of cloistered retreats, with colonnades and quadrangles, the latter opening toward the south."

May 5, 1817, the Trustees directed the erection of buildings in accordance with a plan presented "for buildings about a square." Four days later Mr. Jefferson delineated his connected pavilions and dormitories on three sides of a "square" opening south, "with trees and grass," in a letter to Mr. William Thornton. This letter is reproduced in Dr. Lambeth's chapter. On January 6, 1818, the Trustees described the purchase of land "high, dry, open, and furnished with water," and a plan which provided for adding to the buildings "indefinitely hereafter," "the whole in form and effect" to have "the character of an academical village."

On August 1, 1818, a legislative commission meeting at Rock Fish Gap in the Blue Ridge approved the site and the plans, with the knowledge that "one pavilion and its appendix of dormitories" were far advanced and another under way, and that the one hundred and fifty-three acres of land that were added to the original forty-seven acres included

Jefferson as a Designer of Landscapes

"a considerable eminence" for the erection of a future observatory. This observatory Mr. Leander McCormick, of Chicago, did erect in 1880–81.

Referring again to the reproductions in Dr. Lambeth's chapters, it will be observed that Mr. Jefferson in his first plan located the ranges (dormitories) close to the rear of the lawn, class-room and professors' homes (pavilions), with gardens at the back of the ranges, and then ingeniously reversed the gardens on his plan to bring them between the ranges and lawns by cutting out and reversing a part of his drawing. This last arrangement permitted a direct access by stairs to the gardens from the professors' homes in the second story of the pavilions which were included in one plan and partly built, as indicated by Dr. Lambeth. The service road and yard, used in common by two pavilions, were shut off from the gardens by the serpentine walls. Thus you will see he provided a secluded outdoor compartment for professors' families that corresponded to his Monticello south lawn.

Regarding these changes, Mr. J. C. Cabel, who was Mr. Jefferson's most helpful legislative co-worker, but whose criticism on the style and constructions of buildings were generally not accepted, says, " I was extremely happy to be informed by General Cocke that you had annexed the gardens to the back yards of the pavilions."

In locating the group of buildings, Mr. Jefferson so fixed

the main axis line of his quadrangle that the southerly view to the court was over a rather precipitous narrow valley running across the axis line with a narrow ridge beyond, and then at some distance a high hill view, really a fine outlook. I find no evidence that it ever was Mr. Jefferson's intent to close up this view and this "opening south." Apparently the indefinite extensions he had in view at that time were to be continuations of the lawns and the ranges. The erection of a modern building across this southerly end has shut out the view from the lawn, but not much of the light. This work is so well done, however, that it will always remain as a worthy monument to the skill of the designer, Stanford White.

The rotunda also was placed at the head of a valley, running with the axis line, and through which a most effective view of this structure was to be obtained from uplands a third of a mile to the north.

It will be observed that this orientation of the quadrangle was made to take advantage of the steep slopes and valleys in making both outlook and inlook to landscapes and buildings more effective, in the same manner that similar situations were taken advantage of at Monticello at the fine view on the road up, as well as in the location of the house. That this was a result of a study of his landscape and topography is made evident by the fact that he did not follow the line of least resistance or the exact north and south line. That he regarded the lines thus established as essential elements of his design is indicated by his refusal to accept the recommendation of Mr. A. C. Brockenbrough, his superintendent of construction, who wrote May 1, 1820, that adherence to the plan would require at "Hotel A" of the West Range a "bank 7 feet high and then the cellar to dig out; in order to save some labor I propose advancing the building a few feet in the street and then throwing the street more to the east."

With these references to the landscape phases of Mr. Jefferson's design and a previous reference to his stepping down the building on the Monticello side of the slope, I would have you read Dr. Lambeth's statement regarding the false perspective which he so skillfully developed in his view from the rotunda between the connected pavilions of the East and West Lawns toward the view that he had retained by keeping his "opening south."

Some of the circumstances attending the location and construction of the University, showing Mr. Jefferson's responsibility for the minutest detail, will be of interest.

You will observe Dr. Lambeth's reproduction of the original survey notes made about the time the buildings were located, and Mr. Jefferson's footnotes on discrepancies thereon.

Captain Bacon states that Mr. Jefferson wrote the deed himself for the first purchase of forty-seven acres, which

Jefferson as a Designer of Landscapes

Captain Bacon says "was a poor old turned-out field, finely situated." He also states that Mr. Jefferson negotiated the second purchase of one hundred and fifty-three acres on the "considerable eminence" having "much fine timber and rock used in building the University." These two hundred acres cost $1518.75.

From Mr. Tucker's "Life of Jefferson" (1837) comes the statement that from the spring of 1819, Mr. Jefferson procured the different workmen and superintended the building of the University. "He not only formed a general plan of the buildings, but drafts of every subordinate part were made by him." Captain Bacon describes minutely the event of Mr. Jefferson's laying out the entire foundation of the University with rule, pegs, and twine, and then immediately setting at work upon it the ten men assembled for the purpose. He also described Mr. Jefferson's almost daily visits of inspection regardless of storms or company, and his rigid rejection of poor materials. He refers also to the great time and the crowds that were at the laying of the corner-stone by President James Monroe, who was a Trustee, as were Presidents Madison and Jefferson, both being at this ceremony on October 6, 1817.

It is quite obvious that Mr. Jefferson's interest in gardens and lawns was quite as great as it was in the buildings, and that he intended to have tree plantations made, as indicated

Jefferson as a Designer of Landscapes

by his description of his square "opening south, with trees and grass." The work on the gardens and lawns went on with the building, the cost of back yards and gardens being up to 1821 fifteen hundred dollars. In 1822 he refers to the pavilions with their gardens, to the garden walls and parts of the grounds, and on October 26, 1823, he reports, "the garden walls are finished, the lawn is graded."

While we know that Mr. Jefferson made and executed his own landscape planting studies at Monticello and intended to have trees on the lawns at the University, as stated above, I do not find that any trees were planted under his personal direction or in accordance with any planting plan he may have made. The only record I have of tree planting is that the original trees of the two rows on the lawn were planted in 1840, the present red maples and ash about 1860. Other trees about the grounds were evidently planted at various times without proper consideration, for they almost wholly hide the buildings from every viewpoint.

Mr. Jefferson did, however, have definite plans for the creation of an arboretum, and in the preparation of this he was assisted by the Abbé Corriea de Serra. On April 17, 1826, two months before his death, he sent Professor Emmet a detailed plan of six acres, which included, as he states, the extent of ground to be employed, the number and character of plants to be introduced on it, "restrained altogether to objects of use and indulging not at all in things of mere curiosity, and especially not yet thinking of a hothouse, or even a greenhouse." After having "diligently examined all our grounds" as to the "circumstances of soil, water, and distance," Jefferson recommended a place on "the public road at the upper corner of our possessions where the stream issues from them," a trapezoid one hundred and seventy yards square, the breadth of which would take "all the ground between the road and the dam of the brick ponds, extending eastwardly up the hill, — the bottom ground for garden plants (four acres), the hillsides for the trees (two acres). He would inclose the ground with a serpentine wall seven feet high (eighty thousand bricks for eight hundred dollars), or for a while posts and rails. He would form all the hillside into level terraces curving with the hill, and the level ground into beds and alleys. Lastly, he would secure a gardener with sufficient skill. His source of seeds would be "our seed ships, English gardens and seed shops, our ministers and consuls," and especially "my good old friend Thouin," of the Garden of Plants at Paris, who for twenty-three years had regularly sent him a box of exotic seeds which, he writes, "I regularly sent to the public and private gardens of the other states." He refers also to securing seed from a larch tree at Monticello, and from a marronnier or cork oak tree at Mount Vernon.

Jefferson as a Designer of Landscapes

Mr. Jefferson's biographers have not touched upon his broad conception of landscape which I have endeavored to make clear, wherein buildings are considered as important incidents in a landscape to be definitely and accurately co-related to it. The importance of this co-relation is coming to be more and more clearly recognized to-day, because that profession that designs and constructs landscapes, and arranges for the location of buildings and arrangement of grounds, is securing year by year more effective results in coöperation with that profession that designs and constructs buildings.

If this chapter will help more definitely to differentiate the responsibilities of these professions in the public mind, then it is well that it should have been written.

THE END

Plates Illustrating the Text

PLATE I. Plan of Bremo, showing moat around front of lawn, and the parapet wall separating front from rear lawn, at the same time connecting the end pavilions with the main building.

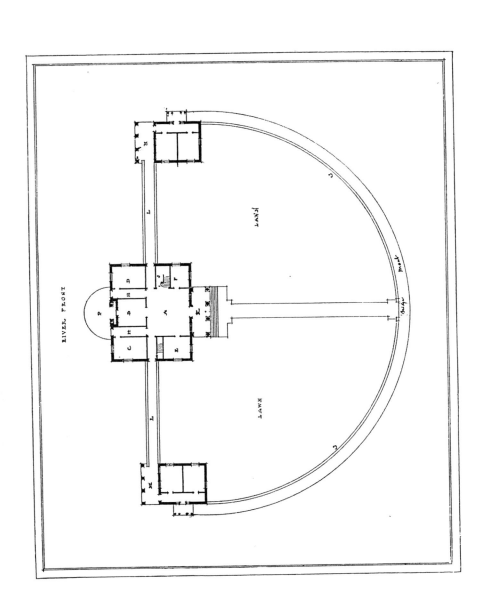

PLATE II. Principal floor plan of Monticello.

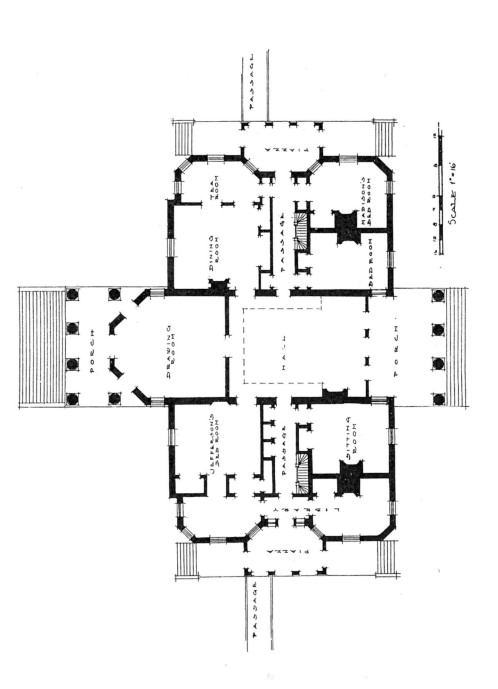

PASSAGE

PIAZZA

TEA ROOM

MADISON'S BED ROOM

DINING ROOM

PASSAGE

BED ROOM

PORT

DRAWING ROOM

HALL

PORT

JEFFERSON'S BED ROOM

PASSAGE

SITTING ROOM

LIBRARY

PIAZZA

PASSAGE

SCALE 1" = 16'

PLATE III. Part of a letter from Jefferson to President of Literary Fund, showing how he attempted to carve his capital from native stone.

another instance was the importation of a foreign Artist, for carving the capitals of the more difficult orders of the buildings. the few persons in this country, capable of that work, were able to obtain elsewhere such high prices for their skill and labor that we believed it would be economy to procure an Artist from some country where skill is more abundant, & labor cheaper. we did so. but on trial the stone we had counted on in the neighborhood of the University was found totally insusceptible of delicate work; and some from a very distant, but the nearest other quarry known, besides a heavy expence attending it, transportation, was extremely tedious to work and believed not proof against the influences of the weather. in the meantime we had enquired and learned that the same capitels could be furnished in Italy, and delivered in our own ports for a half, or third, of the price, in marble, which they would have cost us here in doubtful stone. we arrested the work here therefore, and compromised with our Artist at the expence of his past wages, his board and passage hither, amounting to 1390. 56. these are the only in-

D. C.

-stances of false expence which have occurred within our knolege.

PLATE IV. First lay-out of the University group adopted by the trustees May 5, 1817, together with specifications and estimate, for the first pavilion, which Jefferson placed on the reverse side of the same sheet.

The walls of the Pavilion are 116. f. running measure.

Cellar 2. bricks thick, 10 f. high. 20. bricks to a square foot. 24 x 10 x 116 amount to 277,840. bricks

Upper walls 23 f. high, 1½ brick thick, 18 bricks to a square foot. 18 x 23 x 116 - - - -

the chimney - - - - - - - - - - - - - - -

6. pilasters - - - - - - - - - - - - - - -

the necessary Appendices, passage &c. estimate (61 f. run measure, 9 f. high, 1. brick thick)

each Chamber has 36 f. of wall, running measure.

if 10 f. high & 1. brick thick. 10 x 12 x 36. amount to 4320. bricks.

one half of the chimney (one chimney serving 2. chambers)

2. pilasters

out of the walls be ½ br. thick there must be added - - -

20. chambers to each pavilion therefore will require - -

and a Pavilion with it's 20. chambers will take - - -

The method of making a rough estimate in Philadelphia, of the cost of a brick dwelling house, finished in a plain way, is to reckon the carpenter's work equal to the cost of the brick walls, and the car -penter's materials and the ironmongery equal also to the cost of the brickwalls. but in the present case the carpenter's materials (timber) will either be given, or cost very little, and the ironmongery will be little; I believe therefore the cost of the Carpenter's materials & iron -mongery need not be stated at more than half the cost of the brickwalls. reckoning brickwork therefore at 10. D. the thousand, the cost may be roughly estimated as follows.

Pavilion. walls 817.50 Carpenter's work 817.50 Carpenter's materials & ironmongery 408.75

Appendices. on the same principles.

Chambers. each on the same principles costing 131. 15, 20 chambers will cost - - -

the establishment of a Pavilion & 20. Chambers for each professorship will cost therefore

The estimate above is made on the supposition that each Professor, with his pupils (suppose 20) shall have separate Pavilion of 26 by 34 f. outside, & 24 by 32 f. inside measure: in which the ground-floor (9½ f. pitch in clear) is to be the schoolroom, and 2. rooms above (10 f. pitch clear) and a kitchen & cellar below (7 f. pitch clear) for the use of the Professor. on each side of the Pavilion are to be 10. chambers, 10. by 14 f. in the clear 9½ f. pitch, with a fireplace in each, for the students. the whole to communicate by a colonnade of 8 f. width in the clear. the pilasters of brick to be generally 5½ f. apart from center to center.

The kitchen will be 24. by 14. on the back of the building adjacent to the chimney, with a window looking back: the cellar 24. by 10. also, on the front side, with a window looking into the colonnade. of the Pavilions front -ing South should have their stair-case on the East: those fronting East or West should have the stairs at the North end of the building, that the windows may open to the pleasantest breeze.

Back-yards, gardens, stables, houselots &c. to be in the grounds adjacent to the Square, or the outside.

PLATE V. The upper half of the cut shows an elevation of the first story of the first pavilion. The Tuscan arches on which Jefferson superimposed his doric of Palladio. The lower half shows the plan of the first pavilion, with its side entrance for the Professor's household, also showing the plan of adjacent dormitories, with the Tuscan arcade in front of them.

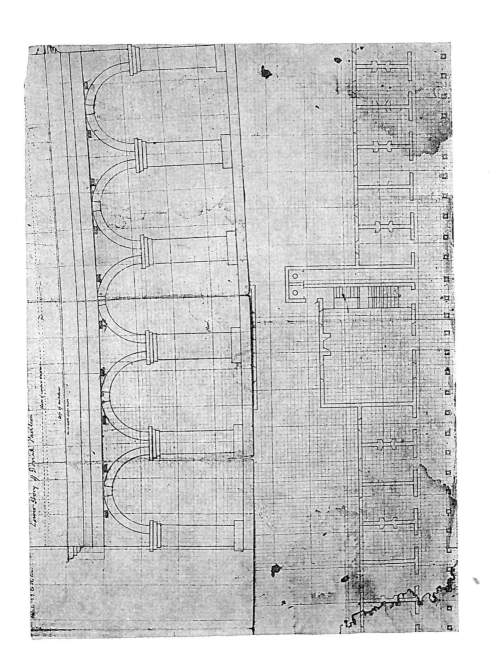

Lower Story of Deputed Pavilion

PLATE VI. A page of Jefferson's pocket notebook containing notes for his first pavilion or the dormitories and Tuscan colonnade attached thereto.

Pavilion no. S.VII.
The upper story of the ~~Doric~~ Pavilion to be Done, with a Pedimn
~~front~~ & Portico of 6. columns. I assume 16. I for their diam.
because the laws of the order will then give us ~~pulls~~ correspond.
with the dimensions of the building proposed.

			9
the base	mo. ' f '	projects 10 = 2.666	0 - 3/4 — .2
	0-30 = 0-8		1— .266
shaft	9-0 = 9-4	+ 9	1 1/4 — .333
capital	0-30=0-8		1 1/3 — .355
	——————— = 10-8		1 1/2 — .4
	8-0		1 3/4 — .466
	mo. '		2 1/4 — .6
architrave	0-30 = 0.8		2 2/3 — .711
frize	- 45 = 1.		3 — .8
cornice	- 38 = 0-10.133		3 1/4 — .866
	——————— = 2-6		3 1/3 — .888
	1-53 13-2		3 1/2 — .933
			3 3/4 — 1.

the axes of the columns ~~are~~ 10.66 within the surface of the arch below
a triglyph & metop. ~~are~~ 20.9.

	9 + 9	
from center to center of column, & trigl. = 80 = 6-8		4 — 1.066
5. columns & intercolns 33-4		4 1/2 — 1.2
+ ~~these~~ 3 diam. 53' = 1-1.866 [say 52 1/3 = 1 2]		4 3/4 — 1.266
breadth of brick work at top 34-5.866 [say 34 6]		5 — 1.333
+ able projn = 2×50' 2-2.666		6 — 1.6
whole span. of pediment 36-8.533 [say 36 9 666]		6 1/2 — 1.733
2/9 of which is 8- 1.096 [say 8-1 9260 or 8 2]		6 2/3 — 1.777
		6 3/4 — 1.8

	9 ' + 9	
an intercolonnation is 80 — 16 = 64 = 5-4		7 1/2 — 2.
		7 3/4 — 2.066
the arches under the portico must be of course 80.9		8 — 2.133
from center to center of pier.		8 3/4 — 2.333
give 1/4 of this to the pier, to wit 20 9		9 — 2.4
3/4 to the opening of the arch 60 9. 9 ' + 9		10 — 2.666
give 1 3/4 squares to the height of the arch 105 = 8-9		10 1/2 — 2.8
which leaves between the void of the arch, & the		11 — 2.933
bottom of the Tuscan ontabl. space for an archi-		11 1/2 — 3.066
-trave of 26' = 6.933 9.		12 3/4 — 3.4
		14 1/2 — 3.866
the impost should be in height 35 = 9.33 ' 9		15 — 4.
it's projection 16 = 4.266 broken into 2. of 2.122		16 1/2 — 4.4
the thickness of the piers is 60' = 16 9. that ~~they~~		26 — 6.933
may correspond with the pilasters of the ~~columns~~		27 — 7.190
the height of their base the same as those of the pilasters!		28 — 7.466
the floor of the portico on a level with ~~lower~~ of dormitory		29 — 7.733
it must decline from the building towds the front.		30 — 8.
the ~~guttered~~ joists must discharge their water thro the		30 1/2 — 8.133
~~cornice~~ of the Tuscan by projecting 1. 9. beyond		33 1/2 — 8.933
it's 1st face, the opening to be masked by a thin squar		35 — 9.333
board, cutting the mouldings of the architrave as the		35 1/2 — 9.466
keystone of an arch does		36 — 9.6
the secret rooflets must correspond with the ~~piers and~~ arches so as		36 2/3 — 9.777
that the guttered joist may fall over their centers		39 — 10.4
the floor of the lecturing room to be 2. above ye of arcade		39 1/2 — 10.533
To admit some light and air into the office below.		40 — 10.666
the floor of the offices 6.f. below the surface of the ground.		45 — 12.
		60 — 16.
		64 1/2 — 17.2
		68 — 18.133

Dormitories to No. VII

The Covered way in front of the whole range of buildings is
to be Tuscan, with columns of brick, roughcast. their diam. 16 I.
but in front of the Pavilions to be arches, in order to support
the Columns of the Porticos above more solidly.

Tuscan. a socle of 12 I. under the whole colonnade to raise
it's floor above the ground, & to
project beyond the base 10' = 2.67

shaft. base 8. 9	1' = .266
just .96.	1½ = .399
capital 8. = 112 = 9-4	2 = .533
	2½ = .666
architrave . . 9.333	3 = .799
frize . . . 6.933	3½ = .933
cornice - . 11.599 —27.866 = 2×3.86	4 = 1.066
139.866 = 11-7.86	5. = 1.333
projection of cornice 43½ = 11.599	5½ = 1.466
	7½ = 1.999

each Dormitory being 11 f. from center to center   8½ = 2.266
of it's partition walls, there will be 2. inter-   9 = 2.399
-colonnations of 4 f. 2 I. each to every Dormi   10 = 2.665
-tory. to wit. 2. intercolns - - - 8-4   12½ = 3.333
      2 pilaston columns. 2-8   17½ = 4.666
            11—   22½ = 5.999

the centers of the intercolns must answer to   24. = 6.399
the centers of the doors & of the partition walls.   26 = 6.933
the cover of the Dormitories & colonnade to be   27 = 7.199
serrite rooflets of 2-9 span, the joists being 4½ from   27½ = 7.266
center to center, declining from front to back   30 = 8.
so that the guttered joist shall discharge all   32 = 8.533
it's water on the backside of the building.   35 = 9.333
these rooflets with their joists & terras floor to   43½ = 11.599
occupy the thickness of the entablature, 2-4.   45 = 12.
the columns being of brick, their bases are 30=8I   52½ = 13.933
high, and project 10' = 2.67 I.   54⅙ = 14.466
the capital of brick 30'= 8I. high, project. 10'= 2.67   60. = 16.
the column diminishes to 45' = 12 I.   66. = 17.599

the floors of the dormitories to be 1 f. above that of the arcade colonnade
the floor of the lecturing room   2 f. above that of the colonnade.

Pavilion No. S. VII.

The upper story of the [   ] Pavilion to be Doric, with a Pediment front & Portico of 6. columns. I assume 16 I for their diam. because the laws of the order will then give us pulls correspond. with the dimensions of the building proposed.

the base   mo. ' +   0-30 = 0-8   projects 10 = 2.666
shaft   3 - 0 = 9 - 4
capital   0 - 30 = 0 - 8   + I
           ——————— = 10 - 8
           0 - 0
architrave   mo. '   0 - 30 = 0 - 8
frieze   .   .   45 = 1 .
cornice   .   .   38 = 0 - 10.133
          ——————————   = 2 - 6
          1 - 53   13 - 2

the axes of the column are 10.66 within the surface of the arch below
a triglyph & metop before 20. I.   I   + I
from center to center of columns & trigl. = 80 = 6 - 8
5. columns & intercolns   33 - 4
+ 4 nom. I diam . 52' =   1 - 1.066   [say 52½ = I 2]
breadth of brick work at top   34 - 5.866   [say 34.6]
+ double projn = 2×50'   2 - 2.666   [say 36 9.666]
whole span. of pediment   36 - 8.533   [say 36 9.666]   + I
2/9 of which is   8 - 1.096   [say 8 - 1.926 or 8. 2]
————————————————————————
an intercolonnation is 80 — 16 = 64 = 5 - 4
the arches under the portico must be of course 80. I.
from center to center of pier.
    give ½ of this to the pier, to wit 20 I
    ⅔ to the opening of the arch 60 I.   I   + I
    give 1¼ squares to the height of the arch 105 = 6 - 9
    which leaves between the void of the arch, & the
    bottom of the Tuscan entabl. space for an archi-
    -trave of 26' = 6.933 I.
the impost should be in height 35 = 9.33'   ' I
    it's projection 16' = 4.266 broken into 3. & 1.422
the thickness of the piers is 60' = 16 I, that same
    may correspond with the pilasters of the columns
the height of their base the same as those of the pilasters
the floor of the portico on a level with lower of dormitory
    it must decline from the building towds the front.
the cut lugged joists must discharge their water thro the
    [   ] of the Tuscan by projecting 1. I. beyond
    it's 1st face. the opening to be masked by a thin square
    board, cutting the mouldings of the architrave as the
    keystone of an arch does.
                                    princ. and
the secret soffits must correspond with the arches so as
    that the gutter joist may fall over their centers
the floor of the lackning room to be 2. f above ye arcades
    to admit some light and air into the office below.
the floor of the office 6 f. below the surface of the ground.

PLATE VII. University of Virginia. A page from Jefferson's pocket note-book showing his plan for adapting the ceiling of his rotunda to the purpose of teaching astronomy.

The concave cieling of the Rotunda is proposed to be painted sky. blue and spangled with gilt stars in their position and magnitude copied exactly from any selected hemisphere of our latitude. a seat for the Operator movable and fixable at any point in the concave, will be necessary, and means of giving to every starilicated position.

Machinery for moving the Operator.
a.b.c.d.e.f.g. is the inner surface of 90° of the dome
o.p. is a boom, a white oak sappling of proper strength, it's heal working on the center of the sphere, by a compound joint admitting motion in any direction, like a ball and socket.
p.q.r. is a rope suspending the small end of the boom, passing over a pulley in the zenith at q. and hanging down to the floor, by which it may be raised or lowered to any altitude.
at p. a common saddle, with stirrups is fixed for the seat of the operator and seated on that he may, by the rope be presented to any point of the concave.
        Machinery for locating the stars.
a.s. is the horizontal plane passing thro the center of the sphere o.
an annular ream of wood, of the radius of the sphere must be laid on this plane and graduated to degrees and minutes, the graduation beginning in the North rhomb of the place. call this the circle of amplitude.   a moveable meridian of 90° must then be provided. it's upper end moving on a pivot in the zenith, it's lower end resting on the circle of amplitude, this must be made of thin flexible white oak like the ream of a cotton spinning wheel, and fixed in it's curvature, in a true quadrant by a similar lath of white oak as it's chord a.n. their ends made fast together by clamps.
this flexible meridian may be of 6.I. breadth, and graduated to degrees and minutes.
the zenith distance and amplitude of every star must then be obtained from the astronomical tables. place the foot of the moveable meridian in that of the North rhomb of the place, and the polar star at it's zenith distance, and so of every other star of that meridian. then move the foot to another meridian at a convenient interval, mark it's stars by their zenith distance, and so go round the circle

bb. ci. dh. el. fm. are braces of window cord for keeping the meridian in it's true curve.
        perhaps the rope had better be attached to the boom at s. instead of p. to be out of the eye of the operator. perhaps also the chord board an had better present it's edge to the meridian than it's side.
        if the meridian ark and it's chord be 6.I. wide & ½ I. thick they will weigh about 135. lb. and consequently be easily manageable.
        if the boom op. be 35.f. long, 6.I. at the but & 3.I. at the small end, it will weigh about 100. lb. and be manageable also

PLATE VIII. First plan of the double ranges of buildings showing how
Jefferson cut out with his pen-knife the piece which contained
West Range facing the lawn. In this plate the original piece
is replaced.

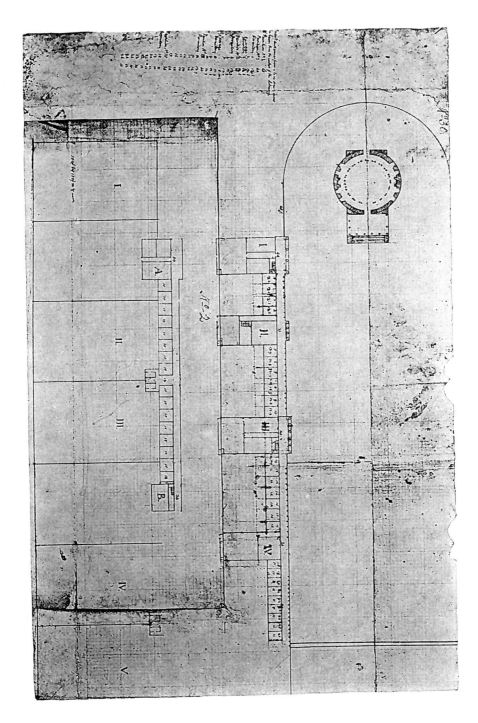

PLATE IX. The same original plan with the piece of paper laid in place containing the revision — the new range now facing away from the lawn.

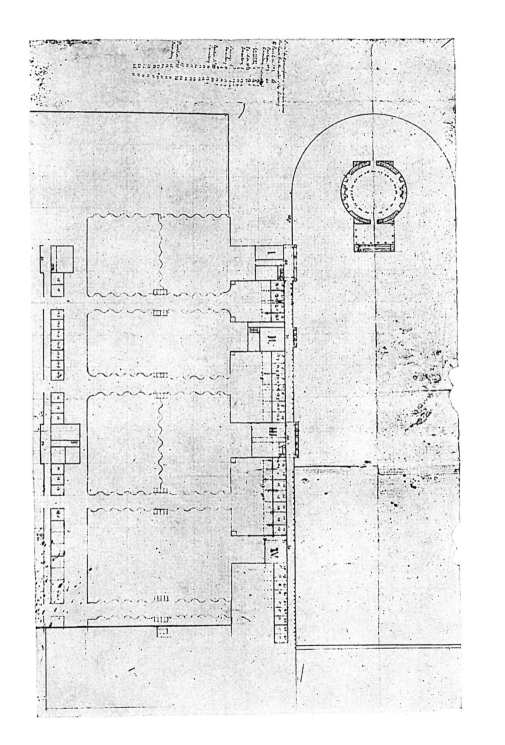

PLATE X. One of Jefferson's detail drawings for the railing above his Tuscan arcade.

railing of Terraces.

whole height from floor 2. 9
total upper rail   4
     ballusters show   18.
     lower rail   4
     opening at bottom   1
                        ──
                        27

ballusters from center to center 4.3.

PLATE XI. Jefferson's specifications for marble capitals he is ordering through Thomas Appleton at Sivorno, Italy.

Specification of the Corinthian & Ionic capitels wanting for the University

1. Corinthian capitels for columns whose inferior diameter is 26. I. English, & its
diminished diam. 25 2/10 I. To be copied exactly from the Corinthian capitel
of Palladio, as given in his 1st Book wherein he treats of the orders in general
and its 17th chapter in which he describes the Corinthian capitel particularly,
the drawing of which is in plate XXVI. Leoni's edition publ.d in London 1721.

for Pavilion Nº. II. West

2. Corinthian capitels for columns whose inferior diam. is 24. I. & diminished diameter 20 8/10 I. to be copied from those of the Thermae of Diocletian at Rome.
this is not in Palladio, but is given by other authors, and particularly by
Errard and Chambray in their Parallele de l'Architecture antique et
moderne. Paris 1766. pa. 79. plate 33. I should prefer however to have only the
ovolo of the abacus carved, and it's cavetto plain, as may be seen in Scamoz:
Chambray's edition B. II. chapt. V. article 8. pa. 150. plate 36. nor would I require
it's volutes or caulicoles to be so much carved, as those of Diocletian's Baths, fine-
ing the simplicity of those in Palladio preferable.

for Pavilion Nº. IV. East

2. Corinthian half capitels, for half columns of the same model as the 2. columns
laster mentioned, being for the same range.

4. Ionic capitels for columns whose lower diam. is 30 I. & diminished diam. 26 1/2
to be copied from those of the temple of Fortuna virilis in Palladio.
and ballusters in their flanks.
observing that the two middle capitels shew volutes in front and back,
and the two corner capitels are what he calls angular, that is to say
presenting volutes in their front & outer flank, and ballusters in their back
and inner flank. see Palladio. B. IV. ch 13. pa. 65. plate 37. Leoni, London edition

for Pavilion Nº. 3. East

6. Ionic capitels for columns whose inferior diam. is 30. I. and dimin.ed diam 26.
to be copied from the capitel of Palladio as given in his 1st Book wherein
he treats of the orders in general, and it's 16th chapt. in which he describes
the Ionic capitel particularly, the drawings of which are in plates 20.22. pa. 25.
Leoni's, London edition, presenting volutes in front & back & ballusters in their flanks.

for Pavilion Nº. III. West

In all these cases the Astragal of the upper end of the shaft must be subjoined to the corinthian capitel
in the same block, because our columns being of brick, stuccoed. it cannot be carved on
them: and to the Ionic capitels must be subjoined, not only the Astragal, but a bit
of the shaft itself as low as the bottom of the Volutes.

to include (besides it's halfround member or Torus) the cavetto & listel below it, which meets the naked of the diminished shaft, and which will be seen in the same plate of Palladio subjoined to the part B. of the capitel.

We have agreed with Giacomo Raggi for 10. bases and 2 pilaster bases for the same columns, according to the agreement inclosed as he is not in circumstances sufficient to answer any failure of contract, we have of necessity been obliged to ask your superintendance of his performance; and he places himself under your attentions as much as he would be under ours were we present. should you percieve any manifest intention on his part to abandon the performance, or any certain incompetence to the fulfilment, we will pray you to declare the contract dissolved and to warn him to proceed no further. but if he goes on diligently and hopefully we wish him to recieve all reasonable indulgence. 50. D I have been advanced here to him on account. should he fail in his contract, I will ask the favor of you to inform me without delay at what price we can get such bases furnished to us as our agreem specifies. this will determine us whether to get them here or there. I will also ask the favor of you immediately on reciept of this, to inform me at what price we can be furnished there with squares of marble to pave the floor of the portico of the Rotunda, polished and accurately squared ready to be laid down, the squares to be 1 foot square   we shall also have occasion in the interior for 40 Composite capitels of wood, for columns whose diminished diameters are 15 $\frac{11}{16}$ Inches English. to be copied from Palladio B 1 c. 18 pl 30.   I will thank you also for the best engraving of the Pantheon. on a single sheet to be had with you.

Dear Sir   Monticello Oct. 8. 23

In my letter of July 10. I informed you that the Ca-
-pitels you had forwarded were then on their way to Richmond.
they came to hand here in August and are now put up.
they are well approved on the whole, and particularly as to the
quality of the marble. but I am instructed to mention some parti-
culars not fully executed

1. in the Corinthian capitels there is a want of the Cavetto and
listel of the Astragal which intervenes between that and the naked .
of the shaft and which should have been subjoined to the block
of the capitel

2. in the Ionic capitels from Palladio, the astragal is plain in-
-stead of being carved. as in Palladio B.1 pl.22.Q.   so also on those
from the temple of Fortuna virilis, the same members are plain in-
-stead of being carved, as in Pallad. B.4. pl 37.

The Visitors of the University had their meeting the day before
yesterday, and I am now authorised to apply to you for the capitels of
the columns of our Rotunda. agreeable to the following specifications.

Ten Corinthian capitels of marble for columns whose dimi-
-nished diameters are 2 feet 8 4/10 inches English measure.

Two Corinthian semi-capitels for Pilasters, or halves of square
columns of the same diminished diameter cut diagonally thus
so as to present a front and flank each at the corners of
the building. all to be copied exactly from those of the Pantheon, as
represented by Palladio. B.4. chap. 20. pl.60. Leoni's edition.

Our columns being of brick, in which no moulding can be worked
it is necessary to subjoin to the capitel the astragal of the column
making it a part of the same block. and the term astragal is meant

to include (besides it's halfround member or Torus) the cavetto &
listel below it, which meets the naked of the diminished shaft,
and which will be seen in the same plate of Palladio subjoin-
-ed to the part B. of the capitel.

We have agreed with Giacomo Raggi for 10. bases and 2 diagonal pilaster
bases for the same columns according to the agreement inclosed
as he is not in circumstances sufficient to answer any failure of con-
-tract, we have of necessity been obliged to ask your superintendance of
his performance; and he places himself under your attentions as
much as he would be under ours were we present. should you percieve
any manifest intention on his part to abandon the performance, or any
certain incompetence to the fulfilment, we will pray you to declare the
contract dissolved and to warn him to proceed no further. but if he goes
on diligently and hopefully we wish him ⟨†††⟩ recieve all reasonable
indulgence. 50. D have been advanced here to him on account. should
he fail in his contract, I will ask the favor of you to inform me without
delay at what price we can get such bases furnished to us as our agreem
specifies. this will determine us whether to get them here or there.
I will also ask the favor of you immediately on reciept of this, to inform me at what
price we can be furnished there with squares of marble to pave the floor
of the portico of the Rotunda, polished and accurately squared ready to be laid
down, the squares to be 1 foot square   we shall also have occasion in
the interior for 40 Composite capitels of wood, for columns whose
diminished diameters are 15 $\frac{11}{16}$ Inches English to be copied from
Palladio B 1 c. 18 pl 30, I will thank you also for the best engraving
of the Pantheon on a single sheet to be had with you.

PLATE XIII. University of Virginia. First page of Jefferson's pocket note-book showing data for July 18, 1817, the day on which he staked out his plan; also additional notes concerning compass reading added about two years later, Dec. 7th, 1819.

Operations at — for the College

July 18 .... m

a. the place at which the theodolite was fixed
being the center of the Northern square and
the point destined for some principal building
in the level of the square l. m. n. o.

100.f   100.f   f

the fall from a. to d. 18.f

✻ from a. to d. the bearing magnetically S. 21° W.
add for variation   2½
                                   S. 23½ W.

n .... +. o

s .... b .... h

? the true meridian was that day 2½ to left of magnetic.
b. is the center of the middle square, and at
g we propose to erect our first pavilion
c. is the center of the Southern square.
locust stakes were driven at l. o. f. g. b. h. i. c. k. and
at d. is a pile of stones.

p .... +. g

i .... c ...... k

each square is to be level within itself, with a pavilion at each end
to wit at e.f. gh. ik. and 10 dormitories on each side of each pavilion
filling up the sides of the square.

r ...... d ...... s

from a. to b. was measured 255.f. or 85.yds, b.c. the same, & c.d. the half.
from the points a. b. c. was measured 100.f. each way to o.f. gh. ik. making
thus each square 255.f. by 200.f. = .8541 of an acre or nearly 17/20 —

from central line of library		f	whole.		from central line of library		f	whole
to Pavilion No. I		68	68.		To Hotel A.		68	68
Pavilion		44	112		Hotel A.		50	118
Dormitory	1	13-6	125-6		Dormitory	15	133
	2	13-6	139.			15	148
	3	13-6	152-6			15	163
	4	13-6	166.			15	178
Pavilion No. II		37.	203			15	193
Dormitory A	5	13-9	216-9			15	208
	6	13-9	230-6			15	223
Passage		6-10½	251-1½		Necessary	12	238
Dormitory	8	13-9	264.		Dormitory	15	253
	9	13-9	270-7½			13	265
	10	13-9	292-4½			15	280
Pavilion No. III		44	336-4½			15	295
Dormitory	11	13-9	350-1½			15	310
	12	14	364-1½			15	325
	13	14	392-1½			15	340
	14	14	392-1½			15	355
	15	14	406-1½			15	370
	16	14	420-1½		Hotel B.	34	404
	17	14	434-1½				
Pavilion No. IV		34	468-1½				
Dormitory B	18	11	479-1½				
	19	11	490-1½				
	20	11	501-1½				
	21	11	512-1½				
	22	11	523-1½				
	23	11	534-1½				
	24	11	545-1½				
	25	11	556-1½				
	26	11	567-1½				

✻ Dec. 7. 19. I took the bearing accurately of the range of pavilions, & found it magne-
-tically. S. 21. W. the variation of the needle being that day 4.° S. of the true N. or to the right. It is
probable that at the operation of July 18. the variation of 15. minutes was inadvertently considered as the true one

PLATE XIV. Part of specification for Rotunda, showing method of reduction after the Pantheon.

Rotunda, reduced to the proportions of the Pantheon and accomodated to the purposes of a library for the University, with rooms for drawing, music, examinations and other accessory purposes.

the diameter of the building 77. feet, being ½ that of the Pantheon, consequently ¼ it's area, & ⅛ it's volume:
the Circumference 242. f.

the height.	foundation	3 - 0	foundation	3 - 0
	basement	7 - 6	basement	7 - 6
	Columns	28 . 6	lower rooms	17 -
	entablature	5 - 7¼	to spring of arch	10 - 4¼
	Attic	13 - 9	to top of wall	12 - 6
		58 - 4¼ = 58.35		58 - 4¼

	height × bricks to a foot × circumference	bricks
3½ bricks thick	3 × 42 × 242 =	30, 492
3	7½ × 36 × 242	65, 340
2½	17 . × 30 × 242 .	123, 420
2	18 - 4½ × 24 × 242	106, 608
1½	12 - 6 × 18 × 242	54 . 450
the whole circular external wall .		380, 310
front & back buttresses of 141. f. area each		263, 275
2 . massive chimnies, serving as buttresses		44 . 800
3 semielliptical partitions of 2. bricks thick.		108, 450
		796, 835
shafts of 12. columns 3. f diam. 23½ f high		315 . 840
		1,112 . 675

to thicken the walls a half brick more from bottom to top adds 84702 b[ric]ks making in the whole 1,197, 377. or say 1,200,000. which is adviseable.

	module		f	
diameter	1		= 3.	
dimin^d diam.	0 - 54		= 2 - 8.4	
base	30	=	1 - 6	
shaft	7 - 50		23 - 6	= 28 - 6
capitel . . .	1 - 10 .		3 - 6	
architrave . . .	38	=	1 - 10.8	
frize	28½		1 - 5.1	= 5 - 7.2
cornice .	45½		2 - 3.3	
Attic base	part 121. . . .	=	3 -	
shaft	363		9 -	13 - 9 .
surbase	69		1 - 9	
				48 - 0

diam. of Attic pilaster 2 f - 8.4 i
intercolonnation 2. diam. = 6 f
projection of Cornice 47½ = 2 f - 5.65 i
Pediment. span 52 f - 5.75 i
height 11 - 8

breadth of Portico 16 mod = 48 f

plinths of Dome 11. f
crown of do. - 8. f
19 . f

. Internal heights

	f
foundation . . .	3 -
pedestal or basement	7 - 6
floor, or step . . .	1 .
lower rooms clear	16 .
floor	1 - .
library. wall	29 - 6
[illegible] of dome above the [illegible] of do.	19 -
	77 -

(library wall and dome together:) 48 - 6 height of dome room

Library.

to get a circle of columns at a proper distance from the wall, and, with their entablature the height of the wall within, to the spring of the ~~arch~~ the diameter must 1 f - 6 i, then [illegible] they are arranged must be 27. f (or 54 f diam.) circumference 113. diameters = 169.5 f
to correspond with the windows there must be 20. intercolonnations.
and that the intercolonnation may not be too large for the Corinthian order we must
an intercolonnation of 3. diameters will be 4 f - 6

2. columns	3 -
space between them 20 i	1 -
	8 - 6 × 20 = 170 f

PLATE XV. Section of Library or Rotunda.

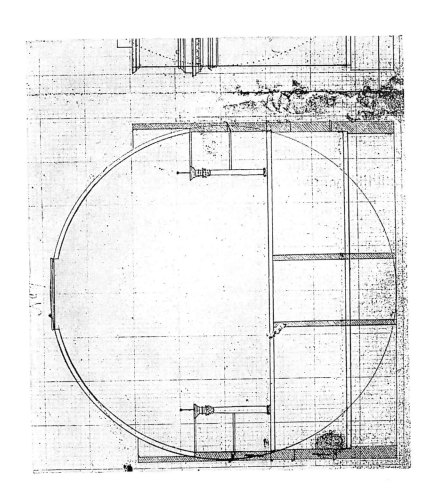

PLATE XVI. Plan of first and second floor of Library or Rotunda.

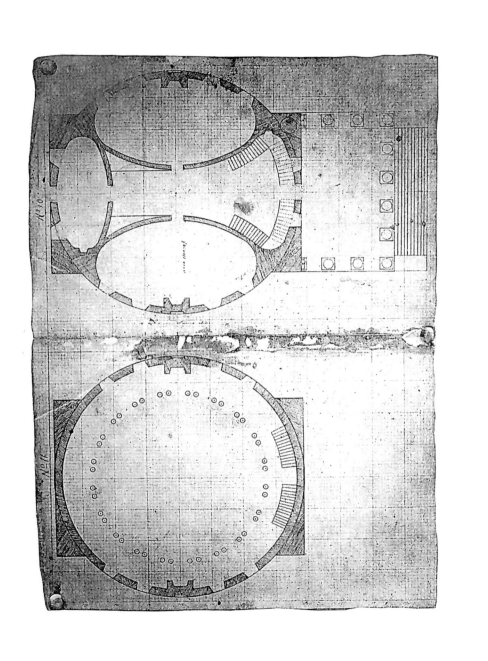

PLATE XVII. Elevation of Library or Rotunda.

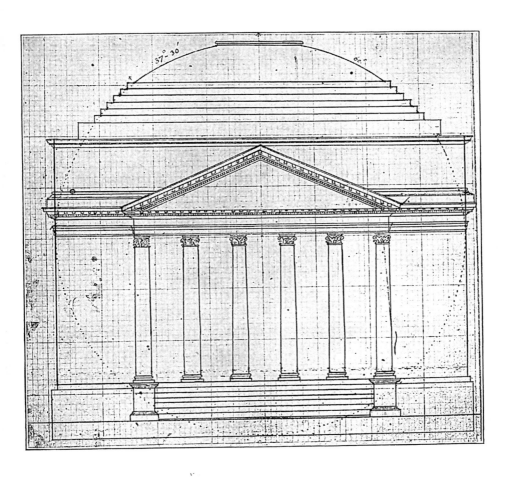

PLATE XVIII. Specification for the domed roof of the Rotunda.

additional Notes for the Library.

The estimate of bricks on the first drawing was _ _ _ _   1,112,675

   if we make the wall half a brick thicker from bottom to top it adds _ _ _ 84,702

                                                               1,197,377.

If we make the attic of wood, instead of brick, it deducts _ _ _ 79,920

   leaving the corrected estimate for the whole Rotunda _ _ _ 1,117,457.

the Terras on each side is to be in breadth equal to the flank of the Portico.
   it will be 61~6, but deducting for the descent of the steps it may be consid'd as 54.f long
      the foundation & Basement being 2.br. thick & 10½f. high. Us such walls _ _ 54,432

so that the Building & it's 2. terrasses will take _ _ _ _ _ _ _ 1,171,889.

The thickness of the wall at top, to wit, at the spring of the vault of the roof is 22.I.
on the top of the wall lay a curved plate, in Delorme's manner, consisting of 4. thicknesses of 3.I. each. 22.I. wide, pieces 12.f. long. breaking joints every 3.f. bolted
   through with bolts of iron, having a nut & screw at their end
on this curved plate the ribs of the roof are to rest.
the ribs are to be 4. thicknesses of 1.I. plank, in pieces 4.f. long. breaking joints at
   every foot.
they are to be 18.I. wide, which leaves 4.I. of the plate for the attic uprights to rest on.
the ribs are to be keyed together by cross boards at proper intervals for
   the ribs to head in as they shorten
the curb of the sky light to be made also in Delorme's way, but vertically.
the fire places & chimnies must be brought forward so that the flues may not
   make a hollow in the main walls. they will thus become buttresses.

PLATE XIX. Specification for pavilion X, illustrating Jefferson's method of determining his attic pilaster, also representing the only time in the entire set of records when the personal pronoun I occurs — using it to acknowledge a personal limitation.

Pavilion N° X East. Doric of the Theatre of Marcellus. the columns to have no bases. diam.= 3.1

			Correction.
the cornice is	$^{(a)}/37.5 = ^{+}/1\sim10.5$	Upper joists = $^{+9}1\sim0$	(a) for 37.5 say 42.5
frise - - - -	45. = 2~3	upper room clear 12~0.75 (d)	(b) 1~52.4 say 1~57½
Architrave	$30' = 1~6$	middle joists 45. 1~0	(c) 9~22½ 9~27½
whole Entablature	$^{(b)}1~52.5 = 5~7.5$	lower room clear 12~0.75 (d)	and add 3.I. to each of the cor-
Capitel	a 30 = 1~6	from floor to zocle 2	-responding measures in feet & I.
Shaft	7~0 = 21~0	20~1.5	(d) for 12~0.75 say 12~1.5
Order entire	$^{(c)}9~22.5 = 20~1.5$	Kitchen cieling above zocle 1.7	(e) 43~11.4 34~0.6x4=15.2
dimin diam. 48 = 28~8		from Zocle to kitchen floor 7 } Kitchen 8.4	(f) 9~9.2 7~0.367
1' =.6². 60' = 36.1.		To bottom of foundation 2	
		10.	

the Portico Tetrastyle. the front as follows.
{ wing 1. Triglyph 75' = 3~9 +1. dim semidiam. 24' = 1~2.4 = 4~11.4
{ Portico 1. dim semid. + 7. trigl + 1. dim semid. = ... ~28~7.8
{ wing 1. Trigl + 1. semid. - - - - - - - - - . . 4~11.4
              whole breadth of building - - - - - - - . . .~38~6.6

projection of Cornice 54 = 2~6.4   Shaft of Chimney 43. by 44.
Pediment. Span. 43~11.4 $^{(f)}$ height 9~9.2   to wit 6 flues of 9. by 16 clear.
from zocle to upper floor   - 15~0.75   Stairs. 18. risers of 8½ I
deduct Tuscan order entire   11~7.86   17. treads of 10 I
descent from upper floor to terras 3~4.89   to wit 1st flight 8.}
                                              quart place 1 } = 17.
                                              2d. flight 8 }

The Attic I have never seen an Attic pilaster, with the measures of it's parts minutely expressed !:
except that of the Temple of Nerva Trajan Palladio. B. III. Pl. 19. that temple is overloaded with
ornaments, and it's Pilaster frittered away so minutely, in it's mouldings. as to lose all effect.
I have simplified these mouldings to suit our plainer style, still however retaining nearly their general
outlines and proportions.

Our pediment being 7~8.25 in height, the base & die of the Attic must be that, or ever so
little more. the whole height of the Attic being divided into 8. parts, the cap or surbase is 1. parts
the die 5. parts, and the base 2. parts. -
Take 13½ I. for a part and the base and die will be 92.75
                    deduct the height of the pediment   9. 25
leaves the spare space between the apex & cap only   .5 or ½ I
the cap or surbase will be 1. part = 13.25
    die - - - - - - - - 5. parts = 66.25
    base - - - - - - - 2. parts = 26.50
whole height of Attic - - - - - 106.   or 8~10
the whole height being 8. parts of 105' each or 840'. these divided by 106. I. give to nearly.
8'. to 1. I. that the small mouldings of the cap & base may be calculated at that without sensible
    error
he Cavetto above the cap is not reckoned a part of it. it should be on this case 70. or say 9. in height.
and 85' or say 11. I. within the projection.
the breadth of the pilaster is that of the diminished diameter of the column, to wit. 28.8

PLATE XX. University of Virginia. One of Jefferson's plans for an observatory which he later condemned. (The specifications for the building are written on the back and are printed in this text.)

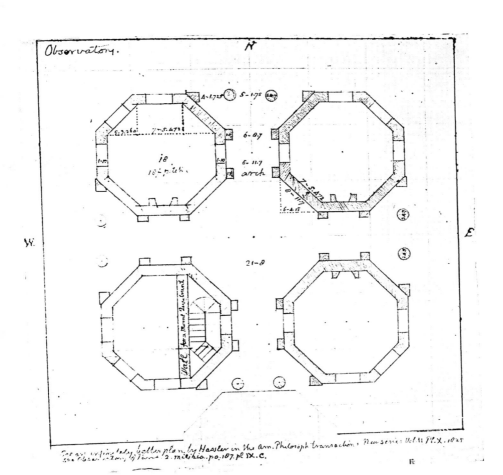

PLATE XXI. University of Virginia.   Jefferson's sketch for a bell which would ring the hours automatically and yet permit of being rung independently.

Plan of a clock for the Rotunda, the bell to strike for praying also.

The bell to be raised communicates on a system of 4 wheels... the striking also.
the different plates to bear the center of the telegraph program of the regiment,
the different plate to vibrate thingoeketioned... so that... with... weight...
the bell clock hammer to vibrate... open... the... the... rod of great use in the bell.

the bell temper to vibrate on a plane at right angles with that... each of the... movement

This clock weights to dipped... on the cylindrical cavities of the well on each side.
the bell remain in one of them.
the clock to have an hour hand only with divisions for 60' between each hour of the pind
to be... happy up by 21', and the minute 0. 368?
to be... up on the back side of the wheels

scale in view showing bell hammer &

→ the steen jacks as well for sits ... will make a vacancy for the bell barges to which few...

front view showing bell hammer &

$\frac{1}{3-3}$

to vibrate seconds

bell rope

PLATE XXII. University of Virginia: plan of existing conditions.

UNIVERSITY OF VIRGINIA

CHARLOTTESVILLE – VA.

PLAN OF EXISTING CONDITIONS

SCALE 1 INCH = 500 FEET

500   300   100 0   500   1000   1500

WARREN H. MANNING   LANDSCAPE DESIGNER
BOSTON, MASS.   MARCH 11, 1913

NO 760-84

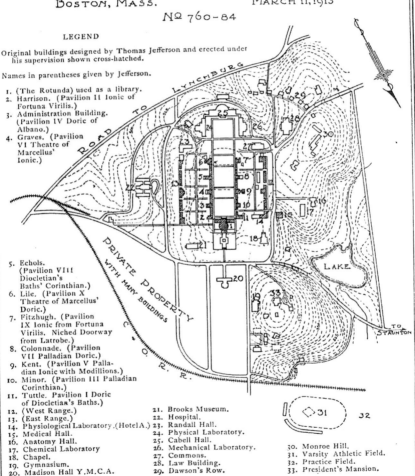

LEGEND

Original buildings designed by Thomas Jefferson and erected under his supervision shown cross-hatched.

Names in parentheses given by Jefferson.

1. (The Rotunda) used as a library.
2. Harrison. (Pavilion II Ionic of Fortuna Virilis.)
3. Administration Building. (Pavilion IV Doric of Albano.)
4. Graves. (Pavilion VI Theatre of Marcellus' Ionic.)
5. Echols. (Pavilion VIII Diocletian's Baths' Corinthian.)
6. Lile. (Pavilion X Theatre of Marcellus' Doric.)
7. Fitzhugh. (Pavilion IX Ionic from Fortuna Virilis. Niched Doorway from Latrobe.)
8. Colonnade. (Pavilion VII Palladian Doric.)
9. Kent. (Pavilion V Palladian Ionic with Modillions.)
10. Minor. (Pavilion III Palladian Corinthian.)
11. Tuttle. Pavilion I Doric of Diocletian's Baths.)
12. (West Range.)
13. (East Range.)
14. Physiological Laboratory. (Hotel A.)
15. Medical Hall.
16. Anatomy Hall.
17. Chemical Laboratory
18. Chapel.
19. Gymnasium.
20. Madison Hall Y.M.C.A.
21. Brooks Museum.
22. Hospital.
23. Randall Hall.
24. Physical Laboratory.
25. Cabell Hall.
26. Mechanical Laboratory.
27. Commons.
28. Law Building.
29. Dawson's Row.
30. Monroe Hill.
31. Varsity Athletic Field.
32. Practice Field.
33. President's Mansion.

PLATE XXIII. University of Virginia: study for development.

UNIVERSITY of VIRGINIA
CHARLOTTESVILLE Va
STUDY for DEVELOPMENT
SCALE 1 INCH = 500 FEET

500 300 100 0   500   1000   1500

WARREN H. MANNING   LANDSCAPE DESIGNER
BOSTON, MASS.   MARCH 11, 1913

NO 760-85

EXISTING BUILDINGS ■   PROPOSED BUILDINGS ▨

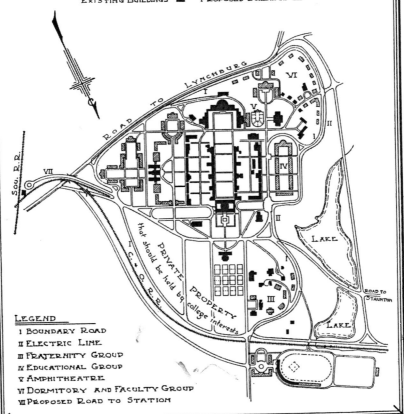

ROAD TO LYNCHBURG

Sou. R.R.

C. & O. R.R.

PRIVATE PROPERTY that should be held by college interests

ROAD TO STAUNTON

LAKE

LAKE

LEGEND
I BOUNDARY ROAD
II ELECTRIC LINE
III FRATERNITY GROUP
IV EDUCATIONAL GROUP
V AMPHITHEATRE
VI DORMITORY AND FACULTY GROUP
VII PROPOSED ROAD TO STATION

LaVergne, TN USA
23 July 2010
190728LV00001B/125/P

Negotiating Racialised Identities

Indigenous Teacher Education in Australia and Canada

Carol Reid

Negotiating Racialised Identities

Indigenous Teacher Education in
Australia and Canada

Carol Reid

COMMON
GROUND

This book is published at theLearner.com
a series imprint of the UniversityPress.com

First published in Australia in 2004
by Common Ground Publishing Pty Ltd
www.theLearner.com

National Library of Australia Cataloguing-in-Publication data:

    Reid, Carol.
    Negotiating racialised identities:
    indigenous teacher education in Australia and Canada.

    Bibliography.
    ISBN 1 86335 539 1 (pbk).
    ISBN 1 86335 542 1 (PDF).

    1. Teachers — Training of — Australia. 2. Teachers — Training of — Canada.
    3. Indigenous peoples — Education (Higher) — Australia.
    4. Indigenous peoples — Education (Higher) — Canada.
    5. Aboriginal Australian teachers — Training of. I. Title.

370.711

Cover design: The circle represents a meeting point for Indigenous Australians and
Indigenous Canadians use a 'talking circle' as a central communication style. The
colours (red, black, and white) represent the racialised skin categories of Indigenous
peoples in both countries and the white text over the two tones suggests both racialised
'whiteness' and colonial relations.

Cover designed by Katie Czerwinski.
Typeset in Australia by Common Ground Publishing.
Printed in Australia on 80gsm Offset.

Dedication

To my mother and father, Eric and Phyllis Hutchin, for providing a resilient and stimulating working class home full of debates, crafts and ideas; for a questioning stance towards authority and consistent respect for people in all their diversity.

Foreword

Carol Reid

One feature common to both Canada and Australia is the relatively poor educational outcomes for Indigenous people. Both countries have responded to this by, among other things, introducing programs to increase the number of Indigenous teachers. This book compares and contrasts the negotiation of difference in two Indigenous teacher education programs in Australia and Canada.

The book employs a theoretical approach based on the concept of racialisation, Bourdieu's theory of practice, and the notion of culture-as-negotiation. This theoretical framework is used to interpret and understand interviews with Indigenous and non-Indigenous teacher education students, administrators and teacher educators at the Northern Teacher Education Program (NORTEP), Saskatchewan Canada, and the Aboriginal Rural Education Program (AREP) in New South Wales, Australia.

The book outlines, through this comparative study of the AREP and NORTEP, how the tensions and contradictions of Indigenous teacher education can be productive. The book identifies critical issues of education in diasporic communities; highlights the politics of colour in higher education; signals how privilege is reproduced through education; shows how culture emerges as pathology and demonstrates the importance of creating a third space for the constant negotiation of the meaning of cultural difference in education.

Acknowledgments

Like many that begin this journey, it has taken me a long time to reach the end. I could not have done so without the support and encouragement of a number of people. Firstly, I would like to thank Dr Ken Johnston for his gentle encouragement and understanding of the purpose of this journey and his comments on draft after draft. In addition, his knowledge of the field that we shared was an invaluable source of intellectual support. Thanks also to Betty Johnston, who asked questions and shared her ideas. I would like to thank my Indigenous and non-Indigenous colleagues and students at the University of Western Sydney and Indigenous friends who have, over the years, challenged and encouraged me. In particular, I greatly enjoyed the coffee 'discussions' with Scott Poynting, Kelvin McQueen and Ann Coleman when we could grab the time. Special thanks to the staff at the Northern Teacher Education Program (NORTEP) and students for being so open and supportive during my stays at La Ronge, Saskatchewan, Canada. Thanks also to Helen Velissaris who listened to my ramblings and to the University of Western Sydney for funding support over the years. I would like to also thank Colleen Mitchell of Clear Concise Communication for editing beyond the call of duty. Thanks also to the team at Common Ground, namely Bill Cope, Katie Czerwinski and Kathryn Otte. Finally, thanks to my family – my parents, Phyllis and Eric Hutchin, my children Julian and Naome and their partners Ikuyo and Rob, who, as always, kept my feet on the ground. Lastly, to Jock Collins, my partner for more than 20 years who has always encouraged and supported my work and provided intellectual, emotional and physical support.

Contents

Chapter 1

Introduction

> Coming into a racially divided society with good and no doubt
> naïve intentions towards the Aborigines, we went out of our way
> to display our lack of prejudice, our colourblind virtue. This often
> involved assuming a form of inverse racism – automatically taking
> the Aboriginal side in public debate, speaking not just of them, but
> for them. It was no doubt a better way to proceed than being
> prejudiced against Aborigines and always assuming the worst of
> them. But it was prejudice nevertheless. It clouded judgement and
> led to special pleading, double standards and a measure of
> hypocrisy, although we didn't realise that at the time.
>
> From Henry Reynolds, *Why Weren't We Told?* 1999:50]

Introduction

Henry Reynolds was writing about a **different** place and a different
time to the themes of this book, which **looks** at Indigenous[1] teacher
education in New South Wales (NSW), **Australia** and Saskatchewan
(SASK), Canada in the 1990s. However, **Reynolds** reflections on
being a *migloo*[2] a few decades ago **in northern** Queensland resonate
with my own experiences as a *gubba* – **or white** person in Aboriginal
terms – in metropolitan NSW. From **the early 1980s,** when I began to
teach in an inner urban school in Sydney – where Aboriginal student
numbers gradually increased from 10% to 60% of the total student
body over five years – I, too, felt these tensions. In environments such
as these, as far as Aboriginal aspirations are concerned, you could find
yourself positioned as either a 'fellow traveller' or as 'the opposition'.

---

[1] The term Indigenous is used when speaking generally about the experiences of
Australian Aboriginal peoples and Canadian aboriginal peoples. The term Aboriginal
with a capitalised 'A' refers only to Australian Indigenous peoples. The term
'aboriginality' is used when discussing identity issues in relation to Canadian contexts.

[2] A term used to describe 'whitefellas' in northern Queensland, Australia.

I abhorred the racial discrimination against Aboriginal people in our society, but did not really know Aboriginal people and so I thought *if I knew them better* I would know how to respond to the educational needs of their children.

Growing up as an Australian born daughter of British immigrant parents in Sydney's working class western suburbs in the 1950s and 1960s had made me aware of injustice and of the way in which education can be an alienating force for the less privileged (Ryan, 1976). I knew about social class and how it intersected with ethnicity in shaping educational outcomes in Australia, but little about Aboriginal people. However, as Reynolds (1999) observed in the quote that leads off this book, class was a very different reality to that of race because class "could be learnt and therefore modified by slight adjustments to accent, vocabulary, gesture and stance" (p.50). For me, despite experiencing some of my parents' 'anti-Pom' prejudice, there was still much to learn about the way in which 'race' shaped the lives of Australians.

While doing the research included in this book, I found these sentiments were shared. I had moved from being an inner-city primary school teacher to a university academic teaching undergraduate students to become teachers. Part of my job was to teach in and co-ordinate the University of Western Sydney Macarthur (UWSM) Faculty of Education Aboriginal Rural Education Program (AREP) which was established, like other programs in Australia, to increase the number of Indigenous teachers. Along with many of my tertiary education colleagues and our students, we tried to make sense of our racialised identities. This was often a process full of contradiction, humour and frustration. I would like, therefore, to stress the complexity of the processes that we were part of observing and shaping. There is a history of racialisation that we need to understand without somehow dragging it along with us in a simple untangled thread. Keeping the tangles "without diminishing the simultaneous presence of the most disparate elements that converge to determine every event" (Calvino cited in Bottomley, 1994:1) is a part of the struggle for meaning. As a 'white' teacher of young people from working class, immigrant and Indigenous backgrounds, and, later as an academic writing about Indigenous teacher education in Australia and Canada, I have tried to unravel the intertwined complexities that bear on the field of Indigenous education at all levels.

2

One of the reasons I made this a comparative study relates to the fact that Indigenous education in Australia and Canada has been a site of struggle since colonisation. The focus of struggle has shifted over this period from issues of Indigenous access *per se* to issues of Indigenous control over curriculum, funding and administration. More recently, there have been additional calls in both Canada and Australia to 'Indigenise' or 'Aboriginalise' sites of education for Indigenous students. The two enclave[3] programs for the training of Indigenous teachers which are at the heart of this book – the Aboriginal Rural Education Program (AREP) in Sydney, NSW and the Northern Teacher Education Program (NORTEP) at La Ronge, Saskatchewan – reflect these shifting struggles. The two enclave programs were established specifically to increase the number of Indigenous teachers, and almost exclusively taught to, Indigenous students. They were developed at a time when increasing Indigenous access to educational structures was the primary consideration. Since that time, Indigenous access to tertiary education in Canada and Australia has increased, and other issues related to the culture of tertiary institutions have become the centre of debate. However, despite greater participation in tertiary education in Australia and Canada and the fact that 0.8% and 4% respectively of the Australian (Australian College of Education, 2001) and Canadian (email exchange with Department of Indian and Northern Affairs, Canada who based this figure on 1996 Census data) teaching forces are Indigenous, the legacy of inequitable educational outcomes at all levels of schooling since colonisation in both countries remains an issue of major importance and much debate at the level of theory, policy and practice.

This book is a contribution to the field of Indigenous education in Australia and Canada. In each country there has been substantial analysis of this field, often with a focus on the way in which cultural differences impact upon educational outcomes. To some extent this has become the standard approach to Indigenous education in both countries and has constituted a kind of *cultural determinism*. That is, cultural difference has been 'read off' as if static (McConaghy, 1997a). The most extreme manifestation of this practice has been the use of a series of checklists comparing and contrasting Indigenous and

---

[3] Separate academic support systems that were established for Aboriginal people in teacher education courses.

non-Indigenous peoples' cultural 'attributes'. In other ways, 'culture' has been a useful veil for racism (Haig-Brown, 1995:238).

This book is a departure from these approaches in the sense that it returns to the theme of 'race', not as a biological construct but a social construct (de Lepervanche and Bottomley, 1988). Utilising the notion of *racialisation* (Miles, 1982), the study attempts to understand the on-going impact of race as an ideological and political process in Indigenous education. Miles uses the concept of racialisation to "explicitly indicate the existence of a social process in which human subjects articulate and reproduce the ideology of racism and engage in the practice of racial discrimination, but always in a context which they themselves have not determined" (Miles cited in Collins, 1991:200).

This approach is important since many empirical studies in Australia – often in the form of ethnographies – have focussed on children and the cultural mismatch between non-Indigenous teachers and Indigenous students (Malin, 1990; Harris, 1990). Often, this 'culturalist' explanation has just been layered onto adult Indigenous learners as well as in comparative Australian/Canadian studies (cf. Hughes and More, 1993). However, there is little empirical work available to challenge simplistic culturalist explanations (McConaghy, 1997a:128). Furthermore, there is a need to adequately conceptualise 'race' in discourses about Indigenous education policy and practice (*ibid.*). This book aims, in part, to fill this void.

Specifically, the book is concerned with the way in which – mainly non-Indigenous – administrators, teacher educators and Indigenous student teachers negotiate racialised difference in two Indigenous teacher education programs in Australia (AREP) and Canada (NORTEP). It seeks to illuminate the tensions and contradictions that arise as a consequence of centuries of racialised relationships between Indigenous and non-Indigenous peoples. The two case studies permit an understanding of how this racialised process has been negotiated, reproduced and changed over time.

An exploration of the complex and contradictory processes of racialisation, and the way in which differences are negotiated, requires a multi-level analytical structure. Bourdieu's concepts of *field and habitus* are introduced as a useful scaffold to develop a *theory of practice* in Indigenous teacher education. This is because Indigenous educational experiences cannot be understood in isolation from the forces from which they have been created and are being created. Too often, interactions between Indigenous and non-Indigenous people are simply 'read off' (McConaghy, 1997a), treating race, or its reincarnation 'culture' (de Lepervanche and Bottomley, 1988) as a one-dimensional, static given while, paradoxically, denying any dependence upon biological racialised identities. But Indigenous and non-Indigenous peoples *are* constructed as 'races', in complex and changing ways that stretch from the way in which the colonial and post-colonial State has defined and categorised Indigenous people in both countries, through to the ways that individuals think of, and conceptualise, Indigenous and non-Indigenous peoples. These processes are often contradictory and variable over time. Through using a comparative Australia/Canada framework it is possible to understand better these complex processes of racialisation – to identify the similarities and differences in the two countries – and how they impact on Indigenous teacher education.

A multi-level analysis includes the macro, meso and micro aspects of the field of Indigenous education in Australia and Canada. At the macro level, the book outlines political and ideological dimensions of racialisation of Indigenous peoples in society in general, and in the history of Indigenous education in particular, in both countries. However, to avoid a reductionist approach, it is necessary to examine the local interpretation of wider policies and practices. This meso or institutional level analyses the specific local conditions that gave rise to the two enclave programs of AREP and NORTEP. It maps out the objective relations in the field so that the formation of the two programs is understood as a function of and a response to the constraints of national policies and local desires. Finally, the study incorporates a micro-political analysis that focuses on the re/formation of teaching identities, individual perceptions of the programs, the issues arising within each program and their negotiation. The emphasis here is on the continuing constitution of, and challenges to, racialised identities within the field of Indigenous education in Australia and Canada in general and in the AREP and NORTEP programs in particular.

Defining the 'problem'

At the start of this chapter, I wrote of my early years in school education and later tertiary education working with Indigenous and non-Indigenous students and their parents. This was outlined because

5

it is important for the reader to know that this book has grown out of "an amalgam of practical problems" as Grenfell and James (1998:177) put it. These practical problems arose during my 10-year period as a teacher in an inner Sydney public school with high Aboriginal enrolments. Later they arose as an administrator in charge of, and lecturer in, an Aboriginal Rural Education Program. These experiences have revealed the need for a complex eye over the theory and practice of Indigenous educational issues.

The practical problems encountered at both primary school level and university centred on negotiating differences in contexts that were highly racialised. Dissatisfied with the ways in which the dominant approach to Indigenous education – that is, 'culture-as-explanation' – explained the struggles that participants were experiencing, led me to reconsider the place of 'race' in theorising Indigenous educational contexts. I have not been alone in this journey and I have found the work of anti-racists such as the late Barry Troyna (1993, 1994, and 1998) critical to my understanding of the complexities of the concept of racialisation and its usefulness for the field of Indigenous education. Racialisation also provided a useful lens through which to consider a comparative cross-cultural approach of Australia and Canada. In addition, I have been influenced by a range of scholars whose work also grapples with post/anti-colonialist readings of Indigenous education, but from different perspectives. In this book I have drawn insights from feminist and post-structuralist accounts of Indigenous adult and school education in Australia (McConaghy, 1997a; Nicholls et al., 1996) and Canada (Haig-Brown, 1995), and neo-Marxist analyses by Keeffe (1992) in Australia and Hesch (1996) and Wotherspoon (1991, 1998, 1999) in Canada.

Drawing on the insights of scholars in the field, and my own concrete experiences, I have framed the central problem of this book in a way which attempts to take into account not only the problems which arose from practice, but the methodological issues involved in research relating to Indigenous/non-Indigenous relations. The central question then, is: *How does racialisation shape Indigenous teacher education programs in Australia and Canada?*

From this central research question, a number of subsidiary questions become apparent and are as follows:

- What are the legacies of colonisation in Australia and Canada for Indigenous education?

- Why were enclave programs for Indigenous teacher education students in NSW and SASK created? What form have they taken and what have been their experiences – successes, failures – to date?
- In what ways do administrators of Indigenous teacher education programs reproduce and/or contest the racialised spaces within educational institutions?
- What assumptions underlie teaching philosophies in AREP and NORTEP and how are they challenged/reproduced, reframed and/or transformed?
- How do the teaching staff and students negotiate racialised identities in both programs?
- How do Indigenous students in AREP and NORTEP construct an identity as *Indigenous teachers*?
- What similarities and differences emerge in the Australian and Canadian case for all these questions and how can these differences and similarities be understood?

These questions are aimed at examining the contexts and processes through which racialised differences have been negotiated within the AREP and NORTEP Indigenous teacher education programs. The discussions and interviews conducted with administrators, fellow academics and student teachers during the research for this book resulted in opportunities for participants to explore tensions that had been encountered in the two programs. Participants in the research journey that shaped this book also spent some time justifying their perspective by drawing upon the processes and relationships constituting their own identities as Indigenous and non-Indigenous administrators, teachers and future teachers.

Theoretical underpinnings

As explained earlier, the fundamental concept to this study is *racialisation*. Racialisation is "a political and ideological process by which particular populations are identified by direct or indirect reference to their real or imagined phenotypical characteristics in such a way as to suggest that the population can only be understood as a supposed biological unity" (Miles cited in Troyna, 1993:28). There is a range of other terms such as ethnicity, culture, nationality and heritage that have replaced the now discredited concept of biological 'race' (Keeffe, 1992; Troyna, 1993). What is consistent across all forms of usage is the problem that emerges from the homogenising way these terms are often operationalised, which renders all those who are named and categorised, as the same. In part then, racialisation is the use of categories that produce homogenised understandings of very diverse groups of people.

Therefore, although we may accept that race is a social/cultural construct, not an objective biological reality, we still need to examine why people still act as if there are races. In the case of Indigenous peoples in Australia and Canada, racialisation shaped Indigenous relationships with the white invaders/settlers and each other. Historically, policies and practices in both countries shifted from neglect, to segregation, to assimilation and integration, to self-determination/self-government. These changes in Indigenous policy in both countries demonstrate that racialisation processes are dynamic and often contradictory.

Racialisation also occurs through the absence of overt racial categories. This has been called a process of *deracialisation* (Reeves, 1983, cited in Troyna, 1993:28). That is, there is a covert use of racial evaluations. It is possible to see how deracialisation operates when examining what appear to be benign statements, such as in the case of the AREP, where it was often argued that the program was a strain on educational resources because of the small group numbers involved. Heated debates centred around diverse issues, such as the need for 'standards' to be maintained in AREP – a reference to the comparison between AREP and mainstream teacher education courses – or the notion that group conflict within the AREP students themselves was 'bad for the cause'. Racialised, homogenising and essentialist notions of the Indigenous students and mainstream students were central to such debates. As Troyna (1993:29) put it: "This covert use of racial evaluations serves important political purposes… because it is often capable of 'justifying racial discrimination by providing other non-racist criteria for the differential treatment of a group distinguished by its racial characteristics'."

However, the answer is not simple. Indeed, deracialisation as an ideological practice can contribute to ongoing inequality once students begin teaching. Hesch (1993) argued in his Canadian study of the Saskatchewan Urban Native Teacher Education Program (SUNTEP) that ideological practices, such as behaviourist pedagogical theories, contributed to future exclusion of aboriginal youths from school. "The demand that preservice teachers implement behaviourist 'effective teaching' strategies which largely standardise the experience of both students and teachers, and which limit the possibility for curriculum innovation, recreate the same problems which earlier drove many of these same preservice teachers out of schools in their youth" (Hesch, 1993:14).

While racialisation is a central analytical tool in this book, it was not enough to understand AREP and NORTEP through this lens only. The focus on racialisation presents a number of methodological problems, which I take up in the next chapter. To be able to compare and contrast the two programs, I have also used a multi-level analytical structure based on Bourdieu's theory of practice. This was done through an overview of the *field* of Indigenous education in both countries. At another level, I examined the meso or institutional arrangements of AREP and NORTEP and the struggles of individuals within the programs. Again, Bourdieu was useful because through case studies it is possible to see that institutions are "structured and structuring" (Grenfell and James, 1998:174). The micro-political dimensions to this study – the focus on individual and collective struggles – revealed the way in which *habitus* not only shapes the *field* of Indigenous education but how it is in turn shaped by it. Using this theoretical framework provided an opportunity to reveal the agency by which, within constraints, Indigenous peoples have shaped Indigenous education in both countries. This approach necessitates a move beyond culturally deterministic models of Indigenous education.

Purpose of the book

The book has three main purposes. The first is a *theoretical* purpose: to develop a theoretical framework based on the notion of racialisation that can contest 'culturalist' explanations by providing a more complex explanation of Indigenous teacher education in Canada and Australia. The second has a *policy* purpose: to examine the possibilities and limitations of initiatives in Indigenous teacher education in general and enclave type programs in particular and their relation to the 'mainstream'. The third purpose is to examine *practice*: to provide data for reflection and examination of the two enclave programs.

As stated earlier, this study grew out of a range of issues and problems in an Indigenous teacher education program that had to be dealt with on a day-to-day basis. While examining other models of

Indigenous teacher education and the paradigms used to understand Indigenous education in general, I was struck by the dominance of 'culture' as an explanatory tool. Furthermore, the focus on culture seemed to be creating a situation whereby more and more research was being done yet the debate was not moving forward (Nicholls et al., 1996). Firstly then, the purpose of this book is to provide some fieldwork in Australia and Canada that permits a comparative study of the continuities and discontinuities of racialisation and the way that this shapes the life and educational experiences of those involved in Indigenous teacher education. This fieldwork is described in more detail in the next chapter. The comparative approach should make it possible to compare local responses and identify similarities and differences, rather than operating on binaries that have plagued the research in this area. So the first purpose is to shift the debate further through providing a different window onto theory and practice.

The second purpose of this book is to provide a basis for discussion about the ongoing possibilities for Indigenous teacher education in Australia. A critical history should permit new directions to be identified. Relative to Canada, Australian Indigenous education has taken a long time to move towards community control of schools and programs. While this is happening now, what is the justification for this direction? As in girls' education, in Indigenous education '*separate*' meant '*less than*' a generation ago. However, a long list of class, linguistic and religious groups has operated schools and institutions separate from the mainstream in Australia. There are Catholic schools, Jewish schools and international schools, to name but a few, among the private sector of Australian school education. Separate seems popular in Australia in the contemporary period. This book aims to contribute to this debate through an analysis of the ways in which community-controlled education generates the promotion, as well as the containment, of diversity.

Finally, since administrators, teachers and teacher education students within these programs are always struggling at the cutting edge and have little time for reflection, it is hoped this book contributes to a greater understanding of the forces that contain and create agency in Indigenous teacher education.

Significance of the book

There has been no comparative study of Indigenous teacher education in Australia and Canada that looks at processes of racialisation. Some work published by Hughes and More (1993) compared the learning styles of Indigenous students in Australia and Canada. However in Chapter 4 I present a critique of the 'learning styles' form of analysis that has been so dominant in Indigenous education at all levels. So the first significant aspect of this book is the break with dominant forms of explanation – such as learning styles theory or reified culturalist explanations – in Indigenous education.

The book is also significant because it makes a break from victim discourses by conceptualising 'cross-cultural' contexts as sites of negotiation. The book seeks to explore the ways in which people act rationally to improve their material circumstances but also how these decisions are constrained by historical and contemporary relations and structures. This is done through an examination of the strategies and responses made by administrators, teaching staff and students in the programs under study. The book seeks to highlight not so much the differences in relationships – although these exist and will be discussed – but what Nakata has called "complementarity" rather than separateness (Nakata, 1995:25 cited in McConaghy, 1997b:131). This is a fundamental epistemological break from other empirical research in this area. Cultural dissonance has dominated discourse in Indigenous educational policy and theory with the resultant reinforcement of notions of the 'specialness' of Indigenous students which then equate with notions of 'less than', 'unable to change or adapt' and a range of other victim discourses. It is my contention that victim discourses are also made to capture the agency through which Indigenous peoples in Australia and Canada fight to shape their lives in general and their educational opportunities in particular.

Structure of book

Chapter 2 introduces the research design and theoretical framework. It provides an overview of the methodological issues in undertaking comparative studies as well as 'cross-cultural' research. This chapter outlines the fieldwork that was conducted in Sydney and La Ronge while a more extensive literature review is taken up in Chapters 3 and 4.

11

Chapter 3 outlines the historical context that bears down upon – shapes, constrains, allows – Indigenous education outcomes in Canada and Australia today. It outlines the ideological and political dimensions of racialisation. A comparative history of state/Indigenous relations in Canada and Australia is presented to provide a context for understanding the two programs, AREP and NORTEP, which are the focus of the study. The historical roots of Indigenous political activism and challenging of state governance by Indigenous peoples in both countries help to situate the two programs in an on-going struggle for self-management.

Chapter 4 maps the dominant paradigms in Indigenous education. It reveals the hegemony of culture as an explanation for difference and Indigenous educational inequality. These dominant paradigms are critically assessed through the theoretical framework developed from combining Miles' concept of racialisation with Bourdieu's concepts of field and habitus.

Chapters 5 to 9 draw on secondary historical analysis and on primary data gathered from fieldwork in Sydney and La Ronge. Chapter 5 describes the history of the Aboriginal Rural Education Program (AREP) at the University of Western Sydney, New South Wales, Australia. It analyses the changing form and content of the program – and the accompanying debates about institutional arrangements, struggles over pedagogy, Aboriginality and funding.

Chapter 6 examines the Northern Teacher Education Program (NORTEP) in a similar light but spends a little more time describing the Indigenous struggle for control over education. This is because Indigenous peoples in Canada have pushed more into this area and we can learn from their struggles. Indigenous struggle in Canada has led to a much greater degree of Indigenous control of Indigenous education programs such as NORTEP, than in Australia. This highlights one important difference in state/Indigenous education between the two countries.

Chapter 7 analyses the ways in which important administrative and academic personnel in the AREP and NORTEP programs have managed the political, cultural, economic, social and educational nature of the two programs in this study. The data in this chapter is largely drawn from interviews and is concerned with managing diversity.

Chapter 8 continues the micro-political analysis that began in Chapter 7 but this time examines the pedagogical and philosophical principles espoused by teaching staff. In addition, the identity struggles that take place in teaching and learning contexts will be discussed. In this chapter it is possible to begin making some generalisations about the ongoing ideational processes of racialisation in the teaching and learning context.

Chapter 9 explores the formation of neophyte teachers. This is achieved through an examination of their histories in relation to schooling and the program so far; their understanding of 'community' and ideas about pedagogy. The chapter also analyses the often-contradictory production of student identities as future *Indigenous* teachers, thus revealing once more the on-going dimensions of racialisation.

Chapter 10, the conclusion, returns to the central concerns of this book and gives an overview of the essential themes arising from the study. It will consider policy implications and the usefulness of theoretical and methodological frameworks.

Chapter 2

Making Meaning in Cross-Cultural Studies

Methodological and Theoretical Perspectives

Method

A range of methodological 'problems' shapes the research questions that are at the heart of this book. A short discussion of these will be developed to set the parameters as well as interests and approaches used in this book.

One of the central concerns was to remove a focus on the 'Other' as a self-contained category (Nakata, 1997). That is, I wanted to focus on students and their teachers, not in terms of their difference, but in order to gain an understanding of the way that racialised identities are negotiated in relations of unequal power. For Indigenous students and their Indigenous and non-Indigenous staff, the struggle to make sense of their lives created opportunities for empowerment and at times, confusion, on the part of all involved.

One of the problems with studying people as 'self-contained' categories is that this approach often leads to the categories in social life being taken for granted and the relationships between them studied (Connell, 1996). What is in fact complex and different is presented as homogeneous and simple. Connell has shown that this categoricalism biases research towards a concern for what is normative (that which is expected or approved) rather than 'common' or the way things usually happen (*ibid.*). In research involving Indigenous and non-Indigenous participants, normative approaches can take the categories of analysis for granted (i.e. as cultural absolutes) and foreground social relationships solely in terms of ethnicity.

As far as confusion is concerned, there was a set of difficulties that I encountered in my role as a non-Indigenous researcher. The study, as I suggested earlier, grew out of my involvement in Aboriginal education for the past eighteen years and had been shaped by the urgent daily matters that I faced as coordinator of the AREP. My research role could perhaps be best described as *participant objectivist* (Grenfell and James, 1998:176). My history in the AREP was not from a dispassionate, distanced and detached position as in the participant observer tradition. What this means, is that the observations made are not value-free or neutral because I am also "positioned in a field, which structures the representations" (Grenfell and James, 1998:176) produced. Yet, even with this awareness I will only be telling a partial narrative. As a participant objectivist, I bring a practitioner's perspective to historical documents and theoretical paradigms to the interviews and analysis in this book. I also bring a gaze shaped by a gendered white racial identity and working class background and the privilege that might or might not carry with it. The participant objectivist orientation provides space for these experiences, which are generally outside of the analytical framework that circumscribes or shapes data gained from formal interviews (Hammersley and Atkinson, 1995:140). As a reflexive sociologist however, I also attempt to maintain a reflexive stance. An insider epistemology is useful but there's always something going on behind your back!

My aforementioned 'whiteness' will be seen as part of the insider/outsider epistemology. Should a white woman be talking about Indigenous education? There are many debates about the role of non-Indigenous researchers who research Indigenous issues. These are important because they alert us to the ethics of what we do as academics (Brady, 1992; Troyna, 1998), and in this instance extending to teachers in schools. Questions of power – in terms of how the research is constructed and for what purpose – alert us to the political nature of intellectual work (Katz, 1992). Where unequal power relations are part of what is being evaluated, then it is necessary to critically scrutinize how power works through the research process itself.

In addition to the recognition of power in the research process, there is also the need to address the issue of authenticity. It could be argued that not being a 'cultural insider' is one reason for rejecting non-Indigenous researchers' claims. Fay (1996:9) calls this argument solipsism and suggests that such an approach "is the theory that one can be aware of nothing but one's own experiences, states, and acts". Such 'one-self-ism', sees the self as a thing rather than as a process, Fay further argues (*op.cit.*:232). Fay's model of culture is of an "interactive zone of activity" through which the self is formed, in interaction with others (*ibid.*). Seeing culture as a process is a powerful insight that helps shape the analysis in this book. It means that all people engaged in the research process are part of cultural production.

There have been real concerns about the historic misrepresentation of Indigenous cultures by academics, which has contributed to a negative categorisation of Indigenous peoples. This is the consequence, in part, of these researchers failing to make explicit that which remains hidden – their subjectivity. The subjectivity of the researcher includes their life history, theoretical orientation, and power in relation to the participants and practical purpose. Nakata (1997) alerts us to this problem. Methodologies that conceal the interests of the researcher have produced a fetish for "anthropological explanations by educationists" that encourages "a blindness to the *reality* of situations in favour of making visible an external referent culture" (Nakata, 1997:426). Neo-colonialism continues in organisational and legitimating forces such as research paradigms.

We can explore this process through examining a debate between Williamson (1997) and Nakata (1997). Williamson uses an interactionist framework to analyse the history of schooling for Torres Strait Islanders from 1873-1941. He uses this framework as well as a grounded theory method to analyse his data. He is hoping to avoid what are known as 'victim discourses'. This approach, he argues, allows for the agency of the actors to emerge and for theory to be developed from such data rather than being theory-driven like most historicist 'official' accounts (Williamson, 1997:413). Nakata argues, in response, that if there is no positionality (such as Williamson's) or any understanding of the fact that interviews are "cultural negotiations" then he misses the "systems of thought" that mark out what Nakata (1997:430) calls the "epistemological locatedness" of the interviewees.

Nakata argues that Williamson's theory of Indigenous education is caught in the new conventional orthodoxy. This orthodoxy relates to the use of dualisms which are inherent in the race-relations framework, a concern which is taken up in Chapter 3. There is no questioning of categories or an attempt to understand the way in which hierarchies of power shape these categories. Williamson accepts the words of his informants as representing Torres Strait Islander culture through a focus on their cultural *difference*. Nakata

17

argues that, consequently, explanations for Torres Strait Islander responses are always understood in terms of their approximations to whiteness (1997:428).

Working with Indigenous academics has heightened my awareness of the importance of these 'positionings' and alerted me to seeking new ways of framing issues in my research. Any framework that seeks to do this must rely less on cultural attributes as a way of describing difference and focus more on how power is produced and reproduced within specific contexts. This is more in keeping with a *realist* approach than positivist. The main difference, as Fowler puts it, is that "realists accept that explanations may involve analysis in terms of unobserved entities" (Fowler, cited in Grenfell and James, 1998:72). The purpose of research from this realist perspective is to reveal the pretence of an observable, rational truth.

The focus on *racialisation* in this study is an attempt to move away from a focus on 'culture-as-an-explanation' in Indigenous education. Chapter 4 outlines the debate more extensively, and builds on the above concept of culture as a process or culture as a social relation (Chan, 1997:70). Using Bourdieu's theory of practice, it is possible to situate the formation of cultural practice within a broader *field*, which Chan (1997:71) defines as "a social space of conflict and competition, where participants struggle to establish control over specific power and authority, and, in the course of struggle, modify the structure of the field itself".

In developing a framework to analyse this process using the case studies of two Indigenous teacher education programs, AREP and NORTEP, there was a need to acknowledge that negotiation, struggle or agency occurs from positions of inequality. These *systems of power hierarchies* (Grenfell and James, 1998:169) can be analysed in any field. In Indigenous teacher education, the field consists of the historical relationships between the State and Indigenous peoples; the disciplinary knowledge used in education systems and which have reproduced and legitimated practices that produce inequality; and the way that Indigenous education has been racialised. It also consists of the power that is invested in educators over (Indigenous and other) students in classrooms via the regimes of assessment, standards and routines.

Change occurs to this field through the interaction of *habitus* and field. Habitus is "the systems of dispositions" that agents "have acquired by internalizing a determinate type of social and economic condition" (Bourdieu and Wacquant, 1992:105). Administrators, teaching staff and students all bring "a feel for the game" (Chan, 1997:71) which is enacted in relation to the field. In the case studies of AREP and NORTEP, a rupture often occurs when habitus meets the field and someone feels like a fish out of water either as a student or teacher. The analysis of the way in which specific forms of racialisation manifest at one particular level and come to influence or be taken up at other levels, becomes the final object of this process (Connolly, 1998:133). Racialisation shapes the field as well as the "feel for the game" that the various agents bring to the 'habitus' of Indigenous teacher education programs.

Data collection and analysis

Macro level

The field of Indigenous teacher education, which is the focus of this book, is situated within a much broader field of power, namely Indigenous/State relations. This governance shapes possibilities for agency at all levels. In no other area of education has the role of the state been so continuously invasive.

In gathering data about the role of the state in Indigenous affairs including education, I have drawn on historical documents, reports and evaluations of the programs and first hand accounts through interview materials. This data enables a contextualised understanding of the social relations producing the conditions in which the two programs operate.

The study is also cross-cultural in the sense that it compares the Canadian and Australian contexts. This was done to highlight ways in which neo-liberal States simultaneously constrain and create conditions for change, but they do so in different ways in different places at different times. Chapter 3 will examine this process.

Understanding the macro aspects of this study was challenging from the point of view that while I was part of the AREP, I was an outsider to NORTEP. This meant I knew less about the relationships between the Canadian nation and Indigenous peoples than I did about the Australian context. Indeed, the focus on teacher education was a consequence of serendipity.

I first became aware of NORTEP when I travelled to Canada in 1992 hoping to do a comparison of elementary schooling for Indigenous students. I met a woman in Saskatoon, Saskatchewan at an

Indigenous language forum organised by the University of Saskatchewan where I was visiting at the time. By chance she was travelling to La Ronge the next week and proffered an invitation. We visited Stanley Mission and discussed reserve life and teaching on reservations, and I was invited to talk to her students at NORTEP about Aboriginal English.

After a week I left La Ronge and thought no more of NORTEP until I began coordinating the AREP in 1993. It was at this point that the urgency of day-to-day issues – and the prompting by one of my supervisors – changed my focus to comparing the two Indigenous teacher education programs rather than schooling systems.

So, I was a cultural outsider – non-Canadian – and had little time or opportunity to replicate my involvement and understanding of NORTEP in the way in which I had come to know AREP. Therefore, my analysis was focussed on how NORTEP, as an Indigenous teacher education program, might help me better understand the AREP by providing a 'new window' onto some of the same issues.

During my time in Canada, I immersed myself in the media and in libraries to get a sense of the historical formation of the Canadian nation. As will be discussed briefly, the formation of the nation in Australia and Canada required creating a space for Indigenous peoples. The continuities in terms of racialised taxonomies which were used as justification for governance were striking, though the form of governance differed in Australia from Canada. Thus, the actual consequences for Indigenous groups were markedly different in terms of rights. This will be taken up in Chapter 3 and more closely again in Chapters 5 and 6.

I read extensively about the history of Indigenous education in Canada while visiting in 1992. When I returned in 1996 I spent three months at the Ontario Institute for Studies in Education (OISE) in Toronto where I had some wonderful support from Professor Barbara Burnaby who had a lot of involvement with Indigenous language issues in Canada. From here I returned to Saskatchewan and continued to research the various Indigenous groups' struggles to gain control over education in that province specifically.

A number of days were spent at the Saskatchewan Teachers' Federation looking through their archives which revealed their long association with Indigenous activists. Conversations took place with the director of international programs at the Saskatchewan Indian Federated College (SIFC) in Regina regarding funding, philosophies and future directions; and workers in the Indian Teacher Education Program (ITEP) at the University of Saskatchewan and I also attended a twenty-year celebration of NORTEP back in La Ronge. In short, I came away invigorated and committed to Indigenous control over education. This did not mean there were fewer complexities in Canada. Nor did I maintain such a simplistic analysis as the study progressed.

One of the reasons for this related to the way in which the Indigenous population seemed to be so heavily racialised in terms of the classificatory system that governed their rights. I saw this taxonomy – Status Indian, non-Status Indian, Inuit, Métis, Bill C31 – as anathema in my understanding of race-relations. I had yet to learn that it also created diversity and access to on going rights – something that was sorely missing back home.

Interestingly, I came home and began to share some of these observations. I was confronted with responses that included seeing the Canadian system as more highly racialised and akin to apartheid. How, for example, were they ever going to 'learn about' Indigenous people if *they* were kept separate? This wasn't that different to my initial response. There had always been a concern that having AREP separate was no good for the 'other' students.

So the comparative aspect of this study provided a new lens through which to understand 'race' as an organising category and as a political tool in general but specifically in education. I also saw more sharply the contradictions of racialisation and therefore the *possibilities* for advocacy.

For example, from this analysis it was possible to understand the call for control over education in Canada and the different types of educational policy making in each country. This macro analysis enabled a better understanding of the politics of difference situating struggle in a broader context.

Meso level

The case studies of AREP and NORTEP are *institutional* case studies. Situating both programs in the broader historical context allows important connections to be revealed. This means that it is possible to examine the way in which institutions are, as Grenfell and James (1998:174) put it, "structured (organisationally, managerially, ideationally) and structuring (in terms of their constitutive effects on

21

local activities) structures". That is, it is possible to see local interpretations within constraints. While staff within the AREP and NORTEP are constrained by – similar but different – issues such as funding, issues of curriculum control and staff development, they nevertheless act within these constraints to bring about transformation.

Again, to understand and explain the two programs, a range of data sources has been used. In the case of NORTEP, Carnegie (1991) provided a particularly useful review of the general background to the philosophy, aims, obstacles and pedagogical debates of NORTEP since inception. This helped locate and organise a range of histories and statistical data that was provided to me by the director of NORTEP. Material obtained from libraries at the University of Saskatchewan and the Saskatchewan Teachers' Federation provided a diversity of narratives from Indigenous and non-Indigenous activists. I attended the World Indigenous People's Education Conference, 1996, in Albuquerque where Keith Goulet (MLA, Saskatchewan) talked about his role and others in the struggle to get NORTEP up and running.

A much smaller and less useful review of AREP (Centre for Indigenous Australian Cultural Studies, 1996) provided some outlining of the program's development. Another study of the enclave model (Lynch, 1990) provided some insights to the processes of racialisation in the early development of the program – in particular the ideologies concerning Indigenous people circulating in the parent institution at that time.

I made much use of minutes of meetings, some archival bits and pieces such as memorandums, plans for restructuring, debates about future directions and other day-to-day materials. As I was the keeper of these documents – and sometimes the producer – they were well synthesised in my thinking about the issues. In addition, data was produced which provided figures related to retention rates, length of course until graduation and dimensions of gender. This immersion is typical of standard ethnographic practice.

Both analyses were supplemented by interview material of administrators in each program as well as the researcher's own observations and history in the AREP as coordinator and lecturer. These interviews are discussed in the next section. There is no attempt to compare the two programs with other Indigenous teacher education programs.

Micro-political relationships

Interviews

In this study, I interviewed administrators, academics and students of the AREP and NORTEP programs to provide an insight into the micro-political aspects of teaching and learning. The problem became one of analysing the way in which those at the coal-face – the administrators, teachers and students in these programs – negotiated difference.

The analysis contained in Chapters 7 and 8 is drawn from transcripts of 19 academics and administrators – five from NORTEP and 14 from AREP. Chapter 9 is based on interviews with 16 students from AREP and NORTEP. In the NORTEP program I interviewed five out of eight permanent staff members (including two Indigenous staff) and eight students (including one non-Indigenous student). In the AREP 14 staff were interviewed and nine students. They were semi-structured interviews and with all participants I discussed the following:

- The program – curriculum and teaching/learning processes.
- Life histories in relation to education to gain a sense of their formation of identity as a teacher (staff) and future teacher.
- Inter-cultural experiences prior to the program and since. Success or not of enclave mode.
- Reasons for participating in the program.
- Future plan (pedagogical change, jobs).
- For staff involved in administration, we discussed the early and on-going development of the program to gain a sense of the shifting political and pedagogical frameworks.

While most interviews covered this terrain, in some instances not all areas were covered. In relation to AREP, I knew all of the students, had taught them at some stage, was the coordinator of their program, and felt a responsibility to allow them space to talk about the issues as they saw them. This does not deny power in the interview situation, rather it seeks to diminish its effect and avoid *symbolic violence* (Grenfell and James, 1998:124) towards the interviewees. In effect, it means allowing the interviewee to treat the process as one of cultural negotiation rather than one of imposing categories. This form of reflexive ethnography (Hammersley and Atkinson, 1995:20) acknowledges that I am part of the research and that by imposing categories on the interviewees, I am objectifying my own subjectivity and research. In the next section on analysis, I expand on this process.

In terms of NORTEP staff and students, I was an academic visitor with minimal knowledge of the Canadian context. I felt that the students who spoke with me were partly there through curiosity (Australian film star and icon Paul Hogan and a dolphin were starring on a telemovie the week I was interviewing), partly through the possibility of student exchange but largely because *they* had something they wished to tell me. The interviews themselves were, as Nakata (1997:430) suggested, cultural negotiations.

Analysis

Since most of the interviews were free flowing narratives, the participants constantly negotiated meaning (Mishler, 1986). This narrative approach provided rich data but made analysis extremely difficult particularly in relation to coding. Following Mishler, I consider the narratives were joint constructions.

> Labov's notion that respondents appear to be partially "reliving" their experience when they tell stories about dramatic or stressful events in their lives and therefore do not "monitor" their talk is neither reasonable in terms of our general understanding of discourse nor in accord with what we know of the interview process...the interviewer's presence and form of involvement – how he or she listens, attends, encourages, interrupts, digresses, initiates topics and terminates responses – is integral to a respondent's account. (Mishler, 1986:82)

Acknowledging that narratives are joint constructions immediately sets up a situation that demands attention is paid to the *social* functions of acts and events in the real world as expressed in the narrative (Mishler, 1986:84). As I outlined above, participants were given the option of asking me questions or adding to their narrative (outside of the guiding questions) at the end of the interview. In many instances, this elicited additional material that showed that participants had a sense of purpose in the process of interviewing. Some sought clarification in a kind of mutual sharing of perplexing issues, while others wanted to reiterate specific elements of the discussion or return to themes that had not been fully explored. The following response from a student at NORTEP illustrates this point:

> ... up here where you say, "What's the worst thing about school?" I found that the community that I was growing up in... I didn't want to bring up anything that was negative... [Jessie: 9, lines 9-12]

What was of interest was that this student had intentionally decided not to speak of negative events and when she did it was intensely personal. This alerted me to the fact that being a cultural outsider in Canada carried with it certain limitations and that perhaps Indigenous students are wary and tired of telling stories of oppression (Jones, 1998).

Invariably these final questions and statements gave *coherence* to narratives. In many of my interviews the interviewee controlled the narrative which left me with little idea of how to work with the data. In the end it was the themes arising from interviews – created by elaboration, reiteration and expansion – that provided the analytic categories (Mishler, 1986:89). This approach, after Bourdieu, is reflexive because it will "implicate the researched and the researcher in the same theory of practice" (Grenfell and James, 1998:157).

However, the process could not be described as 'naturalistic' since there was no attempt to describe and "tell it like it is" (Hammersley and Atkinson, 1995:205). Bourdieu's multi-level analytical structure for a theory of social practice produced a 'way of seeing' the material.

In the generation of concepts for this book, I was guided by evidence of knowledge, beliefs and actions located in the general analytical framework of racialisation within the field and habitus. Concepts were also generated by the participants in interviews – another dimension of agency – and provided insights into the overall development of a theory of practice. These are 'sensitising concepts' which give a general point of reference rather than defining prescriptions of what to see (Hammersley and Atkinson, 1995:212).

In interpreting the interviews, I kept in mind the advice of Solomos and Back (1994:157) "to decipher the meanings of racialised identities without attempting to prioritise one classification as more legitimate than another". The dominant discourse surrounding Aboriginal education has focussed on 'culture' in a way that Solomos and Back would call the *metonymic elaboration* or the coding of 'race' as culture (1994:156). However, this discourse is filtered in specific, local contexts and articulated to the social relations.

Each interview or narrative was treated as a 'case study'. A case study "involves the investigation of a *relatively small* number of *naturally occurring* (rather than researcher-created) cases" (Hammersley, 1992:185). A case study can give you different insights to an issue than a survey can. When analysing the teachers' narratives it was important to understand how the conditions and the experiences they have had shaped their understandings. To that end it is also necessary to consider the personal histories of each or the intersection of their biographies with history to understand their ideological discourses, pedagogical philosophies and practice.

This is of course what Bourdieu (1990:54) calls habitus. "The *habitus*, a product of history, produces individual and collective practices – more history – in accordance with the schemes generated by history. It ensures the active presence of past experiences, which, deposited in each organism in the forms of schemes of perception, thought and action, tend to guarantee the 'correctness' of practices, and their constancy over time, more reliably than all formal rules and explicit norms." Racialisation is then part of the habitus of all of us on the one hand since we interact with a racialised field, but it is also different depending on our positioning within that field.

Limitations

In the introduction, I insisted upon an anti- or post-colonialist approach to this book. I did this because I did not want to continue operating on simplistic binaries as if we – Indigenous people and others – are unknowable to each other. However, it is also true that by my very position as AREP co-ordinator, and as a white female, I carried in some instances power or lack of power into the research contexts and processes of the book.

As a result, I do not claim that everything in this book is 'truth'. Indeed, I have made it clear that my concerns emanated from daily matters as co-ordinator of AREP. There were struggles around standards, competencies, outcomes, teaching and learning styles, resistance, language, assessment practices and so on, which were daily concerns of the AREP co-ordination process. These seemed to be a continuation of the same issues that I had faced in a predominately Aboriginal primary school working with Aboriginal *children*.

This suggested the dominance of particular racialised ideologies in the cultural dissonance thesis. Unlike my earlier work in schools, I was no longer happy with the culturalist approach that explained student behaviour and inequitable outcomes in terms of cultural difference. This approach cannot account for difference within Indigenous students themselves and within the 'whites' that dealt with Indigenous education at all levels. In this sense I was, and I still am, captive to theoretical fashion (McConaghy, 1994). Yet, I began to move back and forth between my gut responses and theoretical claims. Relating rather than observing seemed to be a way of bridging differences: it was important to acknowledge and cast off the hegemony of objectification.

In this sense, my analysis is shaped by these experiences and limited by my concern for a theoretical approach that gives agency back to actors in these contexts rather than one that explains them away through overly deterministic structural arrangements. Yet, as I am aware how constraining and limiting these structures can be, they are at the same time central to examining how and why and what people do to transform their lives.

The relationship to education that I have developed also limits my analysis. I am aware that behaviourist traditions of schooling go a long way towards rejecting children, despite their proficiency at academic tasks. The hidden curriculum of conformity to middle class norms – themselves often idealistically constructed – tends to be valued and rewarded more than just academic performance. Hence, the overwhelming focus on 'culture' as a way to deal with differences in values and behaviour. Such positivist or normative research paradigms are concerned with defining the 'aberrations' of Indigenous students and with shaping them into – and judging them by – 'white', middle class normative outcomes.

The book is also limited by the fact that it does not attempt to describe and analyse the policy shifts in Indigenous education since these have been done well elsewhere (McConaghy, 1997b; Nakata, 1991; Haig-Brown, 1988; Barman et al., 1986; Burnaby, 1979). The purpose is mainly to provide an understanding of the context in which each program was created; what each program hoped to achieve; the difficulties faced, and the influences shaping future direction. These two programs provide moments during which the complex and changing processes of racialisation of Indigenous teacher education can be observed and their contradictions highlighted.

In trying to understand the Indigenous student trajectories in relation to the field of education, I was interested in their "sense of identity of interest" (Connell, 1985:158). The interviews were therefore focussed partly on their paths to teaching including schooling experiences past and present, as well as significant others in forming one's identity as a future teacher. Their experiences of AREP and NORTEP were also central issues in the interview process. The research became an exploration of the 'generative principles' (Bourdieu and Wacquant, 1992) that structured, and were structuring (Grenfell and James, 1998:174), racialised discourses and social relations in the two programs. The same principles were explored through an examination of the habitus of administrators and teaching staff in interviews.

The limitation of this approach is that 'meaning' is constructed by me from and with the interviewees in Canada and a combination of observations and interviews in Australia. I do not imply that what is said is done. Rather, I am concerned with the meanings that people attach to their activities, and how this meaning can be understood. This is in terms of the broader institutional and narrower individual subjectivities that are part of the processes of the racialisation of Indigenous and non-Indigenous people in Australia and Canada.

Conclusion

The relation between different levels of analysis can be explored through an example from one of my interviews with an AREP student. At the macro level, Aboriginality in Australia is defined by important gate-keeping institutions as self-identification, community acknowledgement and/or descent. You must be Aboriginal to attend the AREP and receive financial support. The AREP itself is a result of recognition of the need for Aboriginal teachers in any strategy to reduce Aboriginal educational disadvantage. The impact of classifications based on race is starkly portrayed in the story of Gladys.

Gladys accompanied another student I interviewed (with my and the interviewee's permission) because she "wanted to see what it was all about". She hadn't originally volunteered for an interview. At the completion of the interview she said: "Well that's alright then, can I come and talk to you?" During the eventual interview with Gladys it became clear what her purpose in speaking to me was – the assertion of identity. During the sociology of education class that I taught to the AREP students I had used a reading from Kevin Keeffe (1992) on Aboriginality-as-ethnicity. The reading caused a degree of discomfort and anger because it challenged the taken-for-granted idea that Aboriginality was *inside* the person (essential). Gladys and another student became very quiet in class. Gladys also became upset and was crying during the interview claiming that I had denied her identity using the Keeffe argument because as a stolen child there was only *this knowledge in her heart* to confirm her identity.

Gladys finished her degree and is doing casual teaching. She is also being investigated by education authorities as to her 'true' identity. If found not to be a 'true' Aboriginal, she will have to pay back the financial support given to her during the AREP course. Gladys was given an identity by the State, had it stolen, reclaimed it and now is having it taken away again.

Racialisation is therefore central to any understanding of the educational and life experiences of the Indigenous and non-Indigenous participants in the two programs – AREP and NORTEP.

policy context:
space invaders
diversity
past.

Chapter 3

Comparative Perspectives on Race and Culture

> [The ideology of racial inferiority]... is, after all, the baggage that your forefathers and your fathers and mothers, your teachers and your leaders, all those who have loved you and whom you loved, have given you. It is a troubling inheritance. Because to deny it is to deny something of yourself. (Noel Pearson, *Sydney Morning Herald*, 11.11.93. p.11)

Introduction

The aim of this chapter is to explore some of the dimensions of 'the baggage' that Noel Pearson refers to in the above quote, in particular how it is carried in the changing dimensions of racialisation that have created special relationships between Indigenous people and the wider society in Australia and Canada. A cross-cultural comparison involving Australia and Canada is useful for illuminating the *different* and *similar* processes and contexts in which racialisation takes place. It also helps make sense of broad policy changes from assimilation to self-determination/self-government by examining the way in which *race* has been used to develop Indigenous policy in general, and Indigenous education policy in particular.

The history of State/Indigenous relations will be explored with particular reference to the prevailing constructions of 'aboriginality'[1] and the ways in which these shape policy for Indigenous peoples in both countries. The significance of racialisation to this study can be demonstrated through examining the historic policies of removal and 'training' of Indigenous children in Australia and Canada. These types of policies, which have led to what are known as the 'stolen

---

[1] Aboriginality is used here in the generic sense to describe all Indigenous peoples.

generations' in Australia and residential schools in Canada, have contributed to ongoing cultural, social, economic and political inequalities. Using the concept of racialisation, it is possible to develop a framework that has explanatory power in relation to the tensions that are produced in the two Indigenous teacher education programs that are at the heart of this book. The comparative nature of this study also provides an opportunity to examine how processes of racialisation are *challenged, reproduced* and *transformed* in different contexts, thus revealing agency within constraints.

We have witnessed the changing dimensions of racialisation during the past four decades in Australia and Canada in a number of ways. In this period, there has been intense renewal and change in terms of the rights of immigrants and, in particular, Indigenous peoples. The Australian nation has debated republicanism, the 'Mabo' judgement of the High Court established new possibilities for Land Rights while a Reconciliation process has accompanied reports on *Aboriginal Deaths in Custody* (Muirhead, 1988) and on the stolen generation (National Inquiry into the Separation of Children from their Families, 1997). Canada has also been undergoing constitutional change in recent years. There have been historic decisions such as the establishment of an Indigenous province, Nunavut, while debates about national identity have accompanied the challenge of Quebec to secede from Canada. In the attempts by governments in both countries to redefine national identity there has been a review of the relationship between the State and Indigenous peoples. This has provided the space for the contestation of social constructions of 'aboriginality'.

The paradoxes created through historically racialised identities are revealed in this book through the case studies of AREP and NORTEP. That is, while policies and practices have been aimed at addressing educational inequality, which is the consequence of historic racialisation, they also continue to maintain the racialised politics of categorisation. Troyna calls this the *benign* process of racialisation because it aims to provide access and equity to hitherto disadvantaged groups (1993:29). Some understanding of the historical process of racialisation theoretically and empirically is therefore in order.

'Race-relations' and colonialism

While there are remarkable similarities in the contemporary status of Indigenous peoples in Australia and Canada we need to understand these similarities as emanating from historical factors of colonisation and settlement that have occurred in both countries. Given that Indigenous peoples in Australia and Canada have had somewhat different post-contact experiences it is interesting to note the striking similarities in contemporary rates of Indigenous unemployment, recidivism, school *rejection* rates (Coolangatta Statement, 1993:6) and health status. One of the reasons for this is that the relationship between Indigenous and non-Indigenous peoples in both countries has been characterised by institutional and individual racism. Institutional racism is "both a racist theory and a social practice embedded in institutions that systematically exclude subordinate members from equal participation and treatment in society" (Bolaria and Li, 1988:30). Individual racism centres on the discursive frameworks that construct as inferior those who are 'coloured' or seen as different 'races' of people. The problem, however, with the concepts of individual and institutional racism is that they often fail to account for processes of change. They become phenomena to study rather than ways of explaining negotiation and change.

Interaction between Indigenous peoples and the State[2] is a central part of any analysis of how these conditions have emerged and more recently have been transformed. Change must be seen as resulting from "action within and upon" the limits set down by society (Fleras and Elliott, 1992:ix). The State in both Canada and Australia, from the first moments of contact with Indigenous peoples in the periods of land appropriation, constructed policies based on assumed Indigenous racial inferiority. However, the concept of agency is also central to understanding how change has occurred despite oppressive State policies and practices. Indigenous peoples in Australia and Canada (and some non-Indigenous peoples working alongside them) have resisted racism and fought for fairer, more inclusive, outcomes.

While historical atrocities are now widely recognised and documented, the legacy of racialisation continues today. The *Report of the National Inquiry into Racist Violence in Australia* found in 1991 that "racism and racist violence permeates the day-to-day lives of Aboriginal and Islander people" (Human Rights and Equal Opportunity Commission, 1991:72). This, it was claimed, had a cumulative effect that expressed itself in feelings of hopelessness,

---

[2] The State being the original colonising powers such as the British and the French, and later the nation-state.

33

powerlessness, anguish, distress and emotional disorders among Indigenous people. It is important to stress that these psychological effects are not the result of cultural disintegration but of continuing legal, political and economic discrimination. For example, Justice Muirhead (1988) found that sentencing was often harsher for Aboriginal people and more likely to be handed out than alternative measures such as bonds or community service. Furthermore, medical assistance was often not procured when the prisoner appeared in distress, resulting in a high number of Aboriginal deaths in custody.

Frideres (1988) pointed out that life on reserves in particular in Canada was no better. These areas are often targets for heavy-handed police activity in terms of surveillance and constitute a continual threat of physical violence. Racism in the police force, lack of employment, poor housing and shortages of water and sewerage systems are factors influencing health and well being of Canada's Indigenous peoples. On reserves in Canada "fewer than 50% of Native homes have sewer or water connections; another 50% can be described as overcrowded" (Du Charme, cited in Fleras and Elliott, 1992:6).

Illness has a critical impact on educational success. In Australia, childhood illnesses such as chronic ear disease result in between 10% and 40% of Indigenous children with hearing loss "significant enough to interfere with education" (Reid and Trompf, 1991:58). Almost three times as many Indigenous children contract diseases such as meningitis, pneumonia and respiratory tract infections. This rate is also twice as high as that for the Inuit and Navajo in North America. Childhood in Australia for Indigenous people is the beginning of a relationship with hospitals that will see them admitted two and a half to three times more often than for children in the total population (Reid and Trompf, 1991:50).

In both countries, Indigenous people are more likely to suffer from diabetes, heart disease and diseases of the respiratory system. All of these diseases are chronic and affect potential for access in life. The impact upon families is underestimated. Children miss school to tend sick relatives or because of their own illnesses. Parents are deprived of the support of grandparents. In addition, illness and death are occasions for familial and community responsibility. In the AREP and NORTEP students speak of the difficulties of leaving home and often have to return to bury or tend sick relatives. In Australia, this responsibility is often ridiculed in the racist term 'gone walkabout'.

The financial stress placed on communities is exacerbated by the high dependency ratio resulting from unemployment and the number of children of school age. Often it is the most able who leave to seek work in urban areas thus taking potential income with them. It is also the most able who attend AREP and NORTEP. When they attend these courses, they not only carry their individual hopes but also those of their families and in many instances, whole communities. But because both programs are residency-based, attending the courses requires absence from the very people who most rely on them.

These are some of the legacies that have been outlined many times and which have been the subject of royal commissions in both countries – the *Royal Commission on Aboriginal Peoples* (1996) in Canada and the *Royal Commission into Aboriginal Deaths in Custody* in Australia (Muirhead, 1988). The socio-economic circumstance of Indigenous peoples in Canada also reveals inequalities in Canadian society. Unemployment rates are three times the average of non-Indigenous Canadians. Nearly half (45%) of registered Status 'Indians' depend on some form of social assistance, two and a half times the Canadian average.

> On certain reserves up to 95% of the population subsist on welfare or unemployment benefits. Alcohol/substance abuse and broken families are all too common, and leave youth permanently scarred – income levels are well below average both on and off the reserve, with family incomes of about $9,300 – less than half the national average. (Fleras and Elliot, 1992:16)

Our understanding of Indigenous teacher education is severely limited without some understanding of these conditions of Indigenous inequality and of how they were produced, and are reproduced today.

However, while this sort of macro knowledge provides insights into the material conditions of Indigenous peoples in Australia and Canada, there are some central problems with using this approach. In developing a theoretical framework for this study, it was necessary to examine this dominant approach to Indigenous and non-Indigenous relations. Known as the 'race-relations' problematic (Miles, 1993) this paradigm has been used, as I have done above, to explore historical oppression and to explain on-going disadvantage. However, it has also been harnessed by those advocating that Indigenous students have different 'learning styles' (Hughes and More, 1993; Andrews and

Hughes, 1988) and in ethnographies charting the culturally different ways of understanding the social relations of the classroom for Indigenous students (Malin, 1990; Harris, 1990; Barman et al., 1987). While these have been useful in challenging assimilationist models of schooling there is a danger of cultural determinism inherent in such approaches (Nicholls, Crowley and Watts, 1996; Haig-Brown, 1995). This is why it is important to explore the nature of such an approach as a dependency upon the existence of 'races' renders the 'race-relations' approach problematic.

Miles (1993) provides one of the most vigorous theoretical overviews of the concept of 'race' and 'race-relations'. In his work *Racism after 'race relations'* he explored the ways in which race is operationalised in different historical contexts. He points to the ideological and political nature of racialisation:

> There are no 'races' and therefore no 'race relations'. There is only a belief that there are such things, a belief which is used by some social groups to construct an Other (and therefore the Self) in thought as a prelude to exclusion and domination, and by other social groups to define Self (and so to construct an Other) as a means of resisting exclusion. Hence, if it is to be used at all, the idea of 'race' should be used only to refer descriptively to such uses of the idea of 'race'. (Miles, 1993:42)

The beliefs about 'race', those that circulate as common sense, are therefore ideologically and politically constituted. The 'idea of race' has a long history. 'Race' is not an invention of modern times because there is evidence to suggest that the concept existed prior to capitalism and colonialism (Miles, 1993:7) but it nevertheless gained *ascendancy* during the 18th century and continued to grow throughout the 19th and 20th centuries. This was in part due to the growth in science and the notion of a 'natural' order of inequality. The idea of inferior races proved useful in supporting the imperialist desire to appropriate land in the new colonies.

Most of the early developments in theories of racism and ethnicity have occurred in the USA and the UK, within the disciplines of sociology and political science, although economic theory has also developed a theory of racial discrimination in the labour market. Broadly grouped, sociological theories of race and ethnic relations fall into a number of opposing camps. Firstly, there are those concentrating on the biological determinants of race and racial behaviour. Secondly, there are assimilationist or cultural theories and, thirdly, political economy or neo-Marxist theories. More recently, there have been feminist post-structuralist and post-colonial revisions of these theories. Within each strand of theory, there are great variations.

Biological theories of race

Biological theories view race as a scientifically observable phenomenon. Racial differences are seen to be a result of the 'objective' differences that arise because of perceived physical differences between peoples, with races defined as groupings of people with a set of physical traits similar to other members of the race in question, but significantly different from the physical traits of other races. Racial differences emerge because of either physical difference on the 'inside' – genetic differences or *genotype* – or physical differences on the 'outside' – such as skin colour, hair texture, eye shape or *phenotype*. Races are classified as Negroid, Mongoloid, Caucasian, Asiatic and so on. As Wilson reminds us, "it is only when social and cultural attributes are associated with physical features that the concept racial and hence that of racial groups takes a special significance" (1973:6).

Tucker (1994:12) argues however, that there were many contradictions in scientific research related to 'race' that can only be explained by politics. An example is social Darwinism,[3] which he described as "a mixture of oversimplified biology and opportunistic politics that arose as the dominant sociological thought of the late nineteenth century" (*op.cit.*:26). In this typology of races, the 'white races' or Caucasians were viewed as the superior race, with greater intelligence or ability than other 'coloured' races. The resulting racist ideology was invoked to justify both the inferior social position of coloured people in western societies and the oppression of Indigenous people in colonial societies. In Canadian and Australian history, these theories of white racial superiority were often linked to notions of the religious superiority of Christianity (cf. Bolaria and Li, 1988; Evans, 1975), with the Indigenous peoples of both countries viewed by

---

[3] Social Darwinism was taken from Darwin's work and stressed the 'survival of the fittest'. Herbert Spencer is the major exponent of this normative framework for moral principles (Tucker, 1994:26).

colonialist regimes as both physically and spiritually inferior (Castles et al., 1990; Frideres, 1988). This racist ideology justified the white invasion and the subsequent dispossessing of Indigenous people of their land by British and French colonialists.

Its main persuasive power lay in its belief that the weaker would die out as the species evolved. In fact, this belief was so strong that Australia and Canada had 'white only' immigration laws thus making invisible their resident Indigenous populations.

> By the time of Federation in Australia (1901) and Canada (1867) immigration policy was explicitly racist. Given that the "White Canada" and "White Australia" policies were not formally abandoned until 1962 in Canada and 1973 in Australia, immigration policy was, for more than a century, based in both countries on unambiguously racist attitudes. (Collins, 1993a:3)

It is possible to see other developments from the 18th century to the late 19th century in the concept of 'race'. Malik (1996) presents a thesis in *The Meaning of Race*, which points to the period of the Enlightenment during the 18th century as the philosophical roots for the modern discourse of 'race':

> I want to show that the Enlightenment and the emerging capitalist society that accompanied it, established for the first time in history the possibility of human equality but did so in social circumstances that constrained its expression. The tension between a profound belief in equality and the social limits on its articulation... has been central to the modern articulation of race. (Malik, 1996:40)

We have here an important new link to contemporary racialisation. Racialisation now exists in the context of class relations, of unequal social relations; it does not simply have a 'life of its own' (Miles, 1993). The modern discourse of 'race' is particularly pertinent to this study. Colonisation of the 'New World', including Australia and Canada, led to nation-states that were developed on the principles of the Enlightenment. Policies emanating from the imperial centres reflected the racial ideology of the time, resulting in inequality or exclusion for 'coloured' others. However, it is also true that the agents of the colonising powers carried with them a *range* of racial ideologies that continued to circulate regardless of 'official' accounts.

In other words, as Stephen Castles (1996:18) put it "it is no longer useful (if indeed it ever was) to speak of racism. We need to examine specific *racisms*, as they affect particular groups in various locations and times." Therefore, while humanitarian policies related to welfare provisions were the official goal of racialised policies, racialised practices were often less than humanitarian in the distant colonies.

Assimilationist theories

Assimilationist theories of race and ethnic relations first emerged in the USA in the 1920s with the work of Robert Park (1922), who studied the ethnic diversity of American society through the prism of a 'race relations cycle'. This cycle, according to Park, started with the initial contact of new ethnic groups with the host society, after which competition would emerge over scarce resources, such as employment and housing, leading to ethnic conflict. Eventually these conflicts were accommodated and the new ethnic group became assimilated. With the arrival of a new ethnic group to the USA, the assimilation cycle from ethnic conflict to harmonious assimilation was repeated. In Park's theory, assimilation was narrowly defined (cf. Ujimoto, 1990:213-20), but later proponents to the assimilation school, such as Milton Gordon (1964:71), introduced variables such as prejudice and discrimination into the assimilation process. He viewed assimilation as a more complex phenomenon dealing with cultural, behavioural, structural, marital, identification, attitudinal, behavioural and civic aspects. The assimilationist model became the dominant mode of studying American race relations. As Pierre L. van den Berghe (1967:7) put it, "the field has been dominated by a functionalist view of society and a definition of the race problem as one of integration and assimilation of minorities into the mainstream of a consensus based society".

The assimilationist theory of race relations has been criticised on theoretical grounds by Richmond (1973) on the basis that it is doubtful if complete assimilation would ever occur, and by Rex (1983) who doubted the universality of value systems and race relations systems that assimilationists claimed. Rex suggested that pluralism might equally be expected as the outcome of ethnic conflict as singularism or assimilation. African-American scholars have been particularly critical of assimilationist theory in recent years since the 'assimilation' of peoples of colour in the United States has not taken place (Carmichael and Hamilton, 1967 cited in Collins and Henry, 1994; Omi and Winant, 1993). Proponents of the political economy or neo-Marxist school reject the 'culturalist' focus of racism that is implicit in assimilationist theory and its emphasis on the immigrants' cultural 'baggage' in explaining the dynamics of immigrant life in their new adopted countries. Bolaria and Li (1988:20) argue that in order to understand the social construction of racism in Canada for example, it is necessary to focus on the structure of Canadian society and the historical way in which immigrants have been introduced into capitalist society, particularly in relationship to the labour market. They view 'race' problems as beginning with labour problems, and view racism as something inherent to the process of capital accumulation rather than external to it as the 'cultural differences' approach of the assimilationist school suggests.

Even though the United Nations Educational, Scientific and Cultural Organisation (UNESCO) have argued there is no scientific basis for the concept of race, the legacy of colonisation continues. While race is a socially constructed concept, not an objective difference based on phenotype – physical appearance – or genotype – genetic difference (Bolaria and Li, 1988:16-17), the power of racial categories resonate through time.

Colonialism and the Indigenous Diaspora

In viewing the colonial past there is a tendency to only see the relationship of the government and/or dominant culture to the Indigenous population. This is usually the result of examining policies and measuring their failure or success of the relationship of Indigenous people to the wider society in terms of socio-economic indicators. The categories used to speak of, describe and legislate for Indigenous peoples in Canada and Australia are therefore highly racialised. This is because the categories are often applied as if they were homogeneous and static, which allows some socio-economic trends to be revealed but also conceals important differences within the Indigenous experience. The problem here is that Indigenous identity becomes reified and constructed in terms of indicators that do not allow an understanding of all the dynamics of day-to-day living.

One common denominator for Indigenous experiences in Canada and Australia is in British colonialism, although for Indigenous Canadians French colonisation was also important. Patterson suggests that we could look at colonisation as the latest in a series of events in the life of the 'Indian':

> The Indian is the norm; the others are the outsiders. He is the native. If he goes into the white man's world he is expanding his identity to include aspects of the new life introduced by the outsider. This view or something like it is the one held by many 'Indians', especially the younger militants. Without the 'Indian' and the 'Canadian' view together, the story will not reach the heart of Indian history. (Patterson, 1972:4)

Yet, it is not merely a matter of choosing to take on aspects of the dominant culture. The parallel experiences have been about the role of colonialism and imperialism in each country as well as the freedom of the individual to negotiate new cultural forms, but within the constraints of racialisation.

While Indigenous peoples in Canada and Australia were very different groups of people, from London, England where imperial control originated, "'Indians' were as much a part of the colonial situation as were Africans, Australian Aborigines or Maoris" (Patterson, 1972:12). Patterson argued that emerging national histories forget about these colonial parallels due to a concentration on the emergence and construction of the new State (1972:12).

Of critical importance in the colonialist trajectory was the Poor Law of 1834 (Armitage, 1995), which set out the first welfare system to contain the growing urban poor in England. In 1837, a select committee on Aborigines used the Poor Law as the basis for dealing with people who were living 'outside' the 'system'. The concern for social order was paramount. This approach by the British State shaped the futures of Indigenous people in Australia, Canada and New Zealand. The areas of education, law and religion were given special attention. According to Armitage (1995:4) important components of this approach included:

- Special recognition for the situation of children, who were considered particularly open to change, education, and salvation
- A recognised place for organised Christianity as an essential element in the process of producing citizens

- A commitment to a legal and regulatory process anchored in a separate law for those outside the mainstream of society, pending their full citizenship.

It is clear that through a focus on religion, education, law and civilising processes, the *intended* outcome was cultural genocide for the Indigenous peoples in both countries. The 'welfarist' approach to governance in Indigenous affairs still permeates Aboriginal/State relations in both countries, and has been referred to by Hesch (1993) as neo-colonialism. An important feature of neo-colonialism is the intrusion of the State into the lives of Indigenous peoples – to provide important welfare and other services – but in a racialised and often-contradictory way. As Noel Pearson, quoted at the start of this chapter argues, therein lays the neo-colonial paradox. State welfare for Indigenous peoples is an important, belated right, but welfare dependency or what Pearson has called 'passive welfare' can become a problem for Indigenous peoples in Australia, and possibly Canada, today.

Part of the benefits of State intervention has been the creation of space in education for special programs and entry provisions for Indigenous peoples – with AREP and NORTEP manifestations of this – but at the same time financial pressures always threaten the viability of the programs. All the while, aboriginality is the central organising and/or legitimating principle for both of the programs' existence. Therefore, Indigenous *identity* and *control over its construction* is a site of struggle in both Canada and Australia.

The colonial past is therefore central to the political and economic significance of 'race' in Indigenous affairs. If we place Indigenous people at the centre of the narrative, we can see the familiar trajectories of colonisation, assimilation, integration and self-determination/self-government. In the case of Australia and Canada – both countries experiencing large-scale and culturally diverse immigration programs – the development of State policy for Indigenous peoples ran hand in glove with that of immigrant minorities. Indigenous and immigrant groups are similar in one regard: both groups have been racialised (and in the process so have the rest of the two societies), with the public and private sector relating to them through the gaze of racial difference (Collins and Henry, 1994). Evaluations and expectations of those overtly racialised have resulted in unequal opportunities and outcomes.

Yet, important differences have united Indigenous peoples globally and make their situation different from immigrant minorities. Land is politically, and often economically, central to the Indigenous diasporas: having had it stolen, reduced, bought or controlled. Indigenous groups have expressed a wish to retain their lands, while immigrants dream of lands voluntarily and sometimes involuntarily, left behind. Therefore, the relationship of land to the nation-state needs examination.

The building of nation-states

Nation-states cannot exist without a land base. All activities such as religion, rites of passage, and patterns of movement, social exchanges, economic independence and education relate in some way to land. As a physical, spiritual and economic space, land is the defining feature of Indigenous/non-Indigenous conflict. Traditional Australian and Canadian Indigenous stories relate to the earth as a thing to nurture, to feel responsible for and to protect. It is however the differential State treatment of the rights of Indigenous people to land that marks out some of the differences between Canada and Australia.

Up until confederation in 1867 Europeans (British and French) and Native peoples of Canada had developed some economic relationships. For Canadian Indians, hunting for fur-bearing animals to trade with the white economy largely replaced previous subsistence hunting and migratory patterns (Burnaby, 1979:32). From the late 17th century the Métis[4] were an identifiable group playing a crucial role as 'middlemen': interpreters, guides, canoeists, trappers and at times traders at trading posts (Redbird, 1980:3). Very little contact was made with the Eskimo[5] people, as the Inuit were then known.

Relations changed during the 19th century when a range of land treaties were signed with Indigenous groups so that Canada could become a federation.[6] These changes were hastened by concerns that the United States of America (USA) was encroaching on Canadian territory, particularly in the central Prairie Provinces. In addition, Canadians did not want the same type of bloodshed that had occurred

---

[4] The Métis were originally identified by their dual French and mostly Cree ancestry. More recently this definition has changed to include mixed ancestry of any Indigenous and non-Indigenous community.

[5] Now known as the Inuit with their own land base restored to them called Nunavut. Inuit also live outside Nunavut.

[6] Chapter 6 discusses these in greater detail with particular reference to Saskatchewan.

in the USA between 'Indians' and settlers, so they sent out the Royal Canadian Mounted Police to engage in negotiations for treaties.[7] In Canada, numerous treaties were signed to extricate the land from the Indigenous population during the development of the nation-state (Frideres, 1985). But it was these treaties, and the negotiated rights contained within, that mark out some of the contemporary differences among Indigenous peoples in Canada.

The *British North America Act* (1867) united the new nation and gave the government of Canada legal right over the affairs of 'Indians'. This was followed by the *Indian Act 1876*, which gave the Federal government total control over Indigenous affairs including education. In the signing of treaties, it is possible to see the relationship between the requirements of the nation-state and the business interests[8] it served, and the changing racialisation of Indigenous peoples in Canada.

Bolstered by increased numbers through immigration (Hawkins, 1989) and a diversified economy, the colonisers began to view traditional pursuits and traditions of land ownership of Indigenous peoples as a hindrance (Burnaby, 1979:33). This was followed by the dispossession of Indigenous land, which occurred largely by treaty in Canada. In Australia, particularly NSW, Indigenous peoples were simply driven off their land – not without struggle – by white settlers, since the doctrine of *terra nullius*[9] removed the need to consider compensation. When Indigenous people in both countries got in the way of expanding agricultural needs their lands were further appropriated, while they, the rightful owners, were moved to 'protected' reserves and sometimes given training to farm them (Goodall, 1996; Buckley, 1993). Buckley argues that Indian policy in the prairies that attempted to do this failed because training for farming was "part of the framework of civilizing" and because the tools provided were inadequate (1993:39).

Civilizing pedagogies were scaffolded by particular racialised ideologies. In Australia, it was commonly thought for example, that

---

[7] This history is well documented on the Royal Canadian Mounted Police website at http://www.rcmp-grc.gc.ca/html/125news.htm .

[8] The Hudson Bay Company with whom many Indigenous trappers and traders worked, wanted to protect its interests and land treaties were an important part of their relationship with the State. (See Bourgeault, 1988.)

[9] The British Government determined in 1785 that Australia was a 'no-man's land'. In other words, empty (Attwood, 1996).

the 'indigene' was 'child-like' (Fletcher, 1989a:149-51). Consequently, training, employment and education were limited by racialised assumptions about intelligence and morality. Civilizing pedagogies created exclusionary practices through denial of Indigenous cultural knowledge and the narrow range of employment options available to Indigenous peoples. The Church also participated in civilizing pedagogies independently and in association with the State (Buckley, 1993). Protection that would 'soothe the pillow' was seen as the best thing for those who 'through no fault of their own' would eventually die out (Patterson, 1988; Reynolds, 1981).

As in Australia, early conflict in Canada developed over land used for farming by the colonisers and land used by the Indigenous groups for hunting. There is an important difference, though, as already noted. In Canada the result was a series of treaties between the State and Canadian Indigenous peoples, whereas in Australia the concept of *terra nullius* prevented any such treaties being made (Rowse, 1993). The very act of drawing up treaties in Canada meant that the land in question was actually acknowledged as being owned by some Indigenous people and that there could be a continuing legal basis for compensation. But the treaties did more than this; they effectively gave the government control over the land – and the people who once owned it – for hundreds of years. Indigenous peoples in Canada are categorised by the State before access to educational or other programs is permitted. Indeed, rights of access to many Indigenous education programs depend on this categorisation. The modern expression of this was, until recently, that many rights for Canadian Indigenous people depended on living in separate reserves as 'Status Indians'.

In Australia, the land was considered *terra nullius* (Reynolds, 1981) which was coupled with the fact that the British did not attempt to understand Indigenous land tenure and social organisation. They presumed that Aboriginal people were too primitive for such developments. In keeping with the ideology of Social Darwinism, British colonialists deemed themselves superior to – and took their so-called 'rightful' place in dominating and controlling every aspect of – Indigenous life. These relationships between white settlers and the Indigenous peoples in Canada and Australia were shaped by the racial prejudice of individuals as much as by official State pronouncements. For example, in Australia there was a directive from Britain that the 'natives' should be treated with respect and that no violence was to ensue from the process of 'settlement' (Goodall, 1996; Reynolds, 1981). In practice, the land was taken when needed – often violently because of resistance – with no treaties and no compensation.

The Mabo[10] judgement over turned the notion of *terra nullius* and it was hoped that this would set the stage for a new relationship between Indigenous people and the Australian State (Rowse, 1993; Pearson, 1993). But this has not eventuated because in the Mabo judgment only those Indigenous Australians who could claim relationships to land in anthropological terms or provide evidence of continuous occupation had a right to land rights (Armstrong, 1996). In a country where the dispossession of land from Indigenous people was the key policy, it is not surprising that only a few that still live on traditional lands can claim continuous occupation.

Such ethnocentrism, which was enmeshed in the colonial view of the 'proper' use of land, individual ownership of property and the rightness of Christianity were the hallmarks of racialised policies Indigenous peoples lived with throughout the 19th and into the 20th centuries.[11] At the frontiers in both Canada and Australia Indigenous people were critical to frontier expansion. In Canada the key was the fur trade, in Australia it was livestock, mainly cattle and sheep. Even though their knowledge and skills were critical to their employers, payment and opportunities for Indigenous workers were dictated by the desires and needs of the colonisers.[12] In Australia in the latter part of the 19th century Indigenous workers were paid in rations while immigrant minorities like the Chinese and *kanakas* were paid, albeit low, wages (Collins, 1991:203-4). The development of the nation and a desire and belief in progress framed social policies and political action which in turn shaped Indigenous, and non-Indigenous lives in Canada and Australia.

---

[10] The Mabo decision was handed down by the High Court of Australia in June, 1992. While it could not recognise Indigenous sovereignty, since this was an international matter, it could recognise common law. Common law in Australia, upon colonisation stated there should be "respect for the rights and privileges conferred by native title" (Rowse, 1993:5).

[11] For an excellent Australian history of this process see Goodall (1996) *Invasion to Embassy: Land in Aboriginal Politics in NSW 1770-1972.*

[12] The report into the *Stolen Generations* outlines the impact of race-based policies in the area of training girls for future work as domestics and boys as farm labourers at http://www.hreoc.gov.au/social_justice/stolen_children/index.html.

Nationalism and identity

Benedict Anderson (1991:7), when examining the cultural roots of nationalism, argued that it was unequal social relations and the pluralism of religion exposed during the Enlightenment that created the conditions in which the sovereign state emerged. The concern for the common good over the individual saw the beginning of the concept of citizenship and mass participation within a nation. The idea of community, as a vehicle to express unity regardless of inequality, was born. Nationalisms and unifying symbols – flags, language, and often religion – conceal many differences and various forms of inequality.

At the end of the 18th century the nation was a voluntary, political association that had no concern for ethnicity because it was concerned about the 'common good' (Malik, 1996:134-35). While nation-states in the 19th century began to consider issues of ethnicity and language, the initial concern was about overcoming parochialism to encourage a more outward looking community (*ibid.*). This historical denial of particularism still manifests itself in contemporary struggles around 'place' or 'space' within the nation-states of Australia and Canada. Indeed, the contemporary global struggles around ethnicity illuminate the tension between 'community' and how it is constituted and the freedom and rights of the individual.[13] Conflict is therefore central to the nation-state as it tries to manage the manifestations of inequality. The education system, controlled by the State, has, since the creation of mass education, been "called upon to manage conflicting pressures for conformity and diversity" (Wotherspoon, 1995:45).

One of the consequences for Australia of this 'imagined community' free of differences was the persistent belief until the 1970s and 1980s among mainstream Australia that Aboriginal people had largely disappeared, or only a handful of 'half-castes' remained (Reynolds, 1981). Beliefs such as these had also been supported by the use of racial taxonomies, which the State used to implement policy. The reason that this view changed (and consequently official numbers of Indigenous peoples in Australia rose) was because the

---

[13] Mary Two-Axe Early argued in Canada that as an indigenous woman she did not want to be excluded from the Charter of Rights and Freedoms and left to the governance of indigenous men. This she argued was because those men had often been her oppressors *The Globe and Mail* (29.5.92).

State definition of Aboriginality changed.[14] Before this time, the relationship of Indigenous people to the nation-state depended on gradations of colour.

> They were graded, Colleen and Margaret. We got a letter stating that Margaret was one-sixteenth of an Aboriginal; Colleen was one-fourteenth of an Aboriginal. I don't know how they worked that out: same mother, same father. It was their shades of Aboriginality. (Rintoul, 1993:279)

It was commonly believed that the only 'real' Aboriginal people were those who were black, spoke an Indigenous language and lived in remote areas. Anyone else was a half-caste, quadroon or even an octoroon (Fletcher, 1989a; McConnochie, Pettman and Hollinsworth, 1988). The myth that Aboriginal people were dying out or were being assimilated not only helped sustain the belief that Australia was a nation of bronzed Anzacs, it also justified removing children from their parents. (This view of course forgets that Aboriginal soldiers did fight in the first and second world wars, but they too were forgotten as soon as the troops came back home.)

It is possible to get a sense of this ideology in the following comments by government officials regarding residential schools as early as 1847 in British Columbia, Canada:

> Their education must consist not merely of the training of the mind, but of a weaning from the habits and feelings of their ancestors and the acquirements of the language, arts and customs of civilised life. (Prentice and Houston, cited in Haig-Brown, 1988:29)

In Australia, at this time and for the best part of the next century, Aboriginal people were consistently judged in terms of 'blood'. Children were stolen from their parents if they had any 'white man's blood' in them because it was believed they could assimilate. 'Full bloods', on the other hand, were thought to be noble yet doomed. However, because of the dominance of Christian morality at this time

---

[14] An Aboriginal person is defined as a person who is a descendant of an indigenous inhabitant of Australia, identifies as Aboriginal, and is recognised as Aboriginal by members of the community in which she or he lives as Aboriginal (Langton, 1993:29).

and the general belief that Indigenous peoples were a lesser race, the children of black/white relations were often denigrated.

> I do not know that either physically or morally the half-caste is as good a man as the full-blood. There is a very good reason for that. The fathers of the half-castes are naturally the most depraved white men, and if heredity counts for anything, it must mean that those children are worse than the full-blood children. (Fletcher, 1989a:97)

The spectre of hybridity, as well as recognition of some hidden sexual violence, was a reason for keeping races apart. As Young (1995:25) describes: "... attention was immediately focussed on the mixed race offspring that resulted from inter-racial sexual intercourse, the proliferating, embodied, living legacies that abrupt, casual, often coerced, unions had left behind."

Rather than denying multiple ancestries, the Métis celebrated their unique positions in Canadian society as an Indigenous yet non-native people. Their Christianisation by the French speaking Oblates meant that the sudden migration of the Protestant English into their territories during the mid to late 19th century meant not only loss of land (as part of the Hudson Bay Company's transfer to Canadian ownership) but also religious and linguistic domination (Flannagan, 1971). The term used to describe Métis – half-breed – reflects the racialisation processes but not the meanings attached to the term. The celebration, rather than denial, of multiple identities is a significant difference and can be explained in part by the involvement of the French and their opposition to the British. The Métis were not officially recognised as Indigenous until 1985 and are still struggling for a land base at Red River, Manitoba, the scene of an uprising in 1869-70 over the incorporation of the 10,000 strong Métis community into the Canadian Nation (Flannagan, 1979:28-29). But a Métis class never developed in Australia in the way that it did in Canada, an interesting difference that has not been researched in any detail.

Canadian categorisation of Indigenous people by the State is quite complex. The major categories of *Status 'Indians'* and *non-Status 'Indians'* included groups using 'tribal' names such as Dene and Cree, as well as the Métis. Again, the generic term 'Indian' is still used but is generally considered politically unacceptable because of its colonialist roots and its tendency to homogenise. The term 'native' is also sometimes used. Again, usage has changed in recent years to reflect the diversity of political struggles both locally and globally.

Australian and Canadian colonising powers made invisible the diversity of Indigenous cultures and languages through racial categorisation and in some ways this is a deconstruction and renaming process which is a regaining of symbolic power. In the case of the North American continent there were over 500 nations with more than 600 languages and dialects. In Australia there were over 200 languages, 600 dialects and 400 nations. Calling such a diversity of people 'Indians' and 'Aborigines' assisted in homogenising a diversity of groups, a process necessary to the developing nation.

However this homogenisation had a contradiction: it also shaped an Indigenous political unity which was critical to contesting oppressive social arrangements. In Canada previously separated groups of Indigenous peoples were suddenly thrust together. When this racialised process was coupled with the growing European presence, the high mobility of the Plains Indian, and the boarding school experiences in the 19th and 20th centuries, Indigenous people created a sense of common identity (Patterson, 1972:8). This identity was created out of a specific set of events, an (imposed) shared history, not a 'racial' essence (Hall, 1995). The growing tendency to collective resistance was fed by and through such practices in Australia as forcing disparate groups to live together on missions for the purpose of civilising (Goodall, 1996).

Therefore, the contradiction of these periods which were aimed at assimilating and civilising groups on the basis of a constructed 'race' provided space for people who were previously unknown to each other to come together to redefine and shape these same categories towards achieving political, economic, social and cultural goals.

In summary then, the removal of ancestral lands in both countries created 'a problem' for white administrators which they have historically grappled with, in a paternalistic manner. Policies have changed from 'protectionism' through to blatantly racist policies of assimilation which saw the development of residential schools in Canada (Haig-Brown, 1988; York, 1990:22-53) and led to the 'stolen generations' in Australia (Read and Edwards, 1989). The resulting legacy was one of distrust, alienation and cultural suppression between Indigenous peoples and their white colonial masters.

The periods of large-scale immigration to Canada during the latter half of the 19th century (Hawkins, 1989) contributed to the creation of

50

reserves. It is no coincidence that the *Indian Act* (1876) was established at this time and that the *Indigenous Protection Act* (1909) was established during Australia's highpoint of 'Anglo-ness' (Kalantzis, 1990).

So the legacy of 18th and 19th century racialised taxonomies created particular forms of Indigenous identity in Canada and Australia. These were created through language, in terms of 'naming' groups; economically in relation to payment for work and access to land, and in other forms of social organisation such as education and religion.

20th century (re)visions

Racialisation is a political and ideological process that constantly changes over time because as a process and a practice it has emanated from particular contexts and particular interests. The 20th century has seen the re-imagining of citizenship and national identity in Australia and Canada and the subsequent revision of racialised policies and practices. These changes have occurred as a result of State intervention, of changing demographics and of Indigenous activism.

As the early 20th century dawned and immigration continued to change the shape of Australian and Canadian societies, outdated racialised policies and practices were sharply drawn into focus. During the late 1880s to the late 1930s in Australia there was a period of intense nation building. Australia developed a 'protectionist' stance which was essentially inward looking (Kalantzis, 1990:66). This was the period from 1901, of the 'White Australia Policy', a policy that protected the local labour market through a racist immigration policy as well as 'protecting' Aboriginal people "by separation, by drawing boundaries of exclusion" (*ibid.*).

However, labour was needed in both countries for nation-building (Wotherspoon and Satzewich, 1993:29). Large-scale immigration occurred in Australia and Canada from the middle of the 19th century. Racial pecking orders were established. In Australia, in the late 19th century, Chinese workers, who earned more than Kanakas ('blackbirded' from Fiji), earned much less than Europeans. At the bottom of this racial hierarchy, Aboriginal workers worked not for wages but for rations of sugar, tobacco and flour. The first immigration legislation in the Australian colonies in the 1850s was to restrict Asian immigration (Collins, 1991). In Canada in 1885 a poll tax was imposed on Chinese residents and between 1823 and 1943 Chinese immigration was prohibited entirely (Li, 1988). This was the period in which discourses of 'white nation' were created (Hage, 1998:180) and attributes of 'whiteness'[15] were created in opposition to non-whites.

The major difference between 'White Australia' and 'White Canada' was the explicit nature of the former, and the discrete nature of the latter. As Hawkins (1989:8) put it: "In Canada, in a national sense... the whole episode of White Canada is often downplayed, or clothed in discrete silence... In Australia, however, this was not the case. Their White Australia was a public policy in the plainest sense of the term.

In both Australia and Canada in the early part of the 20th century, and after the First World War and during the depression, reserve lands were taken from Indigenous peoples and given to white immigrants and returning soldiers (Wotherspoon and Satzewich, 1993:33-34; Parbury, 1986; Goodall, 1996). These policies destroyed successful Indigenous farming endeavours on reserve lands in the Canadian prairies and in the wheat/sheep belt of South-Eastern Australia. In Australia, the 1930s were the highpoint of biological determinism where racial taxonomies were developed to control immigration and for mapping the population in the census (Markus, 1988).

Post World War 11

The post-1945 period has seen a marked increase in immigration and the recent entry of Asian migrants to both Australia and Canada. The policy of assimilation in Australia and Canada became severely tested when it became clear that immigrant groups were becoming disadvantaged (Collins, 1993a:13). By the 1970s, the white Australia and white Canada policies were erased from immigration laws. The era of non-discriminatory immigration policy had finally arrived in culturally diverse Australia and Canada (Collins and Henry, 1994). It appeared that assimilation "was so successful... that it created the conditions of its own demise: a culturally diverse society" (Kalantzis et al., 1990:17).

---

[15] The concept of 'whiteness' is currently enjoying a great deal of attention. The arguments are multiple and complex and there is not the space to take them up here. The inclusion of the term is to signal that myths about 'whiteness' also exist.

Throughout the 1950s and 1960s a period of integration saw an unprecedented growth in the internal migration of the Indian[16] population. Between 1951 and 1961 the number of 'Indians' in urban areas tripled (Burnaby, 1979:13). The beginning of the sixties also saw the start of cultural debates in Canada. In 1960, Aboriginal people obtained suffrage and in 1963 a Royal Commission on Bilingualism and Biculturalism was set up and continued until 1971. The Commission floated the notion of the French and English as the "founding races" (Burnaby, 1979:5).

In the struggle over culture in Canada in the sixties, there appears to have been an attempt to include 'Nations' in the concept of the nation-state. However, they were to have no special rights compared to the 'founding races', the British and French. The two official languages, for example, were to be English and French. Here was a deliberate attempt to make invisible the Indigenous presence through the privileging of the dominant cultural/linguistic groups. This was at the same time that Jean Chrétien[17] was arguing that to continue *special* arrangements – such as Federal control of Indian education – was a racist policy (Hawthorne, 1967). Yet, as the Indian was constructed by the dominant as 'Other', they also defined unity among *themselves* as a means of resisting this exclusion and domination.[18] In Chapter 6 there is an exploration of the way in which this marking out of cultural boundaries, specifically in education, produced the seminal paper *Indian Control of Indian Education* (National Indian Brotherhood, 1972).

In Australia, in the late 1960s black and white segregation occurred in picture theatres and local swimming pools, particularly in rural towns. Indigenous activists and sympathetic whites directly exposed and challenged this on *freedom rides* to Aboriginal missions and towns. This was an important example of Indigenous and non-Indigenous activists struggling together for change. Significantly, it wasn't until 1960 in Canada and 1967 in Australia, that Indigenous people were granted citizenship rights.

[16] The term 'Indian' is used here in direct reference to its usage in the text quoted. Currently, *First Nations* is the preferred term, which is inclusive of a range of indigenous groups with various official statuses within Canada.
[17] Jean Chrétien is currently Prime Minister of Canada but was Minister for Indian Affairs at the time.
[18] Refer to Miles, 1993 page 42.

The consequences of the original differences in the basis for land rights still resonates today in Canada where there has been a policy of 'containment' of Status 'Indians' on reserves for much longer than in Australia, despite the drift of increasing numbers of Status 'Indians' to urban areas (Waldram, 1989; Frideres, 1988). Control of education in this context has different meanings to control in Australia where Indigenous students are most commonly found in integrated classrooms in the public system. In Australia the policy of containment of Indigenous peoples on reserves was abandoned in the 1950s (Parbury, 1986) and with it a gradual decrease in Aboriginal-only schools. In the 1960s and especially since 1972, when a policy of 'self-determination' began, there has been a rapid increase in the number of Indigenous people moving to urban areas (House of Representatives Standing Committee, 1992). These differences mean that the delivery of services such as housing, health, education and legal representation should take into account the needs and situations of rural and urban Indigenous peoples (O'Neil and Waldram, 1989).

Despite a number of differences, there can be little question that the parallel experiences, in terms of governance, in Australian and Canadian societies continued beyond colonisation. For instance, Patterson speaks of the "intra-commonwealth influence" (1972:3) whereby minorities in one country seek to emulate the superior position of minorities in another State. In recent years of course, we have seen a global dimension to the Indigenous diasporas[19] with such events as the World Indigenous Peoples Conference in Education, and international youth and health conferences. Also, global organisations such as UNESCO provide a platform for Indigenous groups to take their concerns outside the nation-states.

Identity and contemporary politics

Canadian governments questioned racial discrimination somewhat earlier than Australian governments partly through Aboriginal agitation and agency and partly through the growing global rejection of such a position in Commonwealth countries (Armitage, 1995). There was of course a distinct contradiction within the Commonwealth of Nations: some members of the 'family of nations'

---

[19] Robin Cohen uses the term 'diaspora' to describe those with some common experience. He uses diaspora in terms of immigrant peoples as another way of understanding their experience beyond the ethnic category.

were coloured – India, Hong Kong, Singapore – while others – Canada, Australia and New Zealand – had racist immigration policies that excluded coloured people.

In the early 1970s, Canada adopted a Multiculturalism Policy – since incorporated in their constitution – largely in response to increased cultural diversity and the 'French question'. Australia followed for similar reasons in the mid-1970s in terms of policy not constitutional law. The first major site of the push for rights was education. Demands for English classes and child migrant programs were to forever change the face of education in both countries (Martin, 1978). Previous policies of assimilation could no longer satisfy the demands of an increasingly diverse society. In many ways multiculturalism was a watershed in educational and public policy in Australia and Canada (Collins, 1993a).

In Canada the social construction of 'visible minorities' and in Australia the social construction of migrants moved from one of assimilation or integration to one that celebrated cultural diversity. Social space, public space, was created for cultural diversity and for immigrants at the same time as – and in symbiosis with – the public space that Indigenous peoples began to achieve in the 1970s. In this process, space was also created for rethinking Indigenous education. After much lobbying, Indigenous peoples in Australia and Canada presented governments with plans for involvement and, potentially, control over their educational experience. In Canada this was presented by the National Indian Brotherhood and was called *Indian Control of Indian Education* and was released in 1972. It was "premised on the two educational principles recognised in Canadian society: Parental Responsibility and Local Control of Education" (Barman et al., 1987:2). In Australia, the National Aboriginal Education Committee (NAEC) was formed in 1977, followed by Aboriginal Education Consultative Groups (AECG) in each State soon after (Sykes, 1986). These Indigenous organisations became institutional hearts for Indigenous agency in shaping educational outcomes in both countries. Resourcing based on cultural difference was a hallmark of changes to educational policy from this point on.

However, multiculturalism placed greater pressure on national identity, and events in Australia and Canada over the last decade or so point to a redefining of nation. In Canada the Meech Lake Accord (1987) produced ongoing debate about protection for minority groups in the Charter of Rights and Freedoms (Kallen, 1990:77). In 1990 a

55

struggle developed over the attempted decentralisation of constitutional reform. First Nations MLA, Elijah Harper, voted NO in the Manitoba parliament to accepting the terms of the Meech Lake Accord after all ten premiers and the Prime Minister had not consulted with any First Nations leaders. Also during 1990, an armed struggle at Oka within the Mohawk nation over ancestral burial grounds indicated that the Canadian government's treaties were not meaningless (Boyko, 1995:175). "We had to keep telling them we wanted the barricades down, too. We wanted the police and the army gone, but the first step was a real framework for change, not new grants or different agencies. Real, fundamental changes – the people on our land dealing with the people on their land" (Hornung, 1991:241).

During this period, the Inuit have been granted their own land Nunavut, although not all Inuit live in Nunavut. In Australia, reconciliation between Indigenous and non-Indigenous people has received pressure from Aboriginal groups to include land rights with the resultant High Court *Mabo* decision overthrowing the legal lie *terra nullius*. The republican movement in Australia could also provide fertile ground for Indigenous involvement in contesting the social construction of Aboriginality in Australia and for the redefining of national identity. The republic referendum was defeated in 1999, largely due to the political cunning of the monarchist Prime Minister, John Howard but will return when concerns about constitutional change are addressed more comprehensively.

The new identity politics are not just a feature of contemporary Australian and Canadian societies. Old ethnicities have been breaking down the hegemony of the nation-state in the former Yugoslavia, Indonesia and the former United Soviet Socialist Republic. Some of these movements have been around becoming a separate nation within a nation-state, as already occurs within Canada and New Zealand (Fleras and Elliot, 1992). Burgmann (1993) demonstrates the centrality of identity to such movements in describing the response in 1988 during the bicentennial year to Aboriginal protests. Under the banner of 'Bugger the Bicentennial' protestors were invariably constructed by the media as "not representative or that sections of it lacked authenticity" (1993:26). The question of authenticity goes to the heart of the contemporary politics of difference. The ideologies of racialisation still shape the constructions of who is 'real' and/or 'authentic'.

In Australia, for example, there has been a romanticisation of Indigenous culture (Rowse, 1988) by the white middle classes which has tended to present 'things Aboriginal' as essentially more in tune with the environment, as more caring and sharing and less competitive and market-oriented. The politics of difference in this instance has the effect of presenting or assuming that all Indigenous people are the same, negating the different experiences of those who have been resettled or have moved to cities (Langton, 1981) and who differ in terms of social class (Armstrong, 1996), gender and sexuality. This valorisation of particular forms of culture has led to what Castles (1993) calls the 'new racism' which results in racial stereotyping in the same way that scientific racism did in previous decades. Anyone who does not fit these criteria may have their authenticity called into question.

Yet, there are political dimensions to ethnic nationalism. The key difference between the *nation-state* and the *nation* is "the claim for a separate political collectivity" (Anthias and Yuval-Davis, 1993:25). In Canada, Indigenous peoples are given special status within the multicultural nation-state, as *First Nations*. Not only does this recognise historical realities but it is also enshrined in treaties for some Indigenous Canadians. By contrast, in Australia, there has been much resistance to being subsumed as 'just another ethnic group' until this special status is recognised legally. As Morris (1988) has argued, the new ascription of Aboriginality in multicultural discourse presents government with many contradictions. That is, while Aboriginal people are being presented as the 'First Australians', this ideological representation clashes more and more with their legal status, highlighted by the dramatic events during 1996-97 over the *Wik* decision.

In Australia, the Aboriginal tent embassy that has stood outside the old Parliament House in Canberra since the 1970s was a watershed in Indigenous political history. As a collective display of solidarity the tent embassy reflected the way in which racialisation helped to "draw the ideological boundaries of inclusion and exclusion which are vital for the construction and maintenance of the nation-state" (Castles, 1993:24). The construction of identities in opposition to the dominant group has often included recognition of historically constituted realities. Hall (1995) suggests that *tracery*, the selective construction of identity based upon the past, the present and imaginings of the future, is political. However, Gunew (n.d.) is concerned with the way in which Indigenous groups in Australia, Canada and the United States are playing identity politics: "Indigenous peoples in all three countries appear to appeal to unproblematic notions of identity, which trail guarantees of authenticity in their wake. Their speaking positions are legitimated through speaking itself, via appeals to oral traditions, to speaking on behalf of particular groups, and to ownership of traditional stories" (n.d.:6).

The *politics of recognition*, Taylor (1994) argues, includes a presumption that all cultures are of equal worth, because to assume otherwise is arrogant and morally reprehensible. The contradiction of course, as Taylor succinctly argues, is that the *politics of multiculturalism* through which the politics of recognition is enacted, has an homogenizing effect because it pushes recognition to "favourable judgements of worth" (1994:71).

Multiculturalism has, according to the left, been about incorporation of difference and the papering over of real inequalities (Hage, 1998). According to the right, it is divisive and is watering down the 'good Anglo culture' (Blainey, 1984; Bissoondath, 1994). Rather than replacing 'race' in policies and practices, it has been argued that 'multiculturalism is in fact further evidence of the continuation of racialisation, this time in the form of 'culture' (Rizvi, 1987; Wotherspoon and Jungbluth, 1995). It is important however to consider that "fixity of identity is only sought in situations of instability or disruption, of conflict and change" (Young, 1995:4). Multiculturalism is a contradictory phenomenon in both Australia and Canada: it contains and provides space. In Australia, multiculturalism has had an anti-racist agenda (Vasta and Castles, 1996) because programs and services in the areas of education, health, welfare and so on have been a positive result of multiculturalism, although economic and political equality for non-English speaking background migrants has not been achieved.

While Miles (1993) has been concerned with the reification of 'culture' in the contemporary period because it appears to give 'race' – in the form of 'culture' – a life of its own, Hall (1987) provides us with another window through which to view the current politics of difference. Hall argues, that the "slow, contradictory movement from 'nationalism' to 'ethnicity' as a source of identities is part of a new politics" (1987:46). How do we understand these differing forms of racialisation?

For Aboriginal people in Australia, and for that matter, Canada, the imposition of racial identities has been informed through a process of objectification (Morris, 1988) to provide categories for interpreting social relations. Throughout the historical period of contact, Aboriginal identity has been constituted via the 'gaze' of non-Indigenous people and portrayed in culturally relativist terms. As such, while the "concepts, categories and terminology can change over time... basic perspectives remain constant" (Markus, 1988:46).

Part of the process of constituting difference is to position people as objects of knowledge. Morrow (1984) has described this as "internal colonialism" meaning a way of continuing to maintain relations of power through discourses of the 'Other'. Yet, even when power is negative, it moves against something and in so doing, that object is constituted (Foucault in Lechte, 1988; Miles, 1993). We can understand this through the process of 'naming'.

Naming has been a critical part of the contemporary period whereby Indigenous groups in Australia and Canada have rejected totalising discourses around 'Aborigine' and 'Indian'. First Nations, Métis and Inuit are among terms that replace the colonial forms that were not only incorrect but also contributed to the notion of a biological and/or cultural entity. In Australia, groups are known as Koori (south-east), Murri (north-east), Nunga (south), and so on, as well as tribal names.

The relationship therefore between national identity and Indigenous people in Canada and Australia has become more complex in the post-war years. The political and social policy of multiculturalism has transformed the way in which some aspects of difference are incorporated (Daniels, 1986; Weaver, 1983) while at the same time concealing other dimensions of difference. We can understand Indigenous calls to unproblematic notions such as those outlined by Gunew as a consequence of the particular forms that multiculturalism has taken. In both Canada and Australia – but more so the latter – the place of Indigenous peoples in a new multicultural society has not always been that clear. Many Aboriginal people reject the banner of multiculturalism, but at recent (1996-98) anti-Hanson demonstrations, Indigenous community representatives stood side by side with ethnic community leaders.

In Canada and Australia, Indigenous people have been given space in the nation as first peoples, often in celebratory ways rather than equitable relations, though 'First Nations' is not a term used officially in Australia. Indeed this has been occurring at a time of increasing globalisation and increasing contradictions of nationalism. As citizenship is about identity (Marginson, 1997a) and both Australia and Canada have been experiencing complex struggles around rights of citizenship from women, gays, linguistically diverse groups and Indigenous people, it is not surprising that previous conceptions of national identity are being reworked.

The widespread support for national unity despite diversity is testament to what feminist anti-racists Anthias and Yuval-Davis (1993:22-23) describe as an "expression of the naturalising effect of the hegemony of one collectivity and its access to ideological apparatuses of both state and civil society". The call to unproblematic constructions of identity is of course not only found in Indigenous politics. In the current political climate in Australia, there is a "discourse of Anglo decline" (Hage, 1998) which has recentred racialised identities, in particular 'whiteness'.

Conclusion

In this chapter, I have traced historical processes of racialisation of Indigenous peoples in Canada and Australia. This was done through an examination of key policy periods and their relationship to land issues and the politics of identity. Having examined some of the political and ideological dimensions of racialisation it is clear that it is a contradictory and changing process that is very much context-specific (Solomos and Back, 1996). These contradictions help shape the education of Indigenous people in Australia and Canada.

Haig-Brown (1995) argues that there is always a principal contradiction. In her study of the meaning of 'Indian Control of Education' for students and workers in an Indigenous education centre, the principal contradiction was this: "The Native Education Centre is an institution which prepares First Nations people to participate in an exclusionary, majority non-Native society, while at the same time attempting to enhance their awareness and appreciation of their own cultures and heritage" (Haig-Brown, 1995:237).

The tools by which Indigenous peoples have been able to lay claim to justice have been continuously contradictory. This chapter has explored how the central processes of racialisation provided opportunities for agency but within a racialised constraint. In this current period racialisation often occurs through the lens of culture. In

Australia and Canada, it has been preferable to assimilation which was a deliberate policy aimed at 'absorbing' both Indigenous people and minority immigrant groups into the mainstream (Armitage, 1995). Multiculturalism and self-determination/self-government, or a policy of cultural pluralism aims to preserve each group's distinctive cultural traits. The problem with both approaches however, is the underlying assumption that difference is racially based rather than socially constructed (Wotherspoon, 1991:250).

These seemingly intractable consequences of racialisation can be further examined through an exploration of the relationship between culture and education. It will enable a contextualising of the preceding discussion in the development of Indigenous teacher education programs. This macro level of analysis has been useful for setting a framework that attends to the wider production of culture and its negotiation. Importantly, it has been possible to see the continual negotiation over the meaning of cultural difference.

Chapter 4

Towards a Theory of Negotiating Difference in Indigenous Teacher Education

Introduction

In order to develop a theory of practice in Indigenous teacher education, it is necessary to examine a little more closely the field of Indigenous education in general. In the previous chapter, there was an exploration of the broader field of Indigenous/state relations. It was argued that the historic racialisation of Indigenous peoples created 'special status' that led to similar, but different racialised policies and practices in Australia and Canada.

This chapter continues to explore the notion of racialisation by examining the ways in which culture, difference and inequality have been theorised within educational discourse. Particular attention will be given to the pedagogical frameworks that have been developed to confront the relationship between inequality and cultural difference in Indigenous education. The aim of this chapter, then, is to examine the current understandings of the relationship between culture and pedagogy. I will argue that it is important to move beyond the idea that culture is an impediment, or a resource in education.

This chapter will provide a basis for the empirical analysis later in the book by developing a theoretical framework for understanding culture-as-negotiation. This will be done through an exploration of the way in which the race-relations paradigm articulates with research methods and contemporary ideological discourses within Indigenous education. The chapter firstly addresses the theoretical contributions of studies on pedagogical issues for Indigenous students. One key question here is: How have constructions of Indigenous difference shaped the curriculum, formal arrangements and social relations in the *field of Indigenous education*?

The role of methodological individualism in education is also explored, as it often seems to be the only alternative discourse available. Indeed, the culturalism – individualism continuum in the area of education for diversity more generally, is explored here in a specific form, as a racialised continuum.

Researching culture and difference

In the previous chapter, the processes of racialisation in Indigenous/State relations were shown to have metamorphosed from biological explanations of difference to cultural difference models in the contemporary period. Therefore any methodology that attempts to understand the relationship between racialised culture and education must grapple with the continuation of this 'race-relations' problematic. One way to avoid this problematic is to develop a framework which recognises culture-as-negotiation and education as a process of cultural as well as knowledge production (Gore, 1993). Where Indigenous – and indeed other minority group – students are concerned this has usually been within a race-relations paradigm, which has focussed on cultural dissonance (McConaghy, 1997a).

One example of this dualism is in a teacher education textbook on ethnicity and education (see Figure 4.1). It shows the seemingly natural differences in social worlds of Anglo-Australian babies and Aboriginal babies. A number of students in the AREP teacher education course that I was coordinating at the time were angry that such stereotypes were being taught to future teachers and even more appalled that as Aboriginal people, they had to deal with such insults in one of their classes.

Figure 4.1
Differences in the social worlds of Anglo-Australian and Aboriginal babies

Aboriginal Children	Anglo Children
Baby has contact with many adults and children. Always in physical contact with others.	Contact with a few adults and children. Often alone.
Brief sleeps among many people.	Long sleeps in a room by self.
Little is said to babies. Reliance on nonverbal communication.	Lot of talk to babies.
25% verbal statements to child are abusive.	Few statements are abusive. Most are positive.
Children who can walk are expected to indicate that they want food, otherwise they will not be fed. This develops personal responsibility.	Parent is responsible for child, who is dependent until quite old. The parent anticipates when the child will be hungry.

Aboriginal Children	Anglo Children
Control over food and mother.	No control over food or mother.
Recognises a large number of people.	Limited range of acquaintances.
Few toys or other objects to play with.	Toys used to distract and occupy child.
No punishment.	Reprimands for undesirable behaviour.
Never left alone.	Often alone.
Verbal expression not encouraged.	Verbal expression is encouraged and valued.
Nonverbal behaviour dominant.	Nonverbal behaviour relatively unimportant.
No schedules.	Time is important: schedules for food, toilet habits, sleeping.
Feeding on demand.	Schedule feeding practised by many parents.
No special fuss made of baby.	Baby is fussed over.

Partington and McCudden, 1992:27

While the authors note that the table is developed from the work of anthropologist Annette Hamilton – whose original study was of children in a remote community – the table demonstrates the slippage in the race-relations paradigm from a remote context to *all* other contexts. Nakata (1997:429) argues that a 'fetish for the anthropological gaze' is hegemonic in research and pedagogical approaches in the field of Indigenous education. It is possible to unravel the reasons leading to this approach when examining the ways in which racialisation, as an ideological discourse, permeates Indigenous education.

Racialisation as an ideological discourse in Indigenous education

Nicholls et al. (1996), in an insightful article outlined the ways in which there is a tendency to be trapped in a particular discourse when debating the extent to which culture is implicated in Indigenous educational inequality. Common to this discourse is a focus on culture as explanation and activities that are concerned with working out the best ways to bring Indigenous students into the mainstream. The resulting *culturalism* is often no less assimilationist than previous approaches (Hesch, 1993) and merely provides space for 'white' agency (McConaghy, 1997a). I will argue that the trap, which gets us caught in this circular debate, is the convergence of two very powerful ideological discourses – racialisation as in the race-relations approach; and the deracialised discourse of methodological individualism in the human capital approach. They converge to shape research in the most profound ways yet it is this very binary which contributes to the sense that 'we are not moving on'.

To unravel this discourse it is necessary to see that racialisation is a process embedded in everyday language and social practice (Troyna, 1993; Miles, 1993; Solomos and Back, 1996). That is, it is the 'idea' of race, not as a descriptive mechanism but how it is used (Miles, 1993:42) as a 'feel for the game' (Connolly, 1998:133; Chan, 1997:71) that is of interest. Racialised understandings of difference operate at the level of common sense because bodies are inscribed by ideological discourses of race. The term *ideological discourse* is borrowed from Purvis and Hunt (1993) who argue against the opposition of ideology and discourse. Ideology in this sense is: "... not the practical, really useful knowledge to which the term refers in English – this corresponds to what Gramsci contrasts with common sense as 'good sense'. Gramsci's 'common sense' – *senso communo* – is 'common' in that it is shared; it is the everyday, taken-for-granted assumptions about the world, the inherited commonplaces and conventional wisdom, and so on, common to the mass of ordinary people – rather like folklore" (Poynting, 1995:136).

Discourse is the *process* by which such racialised understandings are produced and reproduced, challenged and transformed. Operating as 'common sense' in every day discourse, racialisation becomes "both a medium of social action and constitutive of the social relations that they reproduce" (*ibid.*:405). While it is not being suggested that racialised ideological discourses are the only discourses shaping the lives of participants in this book, it is evident that it has primary significance in research and pedagogical paradigms in the field of Indigenous education.

It is easy to slip into the *race-relations problematic* because as a methodology, the race-relations paradigm can reveal clear processes of domination and subordination that are racially constituted. Yet, at the same time, the idea of race is reconstituted through such framing. In addition, revealing domination and subordination provides little space for agency and resistance leading to victim discourses. The race-relations paradigm therefore tends to maintain the dualisms that feed on the notion that Indigenous and non-Indigenous people are so different (i.e. racially) that we are unknowable to each other. According to Miles (1993:45): "The analytical task is therefore to explain why certain relationships are interpreted as determined by or expressive of 'race', rather than to accept without criticism and comment that they are and to freeze and legitimate that representation in the idea of 'race relations' as social relations between 'races'."

This is one of the reasons for using the concept of *racialisation* that stresses the contradictions, and role, of agency in shaping the lives of Indigenous peoples in Australia and Canada. It is possible to see the limits to the race-relations approach when policies and practices directed at accounting for cultural difference are examined. An example can be found in the *Policy Statement on Teacher Education for Aborigines and Torres Strait Islanders* (NAEC, 1986) which contains an overview of Canadian and United States Indigenous teacher education programs. There are a number of strategies suggested which draw on these programs. The usefulness of exploring such strategies is offset by an assumption that the same strategies would automatically work in Australia. This ignores the different historical contexts shaping Indigenous rights, educational experiences and patterns of community development. The consequence is an unproblematic reliance on the notion of a 'Pan community' of Indigenous peoples who are all similar because they are all Indigenous or one 'race'.

The *Policy Statement on Teacher Education for Aborigines and Torres Strait Islanders* (1986) consistently used racialised categories to explore difference. "The National Aboriginal Education Committee contends that there are very marked differences between Aboriginal and non-Aboriginal values and lifestyles... In the main, Aboriginal society is structured around the community... Aboriginal society tends not to be materialistic or competitive, rather it practices sharing of resources and cooperation... in comparison non-Aboriginal society is very competitive in the pursuit of material possessions... in non-Aboriginal society the family is usually nuclear" (NAEC, 1986:10).

The consequences of policies that use racialised categories in this manner, is that they lead to responses that fit some presumed homogeneity, ignoring the need to respond to Indigenous diversity (McConaghy, 1997b:130). Furthermore, the *National Aboriginal and Torres Strait Islander Policy* (1989) and the *National Review of Education for Aboriginal and Torres Strait Islander Peoples: Final Report* (1995) continues this culturalist narrative (*ibid.*).

On the other hand, the document *Indian Control of Indian Education* (1972), while not being free of culturalist or racialised language, at least recognised the possibilities for what they then called 'integration', thus revealing less dependence on static conceptions of cultural difference. "Integration is a broad concept of human development, which provides for growth through mingling the best

67

elements of a wide range of human differences. Integrated educational programs must respect the reality of racial and cultural differences by providing a curriculum, which blends the best from the Indian and the non-Indian traditions" (National Indian Brotherhood, 1972:25).

Different contexts produced these policy responses. In Canada, the National Indian Brotherhood (NIB) policy came out of Indigenous resistance. Control over education was to be transferred to the provinces where Indigenous groups had no treaty rights or structural arrangements to ensure their participation. This is discussed further in Chapter 6. In addition, the focus on integration was a sweetener in a climate where the notion of education based on 'race' was considered essentially racist.

In Australia Indigenous education after the war developed in symbiosis with multicultural education policies and very much reflects the additive approach to culture rather than separateness. Before continuing with an examination of the way in which culture has been theorised in Indigenous education, I want to briefly turn to methodological individualism because I will argue that methodological individualism is the *corollary* of – the bedfellow of – racialisation. That is because while it claims to be a deracialised ideological discourse, individualism in fact hides racism and racialised disadvantage. A brief overview of the origins and concept of methodological individualism is therefore necessary.

Methodological individualism

The notion that investment in education would bring individuals and a society benefit was part of a technology/welfarist approach in the 1950s and 1960s (Connell, W.F., 1993:4). This led to a commonsense understanding that "education is a vehicle for social mobility for all", but of course this has been challenged in a number of ways in recent years. Known as the 'human capital theory of education' – a concept emerging from neo-classical economic theory which earned a Nobel prize for Garry Becker (1957) – it has dominated educational programs since the 1960s in Australia and Canada (Marginson, 1993; Wotherspoon and Satzewich, 1993). It is an attractive theory, which leads us to believe that a good education will get anyone a good job because more human capital makes us more profitable to our employers and employers do not discriminate. The theory suggests that educational outcomes are meritocratic and democratic – that is, without discrimination. Its logic suggests that a good education has some direct relationship to labour force participation and earnings since employers pay workers a wage in relation to their marginal productivity – which is itself determined by the individual's stock of 'human capital'. According to this logic, if more Indigenous students finish high school then their labour force participation will increase followed by economic well being. The human capital theory doesn't explain the unequal outcomes for students other than as a consequence of individual effort. Such a theory assumes that if white males are dominating the higher income groups then more money should be spent on their education because the government gets a return for its investment (Marginson, 1993:52).

The central methodological tenet of human capital theory – as of economic rationalism in general – is *individualism*. It is an ahistorical account of differential access and outcomes in education. Neoclassical economists who look at education focus on individuals – non-racialised, non-gendered, non-classed – who maximise the allocation of their resources to education over their lifetimes in the same way that they would decide how many ice creams to have on a weekend.

Individualism has seeped deeply into educational theory and practice in Canada and Australia. Both education *practices* and *processes* maintain the hegemony of individualism. The arrangement of the curriculum into individual unrelated bodies of knowledge and the competitive, selective assessment processes are examples of practices that support the ethic of individualism (Wotherspoon, 1998:83). In the 1970s Bowles and Gintis (1976) argued that the hidden curriculum was pro-capitalist because it failed to challenge the economic and social relations that exist. Education was seen to reproduce the economic and social relations of capitalist society. We were alerted to the reproductive nature of schooling and the ways in which education was a vehicle for the transmission of specific pro-capitalist ideologies as well as skills. But the problem with the Bowles and Gintis (1976) approach was that it was too functionalist, did not look at the contradictions of the role of education in capitalist societies, and did not allow any space for the 'agency' of those within the education system (administrators, teachers, students).

A recent example of the individuating nature of education is the notion of generic skills and competencies. Kalantzis questions generic competencies on the grounds that they are based on "management and training theories that are several decades old and decidedly outdated"

(1992:8). Deracialised discourse is in fact racialised because it assumes individuals are all alike, all just individuals maximising their returns on the labour market in the same way that economists model how individuals decide to invest in human capital via education. In addition, this deracialised discourse implicitly promotes particular skills of "perseverance, self-confidence, appropriate assertiveness and socially acceptable manners" which "reinforce prevailing patterns of privilege" (Slaughter, 1991:75).

However, we have to be careful with this structuralist approach to an analysis of education because while recognising the powerful role that 'capital' has in shaping education to provide a useful labour force, it fails to account for how education change occurs. The impression is that education exists as it is because it is functional for capital. This ignores the way in which agents struggle to shape educational policy in a way to overcome the most glaring inequalities, even if the struggles are not always successful.

The implication of this is that to examine the two programs in this book, we need an approach that exposes the way in which actors negotiate the competing racialised and deracialised discourses in Indigenous educational policy, practice and theory.

The principal contradiction

> There is a large body of literature on First Nations' education that would identify 'the problem' in terms of cultural conflict. This is dangerous in that it assumes cultural determinism, but it is precisely where one looks to define the problem of oppression. (Haig-Brown, 1995:238)

The principal contradiction, as Celia Haig-Brown calls it – avoiding cultural determinism while attempting to attend to cultural difference – emphasises contradictions, the fact that education must be looked at historically and that social life is in a constant state of flux (*ibid.*:235) and always in the process of becoming (*ibid.*:236). In Chapters 7, 8 and 9 this principal contradiction for administrators, teaching staff and students in Indigenous education in Canada and Australia will be explored.

As coordinator of the AREP program for six years, I was constantly confronted with a number of situations in which I was supposed to determine the impact of culture on various aspects of student participation; to work out how to account for culture as an advocate for the program; and how to work with the often contradictory concepts of culture employed by Aboriginal and non-Aboriginal workers in the university. This has not been an easy path for me or others involved in the programs. At times it was difficult to understand moments that led to group solidarity or collective organising by students. At other times there would be self-declarations of difference along a multitude of different aspects of identity. Many of the tensions flew in the face of traditional educational pedagogy, which is individualistic, but also flew against the collectivist/racialised enclave framework in which the program was constructed. Such issues created tensions for all people engaged in the program which in turn created a constant desire to transform pedagogy to take account of 'culture'. The particular perspective of culture that each person brought to the program (habitus) combined with institutionalised cultures (field) created numerous opportunities for conflict and change. The negotiation of culture in these contexts was often contradictory, always dynamic and fluid and, at times, strategic.

To understand the principal contradiction a little better, it is necessary to briefly examine the meanings of culture by comparing and contrasting the etymology of the word with that of their usage in the post war period in Australia and Canada.

Culture

> The complexity, that is to say, is not finally in the word but in the problems which its variations of use significantly indicate. (Williams, 1988:92)

The uses of 'culture' in the contemporary period are not uniform. Raymond Williams states that "culture is one of the two or three most complicated words in the English language" (1988:87). The slipperiness of the meaning of culture is rooted in Enlightenment thought. *Rousseau's Knot*, suggests Roberta James (1997), is the entanglement of liberal democracy and racism which grew out of the French Enlightenment. Reflecting on Rousseau's *Discourse on Inequality*, James notes that two types of inequality are outlined: "...one of which is 'natural' or innate and previous to sociality and which is generated by differences in age, health, strength of the body and qualities of the mind or soul; the other, 'moral or political inequality', is the result of the development of civil society" (James, 1997:54).

The latter explanation is of particular interest in the modern understanding of culture because of the role of the State in Indigenous affairs. The civil state "is governed by the constraint of social relations and sociality" which are hierarchical and have social and economic divisions – as well as cultural" (James, 1997:54). Prior to the notion of civil society, culture had been used to refer to "the *tending* of something, usually crops or animals" and was the dominant meaning in the 17th century (Williams, 1988:97). During the 18th and 19th centuries this sense changed to a metaphorical one assigned to a process of human *development*. The notion of development brought with it class associations as in cultivated and cultivation (*op.cit.*:88) in England. This meaning applies to our understanding of 'high' culture. Williams also examined the meanings of culture in other languages and discovered that around the mid 18th century, the French form of culture was commonly used as a synonym for *civilisation* by Germans.

Culture therefore slides "on a continuum of meaning from culture-as-a-thing to culture-as-a-process" (Keeffe, 1992:9). In terms of Indigenous education this can be a "total way of life" theory or a "changing bundle of ideas, perspectives and mental frameworks" (*ibid.*). It is possible to see in this continuum the basis for multiple understandings of culture in the contemporary period yet when referring to Indigenous peoples, it is usually the 'total way of life' theory that is hegemonic.

One of the prevailing social categories in the contemporary period in Canada and Australia has been that of ethnicity. Keeffe (1992) argues that if we understand Aboriginal people as just another ethnic group then we can get a sense of the way in which culture has been incorporated into Aboriginal education in Australia. He argues that the limitations to curriculum reform in Aboriginal education are located within constructs of Aboriginal *ethnic* identity. A typology is developed showing how Aboriginal ethnicity is constructed through:

- Aboriginality and descent
- Aboriginality and history
- Aboriginality and the Dreaming
- Aboriginality and land

In the constructions of Aboriginality being promoted by Indigenous and non-Indigenous educators there is a focus on primordial ties (Keeffe, 1992:75) that limit culture to static and homogenising conceptions of cultural difference. In a sense such definitions are as constraining as those related to 'blood' (Keeffe, 1992). The Canadian multicultural and Indigenous education policies and practices share this same tendency (Hesch, 1993; Wotherspoon, 1995). The contradictions and limitations of these definitions are revealed in the way in which they are harnessed politically and ideologically. For example, while the State has defined Aboriginality in terms of rights, Aboriginal involvement has often been as "oppositional cultures" (Hall, 1992) inverting negative ascriptions and inadvertently becoming party to the creation of essentialist characteristics (Pettman, 1992). Birthplace, religious practices, ancestry, food, dance and so on tend to displace the political and economic aspects of culture concentrating on the celebration of difference rather than (unequal) relations of power (Keeffe, 1992; Kalantzis, 1988; Ng, 1991). The contradictions of this approach are revealed in later chapters when the two programs are examined regarding pedagogical and administrative arrangements.

The primary understanding that comes out of the preceding discussion is that educational policies in Australia and Canada promote practices – in education and elsewhere – that operate from an understanding of cultural differences as 'readable' (McConaghy, 1997a; Singh, 1998). With this understanding of cultural difference, 'white' agency takes primacy and the agency of the 'Other' is made invisible (McConaghy, 1997a). We all end up in opposition, or so this approach to cultural difference would have us believe. Drawing on the literature from this perspective, we can see how culture has been seen as an impediment to effective solutions for Indigenous educational inequality in Australia and Canada.

Culture-as-impediment

In the period following the Second World War, when mass schooling in Australia and Canada had to respond to increasing cultural and linguistic diversity, education was about assimilation (Kalantzis et al., 1990; Wotherspoon, 1998). The concern was how best to help those of difference to assimilate – to give up their language and culture – to learn English, and become part of the nation. A hierarchical notion of culture, similar to the hierarchical use of racial taxonomies, was imbued in such an approach. The hegemony of methodological individualism within education and society in general, meant that culture was firstly understood as something that created problematic learners. This deficit approach is explored utilising the concept of *blaming the victim* (Ryan, 1976). In this approach, the problems of Indigenous education were to be found in the Indigenous people *themselves* and their 'inappropriate' culture. While this approach sought to overcome inequality it focussed on the 'Other' – collectively and individually – and their deficiencies and saw *culture-as-impediment* when responding to cultural difference.

In tracing the genealogy of difference and education it is possible to locate a process beginning in the late 1960s and carrying through to the late 1970s, when equal opportunity was a dominant social movement in Canada and Australia. Providing access and support for disadvantaged groups became a focus for social theory. During this time, Paulo Freire (1972) developed a strident critique of what he called the 'banking' principle of education. It is a principle, argued Freire, that focuses on the individual in such a way as to highlight their deficiencies and to then 'fix them up':

> To achieve this end, the oppressors use the banking concept of education in conjunction with a paternalistic social action apparatus, within which the oppressed receive the euphemistic title of 'welfare recipients'. They are treated as individual cases, as marginal men [sic] who deviate from the general configuration of a 'good, just and organised society'. The oppressed are regarded as the pathology of the healthy society, which must therefore adjust these 'incompetent and lazy' folk to its own patterns by changing their mentality. These marginals need to be 'integrated', 'incorporated' into the healthy society that they have forsaken. (Freire, 1972:48)

The traditional curriculum or pedagogical framework that underlies the 'banking' principle is essentially assimilationist. The central features of this approach are aimed at cultural and linguistic incorporation (Kalantzis et al., 1990:244). Cultural assimilation could occur at many levels, for example dress, language and religion, as well as custom or the way in which relationships are maintained, such as family. What invariably happened, however, was the overwhelmingly regularity with which it moved in one direction. That is, it was the minorities who had to change.

The contradiction however, is that education is about sorting out students in preparation for active roles in society (Mazurek, 1987). It is no surprise that not all students will exhibit the appropriate

74

qualities. To understand why, we do a vast amount of research related to people's behaviour. In other words, in the process of researching the 'Other' we come up with results that situate the problem in the learner. It is invariably their class, gender or culture that is an impediment. Thus, "education legitimates inequality" (Connell, 1993:27) because it assumes that certain skills and attributes merit reward and that these are *naturally* the best rather than a result of social construction.

The analysis of primary data in Chapters 7, 8 and 9 will reveal ways in which the racialised culture of Indigenous students continues to be seen as an impediment. However, Indigenous resistance to the idea that culture is an impediment has led to a theoretical, political and practical inversion of this approach to one which celebrates culture and treats culture as a resource.

In the next section cultural dissonance is examined as explanation for educational inequality but now the teachers also have to change, not just the students. Culture is co-opted and incorporated to achieve cultural compatibility (Malin, 1997). This 'culture-as-a-resource' paradigm has much in common with the 'cultural maintenance' paradigm of multiculturalism (Kalantzis, 1990).

Culture-as-resource

In contrast to the culture-as-impediment approach to cultural difference and inequality in education, the 'culture-as-resource' approach seeks to recognise, value and work with the cultural knowledge and skills that students bring to the teaching/learning partnership. Such an approach seeks to reverse what Freire saw as the 'banking principle' of education – a non-liberatory kind of knowledge production.

The colonial model of education was useful in explaining how education did more than prepare bodies for the labour force. It pointed to the role of education as a process of social control in the repression of certain knowledges and the privileging of others (Wotherspoon, 1991). This is a particularly attractive model when trying to understand Indigenous experiences of education in Australia and Canada. However, Wotherspoon and Satzewich (1993) argue that the colonial model fails to account for changes in educational policy and practice in Canada. The authors argue that "educational policies and practices are shaped by the labour force needs of a society, but they are also responsive to political agendas and struggles over the kinds of persons and characteristics that are valued by particular social interests" (1993:116). This political/economy analysis is particularly useful in the light of struggles of the past thirty years by Indigenous and minority groups.

In Australia and Canada it is clear that the cultural diversity of the two societies has increased considerably over the past fifty years. Education policy and practice has been redefined in relation to new ethnic minorities and Indigenous peoples in both countries.

In Chapter 3 I used a political/economy approach to trace historical and contemporary aspects of Indigenous experience and education in Australia and Canada. In this way, we saw how political, economic and social factors transformed these societies through different phases of national development. The approach needs extending however to take account of the new processes of racialisation centred on the construction of identity.

Australia and Canada both have multicultural policies and separate Indigenous policies. The literature suggests that the interpretation of these policies into practice in education systems is highly problematic (Kalanztis et al., 1990; Rizvi, 1987; Wotherspoon, 1995; Hesch, 1993). Policy has "de-emphasised cultural pre-requisites of success and power in Australian society" (Kalantzis et al., 1990:22) thus they are more concerned with cultural harmony than social justice. "The project of 'initiation to core culture' [sic *assimilation*] was replaced by self-esteem programs in which one would end up feeling good about one's cultural difference" (*ibid.*:22).

The culture of immigrant and Indigenous education workers is now used as a resource in the development of state-funded positions in schools, colleges and universities. Part of the rationale for employing Indigenous people in designated positions is to draw upon their knowledge of Indigenous culture/s (National Aboriginal and Torres Strait Islander Education Policy, 1989, 1.2.7, 1.2.8; Indian and Métis Education Policy, 1995). Indigenous personnel are also meant to change attitudes, provide input into curriculum development and to act as a conduit between communities and institutions (Wammarra Aboriginal Education Centre, 1992, Vol.1). The Hawthorn Report in Canada argued even more forcefully in 1966 that the 'culture of reserves' meant that there was often a mismatch between the culture of consumption outside and that on the 'inside' (Hawthorne, 1966:56-58). Tapping into those cultural differences was the aim of the First

Nations' seminal 'red paper', *Indian Control of Indian Education* (National Indian Brotherhood, 1972).

One of the consequences of seeing culture-as-a-resource is that instead of changing student behaviour and practices (as in the impediment approach), teachers have to cater for a range of learning styles. Some of the features of this paradigm suggest that cultural incompatibility is the source of inequality (Lipka, 1990) because Indigenous people have different 'world-views' (Hughes and More, 1993). Here is the anthropological notion of culture that is concerned with "embedded practices and meanings" which creates a sense of common identity (Morris and Cowlishaw, 1997:3). The argument here is that Indigenous students have different ways of learning from non-Indigenous students because of these commonalities. The teacher has merely to harness their learning styles by incorporating cultural differences such as specific socio-linguistic forms of expression and social organisation of the classroom and the student will succeed. Therefore, we have a simple inversion from a model of culture-as-impediment to a model of culture-as-resource.

There are a number of critiques of these culturalist models. They stem mainly from the fact that differences embodied by the 'Other' are made to seem *natural*, as if they arise from some sort of essential Aboriginality. This is a central concern for critical theorists who have argued against the development of so-called 'learning styles' theory. The logic of learning styles theory is centred around dualisms which are a 'seemingly neutral scapegoat' (Nicholls et al., 1996:6) in explaining educational inequality. Keeffe (1992) cogently argues that this concern for ethnic absolutism "ignores the vexed questions of the powerlessness and inequality of social groups in favour of explorations into the sources of their identity" (*ibid.*:81).

Part of the reason anti-racists in Britain have rejected multiculturalism is due to this conception of culture in education (Troyna, 1992; Rattansi, 1992). Such approaches have led to the kind of solipsism mentioned previously that would have us trapped in our own little homogeneous worlds remaining a mystery to each other (Fay, 1996:10). This is of course, one of the "unintended consequences of an overwhelming emphasis on cultural difference" (Keeffe, 1992:100). There is a conflation of multiple meanings of cultural difference into one based only upon 'ethnicity' (*ibid.*). Culture becomes a set of practices, meanings and "inherited social relations" (Morris and Cowlishaw, 1997:5). It is therefore critical that a model –

based on culture as dynamic and continually constituted – is developed to analyse the negotiation of difference in Indigenous teacher education.

Culture-as-negotiated

This section will summarise the various approaches to culture and educational inequality as they relate to Indigenous students. It will focus on the general logic of current frameworks using what Connell has defined in *Gender and Power* (1996) as extrinsic and intrinsic accounts. This will assist in finding a way to understand and explain the negotiation of culture without relying upon disciplinary knowledge (McConaghy, 1997a). That is, knowledge from within the field of Indigenous education.

Extrinsic accounts of social and cultural difference provide explanations that are concerned with institutionalised structural constraints. For example, Chapter 3 gave an overview of the impact of policies that situated problems of inequality in the 'race' of particular groups. This biological determinism was not useful since it placed limits on 'development'. Another type of structural determinism is that of internal colonialism, which failed to take account of how the State responds to diversity and how agents work to improve their material conditions. The most common extrinsic or systemic theory at the moment is that of 'culture clash'. Here we have the prolifically documented accounts that chart the existence of differences between *all* Indigenous and *all* non-Indigenous people. The general logic suggests that because non-Indigenous teachers are more individualistic, competitive and future-oriented, they will not be able to understand and cater for their students. This is because Indigenous students are group-oriented, non-competitive and present-oriented. The usefulness of this theory, in terms of highlighting cultural differences, is offset by its presentation of culture as static and homogeneous. Therefore, explanations that depend entirely on the incompatibility of values and norms are culturally deterministic. In these explanations, "social structure is constantly reproduced rather than constantly constituted" (Connell, 1996:44). The categories are static, which makes it difficult to explain change.

At the psycho-social level there are intrinsic theories that focus on custom or learned behaviour which becomes translated into teaching and learning styles. The difference between teaching/learning-styles theory and the notion of culture clash is that one is socially rather than biologically constituted (*ibid.*). For example, learning styles theory has had a powerful impact in all areas of education but particularly in Indigenous education. Indigenous students, it has been argued, learn better in situations that are practical, hands-on and group-oriented. This theory has been useful in that it has been the basis for a politics of reform. Yet, Connell argues, if we understand gender in this same way, "it constitutes a kind of social determinism whereby teachers are at risk of defining and constraining student options through a range of stereotypical expectations" (Connell, 1996:50).

The problem has been that from this position Indigenous people are constructed as the 'Other' and ascribed traits – ethnic, cultural or racial – and their difference becomes an obstacle to progress. Apart from failing to recognise diversity within and between Indigenous and non-Indigenous communities, they have contributed to further stereotyping. There may be political reasons for asserting these characteristics amongst Indigenous peoples and for workers attempting to gain affirmative action for particular groups, but they risk being taken up and used as justification for *negative* discriminatory treatment.

One criticism of multicultural and Aboriginal education policies within Australia has been that migrants and Aborigines will never learn to 'fit in'. This is the conservative argument. It has been argued by Troyna (1992) that multicultural education policies in England have been about doing just that – helping people fit in by finding out about their culture and feeling good about themselves. In this way, just as Kalantzis (1992) has argued, the curriculum has been more about social control than social justice. However, these two counter-tendencies fight and tussle continuously producing contradictory outcomes.

While this critique of multiculturalism may well be useful in many ways there are also contradictions. For within the broader parameters of multiculturalism there has been room to create alternative educational experiences for minorities. Native Survival Schools (Regnier et al., 1988) have provided an education for Indigenous students rejected by mainstream schooling. The Federated Indian College at the University of Regina, Saskatchewan is also another example of Indigenous educational control. In Australia, there has been an increase in the number of independent schools, such as Islamic schools, catering for students whose religious practices are a way of life (Cope, 1993). In remote areas in the Northern Territory, Indigenous schools such as Lajamanu, Yirrkala and Yipirinya offer contexts that are more negotiated due to increased Indigenous community involvement. As well, throughout Australia and Canada, universities have established Indigenous education programs and/or established Indigenous centres of research and teaching. In Australia, a higher education network was established in the early 1990s. These developments are not isolated to Australian and Canadian education systems. Indigenous educational developments are also part of an increasing global networking of Indigenous peoples that transcends national boundaries (Jhappan, 1992).

In summary, culture is increasingly the rubric through which relations of power have been contested. As an overarching paradigm for the development of policy and practice, multiculturalism has placed 'culture' at the forefront of educational change for the last few decades. This was preferable to the previously assimilationist policies which sought to make everyone the same. Critical theorists however, have questioned the risk of homogenising tendencies in the way in which 'culturalist' approaches are expressed in policy and practice (Keeffe, 1992; Nicholls et al., 1996; Rizvi, 1987).

In terms of Indigenous teacher education programs, such paradigms have effects. These are demonstrated in the day-to-day experiences of teaching and learning, in the relationships students have with each other; in the tensions felt by administrators and teacher educators; in the institutional arrangements for such programs and in the schools and communities with which they relate during the course of the students' studies.

If this study is to avoid 'reading' cultural difference in ways which present culture as static and homogeneous then we need a theory of practice that is able to account for how agents in the two programs make sense of their lives. Culture-as-impediment and culture-as-resource are fundamentally underscored by an orientation to the difference of the 'Other'. They are also oppositional and therefore unable to account for change. This book contends that a model of culture-as-negotiation is most useful to understanding Indigenous teacher education. Culture-as-negotiation not only names a process of continually becoming (Haig-Brown, 1995) but it also allows space to consider how Indigenous peoples help shape their destiny. Culture-as-negotiation is also an escape from victim discourses. For non-

Indigenous actors it is possible to be in relationship with Indigenous peoples without having to 'know the other'.

Conclusion

In the contemporary struggle over culture there has been an attempt to recognise past wrongs through the valorisation of Indigenous culture. This leaves a question as to how we should account for culture. It seems important to avoid the construction of a framework based on commonality of experience, blood, spirituality and land (Keeffe, 1992).

Such constructions of culture have been given some authority through the establishment of a range of Indigenous educational bodies at state/province, regional, school and community level. Troyna speaks of this as the 'process' of policymaking whereby broader issues are mediated by education professionals, local government bodies, community groups and increasingly in Australia, business (1992:64). This process occurs within a context (Troyna, 1992:64) which I have shown historically to contribute to educational policies of assimilation, integration and multiculturalism.

The fact that Indigenous groups claim cultural difference as the basis for ongoing inequality is both a consequence of material and symbolic differences. However, to continue to describe these differences as embodied 'traits' that define groups as essentially different from other groups, creates ongoing difficulties for tackling the source of inequality in educational outcomes. Indigenous teachers will find themselves frustrated and powerless if such approaches continue.

Methodologically, there is a need to reposition the object of research to more thoroughly understand the institutional location of 'aboriginalist' pedagogical discourses. The race-relations problematic has, in its attempt to expose power, contributed to the view that difference is determined in some sort of isolation from everyday practice. Culture then takes on a life of its own in the same way in which Miles analysed race used in this way.

Theories that highlight or trace the different trajectories of oppressed and oppressor tell us much about the basis for conflict yet little about the possibilities for change. Attending to moments of rupture, or mapping the contexts in which tensions arise, provides a window through which we can see how issues in Indigenous education are negotiated; how change is permitted in some senses, and denied in others.

Through exploring the institutional arrangements and pedagogical frameworks operating at NORTEP and AREP in the next two chapters, it will be possible to see how a construction of *culture-as-negotiation* might provide valuable insights into the relationship between agency and constraint in Indigenous teacher education in Australia and Canada.

Chapter 5
Aboriginal Rural Education Program (AREP)

Figure 5.1
Map of Australia

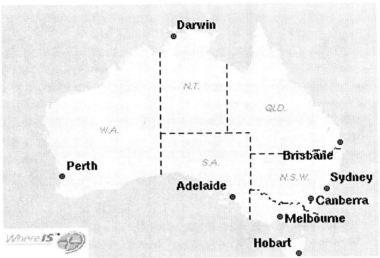

http://www.whereis.com.au Retrieved 25/03/2000

Introduction

The purpose of this chapter is to examine the on-going dynamics of an urban-based teacher education program in Western Sydney, New South Wales, Australia (see Figure 5.1), the Aboriginal Rural Education Program (AREP), which is a program for mainly rural-based Indigenous[1] students in New South Wales. Throughout the history of the AREP, the negotiation of racialised identities has been

---

[1] The nomenclature used in this chapter shifts between Aboriginal and Indigenous. The term Aboriginal will be used in relation to the AREP program and Indigenous used at other times. The term Indigenous is seen to be more inclusive of the Indigenous diaspora within and around the Australian geographic boundaries. Non-Indigenous is also more inclusive and situates the non-Indigenous 'Other' as heterogeneous rather than terms such as 'black' and 'white'.

central in terms of program control, curricula, academic and administrative staffing and funding.

Historical and epistemological overviews of the field of Indigenous education (cf. Fletcher, 1989b, 1989b; Watts, 1971; McConaghy, 1997b, 1997b; Cowlishaw and Morris, 1997; Keeffe, 1992) reveal processes of racialisation that have led to separate and special provision in education. However, while the AREP has been produced out of a struggle within the field of Indigenous education, it is also a site of struggle over what is valued and legitimate. The way in which racialisation works is particularly illuminated when we examine the focus of struggle and the position of the agents within this field.

Inequalities

Aboriginal teachers in NSW are a relatively recent addition to the teaching profession. There were a few untrained Aboriginal teachers in the 19th century and one in the early 20th century. However it wasn't until 1956 (Evelyn Robinson) and 1962 (James Stirling) that the first Aboriginal certificated graduates began teaching. Both were appointed to Aboriginal schools at Burnt Bridge and Cabbage Tree Island respectively. Evelyn Robinson was the first qualified and spoke of her experiences.

> 'It isn't easy to get yourself accepted', she said, 'but once you do, the white man and the aboriginal get on well together. The breach between the two is very unfortunate, but since it has already happened, the task is everyone's to repair it now.' (*She's The First Aboriginal Certificated Teacher: A Credit to Her People*, n.d.)

Evelyn's recognition of long standing differences, the difficulty in being accepted and the desire to move forward encapsulate elements of assimilationist thinking at the time that resonate with the contemporary politics of reconciliation. The particular difficulties that Evelyn faced are echoed time and time again in the literature and policy documents discussed in this chapter.

When Evelyn went to teachers' college, access to tertiary education was mainly supported through the Aboriginal Welfare Board, which provided scholarships for students to attend metropolitan private schools and in a few instances, university (Fletcher, 1989b). In May 1967 a referendum was held and

84

Australians voted for the Commonwealth to have concurrent powers with the states in relation to Aboriginal welfare. This meant, in effect, that the Australian government could now preside over a broad range of Aboriginal programs. Aboriginal people were for the first time recognised as Australian citizens. Shortly after, the *Aborigines Protection Act of 1909* was repealed and the *Aborigines Act, 1969* introduced. An advisory Council for Aboriginal Affairs was established to review submissions from states for funding in the areas of housing, education and health (Fletcher, 1989b:265). From this point, all previous restrictions imposed on Indigenous people in Australia were withdrawn. New rights included the freedom to come and go from reserves, as well as legal rights and access to health, housing and education equivalent to that of other Australian citizens.

During this period and throughout the 1970s struggles over equity issues in relation to immigrants, women and Aboriginal Australians took on new forms that sought to recognise dimensions of exclusion such as language and culture. In this context, issues of racism and sexism were seen to "devalue particular resources of individuals and so deny them the benefits and opportunities available to others" (Lynch, 1990:7). All of these factors helped the push for greater Aboriginal access to tertiary education, in particular teacher education, in the late 1960s and early 1970s (Fletcher, 1989a; Watts, 1971).

Aboriginal Study Grants were introduced in late 1969 (Sykes, 1986) to provide financial assistance to students to allow them to finish school and to enter university. However, it was the 1970s that ushered in a new period in education for Indigenous people in Australia generally. The *National Workshop on Aboriginal Education* reported a number of recommendations in May 1971. Among these were the need for Aboriginal Studies in teacher education courses for non-Indigenous students; the development of flexible entry provisions for Aboriginal people to enter teacher education; and the recruitment of Aboriginal Teaching Aides, currently known as Aboriginal Education Assistants or AEAs (Watts, 1971).

In 1972, there were 72 Aboriginal students in higher education across the whole of Australia (Bourke et al., 1991:3). At that stage, entry to university for all students was via a final test at the end of schooling – the Higher School Certificate. During the term of Labor Prime Minister Gough Whitlam, a mature-age entry path was also introduced, with the first intake in 1976 – of which I was one. Entry was based on age (25 years minimum), interviews, educational and

85

professional experience and a range of entry tests. It was a strategy to overcome gender, class and other forms of inequality in the education system. Mature-age entry went some way towards increasing the enrolment of Aboriginal students but it was the opening up of special entry provisions and special programs at a range of institutions nationally, which began to make a mark (Loos and Miller, 1989; Jordan, 1985).

Intense lobbying from Aboriginal groups pressed governments for changes to education policy with a particular emphasis on increasing the number of Aboriginal teachers to equal representation. The formation of the National Aboriginal Education Committee (NAEC) in 1977 added to the push for new initiatives in the area of Indigenous education. Its rationale, aims and objectives, published in 1980, stressed Aboriginal involvement at all levels of policy making, funding and administration of programs (Sherwood, 1982). In 1979, the NAEC outlined a plan for support mechanisms for Indigenous peoples via an injection of funds to schools and post-secondary education (Bourke et al., 1991). It was from this point forward that an emphasis on teacher education appeared alongside the strategy of 'enclave' programs. Both aimed to improve Indigenous access to tertiary education. However, Indigenous teacher education was aimed specifically at improving Indigenous student outcomes at the level of schooling. A third purpose was to provide Indigenous academic pathways.

Communities

The Indigenous tertiary sector

Some discussion of the concept of 'enclave' and the meanings of 'community' that are operationalised will serve to illuminate the kinds of tensions emanating from special provision. The concept of enclave was first used in the 1970s to describe separate academic support systems that were established for Aboriginal people in teacher education courses. Largely these support systems were staffed by Aboriginal people and the separate nature of the support systems was also intended as a way to maintain Aboriginal identity (Jordan, 1985:34). In 1986, the NAEC emphasised that enclave programs had a defined set of essential elements including special entry provision, academic assistance, separate facilities and the requirement that this should involve a standard teacher education course (NAEC, 1986:15).

An enclave is, therefore, distinct from a group program – which is specifically designed for Aboriginal students only. Enclave support programs had good outcomes increasing the number of Aboriginal teachers from 72 in 1979 to 220 in 1982 across Australia. Deirdre Jordan, however, raised a concern about the reification of enclave as an idea (1985:34) and suggested two consequences of enclave programs: that they would act to exclude programs, despite the fact that they fulfil all the aims stated by the NAEC – that is, that enclave programs limit choice for students and centres would become focused on delivering 'Aboriginal' knowledge; and that adherence to a particular nomenclature in the future will act as a constraint upon the development of very creative programs currently being planned or being implemented to meet new needs in multi-disciplinary institutions (Jordan, 1985:34-35).

Jordan's warning about the constraints of being locked into a single enclave model was rejected a year later by the NAEC, which reiterated instead the positive outcomes of enclaves. The NAEC determined that access to tertiary education, in particular teacher education, was critical if Aboriginal educational outcomes were to improve, and argued that racist assumptions regarding Aboriginal student ability, lack of access to education at all levels; and the cultural insensitivity of educators were all contributing factors determining inequitable outcomes. They argued that educational institutions reinforced this distance between Indigenous and non-Indigenous Australians' educational outcomes through institutional practices, curricula and teaching methods. The concept of enclave support programs, they argued, provided the best way to meet the NAEC target of 1000 Aboriginal teachers in classrooms by 1990, as well as providing a space for the development of Aboriginal academics (NAEC, 1986). The debate between Jordan and the NAEC reflects the tension between special and universal provision and the way in which racialisation creates space at the same time that it contains diversity (McConaghy, 1997b).

The NAEC's stance was reaffirmed in 1991 with the publication of the *Report into Aboriginal Deaths in Custody* (Australia, 1991:96-97, Recommendations 297-299) and the Human Rights and the Equal Opportunity Commission's *Report of the National Inquiry into Racist Violence in Australia* in 1991. The latter report found that "schools and campuses may be accused of perpetuating institutional racism in terms of their educational philosophies and in their roles as

87

workplaces" (HREOC, 1991:346). Migrant and Aboriginal peoples, according to the report, found "their own experiences [were] largely absent from curriculum material or represented in ways that offend[ed] them and also reproduce[d] racism in the wider community" (*ibid.*:353). The report recommendations went beyond simply increasing the presence of women, migrants and Indigenous people in education institutions. They stressed the importance of change to the culture of educational institutions, including the content of curricula, teaching methods and decision-making processes. So the argument shifted from a right to education based on the principles of access and equity, to a concern for the particular form of educational experiences of Indigenous people (Walton, 1997:43).

The debate around special versus equal treatment can be appreciated if we briefly turn to a related policy area. Using a feminist analysis of the same phenomena, Bacchi (1990) examined the response to pregnancy in workplaces. She found that "equal treatment advocates fear that if employers have to make provision for maternity, they might decide not to employ women. Special treatment supporters insist that employers acknowledge women's 'difference'" (Bacchi, 1990:111). Bacchi found that, in general, not acknowledging difference led to an inability to respond to the reality of women's lives – demands of family and personal life – while acknowledging difference "implied that these were women's duties". What this dilemma means in regard to Indigenous education is that programs like the AREP have the potential to acknowledge the historical realities of racialisation and how that may or may not impact on the intellectual, social, cultural and emotional needs of students. At the same time, there is a range of risks associated with valorising racialised constructions of identity, which then situate solutions in Indigenous cultural difference. Later in the chapter I will examine the material consequences of this tension for students, Indigenous and non-Indigenous staff and administrators.

This is the backdrop to the creation and evolution of the AREP program at the University of Western Sydney Macarthur (UWSM). By the end of the 1970s, the government had committed extra funds to improving access for Indigenous students to education. In addition, a range of courses had appeared at a number of universities across the country with annual funding arrangements supporting special provisions for Indigenous students. The UWSM became one of the institutions offering tertiary education opportunities to Indigenous students.

The University of Western Sydney and
Aboriginal Programs

In 1975, the Milperra College of Advanced Education was established as a teacher education facility to serve the southwestern suburbs of Sydney (see Figure 5.2), which was, and still is, home to most NESB immigrants, white working class Australians and many Aboriginal people (Collins and Castillo, 1998). This college mainly prepared elementary school teachers for work in government schools in New South Wales and although students were drawn from throughout Sydney and NSW they, for the most part, came from the suburbs and rural areas surrounding the college. In the intervening years, the name and the overall purpose of the institution has changed as Milperra College of Advanced Education became part of the UWSM, a campus of the third largest university in NSW, however, student diversity has always remained a characteristic of the institution.

Figure 5.2
Greater Western Sydney

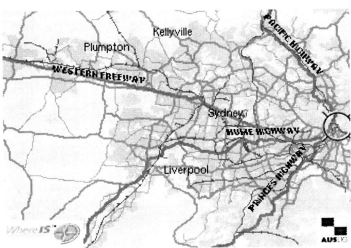

University is near Liverpool. Sydney city centre marked by blue 'crosshair'.

http://www.whereis.com.au Retrieved 25/03/2000

In Australia, the provision of tertiary education places for Aboriginal people who lived in rural and remote parts of the country had been very poor. Along with a number of other institutions which responded to the offer of financial assistance to set up programs for Aboriginal students, the UWS Macarthur submitted a proposal to the Higher Education Board in 1981 entitled *A Proposal to Encourage Aborigines to Successfully Complete Tertiary Studies at the Milperra College of Advanced Education* (Macarthur Institute of Higher Education, 1984:1).

In 1982, Milperra CAE established the Aboriginal Education Unit as an enclave support unit providing an On Campus Bridging Course. The AREP began in 1983 in the areas of primary teaching and social welfare. Initially, UWSM was constrained by Aboriginal education funding processes, which were largely piecemeal, short-term and aimed heavily at student support. Annual changes to models of funding and the range of government bodies distributing funds created a reactive rather than proactive environment for the development of programs. The patterns of funding prevented any long-term development of philosophies and goals. Given these funding constraints, UWSM did well to continue with the AREP.

The pattern of funding changed in 1989, however, when the Minister for Employment, Education and Training, John Dawkins, launched the *National Aboriginal and Torres Strait Islander Education Policy* (NATSIEP). From 1990, funding became triennial to develop long-term Indigenous Australian education strategies. The NATSIEP had four main purposes:

- to ensure Aboriginal involvement in educational decision-making (as a basis for next 3);
- to provide equality of access for Aboriginal people to education services;
- to raise the rates of Aboriginal participation in education to those for all Australians;
- to achieve equitable and appropriate educational outcomes for Aboriginal people. (Department of Employment, Education and Training, 1989:3)

Additional funds were provided by the government under the Aboriginal Education Strategic Initiative Program (AESIP) for three to four trienniums beginning in 1990.

Given that academic programs were controlled by faculties, while academic skill development and cultural support were offered by Aboriginal support units, there was some degree of tension over addressing these goals. In understanding the nature of these tensions it is important to examine more closely the relationship between the AREP and various organisational units at UWSM.

When programs for Aboriginal students at UWSM were being developed there was considerable struggle over creating space in the university for alternative modes of delivery in terms of teaching arrangements, curriculum development and resource allocation. The tension between the universal provision of education for previously excluded students and the need for special provision in terms of support mechanisms produced many difficulties for those involved in the program. In the next section there will be a closer examination of this tension in the context of specific struggles. It is at this level we can see the ongoing impact of racialisation processes and how they both constrain and provide space for agency.

Identities

> But you know in those early days too – and the Aboriginal students didn't start complaining about this for a couple of years – they were given absolute shit accommodation. I mean I'm talking about while on campus. The falling down old buildings that no one else would use. Why were they timetabled in there... down in the rabbit warren? [old demountables] I mean we had a building here that was condemned, an old temporary building, that the students were put into when they came in, because everything else was full. Now that's outrageous. We're not talking all that long ago. (Marilyn: interview transcript)

The 'space' that a program occupies within an institution reveals much about the dynamics of racialisation. While UWSM had attempted to challenge practices that marginalised and excluded Indigenous students in tertiary education in NSW, it had difficulty in developing strategies beyond just enrolling more Indigenous students. One of the ways in which this manifested itself was in the allocation of rooms, staffing for the teaching program and the role of Indigenous academics and administrators in the program. The quote above by one of the non-Indigenous academics in the teacher education program about leftover rooms and facilities was echoed by many of the participants in this study.

> And they were seen as an add-on in terms of rooming, I mean I've had awful battles about rooms and so on. I lived through the situation, and you probably did too, when we had a couple of rooms out the front which were called the mission. And that's where the AREP students went. And I mean they are now quite rightly demolished and so on. So I mean rooming was a difficulty, staffing was always a difficulty. Issues like practice teaching were perennial difficulties. You know, gaining some form of equitable supervision was a real minefield. (Malcolm: interview transcript)

As an administrator in the program, Malcolm was continually faced with the contradictions of racialisation. There were a number of crises of legitimation. For example, the separateness of the program was often seen as a focus for debate. The racialised nature of the program created a set of tensions for teaching in the program.

> There have been stages where I've had to confront meetings of 100 irate school principals and so on, about the quality of the AREP program... the most notable one, was a particular case we had in the North West, where I flew to the town and addressed the Primary Principals Council for that region... and basically convinced them that what we were doing with the AREP students was equivalent to what we were doing with our full time students. (Malcolm: interview transcript)

Judgements from gate keeping bodies have the potential to seriously undermine attempts at reform by making alternative approaches appear less rigorous.

The mode of delivery based on part time attendance at residentials meant the AREP did not have the same institutional leverage as full time programs within the university. The continued marginalisation of the AREP within the university, however, was often dismissed because there was the notion that eventually the 'pool would dry up'. The latter response is troublesome because it assumes a static model of Indigenous culture and an assumed lack of agency which is disturbingly similar to the racialised ideologies during the period of protectionism in Australia, when it was thought that Aboriginal people would all die out. But if the negotiation and struggle for Indigenous control at UWSM is any guide, Indigenous education is dynamic.

If we recall the position from the NAEC (1986:11), which had a concern for "educational processes to work from an Aboriginal worldview", then we have some explanation for the focus for negotiation in recent times over the construction of identity. Much of the struggle since the 1980s over Aboriginal control has been about operationalising this so-called Aboriginal 'worldview'. That one worldview exists became sharply contested in the years 1992-1999 at UWSM. Instead, a diversity of views was revealed when the hegemony of faculty curricula, as well as who taught it, was brought into question. At that moment, the differing perceptions of what constituted an 'Aboriginal' curriculum among the Indigenous community within the university challenged racialised understandings of cultural difference.

In *Taking Control: Power and Contradiction in First Nations Adult Education*, Celia Haig-Brown argues that one of the complexities of Indigenous control in Canada has been the revelation that 75-80% of native children in Canada go to non-native schools (1995:3). This is despite the fact that First Nations people in Canada have increasingly controlled their education since 1971. One of the difficulties has been the overarching dominance of this notion of *one* worldview that has stymied much hard work among Indigenous educators in Canada. The case for localism, Haig-Brown argues – which is also included in *Indian Control of Indian Education* (National Indian Brotherhood, 1972) – goes some of the way towards recognising diversity within unity. The particular struggles for control in our AREP program reveals this Indigenous diversity at the same time that homogeneous readings of Indigenous cultural difference are being reproduced.

The contradictions of racialisation are sharply drawn in the struggle that has been partially told in a document called *Indigenous Higher Education at UWS: A Brief History and Review* (Centre for Indigenous Australian Cultural Studies (CIACS), 1996), which attempts to chart the course of programs for Aboriginal students over the period 1983–1996 at UWSM. One of the difficulties with this document, and with others that have been produced from within the university, is the vested interest that each one has served. None of these reviews have included the voices of students. In this analysis of Indigenous education at UWSM during the 1990s there is an attempt to include the struggles of students to improve their conditions for themselves and for future students.

To understand the negotiation of Indigenous identities at UWSM we need to begin with a close look at the various units, centres and faculties. There have been five different Aboriginal centres or units associated with Aboriginal education at UWSM since 1982. This is in addition to the Faculties of Education and Arts and Social Sciences and more recently, the Faculty of Health.

Until early 1992 MALU was a support unit and the Faculties of Education and Arts and Social Sciences carried out the teaching in the degrees. In response to a range of concerns about attrition, late assignments and lack of support off-campus, which were highlighted at a review in 1992, a two-phased block release mode was proposed (CIACS UWS, 1996:33). Until this time students began and completed their studies in faculties in a continuous program. With the change to two phases, there was an attempt to assign the teaching of some subjects in the new mode to Booloobidja, the newly created university-wide Indigenous centre. In doing so, there was a clear gesture of goodwill flowing from the central concern of the NAEC regarding increased Indigenous contributions. However, Booloobidja never had the full support of all the university network members[2] and failed in its attempt to centralise Indigenous studies. The tensions were centred around Indigenous localism as each network member's Aboriginal unit served a particular political, cultural and social community and each network member was independent from each other in virtually all aspects of university life. There were also political differences between key members of the Aboriginal centres that related to future directions, links with the community and funding arrangements. These differences become more evident when we examine the consequences of implementing change.

There was a crisis in 1993 when the planning for the new two-staged degree began. The degree was to enable AREP student withdrawal after two years with a qualification – a Diploma in Indigenous Australian Community Issues. It was also seen as a way to effectively prevent students going on when they did not have the academic skills – a so-called 'hard' barrier.

---

[2] The University of Western Sydney Macarthur was made up of three members each with their own Aboriginal support unit.

What emerged from this process was a diversity of Indigenous voices related to curriculum development, especially in terms of the way in which Aboriginal identity and knowledge was to be constructed in the new diploma. This couldn't be resolved so there was a split of Booloobidja into two units – one support (MALU) and the other academic (CIACS) – which was greeted with some concern.

> As you are aware I was opposed to the splitting of the Aboriginal administration into MALU and CIACS. I thought that was a backward step and not good for the cause... and I think in hindsight my position was vindicated. I'm very pleased to see it back now in one unit. (John: interview transcript)

But what was the 'cause'? It seems that the split was over that very thing: a definition of the 'cause'. Between 1992 and 1996 there has been a plethora of key documents suggesting changes produced in the struggle for Indigenous control. The negotiation of identities is central to the way in which this control is to be understood.

CIACS signalled their new direction by "referring to the students as 'Diploma students', rather than 'AREP students'" because they wanted to offer their Diploma to "locally based Indigenous as well as non-Indigenous people" (CIACS, 1996:34). The first intake of students was in 1995, although a pilot group commenced in the program in 1994. By the beginning of 1996, it became clear that the implications of a change in nomenclature would be the removal of the word 'rural'. This change created an immediate response from students in the AREP program, as well as from the Aboriginal Higher Education Network – the association of Aboriginal Higher Education Programs (AHEPs) in New South Wales universities, which is the principal advisory body to the New South Wales Aboriginal Education Consultative Group Inc. on all higher education issues.

On April 6, 1996 a letter from a Social Welfare student questioned what he saw as an attempt to 'dismantle AREP' resulting from a 'major power push' to take control of Aboriginal education. Furthermore, it appeared that there was no guarantee that students who had started their degree would be able to continue beyond the end of 1996.

In a meeting held at the motel where the AREP students were accommodated during a residential, students voted for immediate action on the part of the university. They asked for a guarantee that the term 'rural' would not disappear from nomenclature and a promise that the program would receive ongoing university support so that their degrees could be completed. If this didn't occur they threatened to take action to have the funding and the program moved to another, more supportive institution.

The particular dispositions that students brought to these issues had been formed through their work in Aboriginal organisations, as Aboriginal workers in government schools and agencies, and as people residing in marginalised rural areas. They were not passive students without experiences of inequality, nor did they lack organising skills and political rhetoric.

Their concerns were structural in terms of their own educational outcomes but these were not the only concerns. The new centre known as CIACS reconstructed the idea of Aboriginal studies in the light of a new postcolonial revisioning of cultural knowledge. As one of the administrators put it:

> The thing that alarmed a lot of the Aboriginal students, as you are aware, was that in CIACS the word Aboriginal was almost lost in relation to Cultural Studies, racism and other issues. I think that was a major concern. (John: interview transcript)

The objective structure of relations reveals, however, why there was a struggle for the legitimate forms of specific authority – in this instance over what constituted Indigenous studies or 'Aboriginal' knowledge and who should have control. This is reflected in the way in which the university envisaged the role of Aboriginal knowledge.

> Very much the kingpin activity of CIACS initially was to establish an Aboriginal Studies major within the BA – but for that BA, for that Aboriginal Studies major to be available to other members of the university if they so desired. The approach to what CIACS was doing changed with the recruitment of a number of new staff. It was changing under some influence of people who were there already but it really did turn around when the three new staff arrived at the beginning of 1995. At that stage, by that time, CIACS had taken over the teaching, in 1994, of Aboriginal Studies subjects within the Faculty of Education, and to a much lesser extent within FASS [Faculty of Arts and Social Sciences], but they had taken them over, they were doing them. At the beginning of 1995, March or something, I think, I met with the head of CIACS,

and the newly appointed Senior lecturer, who gave us back the subjects. (Malcolm: interview transcript)

These subjects were traditional, historical and anthropological studies of Aboriginality and Aboriginal society. CIACS, even in its name, wanted to radically shift the content of the curriculum and so, the struggle was about whom should have control over constructing the curriculum. There would appear to be some basis for shifting what was considered appropriate and meaningful knowledge for AREP students. One of the lecturers in the program comments:

> I think there may have been just the thought, that if a course was relevant to the regular students in... the same course was necessarily relevant to the Koori group. I think there was that attitude early on... and I don't think it worked. But as I say it had to change and it did change. (Charles: interview transcript)

Yet, there were real problems about who was arguing for these changes and how they were administered. Not only was the new centre overwhelmingly staffed by non-Indigenous people, but the only Indigenous member also had a problematic relationship to the dominant power group – the Aboriginal Higher Education Network.

> I think there were personalities involved. It's always silly to predicate too much of an administrative and managerial decision-making process on personalities, because they can change as we have seen. Both the key players have gone now. (John: interview transcript)

While it is true that personal politics were part of the dynamics, it was also the politics of difference centred on what constituted cultural studies by and for Indigenous students that was at the heart of the struggle. For the students, the fact that non-Indigenous academics were dominant in the struggle and the Indigenous academic who was involved was not part of the powerful Aboriginal Higher Education Network, led them to doubt the legitimacy of the new direction. In addition, some students were concerned that their course would appear different and, therefore, 'less than' to future employees. This was a legitimate concern. Finally, the institution of new AREP recruitment processes threatened the very nature of the program, which philosophically had provided alternative access for students who might otherwise have not entered tertiary education. One of the students commented:

> We were told by this lecturer [in CIACS], that they wanted better students. (Field notes, 10/96)

The role of both the State and the wider institution – the UWSM – in determining the possibilities for Indigenous control needs to be considered if we are to fully understand the other structural constraints placed on CIACS at this particular time.

Firstly, the faculties of Education and Social Sciences had been considerably concerned at the cost to the faculties incurred in running programs where student numbers were small and the number of repeated subjects meant lost EFTSU (individually funded places). AREP was such a program. Furthermore, running the full range of electives was impossible, resulting in a continual piecemeal approach to certain aspects of the curriculum. The transfer of responsibility of electives to CIACS provided administrative relief for the faculties as well as giving the new centre some 'substance'. The faculties had threatened many times to stop running the AREP. The Faculty of Education discussed on an annual basis the on-going viability of the AREP program but always guaranteed that continuing students could complete their degrees. What factors contributed to the burden on faculties?

While the annual changes to funding was transformed to triennial funding in 1989 with the launching of the National Aboriginal and Torres Strait Islander Education Policy (NATSIEP), it became clear that government support for Indigenous programs was beginning to focus on self-sufficiency. Faculties had never set up the programs in this manner, partly through a commitment to the program's role of serving a social need but also because the central administration had diverted some of the annual funding to other points within the university. The funding for CIACS came from the Aboriginal Strategic Initiative Plan (AESIP), which education minister John Dawkins had introduced in 1989 at the same time as the NATSIEP. The AESIP was to cease in 1999 by which time the centre would have to be independent.

During the second half of the 1990s the conservative Howard government, elected in 1996, decreased funding to tertiary institutions, forcing many postgraduate degrees into fee-paying courses. This had the effect of reducing postgraduate numbers, particularly in the Faculty of Education that depended heavily on teachers upgrading qualifications through studying at master's level. The general climate at the end of 1997 was one of great uncertainty for the Faculty of Education and, indeed, the entire university. For CIACS, to gain independence in this climate, it would need to offer very competitive postgraduate courses to survive. When it did not manage to do this, it was dissolved and replaced by Goolangullia Aboriginal Education Centre (Figure 5.3) in 1998. The combination of Aboriginal student and community dissatisfaction, together with these wider fiscal problems, meant that only with united support and an academic Indigenous unit was survival likely.

Figure 5.3
Goolangullia Aboriginal Education Centre symbol[3]

When we consider the relationship between knowledge and power within the university it is interesting to note this struggle over disciplinary knowledge between CIACS's academic concerns regarding the construction of Aboriginality in cultural studies curricula, and the way in which the university was constructing Aboriginality in these processes. The process of racialisation was evident in the space given to Indigenous knowledge – 'Aboriginal studies' – as it stands in relation to what is considered the 'core' of teaching. Keeffe argues that because of the hegemony of racialised understandings of cultural difference, institutions are more able to accommodate traditional cultural studies because it "tends to keep the patterns of domination in place" (1992:83).

The irony, from the point of view of Indigenous struggles over this 'new' cultural studies curricula, is that Goolangullia Aboriginal

---

[3] AREP is no longer controlled by Goolangullia Aboriginal Education Centre.

Education Centre kept the focus on community cultural issues but retained the word Aboriginal over Indigenous. At the end of 1998 the Faculty of Education agreed to transfer control of the Bachelor of Teaching (Primary) to Goolangullia. At the same time the whole of UWSM underwent restructuring and the future for Goolangullia was not clear.

Indeed Goolangullia was disbanded at the end of 2001 after yet another restructuring and the education programs returned to the new School of Education and Early Childhood Studies. Goolangullia did provide a number of pathways for students and these continue. They have, in fact, diversified in terms of teaching, while building up a largely non-Indigenous, part-time teaching staff along with a small full-time Indigenous administrative, support and teaching staff. Aboriginalisation was the policy of Goolangullia but this policy created a new set of tensions to be negotiated.

Conclusion

It is possible, through this overview of the changing structures of Indigenous education at UWSM to see how racialisation continues to shape what is taught and by whom in Aboriginal teacher education, however, the role the State plays in terms of reduced funding arrangements places restrictions on the ways in which Aboriginal activists can work to bring about change in Australian universities today. Unifying discourses are critical at a time of threat, such as when the students feared the rural focus was being removed from course nomenclature. The interactions here between the students and academics created, through struggle, the possibility for new arrangements and the elimination of old structures which depended too heavily on individual goodwill and often paternalistic gestures.

There have been almost 150 AREP teacher education graduates who work in a diversity of positions, including teaching. A number are now school principals, while others have used the cultural capital gained from tertiary education to encourage family members to study. Others are to be found in positions of immense responsibility on Lands Councils, in government departments, or acting as consultants to these organisations.

The success of the AREP is clear and this should ensure its continuation. In addition to graduates it has produced pathways for Indigenous academics. The contradictions produced from the legacies of racialisation will continue however, despite Indigenous control. This is something we would expect and welcome – the power to determine means the power to provide space for a diversity of voices.

Acknowledgement

This chapter first appeared in a similar form as 'Negotiating Identities; Indigenous Teacher Education in Western Sydney' in Collins, Jock and Poynting, Scott (Eds) (2000) *The Other Sydney: Communities, Identities and Inequalities in Western Sydney*, Melbourne, Common Ground Publishing. Thanks to the editors and publisher for agreeing to the inclusion of the chapter in this book.

Chapter 6

The Northern Teacher Education Program (NORTEP)

Figure 6.1
NORPAC/NORTEP symbol[1]

Movements started taking place in the seventies, the very early seventies in the universities. There was a group of people like Keith Goulet who's an MLA now... helped found NORTEP... was a student at the U of S [University of Saskatchewan] you see, and was part of a group that were trying to get a native studies department. Even back to the sixties there were people at the U of S that got INEP going – the Indian and the Northern Education Program – and it was originally meant to prepare non-native teachers, non-Indigenous teachers. The original documents I think talk about giving them at least some sociology and anthropology classes to better prepare them. That was the beginnings of it I suppose and with the seventies the whole negotiation at the

---

[1] This bird is called the Loony and is found all over Canada. The dollar coin pictures the bird and is consequently called a Loony.

political and academic level to get Indian courses, then the Saskatchewan Indian Federated College at the University of Regina um... was the seventies... this is all the seventies this stuff! And it was all a whole kind of political mood... there was a paper brought out in 1972 by what was then called the National Indian Brotherhood – *Indian Control of Indian Education*. This was absolutely seminal, this electrified... I mean I was in the community when this paper came out and it just said what the people wanted you know? There was a whole movement. It became the whole system. You know universities, teacher education, lawyering, doctoring, social work, you name it. There was this move to get Indian knowledge, Métis knowledge, ways of knowing, reflected in the university. And this province very much obeyed. It's got a big population of Indian/Métis people. (Sandra: NORTEP administrator, interview transcript)

Introduction

In this chapter, there is an examination of the ongoing formation of NORTEP, which is a rural-based teacher education program for largely Indigenous northerners living in a range of communities in the north of Saskatchewan. Sandra's summary of the social, political and economic conditions, which gave rise to NORTEP, reveals many similarities with the Australian context. Woven into this anecdote is an overview of two decades of activism and cultural renewal in Canadian society during the 1960s and 1970s. The creation of NORTEP in this instance has been placed in a national, regional, provincial and cultural context outlining the interactions of politically committed education activists alongside Indigenous activists. The field of Indigenous education in Canada therefore parallels the ideological and political movements in Australia at that time. It is therefore possible to give a cross-cultural dimension to the way in which structures continually interact with the activities and cultural knowledge of agents (Chan, 1997:93). This is not surprising given the similar colonial histories and the global movements of people during the post-war period to countries like Australia and Canada.

In this chapter I shall examine these wider social movements, and the specific conditions, which led to NORTEP. Part of this process will include a discussion about 'Indianness' since the racialisation of Indigenous peoples in Canada is somewhat different from that of Australia and a little more complex in terms of the politics of control and political and economic rights. The purpose of this overview is to understand the emergence of the seminal document that Sandra refers to above – *Indian Control of Indian Education* – and the way in which this document created the conditions for a range of Indigenous groups to more actively negotiate the provision of education for their communities. One of the major arguments in this document was that education was where inequality originated through a denial of cultural difference. Accompanied by the demand for a politics of recognition (Taylor, 1994) during the Canadian 'cultural wars' of the 1960s (Burnaby, 1979), and by the ongoing impact of the ideologies and practices of racialisation, NORTEP was an attempt to break with the past by actively engaging with cultural difference. These political and cultural conditions immediately made identity an important issue for NORTEP. This leads to some interesting questions. How did the curriculum attend to issues of identity now that there was the opportunity to do so? What, also, were the politics of control in managing change in terms of the parent institutions and the NORTEP Board of Governors?

While similar issues were confronted by the AREP, NORTEP's relationship to the University of Saskatchewan and the University of Regina was markedly different in terms of day-to-day running. Certainly there were struggles over curriculum content and standards but distance from the parent institution meant there was some space to experiment and respond to local conditions. Yet this separateness did not free NORTEP from constraints since it was, and still is, a multicultural institute that had to deal with a culturally and linguistically diverse Indigenous student population. That is, one of the legacies of colonisation was the historically racialised unequal social relations *across* the Indigenous population. In addition, NORTEP had to deal with the issue of 'northerners' – Indigenous as well as *non-Indigenous* students. The practice of special versus universal provision takes on new meanings in this context.

In earlier chapters, I charted some of these dimensions of the Indigenous education field in Australian and Canadian history, in particular the political and ideological processes of racialisation in national development. The previous chapter, which focussed on the organisational structures in the AREP, revealed tensions as a consequence of historical inequality and on-going racialisation. The struggle for control in the AREP parallels earlier struggles for control in the NORTEP, although the AREP struggle occurred from within rather than from outside the parent institution. Again, these different spatial relationships to the parent institution have implications for structural arrangements of courses. I will tease out these implications in this chapter as well as the particular form that Indigenous control takes in the Canadian context.

Forces shaping NORTEP

'Indianness'

It is useful to see Indigenous educational movements in Saskatchewan in relation to the Canadian government's concern for provincial autonomy in respect of education. Provincial control of education was a deliberate part of the 1867 *British North America Act* (Wotherspoon and Satzewich, 1993:2) as discussed in Chapter 3. However, the *Indian Act of 1876* confirmed and maintained *Federal* responsibility for Status Indians, a responsibility that included education along with health, welfare and economic development on reserve lands. The tension between Federal rights and provincial control – in the case of Status Indians – meant that in the creation of NORTEP, the demand for local Indigenous governance (in the north) was possible while being able to receive continued funding support for the program on the basis of Federal treaty rights.

This tension between local, provincial and Federal control has been evident throughout NORTEP's history and continues today. The particular structural arrangements along with racialised categories of the Indigenous population create a complex system of governance. As this chapter will explain, the (racialised) system of Indigenous rights in Canada has meant differential access to education for Indigenous groups in the north of Saskatchewan (Wotherspoon, 1998:177).

While the generally accepted term in Canada for Indigenous peoples is *First Nations*, there are a range of categories that are invoked by government, Bands and individuals. The Federal relationship to Indigenous peoples takes into account the Status of different groups in terms of land and other rights.[2] There are two types of Status *Indian* – Treaty Indians and Bill C31 Indians. Treaty Indians are those with whom the Federal Government had signed a treaty (see Table 6.1). At the time of signing a treaty the government drew up a

---

[2] I am not suggesting that First Nations see themselves in this way, although they may, rather I merely outline the system of governance as they relate to access to political, economic and cultural rights.

list of names of people who belonged to each Band. The 'Band', as the government recognised organisation of Status Indians (Burnaby, 1979:10), was determined until 1985 on patrilineal genealogy, meaning that women could lose their status through marrying outside the Band – for example, by marrying a non-Status Indian.

Table 6.1

Treaty Rights in Saskatchewan

Name/Date	Indian Peoples Concerned
Treaty 4: 13 October 1874	Cree. Saulteaux
Treaty 6: August, September 1876	Plain Cree, Wood Cree
Adhesion: February 1889	
Treaty 7: September 1877	Blackfoot, Blood, Peigan, Sarcee, Stoney
Treaty 10: August 1906	Chipewyan, Cree

Such structural arrangements demonstrate that "State policies and practices were formulated not only on 'race' and ethnicity, but also on the basis of gender and class" (Wotherspoon and Satzewich, 1993:17). 'Rights by patrilineal descent' was altered under Bill C31 and Status rights were taken up by a number of women, some of whom had regarded themselves as Métis (discussed below) prior to this time, as well as other non-Status Indians who had voluntarily or involuntarily lost their rights. "The amendments ended discrimination against Indian women, restored Indian rights to those who had lost them unfairly, and significantly enhanced the jurisdiction of Indian community governments" (DIAND, 1986/87:8). By March 1986, 50,000 people had applied for Status (*ibid.*). The increase in the Bill C31 population continued to grow by between 5-8% per annum until 1991 (Wotherspoon and Satzewich, 1993:33).

The significance of treaty rights – or the lack of them – is important in understanding the impact of racialisation on people's lives. For example, Bands that had treaties could opt for school buildings and staff rather than gunpowder and gifts (Burnaby, 1979:35). Brian, president of the student council at NORTEP, talked about the free medical and dental care he received plus the opportunities he and others have had in terms of education arising directly from Band funding related to treaty rights. He outlined his Band's contribution to some of its members receiving tertiary education:

... there's three of us here [at NORTEP] and there's some in Regina, some in Saskatoon. Our Montreal Lake Band is funding a total of 53 students... and we've got some three or four students who are living in Arizona, Ontario, Quebec... all over Canada. Like our Band population is spread all over. (Brian: NORTEP administrator, interview transcript)

By the late 1980s, as a result of Bill C31, there had been a doubling in the number of Status students applying for entry to NORTEP (Carnegie, 1991:45). This demonstrates the critical importance of rights related to obtaining Status under the Canadian system. By the 1996-97 intake, the number of applications from Status Indians was close to 50% (NORTEP Information Package, 1996, Statistical Data).

The Métis, on the other hand, are still negotiating their relationship with the Canadian government post 1985. They have not had any formal treaties signed (other than cooperative management agreements in the Northwest Territories) despite the fact that they have associated with particular areas of land in Manitoba – especially Red River – Saskatchewan and Alberta. Initially, the term Métis "applied to the children of 'mixed' Indian and French marriages, but is now used to apply to the children of Indian and European marriages more generally" (Wotherspoon and Satzewich, 1993:32). They were 'go-betweens' in the early days of the fur-trade and often started trading posts, developing their own language – Michif which is a combination of Cree and French – along the way. Many took up positions as middle class intellectuals and entrepreneurs arguing for their own land and style of citizenship.

One of the quite significant differences between Australia and Canada in terms of racialised politics can be found in the notion of 'half-breed', which Métis have been commonly called (Dobbin, 1981; Flannagan, 1971). The notion of half-caste in Australia, which is the equivalent of the concept of 'half-breed', is equated with the denigration of children of mixed relationships as if they were somehow not 'real' Aboriginal people. This is a rejection of the concept of culture based on blood, whereas the notion of half-breed is recognition of the histories of a group of people whose identity was forged at the frontier of white settlement. It is also a reaffirmation of their Indian heritage, which was denied for such a long time.

One impact of historical non-recognition in terms of education is that the Métis have not been recognised linguistically. For example, the NORTEP Board of Governors asked for Michif to be taught, but the Saskatchewan Indian Federated College (SIFC) argued that it was not an Indian language and furthermore, that they had no one to teach it. Cree was the only language the SIFC supported, although Dene is now also included in their programs. This demonstrates the impact of differential rights on the basis of assumed racial purity in Canada. There are some parallels here between Michif (Cree/French) and Aboriginal English as a dialect. Both have been described as 'non-standard' and 'not proper' forms of language despite the fact that they have distinct socio-linguistic characteristics (Eades, 1993).

While there is not the space in this chapter to explore all the groups in Canadian Indigenous society, it is important to background those that appear at NORTEP. One of the other major groups at NORTEP is the Dene. The Dene was forced north when their land was occupied by farming settlements and the resettlement of Plains Cree after confederacy. They live in communities such as La Loche and Black Lake. The Dene have not had the advantages of treaty rights – such as early access to provincial education – so they have actually maintained their language to a much higher degree than other groups particularly at Wollaston Lake (Saskatchewan Indigenous Languages Committee, 1991:177). However, this benefit is offset by their general lack of power in First Nations politics, which means the curriculum has been slow to respond to their needs. In addition, it was the Cree,[3] to which most treaty Indians belong, who displaced them forcing them further north. One of the Indigenous lecturers, Marie – herself a Cree speaking Métis – reflects on her own experiences at school and the relations between different groups of Indigenous students:

> I just went to the school with them and there were a lot of conflicts during junior high between the Cree and the Dene. There was a lot of fights between them. (Marie: interview transcript)

> ... Mostly... probably name-calling and just the usual things like that about the different races. (Marie: interview transcript)

---

[3] Cree students are in the majority at NORTEP. The two Indigenous lecturers speak and teach Cree and Cree is the official focus of cultural studies at the Saskatchewan Indian Federated College in Regina. Dene is now offered at NORTEP.

... they are part of the Blackfoot group.... Navajo's language is quite similar to the Dene. So there's a past history of that... (Marie: interview transcript)

Traditionally, the Plains Cree and Blackfoot (Dene) lived on the plains traversing the current borders of southern Saskatchewan and the USA. With the USA policy of driving away the buffalo to starve the Plains Indians, the Cree and Blackfoot Confederacy came into competition with each other for scarce resources (*500 Nations*, 1995).

One way to understand the impact of differential rights is to briefly explore the Indigenous organisations and whom they represent in Canada. Contemporary organisations include the Assembly of First Nations (AFN), formed out of the National Indian Brotherhood (NIB) which itself was formed out of the National Indian Council (NIC). The NIC originally represented treaty and non-treaty Indians as well as non-Status Indians and Métis. This split in 1968 and produced the NIB representing Status Indians, and the Canadian Métis Society which later became The Métis National Council (Wotherspoon and Satzewich, 1993:231-33). The AFN seeks the entrenchment of Indian rights and sovereignty in the constitution, whereas Métis "do not want to become Indians" (*ibid.*). Rather, they want recognition as a distinct people with a right to land and self-government. When this is set alongside the desire of the Quebecois for sovereignty, the Canadian situation reveals the continuing tensions emanating from its dual colonial origins.

This brief discussion of the differentiation of cultural groups comprising the Canadian Indigenous population is important for understanding that NORTEP is not restricted to one racialised group. The program must accommodate the linguistic and cultural needs of diverse groups. With this knowledge it becomes possible to explain the tensions between the needs of different groups within NORTEP, which is taken up in the rest of this chapter.

It is useful now to turn to the general history of assimilation and integration in Canada to understand the wider context shaping the development of NORTEP. Just as AREP was produced from specific conditions in Australian society, to fully understand NORTEP also requires an examination of the rise of immigration, internal migration and growth of cultural pluralism in Canada.

Federal policy and new social movements

As in Australia, early conflict in Canada developed over land used for farming by the colonisers and by the Indigenous groups for hunting. Bolstered by their increased numbers and diversified economy the colonisers began to view traditional pursuits as a hindrance (Burnaby, 1979:33). The *British North America Act* (1867) gave the government of Canada legal right over the affairs of Indians. The history of this relationship clearly made it difficult for the Federal government to initiate provincial relationships with regard to Indians. They did so through two main ideologies that have been part of Canadian governmentality. Hawthorn (1967) called them paternalistic and democratic. The corresponding periods are 1867-1945 and 1945-1965 (*ibid.*:22-23).

During the period of paternalism Status Indians were contained on reserves. Hawthorn argued that this has had lasting consequences:

> This policy of confining Bands to their reserves and as much as possible preventing contact with the outside world largely contributed to the Indians' continued isolation from the Canadian community at large. Hence the ideology at that time was definitely conservative. It was hoped that the Indians would preserve their traditional ways of life. However, officials overlooked the fact that the Indians' hunting grounds were considerably reduced. Once resources became insufficient, the Indians in increasing numbers were forced to abandon their traditional economic activities to become dependents of the State. (Hawthorn, 1967:22)

In this period the government was interested in civilising the indigene, so education at residential industrial schools was about training for working on farms (Haig-Brown, 1988; Barman et al., 1986). However, the lack of adequate land and inadequate provision of tools meant that an adequate economic base for farming was never successfully established (Buckley, 1993). Yet this notion of 'training' as education dominated thinking well into the 20th century.

Indeed this period in Canada also paralleled that of Australia in terms of a desire to provide Indigenous people with some form of basic training in domestic work if they were female and manual labouring if male. To achieve this, the policy of *aggressive civilisation* (Davin cited in Haig-Brown, 1988:30) had to occur away from the reserve since the 'native' children were less likely to have the ways of the white man inculcated on the reserves:

> The child... who goes to day school learns little, and what is learned is soon forgotten, while his [*sic*] tastes are fashioned at home, and his inherited aversion to toil is in no way combated. (*ibid.*)

Preparation for an agrarian lifestyle was an idea borrowed from the United States' treatment of its Indians (Haig-Brown, 1988; Hesch, 1993). Hesch argues that it was the Anglo-Canadian fraction of the ruling class which looked to the United States for such models which were continued in the period of mass immigration from the late 19th century through the earlier parts of the 20th century (1993:68). Although attempts at wiping out Indigenous knowledge and culture were not entirely successful, the idea of civilising continued along with a low expectation of the educability of the Indigenous population.

Assimilationist thinking can be found in the curriculum from the 1930s. This fact is not surprising given the salience of assimilationist thinking at that time (see Chapter 3). The particular emphasis in Saskatchewan was on vocational training in the 1930s and 1940s (Handley and Kowalchuk, 1969:18; Barman et al., 1986). Following the period of assimilation when a parliamentary committee undertook to revise the *Indian Act*, and integration via joint partnerships with the provinces was in place, many demographics changed.

The post-war period saw white farmers introducing heavy machinery with which the reserve communities could not compete and which effectively supplanted manual labour (Buckley, 1993:67). With the worsening labour market for Indigenous people and a more diverse population, governments began to change their idea about assimilation.

The parliamentary committee established in the 1940s to revise the *Indian Act* recommended that a policy of integration would be more appropriate and contracted the provincial governments to provide education to Indian students in provincial schools, as well as in remote areas where possible, using the curriculum and teachers in the provincial system. The period throughout the 1950s and 1960s saw an unprecedented growth in the internal migration of the Indian population (Hawthorn, 1966). Between 1951 and 1961 the number of

Indians in urban areas tripled (Burnaby, 1979:13). As a consequence of the internal migration of Indians, more than half of the Aboriginal elementary school population was attending provincial schools by the 1960s (Burnaby, 1979:49).

The 1960s saw grassroots civil rights movements 'south of the border' in the USA and student uprisings in Paris. In this context of global change, Saskatchewan Indians formed the Federation of Saskatchewan Indians in 1961 (Barman et al., 1986:14), which eventually joined the formation of the National Indian Brotherhood in 1968. The discontent they voiced over cultural, linguistic and personal rights, however, was 'contained' by the findings of the Hawthorn Report (*ibid.:*15), which outlined Indigenous disadvantage while promoting integration as the answer.

However, during this period of integration a number of other emergent social issues provided opportunity for contesting treaty rights. As previously mentioned, the 1960s saw massive immigration to Canada from a number of non-British countries (Bolaria and Li, 1988) and the start of cultural debates in Canada over cultural and linguistic rights. French Canadians began to argue for separate and special rights and for the recognition of French as one of the national languages. In addition, in 1960 Aboriginal people obtained suffrage and in 1963 the Royal Commission on Bilingualism and Biculturalism was set up and continued until 1971. As a consequence of pressure from French Canadians, the Commission floated the notion of the French and English as the "founding races" (Burnaby, 1979:5).

Aboriginal populations responded very quickly to the presumptuous 'founding races' notion. No longer were they isolated from each other, and they now saw the opportunity to form coalitions to contest their submersion into the dominant French/English Canadian culture. But the 'founding races' notion was not only unsatisfactory for the Indigenous populations; it also enraged immigrant groups. In response, the Canadian government announced a policy of multiculturalism on 8 October 1971:

> Although there are two official languages, there is no official culture, nor does any ethnic group take precedence over any other... A policy of multiculturalism within a bilingual framework recommends itself to the government as a suitable means of assuring the cultural freedom of Canadians. (Whyte, 1983:21)

However, Indigenous people were always governed and legislated for separately from immigrants. The growing discontent among Indigenous groups over their conditions and rights was responded to by the Federal government which "sought to placate the growing criticism by initiating the Hawthorn survey of Indian conditions" (Barman et al., 1986:14).

The Hawthorn Report and 'citizens plus'

Prior to the announcement of the policy of multiculturalism, the Federal government released in 1966 and 1967 the two volumes of *A Survey of Contemporary Indians of Canada* (Hawthorn, 1966; 1967). It was a very comprehensive report shaping the direction of policy in a number of areas for some time afterward. There were ten general recommendations and many more specifically for economics, welfare, politics and so on. Four of the ten key recommendations had a particular bearing on education:

- Integration or assimilation are not objectives which anyone else can properly hold for the Indian. The effort of the Indian Affairs Branch should be concentrated on a series of specific middle range objectives, such as increasing the educational attainments of the Indian people, increasing their real income, and adding to their life expectancy.
- The main emphasis on economic development should be education, vocational training and techniques of mobility to enable Indians to take employment in wage and salaried jobs.
- The Indian Affairs Branch should act as a national conscience to see that social and economic equality is achieved between Indians and Whites. This role includes the persistent advocacy of Indian needs, the persistent exposure of shortcomings in the governmental treatment that Indians receive, and persistent removal of ethnic tensions between Indians and Whites.
- That Indians should be treated as 'citizens plus' because in addition to the normal rights of and duties of citizenship, Indians possess certain additional rights as charter members of the Canadian community.

Furthermore, Recommendation 8 pushed for the education of other Canadians to accept the 'plus' aspect of citizenship and Recommendation 10 called for the end of discriminatory practices in access to all public programs (Hawthorn, 1966:13).

The concept of 'citizens plus' is unique in that it incorporates those rights available to all citizens of Canada in addition to retaining the special rights arising from treaties. The response to this concept, indeed the whole Hawthorn Report, was the *White Paper* discussed below. The Hawthorn Report stressed cultural autonomy (*ibid.*:10) and brought into focus the relationship between level of education and employment in the workforce. "Unemployment generally in Canada has been concentrated among those who have less than a full grade school, and to a lesser extent, high school, education" (*ibid.*:55).

The relationship of education to socio-economic factors and economic development was explored by Hawthorn (1966) through an analysis of United Nations' material on global developments. Education was seen as central to the well being of citizens since "increasingly long periods of formal education and training is required to adjust people to rapidly changing technologies in an increasingly complex world" (Hawthorn, 1966:101). Not only did the report indicate a need for a greater level of skills training, it also called for the development of the social skills required for a ready and willing workforce:

> Fully important as the actual technical and intellectual content of the courses offered are the work habits and motivations which the educational system attempts to instill in people at an impressionable age. A difficult problem of industrialisation lies in the inculcation of work habits regulated by the clock and the weekly calendar, the acceptance of steady (and often monotonous) time schedules and routines, of submission to authority, and other requirements of employment in modern industrial and commercial enterprises. (Hawthorn, 1966:101).

It is clear that the Hawthorn Report was calling into question the very basis of the *Indian Act* – which was essentially assimilationist – by arguing that it was racist. This is because the *Act* was making Indigenous peoples assimilate through a denial of cultural difference without any real attempt to provide access to the dominant culture in terms of employment, health and housing. Integration, Hawthorn argued, should continue in education along with increased rights regarding cultural maintenance. But the *Indian Act* also provided certain rights, one of which was Federal support for education. Without the *Indian Act*, it would be impossible for Status Indians to pressure the government for increased control over the schooling of their children.

The *1967-68 Annual Report* of the Department of Indian Affairs and Northern Development (DIAND) noted that "to facilitate the integration of Indian pupils into provincial schools, changes were implemented in the programs in Federal schools and in the employment of teachers" (DIAND, 1967-68:80). The changes meant that the curriculum became *provincial* as well as the payment and certification standards of teachers. Funds were provided by the Federal government for the pre-service, in-service and out-service training of teachers of Indian students (*ibid.*:81). Increasingly, education was shifting to provincial control and Indigenous Canadians did not have any mechanisms for negotiation in that context.

The *Annual Report* in 1968-69 from DIAND argued that there had been a number of improvements arising from the new policy of integration. It argued that there had been an increase in Indigenous representation on provincial school boards (p.134) as well as a decrease in the use of residential schooling. In addition, the Universities of Manitoba and Saskatchewan provided training for Indian teachers' aides (DIAND, 1968-69:136). So the policy of integration meant opportunities for representation on provincial school boards as well as the opportunity for Indian teachers' aides to assist the integration of students into the wider Canadian society.

In 1969, a few years after the Hawthorn Report was published, the Prime Minister, Pierre Trudeau, promising "a just society", released the *White Paper on Indian Affairs* (Barman et al., 1986:15). It was clear that cultural and linguistic integration of Indigenous peoples at the cost of special status was the preferred direction of Federal government. The paper proposed an end to the *Indian Act* on the grounds that it was racist, as well as arguing for individual equality at the expense of cultural survival (Barman et al., 1986:15). Here we have the paradox of racialisation: on the one hand, special recognition was racist when applied to minorities yet, on the other, it was acceptable when applied to the dominant English/French populations. Indian groups were quick to respond. While they condemned past policies of assimilation, they preferred to maintain their treaty rights with the Federal government and began by negotiating for local control over education following the release of the position paper *Indian Control of Indian Education* issued by the then named National Indian Brotherhood[4] in 1972.

In summary, Indigenous education in Canada since the 1960s has been shaped by Federal, provincial, regional and First Nations interests. What they were struggling over was how to respond to a record of inequitable outcomes in education alongside wider socio-economic disadvantage. While the solutions to this inequality were diverse, education was the key focus.

The state of Indian-Métis education towards the end of the 1960s in Saskatchewan

The Australian pattern of low retention in the schooling of Indigenous people was repeated in Saskatchewan. Handley and Kowalchuk (1969) found that there was a "continuous decrease in enrolment beginning as early as Grade 3 and continuing on with increasing speed until, with Indian students, only .5% are in Grade 12 and in Northern Saskatchewan only .3%, as compared to a total provincial figure of 5.1%" (*ibid.*:1). The report sighted three possible explanations for such a situation. Firstly, that the students were *not being taught properly*; secondly, that *parents were not encouraging staying on*, and finally "the Indian and Métis students *do not have sufficient mental ability* to continue on in an academic stream" (Handley and Kowalchuk, 1969:1). (My emphasis.)

In the 1950s and 1960s there was some experimentation with the curriculum in terms of Social Studies and English. By this stage assimilation had been replaced with a policy of integration. In effect, this meant some recognition of the different lifestyles of children in the north of Saskatchewan and Social Studies content was adapted to represent that difference. However, because over half of the Indian students were in predominately white schools because of the policy of integration, most of the time Indian students were the minority and studied what was appropriate to the majority (Handley and Kowalchuk, 1969:19). Hesch argues that in this way the "canonical curriculum" is reproduced (1993:109). That is, the traditional curriculum is unquestioningly selected and the homogenised and reified Indigenous content is added on (*ibid.*:110).

---

[4] National Indian Brotherhood became the Assembly of First Nations in 1985.

117

As an attempt to break down the hegemony of particular forms of knowledge in schools (Connell, 1993) failed because its implementation was piecemeal. When the core curriculum is examined at this time, it is possible to see more clearly the construction of difference as deficit. For example, English, in particular oral English, was a particular focus. The 'Rose Colliou Oral English' course was introduced with an emphasis on drills and structures (Handley and Kowalchuk, 1969:18). The program failed according to this study because of high teacher turnover, training expense and a lack of resources for the program. Hesch (1993), following Connell, argues that this is the way the hegemonic curriculum works: it serves to fragment and disorganise and render useless the knowledge that the Indigenous students brought to school.

During the 1960s a range of courses at Saskatchewan universities was commenced. The University of Saskatchewan ran an Indian Education Program from 1961. It was within the School of Education and provided subjects for teacher trainees on how culture (and later on language) shaped the curriculum to 'fit' the local community (Handley and Kowalchuk, 1969:28). Education 357 spent much time on these aspects and while recognising difference it failed to change the curriculum in any substantive way. As part of the 'perspective' approach, it failed to recognise the entrenched power relations inherent in the dominant pedagogical relationships.

In 1963, Education 457 provided the opportunity to "analyse and develop principles and techniques of curriculum development in relation to local community resources and needs" (Handley and Kowalchuk, 1969:28). Oral Cree was offered for the first time in the summer of 1967 and taught by a Cree graduate in 1969. Around the same time a master's programme was developed to encourage research into administration, history, cross-cultural and general 'problems' in Indian education. We can see the beginning of particular types of research traditions in this period – especially those that focus on 'resolving' issues of difference.

While Métis existed at this time they were not a recognised ethnic group. As a consequence, they were not a focus for research and their needs and progress were often swallowed up in the general concerns of Indian students, although by the early 1970s their claims are clearly distinct. As stated earlier in this chapter, they did not want to be seen as 'Indian' since this brought with it particular constructions and practices. We can see by this stage that there is fertile ground for change.

By the late 1960s the Indian Affairs Department in Regina, the College of Education at the University of Saskatchewan and the Saskatchewan Teachers' Federation were working together to provide ongoing training and support. Classes were offered to Kindergarten teachers and Indian teacher aides began being hired in 1971-72. The Saskatchewan Teachers' Federation provided short courses on Indian education in response to this demand. As well, teachers were offered short orientation courses if posted to northern schools and were offered bursaries of $200 to take the Education 357, 457, Cree and Anthropology subjects.

The Indian Affairs branch also offered a week to ten-day orientation for those teachers going to Indian schools, but the teachers in integrated schools received little or no special training. So by the late sixties and early seventies, the two major teacher education institutions and the Teachers' Federation in Saskatchewan were working together to change education for Indigenous students.

With the election of the NDP (New Democratic Party) in 1971, Saskatchewan began to revive some of its socialist agrarian roots (Buckley, 1993) which focussed on local representation and governance. In 1972 a Department of Northern Saskatchewan was created with its own minister. The NDP promised the establishment of community colleges to bring education closer to the people in a sparsely settled province. They were to be community-oriented in terms of their educational focus, placement and content. Saskatchewan was the first province to put forward such a revolutionary approach to education (Faris, 1973). The focus was on change beginning with the community college system that started in La Ronge (Goulet, 1996:2). Furthermore, the Métis people were calling for equal Federal recognition and in 1973 formed a new organisation called AMNSIS (The Association of Métis and Non Status Indians of Saskatchewan).

Taking control?

The energy and sense of change revealed in the documentary history above makes it seem as if revolutionary changes are afoot. However, these political struggles and gains conceal the constitutional difficulties that the notion of *Indian control* set in train. There are two important elements to consider: the basis upon which the National

Indian Brotherhood sought control; and the constitutional restrictions around 'special treatment'.

The two recognised principles upon which Canadian education is based are Parental Responsibility and Local Control of Education (National Indian Brotherhood, 1972:3). Harnessing these principles, the NIB argued that through their treaty rights they should continue to receive Federal funding for education but be allowed to control the education of their children at the local level (Ward, 1986:11). To achieve this end, jurisdiction for education would be divided up between the Federal government, local provincial schools jurisdictions and Indian Bands (*ibid.*:5).

However, it was argued at Cabinet level that "there was no legal authority in the *Indian Act* for the transfer of education programs from the control of the Minister of Indian Bands" (Ward, 1986:12). Furthermore, provincial education laws that were 'Indian-specific' were in breach of the constitution because they discriminated on the grounds of 'race' (McPherson, 1991:33). In mid 1982, funding for the education of off-reserve Indians was terminated – that is, to qualify for Federal assistance students had to live on-reserve. It was then that the importance of collective rights began to be voiced by a range of Indigenous organisations. Until the end of 1982, when the Charter of Rights and Freedoms was passed amending the constitution, Band control was fragmented and individually negotiated with the government putting Indians in a *reactive* position (Ward, 1986).

The formation of the Assembly of First Nations in 1985 provided a powerful united front as the "collective representation of individual Bands", while the Saskatchewan Indian Education Council argued that control over education was part of self-government (*ibid.:*20). This two-pronged struggle – Federal and provincial – meant that the increasing control of education by Indigenous groups was not labelled a violation of the *British North America (BNA) Act*. It was argued by First Nations that provincial governments could confer "additional benefits on a broader range of disadvantaged students, including Indian students" (McPherson, 1991:34). So the development of NORTEP was accepted on the grounds that (disadvantaged) non-Indigenous students in the north of Saskatchewan could also attend the college.

By the end of 1991, over 90% of schools on reserves were Band-controlled (McPherson, 1991, Appendix B:37). The *Royal Commission on Aboriginal Peoples* noted that "there was a clear consensus that control over policy, curriculum, and support services is necessary to create an educational experience that reinforces the positive identity of Aboriginal students and enables them to succeed academically" (1996:8). Indeed, statistics support the fact that NORTEP has been very successful in reversing the high turnover of teachers in the north. In the Northern Lights Division, turnover has declined from 75% to 20%, with the percentage of Indian and Métis teachers increasing from 3% to 25% (NORTEP and NORPAC Information Package, 1995). In addition, there is now a clearer policy of devolution:

> The policy is certainly devolution. So, I mean, the meetings we have now with INAC [Indian and Native Affairs Commission] people who support us financially, indicate their role is to work themselves right out of the system... They've really transferred control of education to the local Bands for K-12 and now in the most recent years they've been transferring the power for post-secondary division as well. So, over the years the funding for NORTEP has come from a major provincial grant, from the provincial government, and then we've always gotten our grant from INAC. That's just been a lump sum grant over time. They've been very supportive of NORTEP and now the First Nations people, the Federation of Saskatchewan Indian Nations really are saying that that should cease to occur as well. (Eric: NORTEP administrator, interview transcript)

NORTEP has seen increased diversification of the population and devolution of fiscal arrangements over 20 years. These forces have shaped structural arrangements in particular ways. Having outlined the field in which NORTEP was produced we can turn to the way in which the structure of the program has responded to the issues of control, culture and identity.

The site

Lac La Ronge, the site of NORTEP, is advertised as a fishing destination but also provides a connection to the vast northern system of lakes, ice flows and portage trails. It is a busy settlement with flourishing Indigenous enterprises such as the meat processing plant, the local club and other small businesses used by the local community. There is a Trading Post that still does some business resulting from the traplines.

Figure 6.2
Lac La Ronge (in summer)

Figure 6.3
Map of Canada – Saskatchewan Province

The NORTEP "serves 35 communities in a 350 mile by 400 mile area in the northern half of Saskatchewan, Canada" (Goulet, 1996:1). These 'communities' include Indigenous and non-Indigenous populations but overall around two-thirds to three-quarters are of aboriginal descent (Carnegie, 1991:28). The non-Indigenous inhabitants usually work for government agencies and tend to cluster in particular communities such as Creighton, Ile-la-Crosse and La Ronge, where the NORTEP program is situated. La Ronge is a 'gateway' town situated on Lac La Ronge in northern Saskatchewan, a 'prairie province' in central Canada. It was originally the 'government' town of the north. There are approximately 6000 permanent residents of which about 50% are Indigenous:

> The largest local Band is the Lac La Ronge Band. The Indigenous residents largely make their living from Kitsake Meats, one of their organisations. They run some kitchen facilities in the mines and get employment through that. They have three main areas, fisheries is one too. But they're really not controlling any of the mines. (Steve: NORTEP administrator, interview transcript)

Non-Indigenous residents mainly work in government positions. Since Lac La Ronge has begun selling itself as a fishing and watersports 'resort' it has grown steadily. Between my first visit in 1992 and my second visit in 1996, it had grown to include a large supermarket, video store and an extended urban housing area. There is still a distinct division based on Indigenous/non-Indigenous housing.

At the end of the tarred, dusty (in summer) main street sits a government-designed building called *Mistasinikh Place*. This is where the NORPAC/NORTEP is based. The former is a professional access college for those wanting to study at university in the south. Students complete a range of subjects which are shared with NORTEP students before deciding whether or not they want to do a degree in engineering, science and technology or other courses related to the growing industries in the north.

The building is designed around a central spiral ramp that wends its way up through tropical plants. There is a communal eating area and a generally friendly and cosy feeling, something that has clearly been created in contrast to the frozen lake outside. Students take classes in this building and reside in a series of apartments, along with any visiting faculty from the south, when they are in town. Most students travel long distances over bumpy roads and in winter many have to fly in on 'ski planes'.

Figure 6.4
Northern Saskatchewan Links

Source: Saskatchewan Post-Secondary Education and Skills Training, La Ronge

Source: Keewatin Career Development Corporation Website, Northern Saskatchewan
http://www.kcdc.sk.ca/maps/index.asp

Visiting La Ronge and surrounding settlements reveals that within Indigenous communities there are varying levels of disadvantage mirroring the wider class relations in Canadian society. On reservations some housing is clearly substandard compared to housing designed for Band leaders. In terms of education, many young people have to go to other communities to complete schooling. To understand this, one has to remember that the racialised categories not only created historical inequalities among and between Indigenous communities, but also continue to structure relations between the various groups (Wotherspoon, 1999).

Principles and philosophies of operation

The Northern Teacher Education Program and Northern Access Program Information Package states that the mission of NORPAC/NORTEP is "committed to developing northern people, particularly those of Aboriginal ancestry, in teaching and other professions to become self-sustaining life-long learners based on the traditional values of northern Saskatchewan cultures" (November, 1995:3).

It is important to acknowledge that the NORTEP attempts to overcome the racialised structural inequality through a focus on the 'north' rather than specifying particular Indigenous groups as do other programs in the south. For example, SUNTEP (Saskatchewan Urban Native Teacher Education Program) is primarily for Métis students, and ITEP (Indian Teacher Education Program) is primarily for Status Indian. There is a very strong emphasis on multiculturalism as well as Indigenous 'ways of doing and knowing' within the institution's programs; a deliberate attempt to unsettle dominance and an attempt to deal with differences across the Indigenous and non-Indigenous population. One of these differences relates to the dominance of Cree cultural and linguistic knowledge in educational policy and planning of the curriculum. However, there is an emerging challenge to this as the idea of 'Indian ways' is unravelling.

> You see the Dene communities are um... have been later than the Cree communities at getting schooling kind of thing going and so it's only recently that we've had a group of Dene students in the program. That's when the Crees have realised, some of the Crees have realised their style is not an 'Indian' style, it's a Cree style. (Sandra: NORTEP administrator, interview transcript)

There is some agreement, however, about certain cultural traditions that work for all groups. Figures 6.5 and 6.6 illustrate the enacting of the philosophy of NORTEP through different levels of communication. Figure 6.5 shows that the organisational circle, based on the traditional 'Indian' circle of communication, aims for optimum democracy at the institutional and local levels.

However, Figure 6.6 shows the relationship of all these organisations through the areas of funding, academic, governance and field experience. The following model shows the four major fields involved in inter-agency cooperation. These will be discussed to help draw out the interrelationship of macro structures, in terms of policy and funding, to local provincial and community participation.

Figure 6.5
NORTEP/NORPAC Organisational Circle

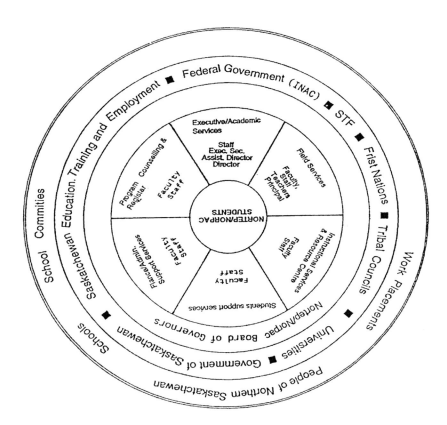

Figure 6.6

Relationships among NORTEP's Cooperating Agencies and Major Fields

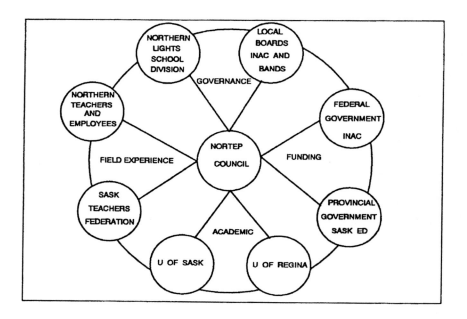

Key: Circumference = Common Project Cooperation; Segments = Special Areas of Cooperation.
Source: Carnegie, 1991: 145.

The circle appears to flatten relations of power although to some extent it is a true model of representativeness. The problem of power and how that shifts is not demonstrated through this model. To understand why Indian control has taken such a long time to occur, *despite* representativeness, one must consider funding, academic programs and issues related to these, governance and field relationships in more detail.

Funding

Funding sources have shifted over the 20 years since the inception of NORTEP. Initially, Indigenous aides were paid 75% of their salaries by the Northern Lights Schools Division (Carnegie, 1991:41). When treaty Indians began attending in 1981 they began paying fully for their study until NORTEP decided this was causing differentiation among students (*ibid.*). Various boards and government departments paid allowances for other students until Saskatchewan Education began funding the program in 1979 (*op.cit.*:42). Some students pay tuition fees.

We can see that previously funding came directly from the government but with devolution there is less need for large representative bodies like the grand council's who sit on NORTEP's Board of Governors:

> The P.A. [Prince Albert] Grand Council used to be the spokesgroup or spokesperson for all of these Bands. Now they're saying: "No... no, you're not a spokesperson for us. We'll tell you what to say but in the meantime we'll speak for ourselves." So Lac La Ronge Indian Band is really autonomous, pretty much in all areas. They are supportive of the P.A. Grand Council in trying to achieve the broader goals, but in terms of the La Ronge Indians achieving their own goals, it doesn't rely on anybody. It doesn't rely on the P.A. Grand Council at all. Whereas in the old, if you turn back the clock less than 10 years we wouldn't be dealing with La Ronge Indian Band, we'd be dealing with P.A. Grand Council. (Eric: NORTEP administrator, interview transcript)

The effects of these changes for NORTEP include a diversification of bodies they are dealing with and an increase in the diversity of students. The funding relationships in this model were changing during 1996 and were leading to a period of uncertainty:

> So that's good in terms of their own self-determination but we were worried. There's been no filtering of those funds. They've always come directly to us. Whereas if they go to all of the First Nations we're concerned that administratively we wouldn't get the same number of dollars here. So it's been very convenient for us. In fact, the simplicity of operating NORTEP in the past was really great from an administrative point of view. The money only came from the provincial government and INAC. That was it. Now, with the transition of funding to First Nations, we deal with all First Nations individually. So it's made it complex but it's fine. It works fine. (Eric: NORTEP administrator, interview transcript)

Academic Programs

The Universities of Regina and Saskatchewan evaluate and monitor the individual programs of NORTEP. The Saskatchewan Indian Federated College (SIFC) monitors Indian Studies and Cree language subjects and their development. No changes can occur without a process of consultation with these bodies. NORTEP has brought about many changes since its inception but they have all had to have approval. One of the areas has been over the qualities that are desirable in a member of the teaching staff:

> Years ago we had more fights than we do now with instructor qualifications. Universities were trying to insist that people had to have PhDs. Well there aren't that many PhDs – certainly amongst the people we used to want to hire there weren't. So we fought. We just fought. (Sandra: NORTEP administrator, interview transcript)

As with the AREP staff, NORTEP staff comes from a wide range of backgrounds in terms of age, gender, experience, current workplace and experience with Aboriginal students. But how were the staff recruited?

> ... they are not full time faculty at the universities; they just teach what they are qualified to teach. Some of them are retirees – whether they are from the university or the teaching profession – and have lots to add. And our students are... it's very much part of the whole cultural tradition, respect for elders. So our students have related well to these people. Like an old white guy might not have been up north before and the students get them and fill them in. There's mutual respect on both sides. (Sandra: NORTEP administrator, interview transcript)

The struggle is not purely academic of course, in the sense of 'standards'. At the macro level, the funding cuts to the universities down south have impacted on NORTEP, leading to more sessional staff and fewer permanent faculty. Again, this is something which has occurred repeatedly with AREP – in part because of a desire to increase the range of lecturers who are flexible and open to negotiating through cultural difference but also because of the increased workload of full time academics in Australian universities.

But having sessional staff is a contradictory process. The relationship with the centre is important in terms of maintaining knowledge of, and access to, the dominant curriculum:

> They are really good for us too. We could get professionally isolated here; having those people come in is really good. Having those new ideas... we often get people who wrote the provincial curriculum. We are at the cutting edge in many ways. Our students often get stuff before the teachers do 'cos they've got the curriculum writers teaching courses. (Sandra: NORTEP administrator, interview transcript)

One of the things that make NORTEP special is the way in which the model is field-based. They have completely turned the degree around into something that utilises knowledge in the field and integrates tertiary study with hands on training. As a consequence, NORTEP is able to employ a range of people for specialised courses. Since they run courses over a one-week block for these subjects, there is an opportunity to use the latest developments in curriculum practice. As many as 30-35 different specialists come and go each year. This model was produced in the 1970s as a response to perceived needs of students and to build on knowledge and skills. As a consequence, it is undergoing some revisiting as an appropriate model for current students. We can explore this through examining the field experience.

Field experience

> I mean really, we began this unique delivery model where you're in for two weeks, out for one week...that was really begun to accommodate in those early years... most of the people that were coming in were women teacher associates in schools for quite a few years. They were saying: "Well why can't I become a teacher? Here I am, a teacher associate. I like what I'm doing and I'm good at it. Besides that I can speak the language. Why can't I become a teacher?" So in order for that to happen, it was necessary that they were able to get them back to their homes and their families because these were all middle-aged women. (Eric: NORTEP administrator, interview transcript)

In her review of NORTEP, Carnegie found that without necessarily defining pedagogical principles as such, NORTEP had "incorporated, deliberately or intuitively, a number of androgogical principles" (1991:109-10). These include life-centred, task-centred, problem-centred orientation to learning as well as building on the readiness, aspirations and resources of individuals and groups (*ibid.*). To some extent these practices *grew out* of the programme based on the kind of student first attending NORTEP more than twenty years ago.

To achieve these principles, close cooperation between schools and school-related bodies was critical. Indeed, teachers working with NORTEP students are called 'co-ops', short for cooperating teachers, rather than supervising teachers. To prepare for this relationship the cooperating teacher is brought in for seminars prior to students commencing field placements. From the outset there is a framework developed for negotiation and a foundation established for a prolonged relationship over a year.

When I left NORTEP in 1996 they were still to determine the future of their field-based experiences because NORPAC, the other aspect of the college, was under pressure to respond to a need for engineers and computing graduates for northern development industries.

Governance

> It's [NORTEP] getting more and more [students] now because the schools are producing highschool grads. We didn't have any ten years ago in the north, now we're getting some. It's largely due to a lot of Band control. You see none of the Bands had highschools a few years ago. They all had to go down south and stay in residential facilities. It didn't produce highschool grads. (Sandra: NORTEP administrator, interview transcript)

The increase in student numbers directly from school and from a greater range of communities was a big change for both the council and the teaching staff. There are now more students from a diverse range of Indigenous groups – and some non-Indigenous – as well as a younger population of students. In Chapter 8 we will see what this has meant for teaching relationships at NORTEP. The changing demographics also require a changing council according to Carnegie's report (1991). Devolution means more self-government, something that NORTEP has always been part of and responsive to:

I mean NORTEP is an example of self-government in its structure, in its Board of Governors. It's specifically taught in native studies classes and I think there might be other... I mean the very fact that you are producing degree people with an education... and many of those have gone on to leadership positions. (Sandra: NORTEP administrator, interview transcript)

Members of the Board of Governors represent school boards, Indigenous groups and professional organisations. Representatives are elected for a period of two years and the council had expanded from nine people in 1976 to 15 in 1996 (Goulet, 1996:8). There is also a Review Committee that meets every Spring.

Conclusion

NORTEP's structure reveals an attempt to provide space for a range of voices on a representative basis. As such, it 'looks after' the overall concerns of the north. These include the turnover rate of teachers; educational opportunities for isolated communities; and maintenance and development of the 'culture of the north'. In a sense then, these broad goals are inclusive of all those who claim to be northerners (those that have lived there for more than 15 years as stipulated by NORTEP's policy). Given the multiple concerns of this teacher education program, and its distinct concern for cultural and linguistic maintenance and development, it becomes important to understand how these philosophies and principles are operationalised in the day-to-day world of practitioners.

AREP and NORTEP have been shown to be similar yet different in their goals. Both programs have concerns about increasing Indigenous access to tertiary education: NORTEP had the additional aim of cultural maintenance. Previous chapters have shown that this was in part a consequence of the way in which the programs were set up. AREP was set up to increase the number of Indigenous teachers nationally with special funds allocated for that purpose. Funding was tied to university funding and institutions had to contribute to the development of Indigenous programs. As an access program, initial concerns were about providing *equal* opportunity with the *same* curriculum and resourcing as for non-Indigenous students studying full time.

In contrast, NORTEP was an affirmative action program aimed at increasing the number of Indigenous teachers while maintaining culture. This difference underscores the differing levels of commitment to understanding and acknowledging cultural difference at the structural level. NORTEP acted on the perceived needs of students in designing their field-based curriculum. NORTEP now faces the challenge of revisiting that structure to see if it works for the current students and new funding arrangements.

One of the differences arising from historically constituted differences is that AREP has not had a guiding philosophy since the students' cultural differences were only a consideration at the individual level until recent years. As a consequence, a critical examination of the curriculum has only been partial and has been consistently couched in terms of 'mainstream' requirements.

Another difference is the physical location of both programs. NORTEP has been more responsive because it is situated in the region in which most students live. With AREP, because of an attempt to paper over differences – to protect students from the criticism that they were doing a 'different' and therefore 'less than' course – there has been a slower response to attending to difference. This is in part a consequence of AREP's physical location in a large metropolitan university, meaning that there is little attention given to the specific conditions in rural areas that students will have to deal with on practicum and eventually when teaching.

Other issues flow from this geographical dislocation. NORTEP has a structure of representation that assists in working through how to deal with these issues. That is, there are educational, Indigenous and non-Indigenous organisations represented on the Board of Governors. At the level of students, teachers from schools work with the academic staff to determine an appropriate experience in the field and back at the campus.

Another way in which the two programs differ is that one is field-based (NORTEP) and the other is campus-based. Again, this mode of study is tied to funding. The AREP support structures at UWSM could be seriously affected if the program was to become more field based. This has the affect of producing particular curriculum decisions and practices, as we will see in the next section. The NORTEP model gives intensive integrated study of particular parts of the curriculum, which are then 'tested' in the field and fed back into the curriculum. AREP on the other hand provides a fragmented curriculum, on-campus and often unrelated to the particular contexts that students are working in. How this is negotiated will be discussed in the following three chapters.

The first chapter in the next section will focus on the way in which administrators negotiate the changing field of Indigenous education in terms of funding, student demographics and increasing Indigenous autonomy. Balancing a universalistic approach to teacher education with the particular cultural issues of Indigenous teacher education reveals how the habitus of administrators shapes, and is shaped by, the field of Indigenous education around wider social movements and increasing cultural knowledge.

Chapter 7
Managing Diversity

Introduction

This chapter is the first of three using primary data based on interviews of administrators, teacher educators and students in AREP and NORTEP. The chapters are arranged according to the habitus of participants rather than conceptually, because it is important to examine the different types of contexts of agents in the two programs under study. In this way, it is possible to see how the tensions and contradictions of racialisation are produced and resolved through the interaction of individual habitus, the field of Indigenous education and the administrative habitus of participants in this study. The purpose is to reveal the specific locations of agents in the system of power hierarchies in NORTEP and AREP.

The system of power hierarchies can be examined by analysing the ways in which key administrative personnel have managed the political, cultural, economic, social and educational nature of the AREP and NORTEP programs. The previous section outlined the ways in which the AREP and NORTEP developed out of important government and community objectives concerning increased educational outcomes and cultural maintenance. It was shown that the character of the two programs was created in particular contexts. The purpose of this chapter is to explore the tensions and contradictions that arise within programs that have been produced out of racialised policies and practices.

I am using the idea of tension to refer to the strains and stresses experienced by program administrators as they attempt to resolve, or arbitrate the conflicting tendencies. As we shall see, negotiating these tensions is often accompanied by a sense of uneasiness, if not hostility. In real life, the tensions rarely present themselves as simple dichotomies. For the purposes of explication, however, it is useful to present them as opposing tendencies, although I should stress that my concern in this chapter is on the way in which the opposing claims are negotiated. There are three broad areas of tension. The first is the *cultural stereotypes versus cultural knowledge* tension leading to the *self-determination versus advocacy* tension. In addition, there were a range of issues leading to the questioning of an *integrated versus separate* program to the mainstream.

The six administrators interviewed for this study have in various ways raised these tensions. As an administrator and teacher in the AREP program I also was very aware of the issues reflected in the interviewees' narratives. The particular challenges for administrators in these programs is rarely understood nor analysed. This chapter presents one approach to understanding the challenges for all working in Indigenous education environments.

The administrators

The administrators who took part in this study were a diverse group of people with a range of experiences and knowledge. At times, I have also used the voices of other participants, particularly teachers, where it adds to the analysis. There were two administrators from NORTEP and four from AREP interviewed for this project. Eric and Greg were from NORTEP. Eric, who was acting in a senior position when I visited NORTEP, had been involved in education for many years and worked at a range of levels including that of teacher and principal, as well as with the Saskatchewan Teachers' Federation. Eric developed his cultural repertoire through a range of experiences overseas, including in India. He provides a useful overview of the history of NORTEP in terms of graduates, and the changing political and organisational structures of Indigenous organisations and how these impact on NORTEP. When describing his role, Eric made it quite clear that politics are a central part of his work and emphasised the need for people coming to the north to be prepared for cross-cultural negotiation.

Greg had only recently arrived at NORTEP but was previously a high school teacher for 20 years in the 'north' so he was not a newcomer to the area. Greg saw himself as a "naïve city boy with no preconceived stereotypes" and as having a personality that simply fitted in with the north. Greg painted a picture of a professional administrator and teacher who avoided the political problems in the community but who was a relaxed and comfortable person that talked and listened on the personal level. He described himself as a tolerant, accessible and supportive person. His main task at NORTEP was to set up the field placements and also do some teaching in the program. In addition, he put together an annual report and statistics for NORTEP.

The four AREP administrators were Francis, Marion, Tina and Malcolm. Francis, Marion and Malcolm were all academics who held various senior positions within the Faculty of Education at UWSM. Tina, on the other hand, had been working in clerical positions within the faculty for a number of years and at the time of this study was in a senior administrative position.

Francis had quite a long involvement in Aboriginal education as a linguist in addition to being a teacher. He was always committed to the AREP, and felt that while listening to students' needs, an eye must always be kept to the standards of the profession. This was important, he argued, because it would be detrimental to Aboriginal communities if students did not graduate with the same degree as non-Indigenous students. Francis was committed to social justice and philosophically worked within an access and equity framework.

Marion had worked at UWSM for a number of years in various capacities. She had held a number of positions including classroom primary school teacher, consultant, lecturer and coordinator in the AREP program, as well as holding executive positions within the faculty. Marion was committed to social justice and found no problem with the concept of different curricula although she struggled with the issue of equivalence. Marion problematised every day issues and enjoyed working through them in management terms.

Malcolm had also been a primary school teacher, a lecturer and coordinator of the AREP, and held a senior position within the faculty. Malcolm valued people being treated as individuals rather than focussing too much on culture. He was concerned about the negative consequences of categorisation and how they had already impacted on AREP students and, as a consequence, said he would rather work through the issues as individual cases. Malcolm also belonged to a professional 'gate-keeping' committee that oversaw teacher education course accreditation.

Finally, Tina was a mature woman who had worked for many years in the faculty. She was studying for her Arts degree and had been offered an opportunity to do Honours. Tina was greatly influenced by her studies and brought a particular perspective to her role as the major administrator and keeper of records for AREP in the faculty. Her particular understandings came from anthropological and sociological studies of cultural difference, although they fitted somewhat more easily in the former paradigm. This does not suggest that Tina romanticised the lives of the students, nor indeed does it suggest that they were homogenised. Tina clearly articulated the way in which she used this historical/anthropological knowledge to provide her with an explanation for the students' situations.

In attempting to explain and critique the program and its outcomes, each participant employed a range of ideological discourses related to their particular view of society and social transformation and their role within that process. For example, Francis and Eric shared a deep sense of commitment to social justice emanating from the range of culturally diverse environments that they had encountered. They also shared positions of authority within their profession and therefore were keen to maintain the integrity of AREP and NORTEP respectively. This meant keeping an eye on professional standards while providing space for dialogue.

Marion and Tina were perceptive administrators. The two women were united in the fact that they were unhappy with elements of AREP and shared a desire to change the way in which it was structured. They did not have the power or resources to do this, however, and were more or less left with having to 'make do'. Both gained knowledge through formal and informal processes regarding Indigenous inequality. Their gender may also have contributed to how they responded in terms of the concerns they highlight. That is, they saw and listened to the personal struggles of students and connected them to wider political processes. In addition, they were the two administrators in AREP most likely to entertain increased Indigenous control of the program.

Malcolm and Greg were interesting because they shared a struggle over the potentially damaging effects of patronisation. Both men held dearly to individual development and success. This meant that they had a particular problem about how individual development and success were related to the collective culture of AREP and NORTEP.

At the time of interviewing, all administrators involved in managing the two teacher education programs were non-Indigenous. This fact meant that they had a heightened awareness of themselves as people who were managing 'cross-cultural' relationships. It is possible to see from the thumbnail sketches of each administrator that individual habitus, in addition to their administrative habitus, shaped education at both AREP and NORTEP.

Cultural stereotypes versus cultural knowledge

Negotiating a path in Indigenous education, where cultural stereotypes have contributed to inequitable outcomes, requires a reassessment of dominant ways of thinking about cultural difference. As was discussed in Chapters 3 and 4, cultural stereotypes have been produced by research that focused on culture as static and readable, thus contributing to simplistic understandings of cultural difference. These 'readings' compete with a more contingent and complex understanding of cultural difference, produced at particular moments and situated in particular contexts. Unravelling these competing understandings of cultural difference was part of developing cultural knowledge.

Greg, a field placement officer, reflected on his attitude when he first came to NORTEP and in doing so showed how wider social categorisations of Indigenous students framed his way of seeing cultural difference:

> I think personally I came here thinking/seeing their faults and I, thinking I'd like to change them – I'd like to change them now – and that's bombed...'cos some of them weren't necessarily faults. I just hadn't grasped what was happening and why it was happening this way. Having known this then maybe I wouldn't look at it as fault. (Greg: interview transcript)

Greg is not the only administrator to raise conscious opposition to what Connell (1996) has called *categoricalism*, emanating from a history of negative processes of racialisation. But the problem is that once cultural difference is rejected in favour of a universal or context free response, one ends up denying difference and adopting an approach that sees culture-as-impediment. Yet there are real problems in finding a way through these dilemmas and the path is fraught with contradictions as Greg stated:

> I initially came here thinking that perhaps we patronise the students too much and that may well still be true in some ways. But not in as many ways as I originally thought. (Greg: interview transcript)

By showing a concern for cultural difference, Greg also warns us that if it goes too far and students are patronised, then colonialist attitudes continue with Indigenous students viewed as child-like and not capable, a legacy of racialised policies and practices. From this contradictory perspective, to be culturally sensitive can be seen to deprive someone of their autonomy/accountability. Cultural sensitivity could then be seen as a cop-out.

However, like Greg, the administrators in AREP and NORTEP quickly became aware that culture does matter. The legacies of racialisation are embodied in each student in terms of family and community relationships. The discourses in education, and particularly Indigenous education, contribute to this bind. That is, there is a lack of 'fit' between the hegemonic discourses of individualism, which hold dear Rousseau's notion of the 'freedom of the individual' with that of a more 'culturalist' discourse in the field of education as discussed in Chapter 4. The latter is heavily dependent upon static notions of culture and recipes for teaching and learning targeting specific groups. Some of the administrators, like Greg and Malcolm, are sceptical of the homogenising tendencies of the latter discourses. Yet, stripped of an easy dependence on individualism while unhappy with culturalist explanations, the administrators struggle to make sense of how to account for culture.

A number of important questions emerge from this tension. For instance, what do our administrators think cultural knowledge is and how did they describe its acquisition? Malcolm argued that you need to be sensitive to people rather than have *textbook* [my emphasis] cultural knowledge.

> I wouldn't want to argue that having an understanding of a background and knowing where people are coming from and so on isn't important. I think it is important, and I think you as a teacher need to get that regardless of what group of students you happen to be doing. But sure it would be a lot easier if there were opportunities for people to gain some of that knowledge. Now I think I've had a number of those opportunities. Most of them have come just by simply sitting around talking to the AREP students. You know that's been tremendously enlightening and tremendously useful for me. I must say not so much in terms of teaching the AREP students, but just in terms of understanding another group of people who have perspectives that are different from and who, in many ways have beliefs that are different from

mine... and from each one you can gain lots of interesting perspectives, not only on them but on yourself as well. (Malcolm: interview transcript)

Clearly Malcolm sees cultural knowledge as important yet he believed that sensitivity could provide a similar 'outcome'. Sensitivity is a kind of openness to a different perspective or a stance leading to relationships that are more productive. This is typical of progressivism, valuing difference through dialogue and having a pluralist vision of society. For Malcolm, cultural sensitivity is the prerequisite for building up a *cultural repertoire* (Cope and Kalantzis, 1997:273).

Yet, something else was happening here. Malcolm shifted from a racialised discourse – you need to get cultural knowledge from *"what [ever] group you happen to be doing"* – to a deracialised discourse as he moved from a *universalistic* account to a *particularist* account of understanding cultural difference. In practice then, the *particular* provided insights but also created a series of tensions that were critical to expanding his cultural repertoire.

This is an approach to cultural diversity that bears the hallmarks of liberalism because it sees difference, as Morwenna Griffiths (1993) suggests, as something to be harnessed in a kind of functionalist approach to cultural difference – a selective, non-threatening and non-transformative approach to cultural difference. If it helps to do the job better, it is *useful* knowledge.

Another way in which administrators described the processes of acquisition of cultural knowledge was through empathy. Marion provided an example of the development of cultural knowledge, which involved recognition of unequal power relations based on social and political marginalisation, in this anecdote about one of the AREP students:

She was an AREP student. I supervised her in two different environments up in Tamworth... in a country school and then in a town school. I spent time at her home. I watched her give a seminar one day – after she had to do something with a kid at school who was in fact a recent arrival from Vietnam and had been on a boat. She couldn't handle it. She was just distraught when she heard the story this boy had been through... and we talked forever about the things her kids had been through and her grand kids... but from her, I developed this notion that **had I** been inside an

Aboriginal body, looking at the world, everybody would have treated me differently than had I been inside my own body looking at the world. (Marion: interview transcript)

The process of 'stepping into the shoes' of someone else was achieved in this instance through personal narrative. Although it is not possible to really know the size of the shoes of someone else, personal narratives provide an understanding of the different ways in which people are culturally constituted – as long as they are willing to listen. What makes this account different from Malcolm's account of personal interaction is that Marion had noticed the connections the Aboriginal student was making to particular forms of social exclusion. There was the beginning here of an understanding of cultural difference connected to the social production of differences through racialisation.

Again, personal narrative can be a powerful source of knowledge as Tina also explained. However, wider narratives about, and personal narratives from the students, provided her with contradictory understandings of Aboriginal identity:

I first came across the AREP students in the library and we were given a lot of, oh sort of forewarning that the AREP students were in, and we were told how we had to treat them – which was different to the way we were expected to treat white students. I found that really daunting because I had never really met an Aboriginal person. When they came in they didn't even look Aboriginal. So I was really, quite unexpected for... especially when they had red hair and blue eyes. I think the initial contact... I was really hesitant, didn't really know what I was doing, I didn't know how to handle it. Once I got to know them as people, then that was different. Once I got to understand what was behind them, what they'd been through. (Tina: interview transcript)

Marion and Tina's cultural knowledge involved a blending of personal narrative with a broader historical narrative. Acknowledging loss of power because of the constraints of racialisation led them to an understanding of cultural difference not based on the 'anthropological gaze' (Nakata, 1997:426) – which has a focus on studying cultural practices – but on understanding the legacies of history.

It is possible to understand how these racialised identities constrain relationships and therefore produce understandings outside of direct experience. As Tina said: *"When they came in they didn't even look Aboriginal"*, even though she *"had never really met an Aboriginal person"*. The legacy of processes of racialisation is that there can be no Aboriginal or Indian without non-Aboriginals and non-Indians. Put another way, the labels 'Aboriginal' and 'Indian' have their origins in histories of State control. Therefore, "Aboriginality is a social *thing* [which]... arises from the subjective experience of both Aboriginal people and non-Aboriginal people" (Langton, 1993:31).

There is the potential then, from stories of oppression – when they occur at a personal level – for shifting presuppositions about Indigenous identity. Through combining the broader narrative which is now a public narrative about Indigenous peoples globally, with a kind of particularism, space is created for mutually transformative relations to occur (Stasiulus, 1990). So, even though the State has created objects of Indigenous people in terms of racialised policies and practices, intersubjectivity (of the kind outlined by Greg, Malcolm, Marion and Tina) created space for negotiating difference which "lies somewhere between the individual and the State" (*ibid.*).

Eric, at NORTEP, spoke about the need to be cross-cultural and felt, as a white administrator, it was an enriching process, rather than one of loss. He explored this process while reflecting on the 'culture of the north' in Saskatchewan:

> I mean, I think that it *[the 'North']* reflects that there are the Métis, the non-native, there are the Cree, the Dene... but they do share this land and so there is a cross-cultural aspect of living. I think that culture of the north is what strikes me as a visitor, you either identify and respect that culture or you reject it. (Eric: interview transcript)

Eric's commitment to social transformation leading to social justice is distinguishable from other administrators during our interview by his language of "critique, challenging and changing the status quo" (Grundy and Hatton, 1995:12). Cultural knowledge in this instance comes from intersubjectivity rooted in particular forms of political activity during the growth of Indigenous and immigrant education in the 1970s-1990s.

However, the oppositional choices that Eric refers to were mooted in the introduction to this study. I argued that in a highly racialised context non-Indigenous people had to make a choice as to whether they were going to be 'fellow-travellers' or reject oppositional politics. One of the problems was that these oppositional discursive practices – centres/margins, inside/outside – give considerable power to 'white agency' (McConaghy, 1997a) through a view of social life as a pattern of dichotomous choices. If this is the only way to explain practice in these two programs – as a simple choice between two competing directions – then we fail to explore the substance of the tensions produced in these contexts and how they are negotiated.

To summarise to this point, our administrators describe building up cultural knowledge through processes such as empathy, the ability and desire to 'cross-over', and the need to understand broader historical contexts. How then, is cultural knowledge used, or a cultural repertoire invoked?

Invoking cultural knowledge

If cultural knowledge is something that can be 'learned' and put in one's 'kit bag', we need to know what cultural knowledge is selected as useful, and how it is implemented in practice. Francis has a particular example that demonstrates how powerful 'invoking a cultural repertoire' can be and the kind of contexts in which it is acquired:

> If you can invoke the repertoire… I remember… [someone said] 'look here, I see you spearing fish and what not, then I see you in a suit in a meeting, doesn't that give you deep inner conflict?' 'No' he said, 'it's simple'… because he was so versatile at invoking the repertoires, and he's learnt them well… and I think that that's part of the secret and if society respects that capacity that's the key thing. (Francis: interview transcript)

In practice, "invoking the repertoire" means something quite rational in response to cross-cultural tensions. It suggests openness and some degree of equality in terms of power relationships. Francis acknowledged these power relations when he suggested that power differences can be assuaged through acknowledgement – "*if society respects that capacity*". The politics of identity in contemporary Canadian and Australian societies reveals that this is not always the case because identity is "partly shaped by recognition or its absence, often by the *mis*recognition of others" (Taylor, 1994:25), which is often the source of conflict:

> You don't have the conflict if the worlds are isolated. For instance you shouldn't say your sister's name, personal name. You don't do that. But in the school, the general belief is that when you are among these crazy Europeans who don't know anything about that, you adapt and you might have to do it and that's understandable... that if you can avoid the situations, pull the worlds apart, you can invoke the repertoire that's appropriate. (Francis: interview transcript)

Firstly, we have a view that conflict is resolved through keeping the worlds distinct. The attractiveness of this is that it allows the isolation of elements that are potentially counter-productive. Another attractive aspect of this view is that the 'Other' is accorded agency. Rather than a discourse of oppression and cultural loss, we have a discourse of adaptability and strategic biculturalism. This is of course a tremendous distinction from a victim discourse yet there is a sense of power still lurking unresolved in this situation because we can't always keep the worlds apart.

All of the administrators talked about the rewards associated with cross-cultural relationships but that these 'rewards' often resulted from experiencing tension. Marion recalled an earlier experience (thus demonstrating her cultural repertoire) that provided her with knowledge of racialisation by exploring the unsettling tensions that arise when you are called upon to play a 'buffer' role:

> In Toronto...I coached the Ontario Under 21 netball team, which was nine members West Indian, one member Anglo... and all the girls in that team were literally um... from the wrong side of the track in Toronto. I ended up playing a huge PR buffer role between those girls and the managers of the team that flew out to Calgary. Well these young women didn't follow a traditional well-behaved, quiet approach to representing Ontario. [I said to the leaders] They are highly spirited. They are having a great time. Some of them have never been on a plane before. The other thing I remembered very strongly there. One of the girls made it into the National team, and the world championships were in the West Indies and they were on the island from which she came and she was literally physically harassed and abused by locals who thought she had no right to be playing for Canada. As a young 19-year-old

she found all of that **really** hard to handle and she used me to kind of dump on when she came back about all of the kinds of problems associated with that. (Marion: interview transcript)

In this context Marion is being asked to soak up anger and resentment like a sponge. The kinds of social learning and the forms of cultural knowledge acquired in these diverse ways were clearly at odds with institutionalised deracialised discourses. A deracialised discourse, like the liberal progressivist ideology, commatises important social relations rendering them invisible (Troyna, 1994). Cultural difference approached in this way only posits "race and culture as relevant to the curriculum... in areas of interpersonal relations that help students understand each other better" (Sleeter, 1992:16). Cultural knowledge in this sense downplays the essential role of inequality in society in shaping cultural difference.

This leads to the next tension for administrators – emanating from the acquisition of cultural knowledge. Once we have cultural knowledge, regardless of how it is defined by administrators, there are times that it is used to advocate for change. However, since we can't really know the size of the shoes we are stepping into there is a risk associated with advocacy.

The advocacy/self-determination paradox

In this study, administrators revealed that once they had acknowledged the cultural reality of students they were not altogether sure how they should respond. Indeed, some asked whether they should respond at all. There has been a long history of the colonial mentality in Indigenous education as discussed in Chapters 3 and 4 and it has been mostly revealed in 'victim' discourses where Indigenous peoples have been variously treated as if child-like. In such cases advocacy has been paternalistic and has robbed individuals or communities of the freedom to determine their lives. Given the structural location of administrators at NORTEP and AREP, they must take on an advocacy role at the same time that they try to distance themselves from paternalistic practices. The paradox for administrators was how to recognise the necessary advocacy role, while at the same time distancing them from the paternalism of the past and working towards student autonomy and self-determination. I will look at this tension in two ways – the personal, interactive level; and the broader policy and community level.

Personal advocacy

> I call these adults kids... it's just my nature unfortunately and I
> keep getting chastised for it. 'We're adults Greg, we're adults
> okay?' (Greg: interview transcript)

The tendency in teacher education to call adult students 'kids' is in
part because many teacher education academics were once teachers of
children. It is also true that because they are dealing with pedagogical
principles applied to children they are apt to 'forget' or treat their
adult students as if they were children. It is a somewhat annoying
tendency and one that creates particular problems in the field of
Indigenous education as Greg has alluded to in the above comments.
But Greg's role at NORTEP requires him to arrange field placements
and this is a role that requires some advocacy. In addition, his teaching
philosophy reveals advocacy elements in terms of community
involvement beyond the normal work routine such as organising
sporting trips so that students get a chance to "taste success and know
they are just as good as other students". This is not uncommon for
teachers in Indigenous communities in the north of Saskatchewan. But
what exactly is advocacy?

Earlier I looked at the way in which advocacy – in terms of
Indigenous and non-Indigenous alliances – was essential to the
development of the AREP and NORTEP. We saw that advocacy
through the struggles of the 1960s and '70s had an impact on policy
frameworks and therefore shaped the context for the development of
the two programs. For example, in Canada, various non-Native
societies argued for the furtherance of Indigenous educational and
artistic rights (Haig-Brown, 1995:69). In Australia, the Foundation for
Aboriginal Affairs (a church run organisation) as well as the
Aboriginal Advancement League carried out similar civil rights' work
and they had Indigenous and non-Indigenous members. Indeed a few
of the participants in this study were part of these types of social
movements. There has always been a relationship between advocacy
and self-determination.

However, advocacy can also take the form of speaking for those
who are disempowered. In addition, advocacy is often associated with
speaking for people who can't speak for themselves, such as people
with disabilities; those regarded as too young and those who are
unable to understand the complexities of the law, for example. In

Australia and Canada, there has been a long colonial history where Indigenous peoples, for various reasons, have been positioned as unable to speak or act on their own behalf.

Cathryn McConaghy in the introduction to her thesis *Rethinking Indigenous Adult Education* (1997a) discussed the mistakes that fellow travellers/'whitefellas' can make when working alongside Indigenous people to bring about more equitable educational practices and institutional arrangements. Importantly, she questioned the overwhelming reliance on Aboriginalist educational discourses that have focussed on particular readings of Indigenous cultures in Australia. McConaghy has argued that not only do these 'readings' create objects of Indigenous peoples, they also make invisible Indigenous agency by privileging 'white agency'.

Rick Hesch in his Canadian study of SUNTEP (1993) also pointed to the difficulties he faced when he tried to create a curriculum based on critical pedagogy paradigms[1] that he thought would provide liberatory outcomes. Underlying his approach was the assumption that students needed to know the cause of their oppression so that they could become advocates themselves.

Advocacy is therefore a difficult strategy and can be in a difficult relationship to the moral lexicon of *paternalism*. This paternalism is often found in benevolent acts of kindness that can be well intended but not wanted. Tina provides a snapshot of this potential difficulty of advocacy when she was administrative assistant for AREP:

> ... you were dealing with a different group of students, because they weren't here all the time. So the limited amount of time they were here, I tried to make sure that their journey was a bit easier. I listened to them more than a lot of mainstream students. I don't know why. There was just something there... that I felt I could make life a little bit easier for them... You had to then be careful that you weren't over-servicing them, in that it might not have been what they wanted. You didn't quite always know... They might not have wanted that. Some would expect it and some didn't want it. It was hard to find that line. That seemed to be very much an individual thing. (Tina: interview transcript)

---

[1] Critical pedagogy is a field characterised as a 'radical' approach to pedagogy. Some of the elements of critical pedagogy include the technology of 'voice' and making explicit the relationship between pedagogy and political goals. The work of Giroux (1988) and McLaren and Lankshear (1994) are exemplars of this approach to pedagogy.

We can see the fine line that Tina talks about and the dangers of acting for people based on cultural knowledge that you alone have selected. This discomfort has led Tina to another solution for resolving the difficulties of advocacy: support for Aboriginal centres in universities.

> I just think the Aboriginal Centres here are the ones that should be taking on a greater role, as far as their enrolments and graduation. I don't think Aboriginal people should come to me, as a white administrator, with excuses. I didn't think I ever had that right to ask or judge, because I've never had that understanding. (Tina: interview transcript)

There is a kind of misguided belief at work here: that if cultural difference is considered the problem in the first instance, then cultural knowledge will solve it. The problem for Tina is that she does not have enough of, nor the right kind of, cultural knowledge. We see this view of cultural knowledge repeatedly in this study. However, Indigenous control will not automatically resolve this tension.

Greg has found this tension in his work at NORTEP, which has had considerably more Indigenous input into how funds are controlled, and into the sorts of practices that are considered appropriate. As Greg struggles with the cultural knowledge/cultural stereotypes tension he worries about paternalism and the impact that has on self-determination:

> NORTEP has evolved in its own history of patronisation. At one time everything was provided for the students. We cleaned up their apartments on Fridays when they went back to the home communities. We provided toilet paper because we got all the funding for them. We gave them an allowance... I found that extremely patronising. Some of those practices have stopped over the years. I have personal beefs I guess sometimes that we are very lenient and I think this is the way that's just the north. But NORTEP is based for northern students who haven't had a lot of success therefore we are very tolerant of things. We're quick to give them leaves and extend the leaves and give another leave and... I guess I handle a lot of complaints with that. (Greg: interview transcript)

As AREP coordinator at the time I empathised with his dilemma. From my own administrative habitus where I had to make similar decisions I asked him whether there were patterns to this leave. He responded that there were personal, academic and family reasons. Students miss relatives, have unsupportive partners (some students discuss this in Chapter 9) and often don't need to explain why they need leave:

> I find them... I guess I question some of the reasons. Is it really required or are we letting this person cop out? I still believe – although some of the students have special needs – I still believe we have to have the right expectations for them. Still believe they can grow; that we will have some difficult and some hard times. It would be too easy for us to say 'okay take leave and sort it out next year'. (Greg: interview transcript)

So here we have the crux of the problem for the administrator (and the teacher): how to recognise differences, and acknowledge special needs, while at the same time avoiding the 'cop-out' situation. Both Tina and Greg have pointed to advocacy that falls across the line into paternalism and patronising behaviour.

At this point, it might be useful to move to the second level of analysis, one that looks at the programs in terms of the community. It is this wider context that also helps shape administrative responses within the two programs and it is also where we can see significant differences between the Canadian and Australian contexts.

The concept of community and advocacy

The relationship of the two programs to self-determination – or rather what the programs might mean to self-determination – elicited some interesting responses. I asked Greg how he thought NORTEP was contributing to native sovereignty:

> I think it's contributing to native awareness certainly, native independence in the sense that we're producing educated aboriginal people going back to the communities who are then capable, I believe, of running things in their own communities. A lot of people in the north historically have been run by non-aboriginals. People from the south have been the managers. Now I think that has changed quite a bit. It's still happening but it's changed quite a bit because of NORTEP. The universities are

producing people who are going back to their communities, who are intelligent educated people who are demanding these jobs... and rightly so. So in that sense it's helping the process towards aboriginal independence at the Band levels and at the community levels. (Greg: interview transcript)

Greg therefore sees connections between education at NORTEP and the skills required for self-determination. Interestingly, he sees the skills provided by the institutions of the State as the way to achieve these outcomes. Perhaps in the case of NORTEP this is in a culturally responsive way given the focus on the north and the influence of people from the north in the programs it offers. But it addresses self-determination from the perspective of 'white advocacy' meaning that Indigenous experts are being produced in their 'own image'. This is an example of how the act of mimicry can reproduce colonial relations of power (McConaghy, 1997a).

There are some interesting contrasts here between NORTEP and AREP in this regard. AREP is a program that has been controlled by a faculty with Indigenous support. In Canada, NORTEP has had greater Indigenous input as well as Indigenous directors. There has been a longer history of Indigenous control in education in Canada and we can see that with a policy of devolution some of the structures that NORTEP has dealt with are changing. Self-determination in this context means that administrators are faced with changes that are increasingly related to the politics of difference. Self-determination actually means greater complexity, which Eric acknowledges, rather than less. He explains how this has worked in the north. We can see that fiscal constraints and increasing Indigenous control begin to define Eric's advocacy role because community based advocacy is becoming stronger:

The P.A. Grand Council is kind of like the parent body of probably, like La Ronge Band, Peter Ballantyne Band, The Athabasque and Dene Band, and James Smith Band. And so, they're kind of an administrative parent group. But, once again that is all changing. The P.A. Grand Council used to be the spokesgroup or spokesperson for all of these Bands, now they're saying 'no no, you're not a spokesperson for us. We'll tell you what to say but in the meantime we'll speak for ourselves'. (Eric: interview transcript)

153

But it is not a simple inversion of control that gives one the power to self-determine. Indeed, the degree to which communities are self-determining is also constrained. Murray, who is one of the Indigenous instructors at NORTEP, explains why this is the case:

> I like the idea of self-government a little bit better, I think. You know First Nations like the idea of self-government? You can never be completely sovereign, based on treaties... the funding... this still has to come from the government. (Murray: interview transcript)

So Murray sees that power is relational. He acknowledges that identity is inextricably tied up with the State and that there are limitations to self-determination. For Murray negotiation, or to be able to negotiate, is a critical part of self-government:

> However when you deal with the government you know it seems like they still want to delegate a bit of their authority on you know... Métis' issues or First Nations' affairs. So we're not clearly and entirely free. (Murray: interview transcript)

From Eric's, Greg's and Murray's accounts it seems that advocacy at the individual level in NORTEP is not appropriate in the context of increasing aboriginal representation on government-funded boards and committees in addition to increased individual Band control over funding. To be able to come to the table and negotiate for oneself or one's community is clearly preferable.

There is an important difference between Canada and Australia, where the lexicon through which the politics of community are negotiated is called self-determination. At NORTEP, Indigenous control has meant being able to negotiate from positions of authority. We can examine the difference this makes when we look at Indigenous communities' relationships to AREP.

Malcolm, in his position in the faculty often had to speak at gatherings of school principals and Aboriginal community groups. On a couple of occasions, he had to answer community concerns about the fact that the program was not meeting their needs:

> I mean for example, I remember at one stage going to a Northwest town and it was about at the time that another university was trying to establish a program, and they were doing things

differently. They were sending lecturers up there and so on, and the community basically thought that was meeting their needs better than the AREP program. I suspect they were probably right... but you know... [it was] just a different program. I mean I didn't make any bones about that. I said that there are some people that will come and do the AREP program. There are some people that will do the other one. It's probably better to have two and it's probably even better to have three. (Malcolm: interview transcript)

The difference for Aboriginal communities in Australia as opposed to those in Canada is the involvement of community in determining educational needs. Community in NSW is represented by the AECG and the Aboriginal Higher Education Network who have locally elected representatives, but representatives of local areas do not have direct input into AREP. This is in part because AREP is not focussed on rural interests and was just concerned with delivering the 'mainstream' program. Therefore, while communities have 'voice' they do not have control.

We can see the limitations to self-determination for the Aboriginal community mentioned. Despite the community's organised response, changes were not made to the AREP program. Now we could say that the market would solve it – as Malcolm has suggested – but is there really the diversity available or are we just talking about the *potential* for diversity (Marginson, 1997b:181)? Marginson calls the above a *weak* choice: "A weak choice is choice between pre-given options, the choice of the market consumer" (Marginson, *ibid.*). However, the processes help to make it appear as a *strong* choice. This participatory model "involves the chooser in the process of formulating options... what matters is that the chooser feels (and is) free to open up the whole question of the choices available and that he or she has the power to change them" (*ibid.*). The idea that AREP is filling a particular market niche substantially prevented the course from adapting to the demands of the community or students.

When the concerns of the community are examined, it is clear that individual self-determination was also at stake. Malcolm acknowledged that many of the concerns were over student welfare, such as being away from families, student disagreements between those wanting to study and those wanting to party:

... and there have been a few issues in the accommodation, in classes that have had to be dealt with... sort of relationship issues

155

are boiling over into classrooms and those sorts of things. (Malcolm: interview transcript)

When this is contrasted with NORTEP it is possible to see how paternalistic practices continue in concrete ways such as in the type of accommodation provided for students. Firstly, NORTEP students are housed in residential town houses in small 'family style' units. They are responsible for their meals and have fully equipped kitchens. AREP students, on the other hand, are placed together in motel style rooms with attendant privacy and study issues. In addition, there are no facilities for cooking in their rooms leaving them dependent on having to pay for expensive meals in the motel or having to go out to a restaurant. Not only do these sorts of arrangements reduce self-determination but they also articulate with the lack of community determination to shape the program.

For administrators in the program this created a climate of reaction and put workers in the program into a situation where they had to attend to difficulties students faced in an *ad hoc* and often individual paternalistic manner. Some of these tensions are discussed in Chapter 8. But Malcolm thought some of this could be overcome through providing technological links and more paper-based packages thus enabling students to be more home-based. This advocacy on his part was met with a collective community response:

> The immediate reaction was that if we did that people wouldn't have to come down here in the AREP mode and so on and anyway they don't all have power points. I suspect that most of the students that come down here do have power points. I guess what was disappointing, what I thought was offering an opportunity for people to grab and say we can run with this, and what came back was a feeling that they were under siege. Now this particularly came from the students and from MALU. (Malcolm: interview transcript)

What do we make of this business about electricity power points? In Chapter 5 the struggle that Malcolm is referring to was outlined quite comprehensively. From the point of view of the students, the proposed changes had happened without consultation with the legitimate body – the AECG and themselves. In addition, the response by MALU about power points was one way in which they could protect the jobs of Indigenous workers within the university. This is because the funding structure for staffing Aboriginal support units was

156

based on students attending residential on campus. Other universities had distance education courses but not UWSM. This is a stark portrayal of the use of essentialist politics and their basis. Advocacy on Malcolm's part was removing the rights of MALU to determine the future of the program and their own futures. This produced what could only be considered a somewhat cheeky form of identity politics fuelled by the structural relations that Aboriginal education has within the institution and wider society in general.

How then do we understand this tension around advocacy and self-determination? In the AREP, white administrators with Aboriginal 'support' structures ran the program, while in NORTEP boards comprised of a majority of Indigenous people and representatives of other interested parties had significant control over the program. As a consequence there was more of a tendency in AREP for what Bartra (1977:430) called a "complex system of favours and obligations" to develop. This was a critical difference to NORTEP. Advocacy can then be seen to be removing self-determination since it conceals and builds on a relationship of dependency. For the white administrators, framed by institutional arrangements that position them as advocates through a dependence on their individual goodwill, there is frustration. At NORTEP there is less dependence on the good will of individuals – although that is clearly necessary – because of the structural arrangements. Some of the problems at AREP seemed so protracted that it created a tension about whether or not the program should be separate or integrated. However, this was also an issue for NORTEP but for different reasons. In the next section, this tension is explored through an examination of how administrators understand and deal with the advantages and disadvantages of separate programs.

Separate/integrated tension

> I would like to do something that equipped them to be less hurt when they first arrive in a typical school as a teacher. And I don't know how to do that because I actually quite like a non-integrated program. (Marion: interview transcript)

Marion's anecdote provides us with some insights into the separate/integrated tension. In her comments, we can see the competing discourses of advantage/disadvantage arising from the contradictory logics of racialisation. On the one hand, there is covert acknowledgment that non-integrated programs seem to offer a different experience. We shall come to see the dynamics of this different experience in these final chapters. Yet, Marion is concerned that by removing conflict arising from integrated classrooms, Indigenous teacher education students may not be prepared for such conflict when they eventually begin to teach.

To examine this tension more deeply, it is important to know how the administrators understand and explain the need for, and nature of, the separate Indigenous teacher education programs in this study. In this section of the chapter, we try to come to understand this tension about whether or not programs such as NORTEP and AREP ought to be separate based on the 'ethnicity' of students. While there was general acceptance in Australia for separate Catholic, Protestant, Islamic and other schools, separate programs in tertiary institutions are rare except in remote regions. In Canada, separate schools are rare but a diverse tertiary sector includes community colleges and a range of Indigenous tertiary institutions. These are interesting differences and help shape the nature of the responses that NORTEP and AREP make to community demands.

The tension is essentially over universal (or equal) versus special provision. The dilemma around special versus equal treatment can be appreciated if we briefly turn to a related policy area. Using a feminist analysis of the same phenomena, Bacchi (1990) examined the debate in terms of the response to pregnancy in workplaces. She found that "equal treatment advocates fear that, if employers have to make provision for maternity, they might decide not to employ women. Special treatment supporters insist that employers acknowledge women's 'difference'" (Bacchi, 1990:111). Bacchi found that in general, not acknowledging difference led to an inability to respond to the reality of women's lives – demands of family and personal life – while acknowledging difference "implied that these duties were women's" (*ibid.*). What this dilemma means in regard to Indigenous education is that programs like AREP and NORTEP have the potential to acknowledge the historical realities of racialisation and how that may or may not impact on the intellectual, social, cultural and emotional needs of students. At the same time, there is a range of risks associated with valorising racialised constructions of identity, which then situate solutions in Indigenous cultural difference.

Among our administrators there are those that worry about the separate nature of these programs and base their arguments upon the notion of *social fulfilment*. The discourse of *social fulfilment*, according to Grundy and Hatton (1995:22), suggests an openness to questioning the status quo. Social fulfilment is the idea that individuals have the right to develop all their capacities in the way they see fit. In these programs, administrators use this discourse to argue for an integrated program because they are concerned that Indigenous students and non-Indigenous students need access to each other's perspectives. The ideological discourse of social fulfilment and the competing logics of the debate about special versus equal treatment underpin the perspectives of administrators in this study.

In the first instance then, there is an examination of the selection of students and the advantages/disadvantages of separate programs in terms of students' perceived needs. Secondly, there is an examination of the issue of equivalence as it pertains to the resourcing of the two programs. Once again, the separate/integrated tension arises from the context in which the programs are situated.

Producing the 'Indigenous' student

In Canada, the notion of a separate program is not an issue in the same way as in Australia. Due to a history of separate rights as 'citizens plus', Canadian Indigenous groups have to varying degrees been implementing community-based programs for more than two decades. In addition to Indigenous teacher education programs in Saskatchewan, there is the Joe Duquette High School in downtown Saskatoon, alternatively called the Native Survival School (Regnier et al., 1988). With a recorded urban, native student dropout rate of 93% across Saskatchewan (*ibid.*), separate educational institutions were seen as the only way to arrest inequitable educational outcomes. Indeed, this high school appears to have had some success in terms of retention and educational achievement among Indian and Métis students (Schissel and Wotherspoon, 1998:10).

It is therefore important to remember that NORTEP was established for these very reasons: a shortage of suitably qualified teachers who would assist in maintaining students' Indigenous cultures and to turn around retention rates and the high turnover of teachers in the 'north'. As mentioned in Chapter 6, NORTEP was set up under particular conditions. Indigenous and non-Indigenous activists were able to argue for the creation of NORTEP utilising the provincial concern for providing educational opportunities for disadvantaged students. Student selection at NORTEP therefore reflects this earlier aim.

> When it comes to a decision about who will attend, be it a native or non-native person, our affirmative action policy does give us latitude to, in a sense, discriminate in favour of the aboriginal person. So over time, well over 90% of our student population is always First Nations. (Eric: interview transcript)

While I have argued that NORTEP is largely Indigenous controlled, this is partly a reflection of the physical location of the program where the population is largely Indigenous. We can see that the complexities of the north in terms of a range of Indigenous groups, is increased when the category of 'northerner' is considered. Since NORTEP in policy is not defined as Indigenous only, there has always been a tension about separate versus integrated based on the recognition of general disadvantage in the 'north'. Eric supports affirmative action programs like NORTEP, but talks about the benefits for non-Indigenous students and would not like to see them disappear from the program altogether.

> What I have observed also, the non-native students, in terms of their development... When they leave here after four years, they are so strong in understanding and appreciation of the needs of First Nations people, that when they go back to their communities they're very strong in terms of the leadership they can bring to school staff. Dealing with cultural and native awareness, so I think in many respects it's really healthy to have some of the non-native students here. The community needs it. Any of the communities do need some non-native people who will speak up and be advocates for the aboriginal community. (Eric: interview transcript)

In the chapter on 'Un/Becoming an Aboriginal Teacher', I interview a non-Indigenous student attending NORTEP. The student has a complex relationship to the program but certainly demonstrates the potential for advocacy that Eric has flagged. However, when reflecting on the problems of advocacy in the previous section there appears to be some danger in expecting this to be done by non-Indigenous students without them understanding the limitations to their role. The only difference is that the non-Indigenous students in the 'north' tend to come from predominately non-Indigenous communities, so they may be useful advocates within these contexts.

In Australia however, particularly in NSW where Indigenous peoples are less tied to 'traditional' lands and activities, separate educational facilities at the tertiary level were uncommon until the period of time in which AREP commenced. In Chapter 5 we saw that policies aimed at increasing the number of Indigenous teachers produced programs like AREP, so that now in NSW there are a number of programs operating from nearly every university. There was never any suggestion, in the case of AREP, that a separate program was a long-term strategy. A context such as this – which essentially could have led to a target and then closure – produces particular responses. Since the target was specifically for 1000 Aboriginal teachers, all students attending are Aboriginal (and have to prove it) with a few Torres Strait Islanders having attended during the program's inception.

Malcolm, who was involved with the program from its early days, reflects a particular view of the separateness of AREP based on these earlier assumptions. When asked about the separate nature of AREP, Malcolm points to a degree of concern:

> I have mixed feelings about that [a separate program]. I can see real arguments why you might want to keep the cultural studies subjects separate. Many of those subjects require them to bare their soul or their history and so on and I can see some argument for why they might not want to do that, with non-Aboriginal people. Perhaps we should have, wherever possible, Aboriginal people teaching those subjects. However, I think one of the things that has happened to the AREP program – and it has the potential to happen with Aboriginal education *per se* – is that if it becomes too restrictive, and if it becomes restricted to Aboriginal people, then there are many useful perspectives which are denied the students. (Malcolm: interview transcript)

Malcolm's response reveals the equal/special tension that Bacchi (1990) raised in the sense that he sees Indigenous issues as belonging to Indigenous people and all other aspects of the pedagogical experience are left intact. However, Malcolm is also concerned with social fulfilment, that is, a desire for students to have access to the broader range of human experiences. This means that Malcolm is concerned about the AREP students 'missing out' on something in addition to seeing the transformative possibilities available through maintaining a space for dialogue.

Indeed Malcolm's, and also Marion's concern for students sharing each other's different perspectives is reiterated a number of times in his narrative. However, we need to ask if this is an idealistic representation of classroom dynamics. Alison Jones (1998), a New Zealand feminist academic, presented an interesting conference paper on this issue. During one of her courses on gender issues, she and a colleague decided to split up the students on the basis of ethnicity – Pakehas (non-Indigenous) and Maori and Polynesian (Indigenous) students. The response from both students was quite significant. The Pakehas felt a great deal of resentment emanating from a sense of loss and grief (Jones, 1998:3) at not having the opportunity to learn from (about) the Indigenous students. On the other hand, the Maori and Polynesian students felt able to get on with their learning in an environment where they didn't have to continually justify their perspective or communicate their experiences of exclusion (*ibid.*:13). Jones argued that colonising processes occur in contexts where the oppressed are exploited by a demand for narrative (1998:15). The pedagogy of 'voice' often means Indigenous students sharing their stories of oppression when there may not have been any. It also limits their agency to one of assisting the non-Indigenous to come to terms with 'white' guilt. In addition, "the coloniser's infatuation with access to/unity with the other" (*ibid.*:17) is a romance that is not necessarily shared by Indigenous people. Greg's reflections on the historically constituted inequitable relations in the NORTEP context reminds us why this might be so:

> There's still a strong feeling that non-aboriginals are outsiders here... that we don't belong. Historically we haven't done a very good job. You know we have exploited and continue to do so. There's more and more smokescreens, more than there has been in the past but you know it hasn't been a very positive relationship or impact of non-aboriginals coming to northern Saskatchewan. You know we improved the technology, we have cable TV but there are more negative than positive sides. People are still very conscious and aware of that and would still like to see less of an impact of non-aboriginals. (Greg: interview transcript)

Before moving on to the next section on the notion of equivalence, a story by Marion outlines a little further some of the problems about

162

integrated programs and the pedagogy of 'voice'. Marion wanted to do something about the lack of non-Indigenous knowledge about the 'Aboriginal experience' in mainstream classes. She attempted to bring together Indigenous and non-Indigenous students at a first-year, field studies camp and arranged for someone from the Aboriginal unit to attend the camp as well as local Aboriginal guides. The AREP students were distributed – one each – among the other students in terms of accommodation and for activities but eventually moved again.

> ... okay I made a bad decision there... because our non-Aboriginal students were not comfortable having an Aboriginal person in their room and I didn't think it was fair to put an Aboriginal student through that obvious sense of discomfort. (Marion: interview transcript)

Marion is the only administrator who has revealed possible elements of racism as a factor in integrated programs. She has not named it as such, preferring a polite euphemism such as 'uncomfortable' when naming the non-Indigenous students' responses. The strategy did not end at accommodation. Marion and her colleagues decided to show a film about the Stolen Generations called *Lousy Little Sixpence*. Marion recalls the responses of the students:

> One Aboriginal student [was] sitting in the room watching the video – and watching the non-Aboriginal students response to the video (you know, all that guilt stuff – don't make me feel guilty) – had an uncle who was in the movie and she just burst into tears at some stage or another. And whoever was leading it, rightly or wrongly, drew out of that person just why they were so upset and her whole family story came out. By the end of it, all the non-Aboriginal kids were in tears. I remember that event – not knowing how to handle that, before or after de-briefing anything. And there was another one where a bit of a ding-dong occurred, because both groups were angry at each other for what was happening in the film. (Marion: interview transcript)

We can see therefore that the ideology of social fulfilment has limitations when expressed as sharing across differences. It is a popular 'cross-cultural' strategy among liberal educationalists and is embedded in the culture-as-a-resource paradigm, which presumes culture can be 'read' rather than negotiated.

Before moving on to the issue of equivalence, it is important to reflect on the important aspects in favour of separate programs outlined by all administrators. These include a supportive network, 'bonding' through culture, cultural maintenance and renewal and language revival. Marion's words sum up the general feeling:

> I think the supporting network. I think they can be comfortable, I was going to say 'among their own'. I think they are more likely to be themselves, to share their difficulties, but to be able to have a good whinge and to be able to really call on each other for help. Help at the deepest level as well as the learning level if they are bonded through their culture. (Marion: interview transcript)

It is difficult to understand what is meant by culture in this context but in Chapter 9 it is explored a little more closely by the students. There is definitely a culture *created* in the two programs although some students may never before have had much to do with the aboriginal community before arriving at NORTEP or AREP. Another complexity in the separate/integrated tension that needs to be explored is the notion of equivalence.

The concept of equivalence

> We were talking about equivalence and about all her stuff about equivalence was that she didn't want to carry them over the line. They had to walk over the line by themselves and my whole thing was well what does carrying them over the line mean? What's equality? All of those issues, equal treatments, equal outcomes. What does equivalence mean? (Marion: interview transcript)

In this section, there is an attempt to answer Marion's question through examining the ways in which each administrator saw equivalence. There are important differences between NORTEP and AREP again in this regard. NORTEP has a broad notion of equivalence that equates with 'different but equivalent'. On the other hand, until 1995 students in the AREP were meant to have exactly the same program as full time students who end up teaching in urban schools. AREP therefore operated within the equivalence-as-sameness paradigm.

One of the first ways in which equivalence was talked about was in relation to how students were selected. Greg seems to think that *a lack of retention* at NORTEP (Greg: 8, line 11) was related to the 'standard' of student enrolled:

> I really want to look at what we're doing with students and that includes selection. Taking students who have a higher chance of succeeding. NORTEP has evolved in that area too. It was originally set up for teacher's aides by the Northern Lights School Division... who were generally ladies, who were generally older... you know thirties and late thirties and who were generally not very well educated. So, that's how it was originally set up. That's how its evolved I think. The expectations have become higher and we are a younger institution and we have a higher degree of standing than we had 10, 15 or 20 years ago. (Greg: interview transcript)

Greg's argument was based on the idea that NORTEP's reputation is now equivalent to other prestigious universities, and they could therefore change entry procedures to account for what he sees as changing student demographics. The increasing number of younger students and those with formal qualifications was an outcome of increased participation in general for Indigenous students. Equivalence was then related in complex ways to objective social relations. That is, it was possible to see how equivalence was constructed in relation to the available labour source. Eric also understands equivalence in this way but he didn't worry so much about retention. He explained:

> I know a lot of people like to see that statistic but I've never really gotten too concerned about it, because what I've observed is that even those folks that came in here for several years and departed, so many of them have used this as a stepping stone to other places and so while they may not have found that this was a career they wanted to choose, it's still been a really important stepping stone for career mobility or a job... just employment. (Eric: interview transcript)

Equivalence can therefore mean equal treatment as in Greg's construction and opportunity as in Eric's. Another area in which equivalence was implicated was in resourcing of the programs. NORTEP was an established program, and while it experienced funding difficulties like all tertiary institutions globally, it had a clear mandate to provide education for the 'north'. As long as the Bands, industry and education authorities were involved in the direction of NORTEP then there would be funding.

AREP, on the other hand, was not considered a long-term strategy. Until 1998 when AREP was given to Goolangullia to control, it was clear that the university did not see AREP or Indigenous education at UWSM as dynamic. That is, the assumption underlying the under-resourcing of AREP, was that it would not last. This has proven to be a static construction of Indigenous struggle for educational equity within UWSM. The idea that the 'pool would dry up' – often an explanation for intransigence – resonates through time with the phrase: they'll all die out. The material reality of this ideology was distressing for many in the program:

> Most people got paid extra for doing AREP teaching. It was almost always done on top of the normal load people did. And so, to some extent it was seen as something outside the general teaching that people would do. (Malcolm: interview transcript)

Given that teaching occurred during a contracted period in addition to a full time load led to exhaustion, frustration and dismay at the conditions in which students were studying.

Many of the differences between NORTEP and AREP relate to the structural arrangements within the university system. The reputation of the two programs among the professional and Indigenous communities that they served also reflects the structural limitations to the programs as well as the role of racialisation.

> There have been stages where I've had to confront meetings of 100 irate school principals and so on, about the quality of the AREP program... the most notable one, was a particular case we had in the North West, where I flew to the town and addressed the Primary Principals' Council for that region... and basically convinced them, it seemed as though I convinced them, that what we were doing with the AREP students was equivalent to what we were doing with our full time students. (Malcolm: interview transcript)

This was a significant event for a couple of reasons. Firstly, Malcolm was asked to respond publicly to a complaint made by *one* principal to the chair of the council. Secondly, the basis of the complaint was that *one* AREP graduate had caused concern among teachers and parents at her school. This was a highly racialised response because it called into question the quality of all AREP graduates on the basis of complaints about one graduate. These sorts of contexts are those in which AREP graduates will eventually teach. Such open displays of racism are not uncommon in the north-western region of NSW, which is well known for vigilante style policing of townships.

These examples do highlight the difficulties of curriculum change when students eventually have to live and work in such environments. How, then, can difference be attended to and the issue of equivalence addressed? Malcolm returned to the notion of equivalence and in so doing suggested that the curriculum is in fact a dynamic process based on selection and continual negotiation. This is the pedagogical – rather than syllabus – view of the curriculum (Grundy, 1994:29). The syllabus view suggests that there is no mediation by teachers or students in constructing the curriculum. The pedagogical view on the other hand, acknowledges that the curriculum is produced through selection and negotiation between teachers and students:

> I have always had some problem with this notion of equivalence and I was never too comfortable in sort of standing up and saying, 'these are the same courses'. I never did say that, but I mean basically what I said was that both these courses are training people to be teachers. They are doing the same subjects. They are doing it in different ways and we at the university deem it to be equivalent. (Malcolm: interview transcript)

In the next chapter we can see that equivalence does not mean sameness even if the subjects and course have the same names. The idea of sameness then, is a political strategy which is often required in the face of negative ascriptions based on Aboriginality:

> If you had a separate course that is uniquely designed for Aboriginal people you could get the inference – rightly or wrongly – that it's sub-standard. Now [name of university], they faced that... their course was based on a solid course but there was a general feeling outside that they've done this Aboriginal course therefore it must be inferior. Now that is a real political problem. (Francis: interview transcript)

So there is a delicate balancing act required of administrators when they have to deal with the public response to programs such as AREP and NORTEP. While administrators deal with the public face of their institutions, they need to depend upon teaching staff that are able to negotiate these tensions at the level of practice. In this last section administrators speak about staffing in the two programs and the sorts of qualities that are expected in attending to a complex teaching situation.

Constructing the 'cross-cultural' teacher

> I mean, our mission statement has been such, to drive us, to be sensitive to the development needs of northern people. Those development needs have a lot to do with them becoming strong in their own culture and their own language. And so the self-development, the personal development component in this program is strong in terms of helping them to develop greater confidence and being positive about themselves, in terms of culture, language, self-esteem. (Eric: interview transcript)

NORTEP has integrated institutional functions such as student support, academic development and funding into one administrative structure. As a consequence there was clarity of purpose with Indigenous and non-Indigenous people working together. Indeed, Indigenous and non-Indigenous men have held the position of Director at NORTEP. Some staff have multiple roles resulting in an overlapping of expertise and knowledge. It has become quite trendy to talk of this as a holistic approach but rarely does it articulate into practice. In Chapter 6 the traditional circle shows how this is constructed in theory and it is possible in Chapters 8 and 9 to see what this means in practice. However, when it came to selecting staff there has been some struggle to turn around dominant thinking:

> Years ago we had more fights than we do now with instructor qualifications. Universities were trying to insist that people had to have PhDs. Well there aren't that many PhDs – certainly amongst the people we used to want to hire there weren't. So we fought. We just fought. (Sandra: interview transcript)

The clarity of purpose at NORTEP can be contrasted with that at AREP. Individual lecturers used to nominate subjects they wanted to teach. There was no guiding philosophy, but Francis nevertheless signals some attributes that he considered necessary for staff working in the AREP:

> If the lecturer brings a lot of cultural baggage, and can't see beyond their own culture...I think that that's a problem of language; I think that's a problem. If ideally you've got someone who knows a fair bit about Aboriginal culture... so much the better. Some people I think are better suited than others to be in the AREP program because of a knowledge base and an attitudinal base. A basic belief in people... there must be just a belief in people as people. That they count, they're important and they are to be loved and nurtured. Hence an attitudinal thing is very important. (Francis: interview transcript)

Such approaches reflect Francis' earlier comments regarding the need to crossover and expand your cultural repertoire. Despite this, Francis places clear limitations to what can be done with cultural knowledge in terms of the curriculum:

> I don't think we are doing the AREP cause any good if we have a patronising standard. Now that doesn't mean you set out to fail people or anything like this but unfortunately I do believe that is part of life. I believe as a group of lecturers we should create the idea that there is a standard and we will do everything we can to help you to get to that standard but you must reach it. If you don't, unfortunately you don't get through. I think the mode is such you've got to adapt. (Francis: interview transcript)

Indeed fear of patronising students is often given as justification for not questioning the whole concept of equivalence. Equivalence is something we are all supposed to agree on. It is clear however that we do not and in the next chapter, we shall see how teacher educators speak about this quite extensively. Francis has, however, heralded some difficulties which alert us to unresolved tensions in this area. If we examine the way in which Francis sees culture being incorporated into the curriculum, we see that culture-as-a-resource is the dominant discourse.

> Well I think that if I were designing a course on creative and practical arts for example, I would write assessment items that the average student could address and pursue. But I hope that in

> writing the assignment they could draw on their particular
> background and develop curriculum unit or whatever that related
> to their background. Mind you the course itself should have
> Aboriginal perspectives right through it. (Francis: interview
> transcript)

Using the approach that Francis suggests creates space for culture,
which is kept separate from the core curriculum. This of course
reflects the multicultural approach to cultural studies, as a kind of add-
on or the *perspective* approach. Creeping into the examples are the
commonly cited areas of Indigenous competence, namely the creative
areas of the curriculum. This does not deny the importance of the
symbolic aspects of culture but rather serves to demonstrate the
entrenched essentialising tendencies of cultural differences when
related to Indigenous students.

One of the consequences of this approach is that it takes the heat
off the hard part of examining the core curriculum. It allows the
discourse around AREP to become deracialised and to therefore deny
that anyone is privileged (Wildman, 1996) by the hegemonic
curriculum. In this scenario we have a supposed universal standard
that everyone agrees on and the canon is safe.

Resistance to change may be lessened if some research were
carried out into graduate destinations and contribution to the field.
Unlike NORTEP, where a study has been done on the impact of
Indigenous teachers in the north (Friesen and Orr, 1995), we do not
know how AREP students fare once they are teaching. Such a gap in
knowledge means that concerns over equivalence and competencies
may be unfounded and indeed may seriously misrepresent the
important contribution that graduates are making in rural areas.
Indeed, the lack of follow-up data – other than anecdotal – has created
a reactive rather than proactive environment. The institutional location
of the AREP program, has until the end of 1998, been managed by
many units, and divided institutionally by function and ethnicity.
Racialised practices in this arrangement result in a convergence of
Aboriginal identity with a support role (student services) and non-
Indigenous identity with faculties (academic units). These types of
arrangements have created a kind of balkanisation, which is best
discussed through contrast with NORTEP.

The clarity of purpose at NORTEP is starkly absent at AREP.
Malcolm speaks of the complex systems of 'favours and obligations'

that developed in AREP as compensation for many structural constraints. For example, NORTEP has a nucleus of permanent full time staff that does the majority of planning and teaching. In addition, guest faculty come from the universities in the south to teach the specialty areas. AREP, on the other hand, staffed the program as an 'add-on' to normal teaching loads. This made it extremely difficult to plan in an integrated manner and to have the sorts of discussions that are always taking place at NORTEP.

NORTEP, in recognising the specific histories of Indigenous people in the north, have inverted the hegemony of racist discourses. They have moved beyond the 'different means less than' ideology that fashions the responses and concerns to AREP.

Conclusion

In this chapter, it has been possible to isolate areas of tension for administrative personnel. Learning to manage diversity will be a skill required of all new managers in the human services with increasing diversification and globalisation (Ginsberg and Keys, 1995:125). For teacher education programs, this is also a critical consideration. The tensions and contradictions highlighted in this chapter centre around the need to continually work through what cultural difference means in any given context. We also saw that tensions were commonly produced as a consequence of wider structural inequalities. In addition, the administrators in these programs demonstrated a diversity of ways of knowing difference, which points to some difficulty in attending to cultural difference in any uniform manner. Importantly however, the differing system of power hierarchies operating at NORTEP and AREP were shown to produce and constrain the possibilities for agency on the part of people working in the two programs.

When comparing AREP and NORTEP it is possible to see how institutional arrangements, professional organisations and individuals interact when engaging with cultural difference. Through the narratives of the administrators in the NORTEP and AREP programs it is clear that cultural knowledge is not static or predictable. The essential difference between NORTEP and AREP has been the acceptance in NORTEP of culture as dynamic and negotiable because of their participatory and democratic processes:

The only time you won't get negotiation is when everyone accepts whatever the thing is and TEPs have never been accepting of 'what is' obviously because 'what is' didn't work. That's why in the seventies the TEPs were founded because it was clearly not working. (Sandra: interview transcript)

It is useful to remind ourselves of the reasons these programs were set up in the first place and ask whether the conditions that gave rise to AREP and NORTEP have changed substantially. At one level, there is some indication that as a consequence of increased retention rates in schooling in general, the two programs are experiencing demographic changes such as younger, more formally qualified students. It could be argued that the programs have served their purpose and now ought to be wound down in the case of AREP and more inclusive of non-Indigenous northerners in the case of NORTEP.

At another level, increased communication networks via technology, improved transport and living conditions in towns and on reserves might suggest other ways of providing educational opportunities. Could technological support mean that students could stay at home and carry out the 'standard' degree offered to all students in conventional faculties or schools of education?

Outside the big questions about educational changes in terms of funding and technology, we need to ask some questions about the nature of AREP and NORTEP. What pedagogical possibilities capture the imagination of people who work in these programs? What attracts the students to AREP and NORTEP and not other similar programs? What view/s of the future were constructed in these programs and by whom?

To answer these questions it becomes necessary to explore the dynamics of AREP and NORTEP through the eyes of the teacher educators and students. Their opinions of the programs may well indicate that there are other considerations in addition to those raised by administrators.

Chapter 8

Teaching With and Through Difference

The oppressed are regarded as the pathology of the healthy
society, which must therefore adjust these 'incompetent and lazy'
folk to its own patterns by changing their mentality (Freire,
1972:48).

Sometimes you know Carol; I reckon this course is going to
assimilate us. It's so hard... to hold on to your identity (Denise,
AREP student).

Introduction: Pedagogy and the politics of identity

In the previous chapter the tensions experienced by administrators
centred on cultural knowledge versus cultural stereotypes; advocacy
versus self-determination and separate versus integrated programs.
Through a focus on the teaching staff at AREP and NORTEP it is
possible to see that like the administrators, teacher educators in the
programs grapple with the tensions that arise from cultural knowledge.
On the one hand, they are seduced by the potential for the meaningful
production of cultural knowledge and producing new forms of
knowledge. On the other hand, this new knowledge seems to compete
for space with and in the core curriculum.

What constitutes cultural knowledge is constantly negotiated by
these teacher educators but, importantly, it is produced through the
politics of identity which takes many forms in their narratives. For
example, their self-identification drew upon individual habitus and
included racialised, gendered, classed and professional dimensions.
Interestingly, all teacher educators used 'colour' words in their
constructions of social relations and many spoke of the salience of

colour and its effects on identity. I have called this the *white versus non-white* tension. Collectively, the teacher educators were concerned with the professional cultural formation of their students while trying to make space for students' cultural knowledge. I have called this the *collectivist/individualist* tension since attending to the professional development of students is often framed in terms of producing autonomous, professional, individuals. At times this is contested by students. At other times, teacher educators impose collectivities. The seemingly arbitrary nature of these positionings produces tension. The principle contradiction arising from these politics of identity centres on the relationship between knowledge and power, or what I have called the *cultural knowledge/disciplinary knowledge* tension.

The participants

In this chapter I will be drawing on the voices of 15 teacher educators – four from NORTEP and 11 from AREP. The difference in numbers from each program relates to the fact that NORTEP has a smaller core of lecturers while AREP draws on an entire faculty. In addition, interviewing at NORTEP took place during a residential where the other three staff members were busy. There were two other AREP staff members who volunteered to be interviewed but a range of factors, such as time and opportunity, prevented them from being carried out. The self-selection of participants and the process of interviewing have been discussed in Chapter 2.

The group of teacher educators in this study came from a range of disciplinary backgrounds including mathematics, drama, English as a Second Language (ESL), language, literacy, sociology, educational foundations such as psychology, practice or field coordinators, computing, special education and social science. Two of those interviewed at NORTEP were Indigenous while those interviewed at AREP were all non-Indigenous.[1]

Among those interviewed, eight were female and seven were male. Five of the male interviewees (Malcolm, Eddie, Michael, David and Charles) had experience in a range of school and tertiary institutions while two were relatively new (Greg and Murray) to teacher education. Among the eight women, three had long term experience in teacher education (Marion, Julie and Sandra) – two in particular in

---

[1] Within the category of non-Indigenous there were also a range of ethnicities but the protection of anonymity prevents identification of this aspect of identity.

cross-cultural environments (Julie and Sandra) – while the rest (Pat, Bridget, Marilyn, Simone and Dorothy) had all taught in schools and had come to teacher education some time during the period 1980-2000. Sandra and Julie had also been involved in educational issues concerned with Indigenous people and recalled the changes dating from the 1970s.

Creating cultural space

> But what about schooling now? Have schools stopped being the instrument of assimilation? My children are in school. I became the principal of the school where I once sat at a desk with the other Yolngu kids. Are my kids having a Yolngu education comparable in depth and rigour to what my parents gave me? I would answer a firm yes. But I can only answer yes because for a quarter of a century people, both Yolngu and Balanda, have worked to achieve this. We have transformed the missionary, assimilation ideology into an authentic Yolngu schooling. It took a lot of imagination and struggle. (Yunupingu, 1998:332)

Yunupingu is describing the struggle of cultural negotiation in a school in far north Australia – the same struggle that was evident in my case studies based in NSW. In this section I want to try and get at this process of struggle, and the imagination that it releases. I begin with those moments where cultural space is created through conflict. Through focussing on particular instances, thoughts and/or actions that set up conflict, we are provided with opportunities to explore the relationship between pedagogy and the politics of difference. In revealing these processes of cultural production we can see that the politics of identity creates space. When cultural difference is recognised, rather than denied, there is space created for the kinds of negotiation and dialogue that Yunupingu refers to above.

The relationship between identity and pedagogy has been documented in many studies (Keeffe, 1992; Kalantzis, 1990; Malin, 1990; Hesch, 1995; Barman et al., 1987; Loos and Miller, 1989). Chapter 4 explored these debates (in relation to Indigenous students in general and teacher education students specifically) and argued for a pedagogy that negotiated through and with difference. The preferred way to do that, it was argued, was to listen to what Troyna (1994) called the 'noise of multidimensionality' rather than relying on the pathology of the racialised Indigenous 'Other' as an explanation for

175

tension. Through the lens of 'identity', it is possible to capture moments when culture is recognised as more than an artefact. Understanding what the tension is about is difficult because inherent in the recognition of cultural difference is the revelation that culture is continually constituted as a relation of power. In other words, recognition of identity is also recognition of power.

What then is the relationship between power and identity and pedagogy? It seems a simple question at first but it brings up a range of issues. Some are about power and knowledge, empowerment and access, techniques of teaching and their contribution to on-going determination. Other issues focus beyond the individual student to the wider Indigenous community. We don't always think about the latter aspect of teaching so it is largely unproblematised in teacher education. Those that teach sociology of education can relate to this marginalisation in teacher education programs (Hesch, 1993). Yet, in these programs there is a struggle over what constitutes an appropriate pedagogy for Indigenous students.

In this chapter, the struggle is typified in part as a *collectivist/individualist* tension which is partly explored through the teacher educators' understanding of the relationship between AREP/NORTEP and Indigenous futures. We can gain some insight from this perspective, into the hegemonic understandings of cultural difference in the professional habitus of teacher educators. One of the reasons for this tension around collective and individual identity is that it is now less acceptable to speak of the 'Other' in blatantly racist terms such as in the Freirian quote at the beginning of this chapter. However, simply deracialising discourses does not alleviate the collective/individual tension because it naturalises 'whiteness' as the norm (Troyna, 1994:334). As I argued in Chapter 4, following Poynting (1995), the articulation or disarticulation of discourses will not resolve this tension. The continuities of racialisation are evident, although hidden, in deracialised discourses as we shall come to see in this chapter. For example, we can see that it is the students who highlight deracialised discourses by demonstrating the ways in which colour *is* a marker of difference. They do this through drawing attention to whiteness and strategically depend on white/non-white binaries. The white versus non-white ideological discourse suffuses the Indigenous educational field and the historically constituted habitus of all those working in the program.

Most mainstream students who become teachers have been successful at schooling (Connell, 1985). This means that they have varying degrees of control over content knowledge as well as a positive identification with the hidden curriculum. That is, through schooling they have learned about competitiveness, testing, hierarchy, success, failure, gender roles and a range of cultural understandings (Wotherspoon, 1998:83) with which they identify. This process of *individuation* is where we all learn about ourselves as distinct human subjects (*ibid.*). Our teacher educators identify with this process since they have been shaped by it (Connell, 1985). These sorts of skills, knowledge and attributes are products of education and have been referred to as cultural capital by Bourdieu:

> They [schools] tend to legitimize certain forms of knowledge, ways of speaking and ways of relating to the world that capitalize on the type of familiarity and skills that only certain students have received from their family backgrounds and class relations. (Bourdieu, cited in Aronowitz and Giroux, 1993:76)

Bourdieu's concept of cultural capital stresses power in the relationship between the attributes that are rewarded and those that are marginalised. Certainly, the teacher educators in this study contend that we do need to attend to culture after they have recognised that a universalistic approach sits uncomfortably with difference:

> ... I'd never lived in a small community and I had absolutely *no* contact at all with aboriginal people. I had no idea and then in a sense that was good because I didn't know that there was supposed to be any difference between us. People are people, so I didn't come with a lot of preconceived stereotypes. I just came... and to be honest how naive I was. (Greg: interview transcript)

Greg's comments demonstrate the way in which universalistic conceptions of humanity are unsettled through a greater engagement with the particular. Greg acknowledges a moment of recognition that ever since has meant a deconstruction of his previously universalistic philosophy. Taylor argues that our identity is partly shaped by recognition or its absence and that non-recognition or misrecognition can be a form of oppression "imprisoning someone in a false, distorted mode of living" (1994:25).

In this chapter, teacher educators wrestle with the fact that recognition carries with it the burden of a moral response. This is partly evident in the way in which the interviewees position themselves, as teacher educators, as teachers and as non-Indigenous or Indigenous individuals. They do this through an exploration of life histories, always in relation to current narratives and the way in which shifting ideas have situated prior knowledge in new light. In doing so they reveal that this tension is not only about privileged discourses and practices but also the privilege of the person who is reproducing them. In other words, tension is usually centred on the production of power and the construction of identities through these relations. The non-Indigenous teachers in these programs felt these politics differently from the Indigenous teachers because of their different structural locations and historically constituted subjectivity.

What is evident in the voices of the teacher educators is a filtering of policy and theory into a complex array of responses. They show how using a method of negotiation and dialogue, within constraints, can produce space for the production of cultural knowledge and the critical analysis of disciplinary knowledge. In this way, they provide space for cultural knowledge to reconstitute the curriculum.

Beginning with the *white versus non-white* tension we can see how notions of colour articulate with the ongoing racialisation of subjectivities. Borrowing from literature on blackness and whiteness as privilege, it is possible to explain how tensions are not individual but social. Following this, there is a discussion of the ways in which collectivities form around specific sites of contestation. This is called the *collectivist/individualist* tension. The final tension gets to the heart of the pedagogical debate because it is concerned with ideas about the constitution and production of *Indigenous* teachers. This is called the *cultural knowledge/disciplinary knowledge* tension where teacher educators try to make sense of the cultural knowledge they have gained.

'White' versus 'non-white' tension

There is an increasing array of academic work on the subject of 'whiteness' (cf. Troyna, 1998 on research methodology; Fine et al., 1997 from critical, feminist and post-colonialist theories of education; Hage, 1998 on the relationship between 'whiteness' and the imagined community or nation). In this chapter I am dealing with 'whiteness' as it emerges in the relationships of agents in this study rather than as a philosophical discourse on whiteness as identity. In particular, I want to show how the *politics of colour* highlights deracialisation and the privileging of normative reference points. The work of Barry Troyna is useful in this instance.

In a powerful critique of three studies of teachers' work,[2] Troyna argued that none have "deconstructed the obvious" and therefore "reproduce commonsense racism" (Troyna, 1994:326). This is because none of the authors problematise ethnicity or race in the everyday world of teachers. He argues further that such deracialised discourses collude with hegemonic conceptions of normality (*ibid.*). The enculturation of teacher education students and teachers into their everyday world of work is through professional competencies and standards. These are constructed and measured through outcomes-based learning defined in course and subject outlines, syllabus documents and university regulations. Hesch (1996:10) calls this the "documentary mode of management", which he argues conceals hegemonic conceptions of normality. It is my contention that this is how *whiteness* is often acted out in the examples in this chapter. Therefore, I am not referring to 'whiteness' as a racial category but more as a metaphor for a form of cultural capital that is valued and often defined as 'standards'.

We need to remind ourselves firstly of the various ways in which 'whiteness' has been central to processes of racialisation. As a marker of racialised identities, colour is, and has been, a powerful tool of differentiation. As discussed in Chapter 3, colour has been used to differentiate between those considered civilised and those requiring protection in Australia. The impact of such policies still 'hides' inside families, in the relations between Indigenous and non-Indigenous people and among Indigenous peoples themselves. This hidden history has been discussed more recently in Australia in the acclaimed autobiography of Sally Morgan[3] (1987) and in Stuart Rintoul's *The Wailing* (1993). The parallel experiences among the Métis in Canada reveal similar experiences and strategies such as 'passing'. Murray, an Indigenous teacher educator at NORTEP explained:

---

[2] Connell, R.W. (1985); Lortie, D. (1975); Sikes, P; Measor, L, & Woods (1985).
[3] *My Place* is the story of Sally Morgan's discovery of her hidden Aboriginal family history. In her story she reveals her Grandmother's shame and denial of Aboriginality. Morgan also discusses passing for another ethnicity using a strategy of "tell them you're Indian".

I came to La Ronge for grade 7 to grade 12. I found that really hard in terms of adjustment here. The school I came to was... I would say the class I was in was 90% white students and the rest were aboriginal students although they never admitted it. There was a bit of racism that was going on. In fact the teachers were that way as well to the point where aboriginal cultures were put down; where you didn't really want to admit that you were an aboriginal. I could get away with that but there was another person – he was darker and so on. It was what made it a difficult adjustment coming here to La Ronge. (Murray: interview schedule)

Murray uses colour words as a marker of difference by contrasting the experiences of himself with others. *Passing* for 'white' to avoid negative cultural stereotypes from other students and teachers is common. The phenomenon of *passing* is a very interesting identity strategy. It happens in class societies (eg. the UK) as well: working class (white) individuals *passing* for middle class whites. This throws up interesting dilemmas for individuals. For example, in Australia the official attempt to legitimate *passing* can be found in the government's policy of providing 'exemption certificates' to certain Aboriginal people. Known as 'dog licenses' or 'beer tickets' among Aboriginal people (Parbury, 1986:166), exemption certificates were essentially passes off reserves and missions for those – usually whiter – people who were prepared to separate themselves from their Aboriginal community. For some, this meant the right to drink in pubs, for others the right to have control of their children. Thus a class or caste system developed where those that left reserves came to despise those that did not want to, or could not, relinquish their Aboriginal identity (*ibid.*).

Michael, an experienced teacher educator in AREP, reflects on the impact of such negative stereotypes on students' identities. In doing so he explores the dilemma of recognition, misrecognition and non-recognition in this narrative about a student in one of his classes:

I suppose in a way F's story about... *"Don't tell anyone you're Aboriginal"*... you know you might say "Jesus Christ it's so much easier not to be Aboriginal in Australian society" – which it is – and you could nearly say to someone "you know just don't bother telling anybody". Then of course if people don't know you're a

Koori they'll start saying anything in front of you... and suddenly you'll realise that's a denial of yourself, there's no future in that. Absolute denial of who you are, it's the most destructive thing. (Michael: interview schedule)

But how do we understand the various uses of colour? What kinds of differentiated identities are being constructed? Colour in Michael and Murray's narratives appear as a matter of choice. Yet, choice doesn't make the construction of identity any simpler. Indeed, it is this very choice for some and not for others that highlights the way in which the construction of identity is a political act. At this point, it might be useful to look at the concepts of blackness and whiteness in a little more theoretical detail to explore the significance of colour. While I have chosen 'blackness' – largely because of the large amount of literature available in African-American and British anti-racist struggles – there have been similar concerns over colourism among Indigenous communities in North America (cf. Manyarrows, 1994). The issue is therefore not about 'blackness' and 'whiteness' *per se*, but racialisation resulting in the phenotypical designation of attributes related to colour.

'Blackness'

Drawing on Tajfel – who writes specifically about blackness (cited in Anthias and Yuval-Davis, 1993:135-37) – there are three ways in which colour is a part of ongoing racialisation.

- As an inherited characteristic, it fits crudely into 'scientific' racist genetic theories.
- It is visible.
- It is an expression of historical cultural tradition.

The first two, argue Anthias and Yuval-Davis (1993), can be found anywhere in anti-Black sentiment but cannot explain the interethnic racisms that stereotype people as "red-skin wild Indians or yellow-peril Japanese" (*ibid.*:136). It is the third point that has the potential to explain the rigidity of such stereotypes through generations.

'Black and White', which represent so crudely the differences in the shade of skin between groups of human beings – are used to symbolise distinctions between vice and virtue, hell and heaven, devils and angels, contamination and purity. (Tajfel, cited in Anthias and Yuval-Davis, 1993:137-38)

This latter culturally based explanation has the potential to explain the persistence of colour categories and the multiple racisms they generate because of their embeddedness in the symbolic and psychosocial world of individuals. Such persistence helps also to understand the difficulty or inability of those who are visible to choose assimilation (i.e. exemption certificates) "as long as the inherited characteristic continues to be used culturally as a signifier for racist discourse and practice" (*ibid.*:137). Marion recalls a situation that demonstrates these processes:

> Somebody, somewhere very early in the piece [pause] got in my car – three Aboriginal students and went out to a shopping centre at Liverpool. A female Aboriginal student wanted an outfit to wear to the end of res' do, and the two guys weren't interested in coming clothes shopping with us. So they went and did something else and then they had to hang around the car 'til I got back. When I got back there was a policeman there convinced that they were stealing my car. (Marion: interview schedule)

Marion's anecdote provides a sharp focus on the public culture and the way in which the 'real' world makes colour highly visible. This understanding also helps to explain how a 'lack of colour' is conversely used to deny identity. As in Michael's narrative, those that can pass – that is, have lighter skin or hair – may well avoid exclusion from the dominant society, yet the price is a denial of the self. In the last two decades the association of whiteness with oppressor has meant a partial inversion of negative ascriptions due to skin colour. Those that are 'full-bloods' or visibly more traditional are accorded reverence and often romanticised (Rowse, 1988) while those that are lighter are often seen as not real or having 'chips on their shoulders' (Reid and Holland, 1996). In Chapter 9 I discuss how these generational differences are impacting quite strongly on the students.

It is evident that we cannot understand colour without exploring the issue of 'whiteness'. There is a current literature spanning cultural studies and law that I do not have space to fully explore. However, I will briefly outline what I consider the dominant usage in this study.

Whiteness as privilege

Privilege is a right granted to individuals in systemic ways be it through class, caste or law (Blair, 1989). Wildman (1996:17) summarised the elements to privilege as follows:

1. The characteristics of the privileged group define the norm.
2. Privileged group members can rely on their privilege and avoid objecting to oppression.
3. As a consequence of the conflation of the above two elements, the holder rarely sees privilege.

Therefore, through a process of normalisation, whiteness is made invisible (Wildman, 1996; Sleeter, 1993). As Troyna has argued, this is partly achieved using deracialised discourses. The following example shows how one student tried to expose this process by making visible the issue of 'whiteness'. For Dorothy, the teacher educator concerned, colour was something that she said was irrelevant because as a child she had attended a school with a range of students of colour from different countries and felt that it didn't make any difference to her relationships with them. To some extent Dorothy was attempting to invert or suppress negative ascriptions emanating from colour (Sleeter, 1993). Here she relates an event that occurred while teaching the primary colours to a group of AREP students:

> [It was a] stand off… that they only wanted those colours [black, red and yellow] and I said: "No we're looking at primary colours today, which are these… and we are going to look at secondary colours next week and talk about all the theory and that."… "I will use black" [student response]. I said: "Well it's a neutral colour." "Well what's white then?" [student response]. Then I said: "Neutral as well actually." "What do you mean?" [student] And I said: "When you look at the colour wheel…" I really felt he was playing… I said: "Look you've got neutrals, primary, secondary and tertiary colours and we make the secondary and tertiary by doing this… We make them harmonious by using black and white."… "I want black" [student response]. It was because the red and yellow[4] were there in the primary colours you see… "And I want my black…" "No, you can't…" When it started I didn't realise what he was pushing at… (Dorothy: interview schedule)

---

[4] The colours red, black and yellow make up the Aboriginal flag in Australia.

This was a defining moment for Dorothy; she realised she was being challenged about knowledge being valueless. In addition, it was no longer possible for *her* colour, and therefore *her* privilege, to be invisible. The denial of the salience of colour, or colour-blindness, is common among those with privilege (Sleeter, 1993:161). In a racialised society, colour cannot be ignored.

To sum up, Michael's narrative above referred to a student who had the opportunity to 'pass' as white but for whom to do so would have been a denial of self. Murray told how 'passing' helped him avoid racism in high school. Tina, in the previous chapter, explored the notion of a 'red-haired, blue-eyed' Aboriginal student and her confusion/surprise. Marion highlighted the continuing racism resulting from the cultural tradition of associating colour with 'vice and virtue'. And Dorothy's well meaning attempt at eradicating colour from cultural tradition brought a surprising symbolic avowal of its visibility from a student. All of these instances reveal the way in which 'race' operates as an organising category and how the assignation of one of its phenotypic attributes: 'colour', has a social effect (McConnochie et al., 1988:6).

Bringing these experiences into the world of the classroom, as in the case of Dorothy's student, forces teacher educators to take into account lived realities in pedagogical relationships. Yet, it is often difficult to know how to do this without collapsing into practices that are *ad hoc* or culturalist. To gain some insight into these difficulties the next section of this chapter looks at the *collectivist/individualist* tension.

Collectivist/Individualist tension

> But the students also tell you... we know if the class isn't going well because we get deputations at the director's door. (Sandra interview schedule)

When do communities come into being or more specifically, when do students form a collective body in AREP and NORTEP? In Chapter 6 I discussed the collective response by AREP students when their program was threatened. They responded collectively to a kind of *institutional pedagogy* that was based upon hierarchical structures. That is, they felt excluded from the decision-making processes that would have an impact upon their lives. The only possible response to this exclusion was to use the power available to them, which rested on the *politics of reputation* and the *politics of recognition*. As discussed earlier, the politics of recognition creates the requirement for a moral response (Taylor, 1994). The politics of recognition contains some interesting dimensions when we look at teaching relationships. In the following scenario, Bridget explored an issue around assessment in which students highlighted the relationship between identity, pedagogy and politics:

> For example, one of the students said: "I would love to know *your* experiences of being assessed and evaluated or whatever. Do you think your lecturer or classroom teacher really knew what you knew?" And one of the students said to me that she just faked all her multiple choice, and she came top of the class. Another girl, in her bit she had to label parts of a stove, and she had never seen a stove. [Not] an electrical stove, they only had a fuel stove. And if I asked her about the flue and everything, she would know... and so I began to realise that their educational experiences... (Bridget: interview schedule)

As I have argued above in 'whiteness as privilege', recognition of cultural difference requires a simultaneous recognition of one's own privilege, and consequent power. Bridget provides us with a strong sense of this hidden curriculum[5] when she reflects here on a moment that she discovered herself at the centre of the gaze of the students. Later she surmised that there was 'something in her head' that she had to sort out about these differences. This is what Hall has called the "recognition of the self through difference" (1987:5). In this anecdote, the normative orientation of testing procedures and content is exposed by the students who questioned the teacher educator's claim to pedagogical 'truth' (Gore, 1993). Indeed, the structure and function of assessment is an issue for many teacher educators and students at AREP and NORTEP.

The hegemony of the documentary mode of management (Hesch, 1993) is evident in processes and practices that shape subject assessment, time frames and what constitutes disciplinary knowledge. Sometimes teacher educators are at a loss as to how to respond to the specific needs of the students once they recognise cultural difference

---

[5] The hidden curriculum is discussed in Hatton (1994) by Peter McLaren (pages 40-42). The definition he uses following Doug White is "*the introduction to a particular form of life it serves in part to prepare students for dominant or subordinate positions in the existing society*" (Hatton, 1994:40).

185

because of the power of the documentary mode of management. When they do respond to student assertions of cultural difference it is sometimes within the framework of multiculturalism. The effect is to situate the problem in a lack of respect for cultural difference resulting in a need to boost student self-esteem and to find ways to acknowledge this difference (Hesch, 1995; Reid, 1999; Luke et al., 2000). The pathology of the individual is still evident in this approach and distracts the gaze from normative principles underpinning teacher education. Hesch argues that this type of multicultural education is "a strategy of the State to secure hegemony in the field of race relations" (1995:105), though multiculturalism is a complex and contradictory phenomenon in Canada and Australia.

We can see if this is indeed the case when examining the production of teaching identities through pedagogical relationships. One of the ways in which the teacher educators do this is when they recall particular instances where recognition of cultural difference disturbed a previously taken for granted act, thought or dialogue. In the process of exploring this recognition they reveal what Giroux has called a "soft" oppression (1994:156). In other words, the ways in which cultural difference is denied through common sense notions of what is natural and proper in society and in education (Hesch, 1993, 1995). This is the hidden curriculum of course and the way it works is to frame difference and inequality "through the narrow landscape of essentialism, fate or destiny" (Giroux, 1994:157).

The following voice of one of the students at NORTEP reveals how this works when he discusses the notion of the 'normal' distribution curve that most assessment results have to fit into at universities.

> Yeah, well right now there is a... there's a group of us in a bit of a bind with an instructor. Ah... we got high marks in our mid-terms. The university said no that's too high so... knocked them down and we felt that we earned those marks but the university said to knock them down because that's not our level of achievement or something. (Brian: interview schedule)

The students' struggle in this instance is over the number of students who can receive high marks but it is also over the fact that the students feel they have been *collectively* rejected as '*not achieving that level*'. There is an interesting tension here. The university uses individuating assessment practices but the students feel a racialised collectivity has been imposed based on an assumption about Indigenous ability. At another level, we can see that although NORTEP is self-governing it is still subject to intervention from other institutions, thus limiting the responses that NORTEP can make in this regard.

Racialisation, as a form of collectively identifying people, takes many forms in the teacher educators' narratives. Julie, who had an interest in ethno-specific curriculum studies, enjoyed teaching in the AREP but found "it is easy to tread on their [the students] toes" (p. 9). The following is a fascinating snapshot of reflexivity in action as well as demonstrating the possibility of mutually transforming the hegemony of culturalist pedagogy:

> We were talking about measurement at the time… and I was talking about how Hopi Indians described time or distance and in particular distance and how it often gets linked with time. How you had to interpret it, and how I would tell distances… and I made a comment… that one of the AREP students had talked about the distances being a six-pack[6]… and then I said this to the next lot of students. And I used it as an example and I thought they might not have liked me using that example. (Julie: interview schedule)

Julie was faced with the essential paradox of a culturalist curriculum. She recognised this a little farther on in our discussion, when she commented that she and the students recognised that what she was saying was a 'truism'. A truism relies on stories or myths, which seem 'common sense', yet have homogenising tendencies. A culturalist curriculum, referred to in Chapter 4 as based on the notions of 'culture-as-impediment' and/or 'culture-as-resource', is constructed through a "petrified mosaic of clichés" (Ålund, 1991:97). Julie's narrative merely reflects the hegemony of the culturalist curriculum in contemporary teacher education. However, racialised collectivities are also created through less overt discursive practices.

Deracialised discourses can also produce material effects that arise from particular types of cultural technologies. Bridget explores these issues and stumbles across another dimension to Indigenous experience which reveals *some truth* about Indigenous inequality but

---

[6] A 'six-pack' is a colloquial term for six small bottles or cans of beer.

also, more persuasively, the normative and highly regulatory nature of record keeping. For Bridget the 'documentary mode of management' is a stark example of the way in which cultural technologies make invisible cultural difference. These are hidden aspects of the curriculum but they are central to understanding the relationship between identity, pedagogy and politics:

> They had a seminar to give and it was about keeping records. I was suggesting an alternative way to assess kids would be to keep records and all that kind of stuff. And as a response to that in terms of a seminar, [student's name] got up and said 'keeping records and all that kind of stuff on kids' behaviour and attitudes can all build up to a good picture'. He said 'the same sets of records can be used against kids'. And then he went on to say... knowing about kids in schools... and how that kind of information had been used to prevent kids from coming back to schools, that police could come in and use those records and use them against kids in court and all that kind of stuff. You know his job was involved in court work? (Bridget: interview schedule)

Identity in this instance is not necessarily racialised, for the same 'effect' of this assessment procedure would be felt by other disadvantaged groups in society. Yet it is true that one of the highest incarceration rates is among Indigenous youth. The student was bringing this knowledge to Bridget. This was knowledge gained from his individual habitus, as an Indigenous worker in the courts. Throwing up challenges to individuating practices such as record keeping is not necessarily creating a statement about Aboriginality. But it is challenging the aim of such practices in dealing with inequality.

How do these processes of individuation relate to disadvantage? The hidden curriculum has been well documented in our understandings of the way in which hegemony operates within education. Sennett and Cobb (1972) eloquently outlined the hidden injuries of class whereby educational practices such as individualism and competition make educational failure seem *natural*. Bowles and Gintis (1976) and Willis (1981) explored further the way in which the hidden curriculum reproduced (class) inequality arguing that educational outcomes corresponded to wider social inequality.

The explanatory power of the reproductionist framework cannot be denied and is generally widely accepted – alongside liberal conservative arguments which focus on factors within students' homes as the basis for unequal Indigenous education outcomes (Bourke et al, 1996). However, knowing this and doing something about it are somewhat problematic. Having multicultural education policies or indigenist education policies does not necessarily mean that core normative pedagogical practices such as these will change.

For example in *The Agony of Education*, the participation and performance of African-American students is explained as a *push-out* factor resulting from a range of factors including outright racism to *misrecognition* of black student identity (Feagin et al., 1996). What does this misrecognition possibly mean? In the following anecdote by Pat, we see this process and experience what Troyna (1994:325) calls the *noise of multidimensionality*.

> "... and you know Pat, one of the things that you have to come to terms with"... Which I admit... I accept some of the criticism... "Some of the students fight the most incredible odds to come to uni and have had very poor education. Whereas this woman..." And I do forget her name "has had a privileged background." Has had education etc, etc... and I thought: "Hang on a minute, I'm not sure I agree with... in terms of me raving how good she was... Why should she be almost disadvantaged because she has in fact had education etc, etc? Why should I feel guilty for saying what a good student she is? It doesn't mean that I ignored the ones that have fought against the most incredible odds. I found that difficult in AREP. I think there is some inverted snobbery there... It was more white culture than black culture. That's incredibly derogatory. I mean let's look at the Pat O'Shanes[7] and some other people who've hardly had a privileged background. You know, um... and I found that really hard to cope with. (Pat: interview schedule)

There are a number of consequences of suppressing the noise of multidimensionality and one of them is to impose a racialised collectivity based on certain characteristics. There seems to be a hierarchy, or different hierarchies, operating here and the Indigenous students work with them as well. It's a hierarchy of

---

[7] Pat O'Shane is a prominent Aboriginal magistrate.

privilege/disadvantage and of traditional/westernised. Differences across the group of students point to not only racialisation but also economic disadvantage.

However, what the two voices in the above anecdote are exploring is the issue of cultural capital. The term cultural capital, coined by Bourdieu, refers to "good taste, certain kinds of prior knowledge, abilities and language forms" (Apple, cited in Miller, 1989:135-36). Cultural capital is a consequence of one's habitus, so understanding habitus provides us with a useful way of understanding the multiple dimensions of inequality and difference in education. The reason for this is that racialisation *and* class *and* gender are all in dynamic relationship to each other in the process of cultural production and in shaping field and habitus.

There is also a tension in this exchange emanating from the idea that culture sits on a continuum from most traditional to most westernised represented by the idea of 'more black than white'. When culture is presented in this way, there is the potential for misrecognition of student identity. That is, to do well if you are Aboriginal means 'losing' your Aboriginality. This is what Pat is objecting to because she sees its limitations. The struggle ends up focussing on the differentiation of students along the lines of 'race' and 'class'. To argue that the assessment processes are unfair, or that particular practices privilege the cultural knowledge of a few, would mean rejecting culturalist explanations and exploring other dimensions, such as social class. That is, attention needs to focus on core practices in education and the knowledge they privilege, rather than simply focussing on the cultural attributes of students.

The students' collectivities are formed in some very interesting ways. How the teacher educators understand this process is also interesting. I want to end this section with two more narratives about collectivities – and the educators' understandings of their purpose.

Eddie was an AREP lecturer who had given a student a distinction grade for an assignment. The student approached Eddie and asked him if he would change the grade to a pass, apparently arguing that *being awarded a distinction was taking away the opportunities for one of his peers to gain that distinction* (Eddie: 13, lines 13-14). Eddie had not come across this before from any student. Here he explains how he responded:

> Well I tried to make him recognise that there was some value in him demonstrating to his peers that it could be done. Someone could get a higher grade and that this could be some sort of model and so forth, and some sort of recognition. I think he partially saw that. I said I'm not going to change your grade. I mean legally I wasn't allowed to do it – the assessment system and that sort of thing. But that's another incident that's stuck in my mind that I probably don't even begin to understand what it was. Now he used to come here wearing some clothes that sort of said to the world that he was an Aboriginal person. (Eddie: interview schedule)

This incident highlights two opposing logics: collectivist, group-oriented logic versus individualistic, hierarchical logic. Students also get caught up in this. There is a feeling of comfort in group-oriented contexts, but they also want individual recognition for work. In this instance, the student appears to have made a decision in favour of the former. Perhaps this was done in recognition of a wider politics, which included his greater access and opportunities in education in general compared to some of the older female students.

A dimension of *generational change* and the changing shape of the politics of identity on other students and pedagogy was also revealed in this final narrative from Malcolm:

> I mean, basically the older women wanted to get through the course, but almost felt they deserved to get through the course. And in many ways, I don't want to say that they didn't work at the course, because I think they did, but they felt that success was passing. Some of the younger women, one in particular, felt that success was getting distinctions and high distinctions. She was looked down upon by the other group, and really did have a difficult time in the sense that she was out-stripping the older women who culturally saw themselves as being superior and felt that she should see that they were superior. And so that was a difficulty. That was a real difficulty for her and I think that's been repeated in other groups as well. (Malcolm: interview schedule)

There is a pattern to this politics of difference. The pattern could be generational, as implied by Malcolm. If that were the case then the male student's response is rational. That is, if social exclusion was a consequence of doing better academically, wanting to blend in could be a motivating force. On the other hand, he (and the student referred to above) may have acted out of respect for these women who often were stolen children or excluded from education when they were younger.

The interesting thing about both narratives is the invisible 'whiteness' in the discourses. In both examples, culture is constructed as an impediment to individual progress. The collective versus individual tension is never resolved in this model of cultural difference. These processes make it difficult to acknowledge different historically constituted cultural formations. Rather, culture is seen as pathological and an impediment to individual freedom.

While social closure seems arbitrary in these instances, they nevertheless point to the changing ways in which 'black' and 'white' identities are constituted. Not only are the students' senses of self being forged in these relations but also that of the teachers. I asked Eddie much later what he thought was meant by the male student's actions and he replied:

> What I mean is that I felt his affinity with the traditional was a reaction to his benefiting from a 'white' education. (Email 18/9/98)

So here is an interesting interpretation – one that recognises that the politics of essentialism, discussed in Chapter 4 (Pettman, 1992), is a consequence of collective solidarity. Eddie thinks the student recognises his own privilege and cultural capital in the face of others who have not had this good fortune. The problem becomes that it is expressed in terms of choices: black or white, traditional/non-traditional. Eddie read his actions as an association with the traditional when he could have been challenging the deracialised, privileging practices in the normative curriculum.

In this section, I have tried to tease out the ways in which individualising normative practices create tensions, which can elicit collective responses from students. In addition, I have shown how teacher educators use and question racialised collectivities. There were more tensions in AREP than NORTEP in this regard although not among the students as I will discuss in Chapter 9. For some reason they did not arise in the narratives of NORTEP staff. Perhaps in the next section it might be possible to find an explanation for this absence in their narratives when we talk about how culture is taken into account in the classrooms in both programs.

The collective/individual tension does produce change however, in the way in which programs are structured, assessed, delivered and resourced. Indeed, the collectivist nature of Indigenous politics and Indigenous education in both countries means that curriculum construction is a political process. A curriculum is constructed however, on the basis of some sense of outcome. What are the intended outcomes of Indigenous teacher education programs such as AREP and NORTEP? This leads to the next tension around cultural knowledge/disciplinary knowledge.

Cultural knowledge/disciplinary knowledge tension

> I remember a student did a paper on discipline techniques. She'd been learning about Glasser and reality therapy and that kind of stuff so she decided to investigate traditional Cree discipline techniques... and one of the conclusions she came up with, was that given traditionally they didn't have twenty kids in the classroom with one adult, that perhaps some of those techniques wouldn't work in a school situation. Maybe some would but she was 'iffy' on it because you've got to change the teaching context then. (Sandra: interview schedule)

We know why we have Indigenous teacher education programs, but what impact do we expect the graduates to have on Indigenous communities or the community in general? It seems to me that we need to think this through when making curriculum decisions. Sandra's comments suggest that the two worlds might be separate although she has provided space in the curriculum for this to be explored. Before discussing further the way in which teacher educators negotiated the curriculum at NORTEP and AREP, I want to briefly explore – in the minds of the teacher educators – why we need Indigenous teachers. This will help us understand their curriculum decisions and the contexts in which they occur.

Indigenous teachers as role models

> ... why we need teachers generally I guess. I think too, particularly in the country, we have a really important role to play. A role because there are so many communities that are dominated by Aboriginal people and other parts are dominated by a lot of racism... and I think it counteracts a lot of problems in rural areas. I think the teachers provide a good role model. I think they

understand the situations that children are in. (Julie: interview schedule)

One of the most common reasons given for having Indigenous teachers relates to the concept of 'role model'. In the quote above, the Aboriginal teacher is defined in terms of their empathy with children of the same 'race' or ethnicity. In addition, the presence of Aboriginal teachers will offset the negative attitudes in rural areas about Indigenous people. There is great store placed in 'role model' theory by the teacher educators in this study and it does have some purchase as Sandra at NORTEP, argues:

> You know when I taught grade two and we talked about growing up and what they would be there wasn't a concept that they could be teachers and nurses. Now kids have that concept that it's perfectly possible for aboriginal people. Those people went first; I mean that impact was terrific. Some of the students in the program right now are in the program because their mothers went here. (Sandra: interview schedule)

The relationship between role models and the success of future generations of Indigenous students is an interesting one. Certainly, many students have relatives who have told them about the programs. There is a weakness in 'role model' theory however, and that is its dependence on *voluntarism*.[8] The theory of voluntarism places a lot of faith in individual capacity, and consequently fails to appreciate the constraints upon agency. Conceptually, 'role model' theory is recognition of the relationship between social structure and how that may impact on students' personal formation. As Connell (1996:50) warns in relation to his discussion on gender, placing too much emphasis on the transformative possibilities of the Indigenous teacher as role model, risks dissolving structure into agency and doesn't take account of concrete social relations. In reality, 'role model' theory cannot explore the way in which the politics of identity in Indigenous education places a heavy load on the Indigenous teacher. In the AREP there is anecdotal evidence that oppressive situations in schools have led to resignations and even in one instance, to the suicide of a teacher. This is particularly evident where there was only one

---

[8] For a good discussion of the limitations of role theory particularly as it applies to gender, which I have drawn on for this discussion, see Connell (1996) pages 47-54.

Indigenous person on staff and they were called on to resolve 'all things Aboriginal' as well as combat racist practices among the staff.

Taking on the role of *Indigenous* teacher adds another dimension to role model theory. In a sense, all teachers are considered role models for the community in some way or another. But the added dimension of racialisation creates additional tensions. For some, this takes away the freedom, or some would argue luxury, to choose whether they want to identify as Indigenous. For others, it may involve a more overt and essentialised construction of identity. We can see this tension in a study by Friesen and Orr (1995). In an attempt to understand the lives of Indigenous teachers post-NORTEP, David Friesen and Geoff Orr carried out a study of northern aboriginal teachers in Saskatchewan and outlined a tentative schema for a *northern aboriginal teacher identity*. The teachers involved all demonstrated:

- The desire to live out their aboriginality in teaching – *pedagogical personality*
- The desire to model aboriginality for the students they teach – *pedagogical orientation*
- A commitment to including language and culture that is aboriginal in the curriculum – *political orientation*. (Friesen and Orr, 1995:5-6, Summary Report)

It is not surprising that the concept of 'model' appears in this schema. One of the goals of NORTEP is "to provide aboriginal role models for northern school children" (Carnegie, 1991:39). What is interesting here is the authors' use of the role model concept in terms of aboriginality. This differs somewhat from the sense that Julie used in her comments at the start of this section. Julie added another dimension to this concept through the idea that Indigenous teachers will be able to counteract many problems. Clearly, the role model concept helps in the construction of Indigenous teachers as activists. Part of the weakness of *the Indigenous teacher as role model* explanation, however, is that it is socially deterministic.

Using the Friesen and Orr study once more, we can examine some interesting competing paradigms in the teachers' voices that make taking on the role of Indigenous teacher complex. For example, in their study of the *pedagogic personality* of the participants, a dynamic model of aboriginality competes for space with their *political orientation*. The story of 'Ray' (Friesen and Orr, 1995:15-22) reveals this tension when he discusses the way in which culture is incorporated into the curriculum. The tension is between cultural maintenance via cultural camps in the curriculum (*political orientation*) and what he has actually practiced himself (*pedagogic personality*). Keeffe (1992) provides an interesting critique of 'culture camps' arguing that schools are more likely to focus on Aboriginality-as-persistence – associated with bush skills and other 'traditional' pursuits – than Aboriginality-as-resistance, which is more oppositional because it challenges racist stereotypes. However, while that may be a *political orientation*, Ray doesn't speak of his *pedagogic personality* as Indigenous:

> I had to be open-minded if I wanted to survive in both worlds. I took the good parts and the bad parts and I put them into one big pile and mixed them up. If you're not open-minded and you just have tunnel vision then you're not looking at what's happening on both sides. (Friesen and Orr, 1995:22)

The metaphor of "mixed them up" provides a strong picture of the almost impossible task of separating 'the worlds'. It is only when we actually try to separate them that we have to rely on fixed homogenising categories.

To summarise, role models as envisaged by teacher educators construct the Indigenous teacher firstly as an example of the norm, secondly as a cultural maintenance worker and lastly as an active, dynamic, cultural negotiator. It is possible to see all three constructions of 'the Indigenous teacher' in all the narratives of the teacher educators. Before moving onto the struggle over disciplinary knowledge, I will briefly outline the other major reasons given by the participants for having Indigenous teachers.

They included the idea that Indigenous teachers would be more likely to empathise and identify with children of their own cultural background by giving them a sense of belonging. A degree of support for this assertion is contained in the student narratives. Others argue that Indigenous teachers would help to counteract racism in the 'system'. It is this area where there is the least understanding about the degree of agency available to individual Indigenous teachers. We can see from these comments that racism is seen purely in terms of intersubjectivity. In Chapter 9 we can see the limits to this understanding in the area of language for example.

Those arguing from a liberal progressivist standpoint say that we need a 'mix' of teachers and that there should be a 'representative' population for any group. Again, a dependence on reading culture as closed renders continually constituted social and cultural relations as static. Given these particular understandings of why we need Indigenous teachers, it is important to examine the way in which these understandings structure the curriculum.

Creating Indigenous teachers

One of the key differences between NORTEP and AREP is that NORTEP graduates mainly gain employment in schools where there are high numbers of native students whereas AREP graduates teach in a range of contexts. While NORTEP is producing aboriginal graduates to teach in all schools – provincial and Band – its focus is on the north:

> I think without NORTEP there wouldn't be the pool of aboriginal teachers like there is in the north. In some schools the only teachers are NORTEP graduates. You also have ITEP and SUNTEP graduates and without those programs I don't think you'd have aboriginal teachers. Not too many are choosing to go through quote 'the regular' unquote, programs. (Sandra: interview schedule)

Sandra is arguing about the importance of separate programs and we can see that the general logic of her narrative is that 'different is better' rather than 'different is less than'. This is not surprising when you consider that such a philosophy is also located in the *Indian Control of Education* document (National Indian Brotherhood, 1972) and in the NORTEP's philosophy. However, the preference for separate programs is evident in both Australia and Canada. What is it about the separate experience that students might prefer according to the teaching staff?

> Well I think segregating them, is in a way providing them with some cotton wool. We are saying, not we, my views... "Look I don't think you have to put up with the crap in mainstream, from some mainstream kids, so I'm going to protect you for a while from that and get you educated as a qualified teacher." (Pat: 13, lines 2-6)

The 'crap' that Pat is speaking of relates to a range of concerns including 'soft oppressions' related to language (which I discuss below) and the constant need to justify the cultural knowledge that Indigenous students bring in to the curriculum (discussed in Chapter 9). Many of the teaching staff in these programs recognise that even in integrated university classrooms where the concept of dialogue across differences is promoted, there is the potential danger for students constantly having to 'tell their stories of oppression' (Jones, 1998) or alternatively remain invisible (students discuss this further in Chapter 9). As discussed in Chapter 7, the pedagogy of 'voice' has been shown in these instances to have a colonising *demand for narrative* (*ibid.*).

The separate nature of AREP and NORTEP create an interesting environment in which to teach. To understand the dimensions of this context, the teacher educators compared and contrasted their experiences of segregated and integrated classrooms. Marion recalls a situation where (for the first time) she saw Indigenous and non-Indigenous students separated in a school classroom. It created some confusion because she was worried that this separation was creating a 'ghetto'. This is quite interesting in view of the fact that it was occurring at a Catholic School – nobody talks about religious ghettos. It was a school however, where welfare workers had a close relationship with the school providing interagency collaboration. Aboriginal parents were coming, going, and learning to read. Both Marion and the student on practicum in this classroom observed very happy students:

> Now that feeling inside that classroom, I reckon it's the feeling we have inside AREP among the students, caring for each other. Collective caring, like the outpouring of happiness among that group that graduated this year. When they were all given their awards... in some sense they were all up there... (Marion: interview schedule)

Why would students be 'happier' in separate classes? In part, it is because the students at AREP and NORTEP are engaged in constructing a collective culture that is invigorating and supportive. One of the ways in which this occurs is through communication. In the following anecdote, Murray, a native studies and languages teacher at NORTEP, speaks about his own experiences in high school:

There were more white students. They would put down the aboriginal students when we used to give our presentations. For example, we used to get laughed at by the other students as well as the teacher. So, a lot of our aboriginal students quit talking after a while in the classroom and I was one of those. So when I first went... when I got my first degree I would chop those classes where I had to make an oral presentation and when I got my first real job I had a very difficult time talking to my colleagues as well as making presentations to the people. (Murray: interview schedule)

Utilising Bourdieu's notion of linguistic praxis, we can understand that as language is acquired, a *relation* to language is also acquired (cited in Grenfell and James, 1998:73). This realisation becomes particularly acute depending upon the linguistic *field* being produced. In the classroom, where Indigenous students are dominant, the linguistic field *may* be more similar to the students' linguistic *habitus*. Familiarity is a consequence of the interaction of habitus and field. The linguistic habitus being "those features of language, and consequent thoughts, individuals are disposed to have and acquire in the course of their upbringing and trajectories through life" (*ibid.*:74). One of the advantages of enclave programs is there is space to utilise one's linguistic habitus in the process of learning.

By contrast, and this has significance for the issues at hand, is that linguistic field is "structured in terms of positions and relations within it, which values and revalues features of language as an expression of social differentiation" (*ibid.*:74). Murray and Marie at NORTEP actively engage with the relationship between the linguistic habitus of their students and the linguistic field. Since both are aware of the relationship between language and cultural knowledge, they are actively developing a curriculum that responds to the cultural knowledge that students bring into the program.

Murray is committed to the maintenance and on-going curriculum development of the Cree language at NORTEP:

One of our concerns in that area as it comes to language... If you're a teacher of an aboriginal language especially the Cree or Dene, you're pretty well on your own. You develop your curriculum, you develop your materials and whatever support you have, you have to develop it yourself. You have to phone other teachers to see what they're doing in certain areas so in many ways you know we're duplicating our efforts. (Murray: interview schedule)

Murray and Marie are working at the difficult edge of heritage language revival and maintenance in Saskatchewan. There are a number of Indigenous languages on the critical list (Saskatchewan Indigenous Languages Committee, 1991) and so there is a sense that the task is urgent. Marie speaks about what this means for her teaching practices:

> Yeah, like how I can present this and make the difference so that I can inspire them so that when they go back to their community they will talk about the language with the communities. It has to come from the community and the family is also important and then something can be done. It's been proven that school alone cannot revive the language. (Marie: interview schedule)

So there is a sense of partnership in NORTEP's relationship with communities in the north. There is an articulation of the curriculum with the communities in which students will later be teaching.

The experiences of Murray and Marie can be compared with that of Charles, a non-Indigenous teacher educator at AREP, who is primarily concerned with school based experiences and developmental psychology. In terms of language, there is a different issue, this time in relation to standard English.

> I know our students can be criticised at times... and *are* criticised by the regular teaching staffs in the schools that they go to, for an inability to put together a few simple sentences, punctuate appropriately and that sort of thing. Orally I think our students get away with it pretty well. In fact the students in the class like to hear Koori talk. I don't think there's any problem there at all in an oral form. (Charles: interview schedule)

Yet in other circumstances, Koori talk does not receive such an open and accepting audience. In my own professional work, I have personally dealt with lecturers and school staff who have been dissatisfied with 'non-standard' English. One principal even commented that it was no good having teachers speak the same way as the children! Clearly, linguistic habitus does count in the construction of an Indigenous teacher in this context.

In another example, I had a group of students come to see me regarding what they believed as unfair marking processes on the basis of Aboriginal English. A student gave a seminar in Aboriginal English as a demonstration of how to best interact with Koori kindergarten children in an Aboriginal only preschool. The student was marked down for her use of Aboriginal English. Cultural knowledge in this instance was compared with disciplinary knowledge (of 'proper' English) and found wanting.

Communication styles are part of identity and it is around the issue of literacy that most normative practices are centred. It is not just a matter of how language is spoken because meanings are also different. As Eades (1993:3) put it: "Differences are found in all aspects of language: i.e. phonology (or accent and pronunciation), morpho-syntax (or grammar), lexico-semantics (or words and their meaning), and pragmatics (or the way that language is used in socio-cultural contexts)."

One of the differences then between NORTEP and AREP is a different focus on language. Interestingly, or perhaps more predictably, 'broken' English as staff and students at NORTEP call it, is not seen as a functioning dialect of English. This is a consequence of the concentration on heritage languages such as Cree and Dene. In NSW Indigenous languages have only recently gained support through a maintenance and revival program. The Bandjulang and Wiradjuri languages are documented, and a few other smaller dialects are currently being researched.

This differential attention to linguistic diversity and linguistic habitus impacts in other ways on teaching practices. In general, NORTEP's language and communication processes in their teaching relationships concentrate quite strongly on maintaining a system of participatory, democratic communication. Classroom dynamics are also different in the sense that NORTEP classes intentionally use talking 'circles' based on 'traditional' communication processes where everyone has a say in turn. This philosophy extends into the way in which the curriculum is structured as well as teaching relationships and curriculum content. To begin, the curriculum is structured in an innovative way:

> ... you see there's something sacrosanct about this, 'we are offering courses at 3 hours a week' and if you are doing something different it has to be inferior... [Our students] like having the same

> class of math from nine to three thirty because we get thoroughly immersed in it. (Sandra: interview schedule)

At NORTEP, students are immersed in one subject at a time and complete it much faster. Some subjects run for a week and others for three weeks. The subjects connect to their field placement where they go out and test what they have learned in the classroom. There is a constant process of input, reflection and feedback for the students and staff:

> ... we call it 'the professional development process' which is basically a learning cycle. We try something and get feedback and make changes as a result of that feedback. (Sandra: interview schedule)

We can see the NORTEP philosophy of democratic participation yields a fundamentally different program structure. If we compare that to AREP it is possible to see how the structure of the AREP program and its concern for equivalence as sameness, stalls any real attempts at change:

> ... with AREP right from the outset there was this pretty firm sort of requirement that you didn't sort of teach a different course because they were Aboriginal students. You taught the same course as the mainstream students were learning, but you obviously tried to adapt the delivery of it to the requirements of the students. (Eddie: interview schedule)

AREP still run traditional classes of 3 hours face-to-face or the equivalent in mixed mode delivery and students will study all the subjects that they are enrolled in during a single residential. The same course uncritically delivered is what AREP students commonly resist and challenge. In contrast, NORTEP values student input and feedback and uses this knowledge to make changes:

> Oh yes, and you encourage them to intellectually challenge you. You have academic freedom, so do they. (Sandra: interview schedule)

There is a strong connection between the schools and communities that NORTEP graduates will serve and NORTEP itself has representatives of these bodies on their board of governors. This means that curriculum decisions are made with particular communities in mind. Pedagogically this has an impact on curriculum decisions and methods.

Cultural knowledge and disciplinary knowledge stand in relation to each other – rather than separate – through a language of critique, challenge and transformation. AREP on the other hand is not connected to particular regions or school communities and operates as a loose collective of teacher educators.

In this context we could argue that pedagogy is more about regulation (Gore, 1993) than critique and knowledge production. Yet, although the language of critique and reflection is not institutionalised at AREP, the separate nature of the program provides space for it to occur:

> I did feel that with AREP, students would stop me at any time and make me go back and explain it... and try... and if I wasn't making it relevant or if they couldn't see the context from it, they would make me do that. I found that a bit challenging to start with but really it did improve my teaching, of them particularly. (Marilyn: interview schedule)

> ... you are constantly being challenged about what you're thinking, what you're saying, what you're doing. (Simone: interview schedule)

This might be what one would expect from university classrooms, yet it does not often occur in teacher education courses in the 'mainstream', at least not in Australia. There is much more acceptance of the status quo and a closer identification with the hegemony of the curriculum by full time students according to our teacher educators. The linguistic habitus of AREP classrooms do provide a different style of interaction according to AREP teacher educators. They claim that while it is challenging it is also somewhat more relaxed and informal. Classes are generally smaller in both programs than in the mainstream enabling more opportunities for communication and breaking down of power relations. Julie explains how this happens:

> ... Just a... really playing on words. Simple, making fun of lots of simple things that you're doing... (Julie: interview schedule)

In summary, NORTEP is producing Indigenous teachers in ways that articulate with the demands of community, in terms of the 'north', and with regard to the original philosophical standpoint of the *Indian Control of Indian Education* document. This isn't a unitary process; it is dynamic and critical. Sandra's quote at the beginning of this section highlights a particular way of viewing the curriculum. In asking students to contest the hegemony of positivist pedagogical regimes in teacher education (Gore, 1993:3), she is making visible knowledge that is produced by particular social interests. It is this active questioning of the institutionalised practices and theories in teacher education – rather than just negotiating the curriculum – which has the potential to be liberating. In other words, negotiation is *part* of the process of transforming curriculum. To engage actively in transforming pedagogy requires an unsettling of *regimes of truth* in teacher education (Gore, 1993:143). In addition, the reification of 'traditional' ways of knowing and doing is unpacked enabling students to see through the logic of culturalist challenges to the curriculum. An example of this is Murray's response to the limitations of just focussing on tradition:

> [I like to give students] contemporary issues because I think it's important to understand… that something that happens in BC – a court case – might have implications for Saskatchewan. So I try to make them see these kinds of connections. (Murray: interview schedule)

The shift to studying contemporary issues has also occurred in AREP. Outside of studies on racism, community issues and representation, the mainstream teacher education subjects have also been substantially reworked to make them more contextualised but this tends to be approached via a broad perspective rather than being based on cultural knowledge local to the regions and schools in which they are living and will be working.

NORTEP has been able to break down some aspects of the curriculum that have been considered hegemonic – the compartmentalised, authoritative nature of the standard curriculum. In this sense there is an active engagement between cultural knowledge and disciplinary knowledge. AREP has provided a particularly strong 'cultural studies' component that opens up students to a language of critique, but it does not follow this through with its approach to teaching methods and theory. There is recognition of the potential for AREP students to be 'organic intellectuals' but this is not made explicit. An example of this cultural knowledge, in terms of AREP students, is expressed by Pat:

> I know what else was good in that ... class was that I didn't have to go through all the cultural stuff with them because they understood it. You know what it's like to come from a different cultural background. All those things that I had to deal with mainstream students and talk about changing cultures and the impact of culture on language. (Pat: interview schedule)

With a less rigid curriculum in place in AREP Pat may have been able to explore the dynamics of the students' cultural knowledge and have the students gain a sense of the knowledge that they already had, and on which they could build new knowledge that was really useful for their particular contexts.

There is a sense that cultural knowledge is being used much more at NORTEP rather than being seen as an impediment or just as a perspective type of resource as is the case in AREP. By this I mean that NORTEP investigated community needs and responded to them rather than try to 'adapt', in culturalist ways, a curriculum designed for full time urban-based students. In addition, NORTEP is making connections across disciplinary boundaries, creating a richer curriculum and one that leads students to see the connections and therefore the purpose of knowledge.

Conclusion

In this chapter, I have attempted to demonstrate that teacher educators learn about, and negotiate, cultural difference in pedagogical relationships shaped by the field of Indigenous education. The contradictory nature of this racialised field leads to a politics of identity within the pedagogical relationships at NORTEP and AREP. There is at the one moment reproduction of racialised identities – emanating from the 'separate' nature of the programs – and a challenge to their reproduction by focussing away and looking at pedagogical regimes that are institutionally legitimated. Key differences in the way in which these contingencies were responded to relate to the philosophical and structural differences in each program.

We need to remind ourselves that NORTEP's origins emanated from the document *Indian Control of Indian Education*. Its mandate was to serve a specific geographical region with a fairly autonomous structure. It is also governed by, and has input from, Indigenous as well as non-Indigenous people. This means that there are some creative and productive debates about the place of culture in Indigenous education in Canada. A little vignette demonstrates this type of interaction very nicely:

> Some years ago we had six on faculty, three aboriginal, three non-aboriginal and we had this thing going... about who talked the most at staff meetings. Now I'm one of them right? I talk a lot. So... one person claimed it was an aboriginal/non-aboriginal breakdown and another person maintained it wasn't. So one fella said, "I'm going to keep tabs. Next faculty meeting I'm going to record who talks." And he did. You couldn't break it down into aboriginality... it didn't break down that way. There are talkers and non-talkers. (Sandra: interview schedule)

In contrast, the AREP was produced from the NAEC (1986) document calling for *1000 teachers by 1990*. Rather than an autonomous program, it was linked to the full time program designed for non-Indigenous students preparing to teach in metropolitan Sydney. It never developed its own philosophy. The fact that rural Indigenous students are studying at a metropolitan university quite removed from the reality of their future teaching lives is also significant. Nevertheless, AREP staff and students have also negotiated the curriculum so that it is more responsive, although these structural arrangements severely limit the degree to which the program can take account of cultural knowledge.

AREP and NORTEP share one similarity. The separate nature of the programs seemed to provide a different linguistic praxis that teacher educators found important in the development of Indigenous teaching identities. For example, the pedagogy of voice (whereby students have to address their cultural difference in ways which non-Indigenous students demand – i.e. stories of oppression) is largely absent in AREP and NORTEP. This means that there are narratives of agency: that is, a focus on what is being done and what could be done to improve outcomes for all children but specifically Indigenous children.

The teacher educators presented in this chapter are generally open to the contribution of students but are shaped by institutional arrangements. In addition, they have an attachment to cultural technologies that are used for the purpose of individuation. Often, tensions arise from the process of negotiating what it is about these normative cultural technologies that is lacking when attending to cultural difference. In this chapter, a comparison between NORTEP and AREP has revealed how a more open, democratic and wider community-based input might contribute to a process that enables an active engagement with cultural knowledge in Indigenous teacher education courses. In this way culture is more likely to be negotiated rather than 'read off'.

In the next chapter, there is an exploration of the reasons why students chose the NORTEP and AREP rather than any other teacher education program. It will then be possible to compare and contrast the teacher educators' constructions of Indigenous teaching identities with that of the students themselves. In addition, the chapter explores the impact of the AREP and NORTEP programs upon the students and their plans for the future.

Chapter 9
Un/Becoming an Indigenous Teacher

> And my son is so proud. He comes home and tells all his friends,
> "my mum's a teacher", and that's just like wow eh? And he told
> me the other day: "You know what mum?"... and I said "What?",
> and he said: "I'm going to be a teacher too." I'm like oh... and
> things just like that make your heart burst with joy sometimes.
> (Lucy-Anne: interview transcript)

Introduction

In this chapter I will be exploring the process of becoming an
Indigenous teacher and, paradoxically, about unbecoming an
Indigenous teacher. This will be done through an examination of the
relationship between the individual habitus of the students and the
field of Indigenous education. For example, both the Australian and
Canadian programs include practices that actively seek to address
negative constructions of aboriginality. In so doing, the students'
aboriginality is being constituted at the same time that they are being
produced as teachers. There is some tension in this process for the
students in terms of their own cultural understandings, in the ways in
which they remember the formation of their cultural self and how that
is expressed in relation to their future as teachers. This is a tension
between their *collective* and *individual* identity. As the students learn
about becoming autonomous professionals, they reflect on communal
and familial influences and practices. This can create another tension
between *family* and *study*. Both tensions emanate from a reframing of
students' Indigenous identities and the emergence of a professional
identity.

The informal and formal requirements of them as identified future
Indigenous teachers create a tension between their roles as
professionals and cultural knowledge workers and producers. Since
cultural knowledge and understanding is one of the reasons that

Indigenous teachers are desired, it becomes important to know how cultural knowledge is understood in relation to professional requirements. If Indigenous teachers are meant to make a difference, we need to know how. The students at NORTEP and AREP have gained cultural knowledge as a consequence of their individual habitus. This knowledge is related to informal processes and therefore emanates from culture-as-practice, and from formal processes such as Indigenous educational networks. This knowledge is more in keeping with the idea of culture-as-resource. However, it is the identity of teacher, and the enculturation of students into an *Indigenous* teacher identity, which is the principal contradiction. The final section of this chapter explores this contradiction through the politics of teaching for Indigenous teacher education students.

We can understand teacher formation using Bourdieu's concept of cultural capital. The sorts of cultural capital required in becoming a teacher can be learned, but in the process, this often means *un/becoming* an *Indigenous* teacher in the first instance. The quote from an AREP student about assimilation at the start of Chapter 8 is challenging this tendency. Often theory that is used in teacher education has been predicated on ethnic exclusions (Chow cited in Gunew, n.d.). That is, the universalistic approach to teacher education – as if all student teachers were the same – ignores the different historically constituted cultural and social identities of students (Hesch, 1993). Too often, the competencies and standards required to become a teacher veil assimilationist practices. It is as if competencies and standards were somehow neutral or given, and not open to scrutiny. Indeed, the cultural understandings that students have in the form of a practical ideology (Hesch, 1993:261) is often seen as an impediment while other forms of cultural knowledge are given legitimacy. This leads to a *universal/indigenist* tension centred on pedagogy and, more specifically, the curriculum. To explicate this tension in the final section of this chapter, I will discuss the politics of teaching in terms of the formation of students' teaching identities; and examine their attachment to schooling and the pedagogical understandings they are developing.

In summary, this chapter will explore the complexity of identities that students in AREP and NORTEP bring to teaching and the ways in which these shape and are shaped by institutional arrangements in the field of Indigenous education. Issues here include the mode of study and its impact on family and community life; the curriculum and its relationship to Indigenous cultural knowledge; and finally, the development of a teaching identity and how that relates to constructions of community.

Identities and the student participants

The relationship between the teaching and cultural identities of students at NORTEP and AREP forms the focus of this chapter. Throughout my interviews with the students their self-identification as Indigenous was a common theme, just as it was for management and teaching staff who self-identified as (mainly) non-Indigenous. Students' stories often revealed narratives of triumph over adversity. They were not simple deracialised discourses of individual triumph, but a complex interweaving of individual struggle constrained and facilitated by social relations rooted in historical conditions. Alongside aboriginality or ethnicity, gender, geography and age were also social relations that constituted identity. In addition, the students were beginning to articulate an identity as teacher.

Becoming a teacher for most of the students meant identifying as aboriginal or, in the case of Henrietta who was non-Indigenous, identifying as a northerner. These are the conditions contained in each program's principles of operation. Students who join AREP and NORTEP may in a sense be demonstrating an "attitude of resistance to power" (Carleton, 1994:4). This is because in the process of identifying as Indigenous – or a northerner – student teachers may be presenting oppositional teaching personas. That is, the universal teacher – based on ethnic exclusions – is thrown into question and with it comes a potential for a revisiting and questioning of theories and practices that are valued and protected by professional gatekeepers, but which contribute to inequitable outcomes for Indigenous students.

A total of 16 students were interviewed individually. Table 9.1 shows the breakdown of interviewees by program, gender, 'ethnic' identity, age and year of study. A number of students identified themselves in a number of ways. While some used group identities – such as when an AREP student said that she was Wiradjuri – and others called themselves Koories, all used the term Aboriginal. NORTEP students identified as a group such as Cree, Dene, Northerner or Métis as well as their legal status, namely Treaty, Status, Bill C31 or non-Status.

211

Table 9.1

Breakdown of interviewees by program, ethnicity, age and year of study

AREP	Aboriginal	5 in their 20s	3 final year
n = 2 males, 6 females	1 metropolitan	3 middle-aged	5 third or fourth year
	7 rural		
NORTEP	3 Métis	6 in their 20s	1 final year
n = 1 male, 7 females	3 Status – 1 Treaty	1 in 30s	1 first year
	2 Bill C31	1 middle-aged	6 second or third year
	1 Dene – non-Status		
	1 Northerner – 'white'		

The first area of tension for our student teachers, which reflects the differing spatial realities of students in these two programs, was the tension between family commitments and wider social responsibilities and the requirements of study. It is important to remember that unlike full time students in metropolitan areas, students at NORTEP and AREP have to travel to their institutions for block instruction and then return to field experience or home to study. They are either placed at a distance from their families, or – when back at home – a distance from support structures such as libraries, academic personnel and each other.

Family/study tension

> I don't know, the impact is kind of… in the first weeks I was here my heart was so sore because I missed my baby so much. (Lucy-Anne: interview transcript)

All except one of the male students (from NORTEP) were parents at the time of interviewing. This characteristic is not different from many students in adult education but teacher training is generally not viewed as adult education. NORTEP has attempted to address the fact that their students were mainly adults working in schools by implementing principles of androgogy in teaching and learning (Carnegie, 1991). Despite this, the social and cultural contexts of the students' education create a tension between the demands of home and the requirements of study.

While NORTEP has tried to reduce these tensions structurally through their field-based course – which is largely in home communities – there is still a high degree of stress evident in the student narratives. If students cannot resolve these tensions, they discontinue (two of the AREP students for example, have discontinued since the interviews were carried out). In the process of resolving tensions, familial and community contexts are compared and contrasted with what is considered desirable in terms of positivist pedagogical paradigms.

Positivist pedagogical paradigms neglect experiences and questions which are not observable or measurable (Williams, 1988:239). When this is combined with normative principles in education – outlining what should be done to fit into positivist pedagogical regimes – we end up with some familiar ideas about how 'good learning' is achieved. The accessibility of a 'quiet space' to work, the idea of isolated learning and the development of appropriate attitudes to learning are taken "as given rather than as products of the relation between different power and cultural groups" (Bredo and Feinberg, 1979:322). When we examine the students' reasons for continuing or coming back to education, it is possible to see the relationship between culture and differential power in terms of educational opportunities, and material and social disadvantage.

Gender

I have chosen gender as one lens through which to examine students' relationships to NORTEP and AREP. It was common for the women in this project to speak as mothers and/or women when they discussed their reasons for returning to, or continuing, education. Evident in these narratives is the continuation of hegemonic gender relations within teaching through the notion of nurturing and looking after future generations. When this is set alongside the male narratives, the segmented/spatial nature of the labour forces – gendered and regional – is highlighted. For the male students, there was the opportunity to enter government-controlled institutions such as policing and teaching. That is, for males who were attached to education in positive ways, there was opportunity in professions where role models were considered necessary and Indigenous input was sought.

Young women

A group of students including two at AREP (Debbie and Rita) and two at NORTEP (Lucy-Anne and Henrietta) were teenage mothers. This did not present a problem in terms of their families. Indeed they were generally supportive. However, the desire for 'something better for

213

themselves and their children' was a driving force in returning to study.

One of the young mothers – Lucy-Anne – was at the end of her first year at NORTEP when we met. She had a small son aged four who was born while she was still at high school in a predominately Métis community. Lucy-Anne returned to school to do her final year from which she graduated, and was a valedictorian, in 1992:

> I actually came back to school... It had a lot to do with him and a lot to do with me. I just felt that in the north... like the population there of young teenage mothers has increased over the years... and I just don't want to be put in a stereotype of having this put on you... and *'this is what you are going to be when you grow up'* ... and when you grow up you sit at home and watch your kid. I'm a single parent and I just didn't want that for myself and I wanted more for my son. (Lucy-Anne: interview schedule)

Lucy-Anne was sensitive to the negative constructions associated with gender and aboriginality and wanted to provide a different future for herself and her son. Since the birth of her son meant only a brief interruption to schooling, she was able to graduate. Throughout our discussion she demonstrated acute awareness of what was required to succeed in education and in life in general. The culture of schooling at her predominately Métis high school corresponded with the strict, yet supportive religious background in her home life. Lucy-Anne's positive attachment to schooling had provided her with rewards. However, it was stressful at times for all the students when they had to attend to family and study concerns simultaneously:

> Then when you get home and you have families you've got this and that to take care of plus your kids or your children then you have homework... like this is due for this class, this is due for this class and which one do I work on? Like you have to juggle that... (Lucy-Anne: interview schedule)

Another student, Rita, left school early although she enjoyed her schooling experience. Her reasons for coming to AREP were motivated by a concern for her children and the fact that her mother hadn't received an education. Rita, from the northwest of NSW, was more explicit about the relationship between the knowledge that can be gained from her course and the way in which power can be accessed in the dominant society:

> As an Aboriginal parent I didn't want to be intimidated. So therefore once I get my knowledge, I can go into these institutions and look up the curriculum and their programming, and find out what is best to suit my children's education, and then weigh it up from there. Because I think that a lot of parents don't tend to look [at it] that way... they only send their children to certain schools because of peer group pressure and so forth. (Rita: interview schedule)

This points to the liberatory aspects of education for individual students. In fact, Rita had already begun to distance herself from the community and intended to leave her area when she had finished her degree. She argued that there had been too many problems in her community and she had seen children fail to succeed and eventually find no employment. Nevertheless, although Rita was determined to complete her studies it was not easy because she lacked control over the social context in which her family lived. Illness and childcare issues were a source of anxiety:

> I believe too that we are only down here on borrowed time, just in case an emergency pops up back in our hometown. We've actually got to fly back there. That's why I like to try and keep on top all the time. (Rita: interview schedule)

Hesch argues that in his study of SUNTEP teacher education students, backgrounds such as these provided students with the knowledge and practices to make a difference in the education of Indigenous children. He called this their 'practical ideology':

> It is an ideology which includes the influence of a self-conscious aboriginal subjectivity. The discourse includes sufficient 'flashes' of good sense to support a position that SUNTEP has the potential to produce transformative intellectuals. (Hesch, 1993:237-38)

But as we can see in the case of Rita, systemic inequalities are often overwhelming. In addition, this practical, living cultural knowledge is rarely harnessed because of empiricist and positivist approaches to teacher education (Hesch, 1993). For example, despite

215

the hard work that many students put into their studies, the communities that they live in are often severely affected by poverty, unemployment and substance abuse. Classroom research, which merely looks at interaction or the micro-political aspects of teaching, often ignores these social conditions. This empiricism creates issues for the curriculum, as we shall see later.

For Lucy-Anne and Rita, teacher education holds the promise of alternative futures through the provision of choice for their children and themselves. For Henrietta – a non-Indigenous northerner – coming to NORTEP was also the best possible way to provide a future. As a northerner, Henrietta feels that the program ought to be for all people living in the north. Her own situation mirrors, to some extent, that of native students from the north. She is a single mother struggling financially, but with a different relationship to the north. Her family history does not speak of racism but of the colonisers and the role they played in 'developing' the north. After Henrietta applied to NORTEP for four years in a row, she was accepted. The affirmative action policy at NORTEP was the reason she missed out but she kept on applying knowing that a cousin had managed to get in previously. As one of six children, her family would have found paying for an education 'down south' almost impossible.

Henrietta was a good student at school in her predominately white northern town of Creighton. She felt that she had good teachers during school and now at NORTEP. Henrietta's positive association with schooling means that she has internalised particular attitudes and values (hidden curriculum) that are required to continue and complete education. Like Lucy-Anne, she knows the cultural capital to be gained through education is worth the struggle even though it is difficult to be a student and a single parent.

> It's hard because I miss her [when I leave her with my parents] but it's also better 'cos I'm less stressed out and I don't end up... I find lots of times if I get really stressed I start yelling you know at little things that she's doing (Henrietta: interview schedule)

What was interesting about Henrietta, was that there was another dimension to the family/study tension centred around her identity – as a white northerner. For example, she talked about the fact that 'race' had never been an issue in her life until coming to NORTEP. This new knowledge led her to speak of her educational experiences in contrast to the experiences of some of the Indigenous students at NORTEP:

> They were supportive of my cultural background [at school] because I was majority there (Henrietta: interview schedule).

> I mean I always knew that racism was a harmful thing [but] until you experience it you never really realise the full impact of what it can do to you and sometimes it makes me sad and sometimes it just makes me mad. (Henrietta: interview schedule)

We can recall Eric's comments in Chapter 7, where he suggested that it was useful to have non-Indigenous students at NORTEP because they could help turn around the thinking in some northern communities. Henrietta's experiences of racism refer to some aspects of the course at NORTEP and to some experiences in the town of La Ronge when Henrietta entered an Indigenous-owned premise. Realising that she was part of the dominant culture also occurred when she was excluded from the program based on her ethnicity. In addition, a native studies lecturer who used to work at NORTEP (and who is not part of this study) had some difficulties in dealing with a non-Indigenous student:

> I felt they were really racist against me. They were native teachers and I heard a lot of, you know... white people did this to us and hate the white people sort of thing. But... it carried into after class and staff. One instructor in particular, it was like he didn't even want to greet me. He just didn't seem to want me around at all. (Henrietta: interview schedule)

This was a very interesting tension and will become an important issue for curriculum development in both programs as the Indigenous students in this chapter also raise some of these concerns. Therefore, for Henrietta, studying away from home involved an additional dimension of tension because the program at NORTEP had a major focus on Indigenous student identity.

For all of the four young mothers there was a common class dimension. In smaller towns and communities teachers enter into class relations with locals. Often teaching is a "means of upward mobility from the working class" (Connell, 1985:158). The students' class relations are evident in the fact that many are lacking in financial resources. Often, they rely on family networks to provide support – although male partners have not always been a source. Often, marriages and relationships end during the time that students are studying. There is a *politics of resentment* that occurs from male partners when women achieve educational success and gain independence outside the relationship. Debbie, an AREP student commented:

> I've had no support from the fella that I live with. No support whatsoever. I think that's why I'm determined to get through this and become a teacher, because he just couldn't care less, and that's made it really hard for me. (Debbie: interview schedule)

Since her partner was not supportive, the support of her family was critical. Indeed, it always had been. Debbie's path to teaching was interrupted when she left high school a few weeks before the end of Year 12 to give birth to her son. Her family had sacrificed quite a bit to see their children gain an education. Her older brother was the first in the family to gain a degree and he asked his friends when they graduated to keep an eye out for his siblings. Debbie's mother played golf with the teachers and they often visited her home. It seemed natural, she said, that teaching would be a first choice especially since they encouraged her at school and home. In fact there was a process of *recruitment* (Connell, 1985:158) evident in several of the students' narratives. The process of recruitment, Connell argued, meant that teachers select students with whom they identify, often of a similar disposition, and encourage them to take up teaching. Social relationships spatially inscribed through race, place, class and gender give a "sense of identity of interest" (Connell, 1985:159).

The women in this study, like the four women above, articulated a desire for knowledge that would be useful for themselves and particularly their children's futures. Encouragement to continue education and become teachers was rooted in family networks and positive association with schooling. The tension between family and study was therefore constituted by these relationships which are contradictory. That is, family networks often provide support but are also the source of stress. This was in addition to the difficulty of leaving home and family for regular periods.

I have focussed on all the women above because, as they were young, they were increasingly the majority in these programs. Clearly, the programs' student populations were shifting from older women to younger men and women. The added dimension of non-Indigenous students at NORTEP also highlights some issues for future discussion. Pedagogical assumptions based on the experiences of previous generations will need to shift to accommodate changing student demographics. In this sense, AREP and NORTEP face the same issues of relevance that all institutions face.

Young men

There is also resentment when education becomes a marker of success and failure within the family. Brian, a Treaty or Status Indian student, has found that education means mobility. He changed school a few times during high school, firstly because his Band had sacked a couple of his favourite teachers at the reserve school and secondly because he needed to change schools to go on to Grade 12. He lived with an 'adoptive family' on another reservation since he found them more supportive of his goals. Brian had just finished his second year and originally wanted to join the Royal Canadian Mounted Police (RCMP)[1] but was considered too young when he applied at the age of 19. His high school marks weren't that great so he tried a few times and finally got accepted into NORTEP. He reflected on his relationship with his mother in particular when asked about family support for his studies:

> My mother went for her teacher training a few years ago but didn't succeed. Well actually she was a teacher aide, teacher associate. She got fired from that... uh it was so many years ago... when I came here she tried everything to discourage me. My mother and I don't have much of a mother-son relationship. (Brian: interview schedule)

There was a tension here that came and went during the interview around family and identity. Brian indicated he really wanted a career in the RCMP. Given the high rates of incarceration on reserves

---

[1] "The idea for a mounted police force to bring order to the frontier west was originally proposed by Sir John A. Macdonald, Canada's first prime minister. Mindful of the violence which had accompanied westward expansion in the United States, Macdonald conceived of a force of mounted police whose primary responsibility was to establish friendly relations with the Aboriginal Peoples and to maintain the peace as the settlers arrived". http://www.rcmp-grc.gc.ca/html/125news.htm

(Frideres, 1988), a career with the RCMP could be seen as problematic in the context of reserve life. However, the history of the RCMP in Canada, particularly in Saskatchewan, is more complex. The RCMP's national museum in Regina, Saskatchewan, showcases the long and constructive – though contradictory – relationship it has had with Indigenous groups, particularly in the Prairie Provinces.

This different familial and community history has made Brian a little more hesitant to accept any homogenising representations of 'Indianness'. Indeed, he used humour to dispel some of the myths such as the comment that "I don't really drink coffee in the evenings. I drink tea... that's part of my European blood" [wry smile]. (Brian: 4, lines 39-40). Brian's political awareness has been honed in the politically active habitus of Band controlled reserve life. In the final section of this chapter, we examine what Indian control of education meant for Brian and how that led him to question some of the truisms of his elders. Generational differences as well as a developing sense of being a professional have created more tensions for Brian.

In the narratives of the female students in this study, there was commonly a desire to teach in order to nurture and 'bring up' children proud of their heritage. For males, teaching was secondary to a career which was seen as more masculine – the police force. With Tom, we can see how this choice may have been influenced by historical forces such as affirmative action policies of governments, as well as the educational and employment focus for aboriginal peoples in the social services:

> Well in Year 11 and 12, they bring out Careers Advisers and the Police Force was one idea. I actually worked in the Department of Social Security in a traineeship at the end of my HSC, and hoped to come to AREP. I could've stayed in the Department of Social Security I suppose, earning good money. That's the choices you make. I was pretty lost I suppose. (Tom: interview schedule)

The segmented nature of the labour force in regional areas is reflected in these differing opportunities for men and women. However, in the end it is family *networks*, part of the social capital produced by habitus, that has led Tom to teaching. Indeed, for all the students, networks within their family or community, as well as an often-stated positive attachment to schooling, has led them to teaching. Connell has called this path to teaching the *push or pull* factor (1985:157), and by examining Tom's pathway we can see how this informal process is another significant factor in the decision to teach.

Tom was like many students in the two programs who had relatives that had completed AREP or NORTEP. In this case it was his sister who took him to a residential "to have a look". After coming to a residential and sitting in on classes Tom liked what he saw, especially the fact that Indigenous students were together studying, as well as the reputation of the program:

> I'm quite proud to say I'm doing AREP. It's got a good name about it. It's well known. It's recognised and respected. It's been going for 16 years I suppose. (Tom: interview schedule)

The *push or pull* factor could be called networks of aboriginality, but Henrietta also found family networks via the experiences of a cousin a pull factor. NORTEP and AREP are similar in this sense and both have a good reputation among the students for providing a solid and useful professional qualification as well as creating a collective and strong sense of identity. Since neither program advertises itself widely, nor are they attached to prestigious institutions, these networks are the source of student enrolments.

However, although Tom knew what the program looked like from the perspective of an observer, he did not know about the isolated nature of learning in this mode. These factors really are important elements in students' success or failure:

> The worse part is when you go home to your own community, because I haven't really got anyone to speak to [about] what I do at University. Because my wife – she actually wants to help but she doesn't know what I'm doing. I hardly know what I'm doing. Like I can't sit down and talk the academic jargon that I talk here. She tries to help... she tries her best. There is really not much support back at home. That's the worse part I suppose. (interview schedule)

There is a kind of malaise that develops in the early stages of the students' degrees. This decreases as they develop supportive relationships with fellow students and when they begin to find some sort of sense of what they can contribute when they have finished. Tom says he had no idea in his first year what he was doing in the

221

AREP given his isolation back home. All the students found the first year of study extremely difficult.

We can see from this discussion of Lucy-Anne, Rita, Henrietta, Debbie, Tom and Brian that family and community networks were the source of connections to AREP and NORTEP while at the same time creating tensions for them in terms of their responsibilities. To succeed they have to develop behaviours, attitudes and skills required for careers in teaching. In Connell's (1982) *Making the Difference*, the sort of cultural capital that schools value *corresponds* with the hegemonic curriculum – that is, individualistic, competitive and academic. While it is not being suggested here that our NORTEP and AREP students embody these characteristics, their very survival in the course requires that they at least approximate these criteria. Yet, there is another dimension to the students' lives, that of racialisation, which makes it difficult to sustain a detached self and points to the centrality of belonging as part of identity (Griffiths, 1993). This is once more a tension about individual/collective identity beyond the family.

Collectivist/individualist tension

In this section, there is an exploration of the students' sense of community. This is done through an analysis of the ways in which students acknowledge their collectivities as part of their sense of identity and specifically the way in which this articulates with their developing Indigenous teaching identity.

Some of the students expressed a sense of their collective identity through colour. The visibility or invisibility of 'whiteness' in the student narratives is interesting for the way in which it throws up examples of power in diverse ways. Being 'whitefella', or having attributes deemed 'white', could be related to cultural prescriptions or traditions and/or appearance. When Lucy-Anne is explaining why she thinks being a *native* teacher is important, she consciously expresses her reasons in relation to, indeed opposition to, whiteness:

> 'Cos I know what the kids go through in school like... Sometimes they get... I don't know, they feel inferior sometimes when white people come in and they feel like they don't understand because a lot of native people have backgrounds... like tough backgrounds where abuse is really high and pregnancy. (Lucy-Anne: interview transcript)

Here Lucy-Anne is referring to 'whiteness' as a mark of the other's lack of understanding or privilege and therefore continuing 'soft' role of oppressor. However, the whiteness of the other is not because of *essential* differences. The embodiment of racialised inequality in the form of 'tough backgrounds, abuse and teenage pregnancy' is an historicised understanding of cultural difference. Rather than cultural difference being seen as a consequence of some innate, natural tendencies – as in racist constructions of difference – Lucy-Anne frames them as socially produced. In identifying these differences, Lucy-Anne is constructing an identity as an *Indigenous* teacher. In this moment there is an articulation of a collective identity to a developing teaching identity.

These cultural understandings have provided Lucy-Anne with "partial insights into the ways schools operate to exclude many aboriginal and working class youths of both genders" (Hesch, 1993:ii). These insights are partial because, in the Gramscian sense, they are good sense (Poynting, 1995:61) but also because of the hegemony of empiricism and positivism they are not common sense. The tendency in teacher education towards observation and recording of students' activities at the expense of theoretical analyses means that this good sense is often ignored. In addition, disciplinary knowledge based on research and practice is preferable to argument and critique using their practical ideology (Hesch, 1993:261).

Collective identities are sites of struggle, however, over what constitutes belonging and not belonging. Being racially objectified within a collective based on colour came up constantly in student narratives and needs further attention in relationship to the formation of student teaching identities.

Whiteness is a slippery term because it can conceal a range of meanings such as Lucy-Anne's sense that there was some form of cultural tradition in teaching that constructed disadvantaged 'native' children as inferior based on race. If we turn to Jessie – a Méti student at NORTEP – whiteness had racial and class dimensions that demonstrate the complexities of collective identities. Jessie's father was one of the earlier ex-government employees in the north who lobbied for the establishment of NORTEP. As a late baby in her family, she found herself more isolated from brothers and sisters who were much older. Her peer group became very important and was the source of negative self-concepts:

> I got a lot of negative effect... a lot of negative feedback with my peers and stuff for looking white and I didn't like being white. There was a part of me that I hated. I didn't like white people. I was just prejudiced. Plus a lot of people, too, didn't come from educated families um... a lot of my brothers and sisters weren't... they were already gone, work and stuff like that and I was spoiled. (Jessie: interview transcript)

The intersection of class factors and negative processes of racialisation dominate Jessie's narrative in the latter part of our interview in response to an open question regarding any unraised matters. The notion of 'educated' here is synonymous with 'whiteness'. Jessie is astute enough to see this as a contributing factor to how her 'whiteness' is constructed by others in her community. It is therefore not surprising that Jessie feels that native teachers have helped give confidence to all native students by demonstrating the *diversity* of native people:

> I became a teacher and I wanted to go... "it's okay"... you can nurture them and stuff. I don't see students like that – the way I felt. The hate I had like. (Jessie: interview transcript)

Negative racialised constructions of communities and individuals were common across age groups and gender. John, an AREP student from northern NSW, also spoke of the impact of racialisation upon different groups of Aboriginal people within his hometown. The segregation of 'town and mission blacks' at school informally and formally was seen as a factor in his privilege and a reproduction of their disadvantage:

> I lived in Lismore and the other people come from Box Ridge Mission and a few more others around Lismore. And they had their own little what they called the burial ground, where they sat all the time. (John: interview transcript)

Unlike the other Aboriginal students who lived on Aboriginal missions, John didn't get put into 'Aboriginal' classes, nor was he made to feel his Aboriginality was a barrier even though he did experience one racist incident in his final two years at school. Completing school was, however, a very difficult experience:

I stayed on and battled on in Year 11. But there were no Aboriginal students and that's the difference here. You've got Aboriginal people around you all the time. You can relate to them. They're supportive in whatever you do. (John: interview transcript)

John did not only suffer this isolation and alienation. He noticed also, that even though an Aboriginal Education Assistant (AEA) was employed when he was in Year 11, they didn't stay long:

They didn't last. They were casual off and on. I think the school environment in the end didn't suit them... and the teachers, had a lot of trouble with teachers. (John: interview transcript)

Some school dynamics – marginalisation, isolation and alienation – that are collectively acknowledged among the students in this study are usually offset by other, more productive relationships with significant teachers. There is a constant recognition of teachers who spent time, who acknowledged their aboriginality but without 'tags'. Thus, they were able to experience *individual* success, critical to succeeding in education and essential for negotiating the complex social relations of schooling. They were given social space by these teachers and quite remarkably, the teachers most often acknowledged were those who were connected with sport:

P.E. [physical education]... he was a real person. He was down to earth. What I liked about him was his personality. He saw me as an individual, not being Aboriginal. (John: interview transcript)

Tatz (1987, 1996) has written widely about the importance of sport in Aboriginal communities in Australia in terms of its political and social functions. Often, sport is a way out of unemployment in marginal country towns as well as providing a social focus. One of the NORTEP lecturers, Greg, discussed his role as sports teacher in high schools and the effort he put into after school and community relations. In addition to sport, the curriculum areas of art and music provided many students with the chance to succeed and acknowledge culture. Significantly, most of the teachers who were supportive in high school taught in what are considered the non-core or non-academic aspects of the curriculum.

Mona was another student who enjoyed school. In fact, she felt 'thrilled' each time she found herself back in a school situation. What

225

was it about school that had such positive connotations for Mona? Firstly, she was a 'straight A' student and was therefore academically successful. Secondly, there were students from a range of cultural backgrounds at La Ronge when she went to school. She attributed her social ease with having grown up among a diversity of students, which gave her social confidence and increased her cultural capital. This was not entirely her doing. Mona's mother, who had failed at school and had trouble with English, would not let Mona speak Cree, which was her Indigenous language. She plastered words all over the house so her children would succeed and made them practice their multiplication each night. Mona's mother's fear of failure and the devastating effects that had on her life meant she denied them their Métis cultural background so that they could succeed. However, her mother was giving her more than disciplinary knowledge:

> Sometimes I was frustrated with my mum because she pushed me so much. I got to the point where I was competitive with marks and stuff. I'm not like that... [but] I was expected to be like [that]... but it made her happy I guess. (Mona: interview transcript)

This cultural capital, individual effort and competitiveness were exactly what her mother was able to see were valued by wider society and were the very practices that had excluded her. Nevertheless, these attributes came at a price:

> ... some parts of my background I kind of felt shameful for... like I didn't live on reserves. (Mona: interview transcript)

Mona's ability to pass as white, not only in terms of appearance but also in terms of cultural capital, has given her a different perspective on being Indigenous. These differences in experience in relation to Indigenous identity are in part spatial but also a consequence of agency. In this case her mother was not prepared to reproduce her own situation and actively worked to protect her children from the negative consequences of racialisation. The individual nature of people's responses makes it difficult to generalise about whole collectivities and can pressure students into believing they are or are not really Indigenous. This ideology works in many ways. Tom tries to get at some of these differences and locates collectivities regionally:

> If you are born in the city, you tend to be more isolated, and you tend to lose more of your culture individually. That's generally speaking. Back home where there's more black fellas you can't help but have more culture, more ways about yourself, because you're around black fellas all the time. Down here you're around different people and in the city, the city fellas and the country fellas there's a big difference. And a lot of them don't get on actually. (Tom: interview transcript)

In attempting to show diversity without losing a sense of a collective identity, Tom uses spatial differences such as distance (between communities and later, between individual people). This is difficult while relying on a language of dualisms such as city/urban, more/less culture. The logic of this theory of cultural difference becomes a little unstuck later when he is grappling with a developing professional identity that sets him apart. Tom has some complex understandings of identity that he is wrestling with as he forms a teaching identity. Nevertheless, it is clearly an Indigenous teaching identity that he is forming:

> A lot of people say that when you come to university, you tend to lose a lot of your culture. And that's a very strong idea in the Aboriginal community. They say that you've gone white, or you've changed to white. You don't have to lose your culture. (Tom: interview transcript)

In this section, it has been established that teaching identities in the two programs are being established through a complex interplay of individual habitus and the field of Indigenous education. Individual habitus was seen as spatial in the material, cultural and geographical sense and helped define a sense of relationship to education for the individual students. Common to all students were continuing processes of, and effects of, racialisation. Students spoke of these as explanation for a particular perspective on education and as a way of shaping an emerging teaching identity. At the same time their access to tertiary education depended on their racialised identity.

It is evident that students are able to negotiate the complexities of these social formations although it is not an easy path. This is because the individual habitus of each student has been formed in relationship to the field of Indigenous education. It is a field of immense *disciplinary* knowledge (McConaghy, 1997a). There is the large amount of micro-political studies in classrooms as was discussed in Chapter 4. These focus on the relations between Indigenous students and their (largely) non-Indigenous teachers. Studies such as these have created a heightened awareness of 'race-relations' in education. In addition, many students have been involved in schools and government positions that are identified as Indigenous. To enter AREP and NORTEP they have identified as Indigenous or, like Henrietta, a northerner. The disciplinary knowledge gained from these contexts shapes their pedagogical habitus in ways that produce a much stronger concern for the particular issues in teaching and learning that involve Indigenous students.

To understand further the relationship between pedagogical habitus and the field of Indigenous education, I will examine the formation of the students' teaching identities. This will be done through a focus on the relationship between the personal, political and pedagogical orientations of AREP and NORTEP students.

Personal, political and pedagogical issues for Indigenous student teachers

> I'm more proud of being an Aboriginal person. Because I'm going to be an Aboriginal teacher and I want to give back to my Aboriginal community what I've learnt, and where I've come from. (Gloria: interview transcript)

In the previous sections of this chapter, we saw some explanations as to how Indigenous teachers could make a difference in the education of (particularly Indigenous) children. These included attitudes and practices that would be less likely to pathologise Indigenous children. In addition, in the last chapter, teacher educators thought that Indigenous teachers would provide a sense of identity for Indigenous students. Some of the students felt that having Indigenous teachers would demonstrate that there is a diversity of people who call themselves Indigenous. Some students, like Gloria above, have a very clear desire to 'give back' to the community what they have gained from education.

These attitudes and desires do not spring from the ether but from grounded understandings developed through social and cultural

228

networks. Of particular interest in the formation of such attitudes and desires is the degree to which students identify with schooling and particular types of pedagogic 'personalities'.

What can we learn about the relationship between pedagogy, power and politics through the eyes of the students? To answer this question we need to explore the construction of school cultures from the perspective of the students as well as their reflections on the curriculum at AREP and NORTEP. Some of the students' experiences relate to their own schooling and others to their experiences in the field and classroom during their time as student teachers at AREP and NORTEP. Through drawing on dimensions of their individual habitus students were beginning to create a teaching identity that combines the personal, the political and the pedagogical (Friesen and Orr, 1995).

As I discussed earlier in this chapter, the habitus of students – from which they have gained social and cultural capital via family networks and education – was central to their decision to enter teaching (Grenfell and James, 1998:170). In the earlier sections of this chapter, I have discussed the effects of racialisation on students' lives. At this macro level, we understood cultural traditions and racist historical practices as a factor shaping relationships between students, students and staff and students and schools. However, at another level of analysis, the meso, it was possible to see that institutional changes within schooling systems for AREP and NORTEP students have created a schooling experience that was qualitatively different from that of earlier generations of Indigenous students. At the final level of analysis – the micro – I will extend this focus to looking at racialisation a little more closely in terms of pedagogy. Using Bourdieu's analytical framework based on the aforementioned three levels, it is possible to see that a *system of power hierarchies* (Grenfell and James, 1998:114-116) shapes the students' understandings of the relationship between power, pedagogy and politics.

Pedagogic 'personality' and power

> [Good teachers] didn't treat us like we were an inch tall... (Brian: interview transcript)

'Good teachers' and 'bad teachers' are hard to define but I thought it worth asking students to reflect on their teachers in this way. Brian's response above shows how these questions might be useful in understanding the relationship between pedagogic 'personality'[2] and power. For example, as the students were defining good and bad 'qualities' it became evident that what is called the 'personality' of teachers was judged in terms of *processes*. Commonly, democratic student/teacher relationships were cited as good models. This 'personalistic model' is found in teacher education in North America (Zeichner, 1983 cited in Hesch, 1993:258) as well as in Australia. Given the overwhelming preference for this model in Western teacher education, it seemed important to consider the dimensions of power in the 'personalistic model'.

A personalistic model of teacher education "primarily encourages [preservice teachers] to develop their personal teaching ideologies through the autonomy and dialogue offered by a structured but quite democratic cultural construction" (Hesch, 1993:254). This style is evident in NORTEP's classes and in the narratives of their teaching staff. There is no philosophically driven approach to pedagogy in AREP, but many of the staff spoke about the need to interact in a similar manner.

A personalistic model is based upon co-operation, mutual respect and democratic processes in classrooms. In the 'personalistic model' described by the students, 'good pedagogy' was not just defined as 'teaching style' which often has no ethical or political base (Hursh, 1995). Brian explained what he meant by power, and through this explanation it is possible to gain some sense of the ethical and political issues underpinning pedagogy:

> They made us feel part of the community, part of the school and just to show their trust in us... there was a group of us who liked to work in the evenings... and they trusted us with the keys to the school. They made us feel really good, really proud. And people heard about it and they didn't like the idea of us getting that privilege so they eliminated the teachers. (Brian: interview transcript)

It is possible to see systems of power hierarchies very clearly in this vignette. At one level, the macro, Band control of education resulting from treaty rights meant that the community elders in part

---

[2] Friesen and Orr (1995) use the term 'pedagogic personality' to describe one aspect of a northern Aboriginal teacher identity. In this instance 'pedagogic personality' refers to a "desire to live out their Aboriginality in their teaching" (1995:5).

shaped Brian's schooling experiences. This political dimension to schooling on Band controlled reserves impacted on what the teachers could do.

At the meso level – the institution of schooling – liberal progressive teachers created practices that they thought might challenge institutional arrangements, thus giving students a greater sense of belonging. They were making ethical decisions about their students – a moral response resulting from recognition of schooling practices that were exclusionary. In sacking the teachers, the Band legitimated collective cultural knowledge and power while challenging the professional power and knowledge of the teachers.

This shows the limitations to an ethic of care (Hursh, 1995) in teacher education. The ethics of care is central to the personalistic model, and while it creates safe learning environments, it fails to "consider the contributions of teacher education to reproduction and resistance" (Hesch, 1993:258). This is important, in that if the teacher education students in this study are responding to, and reproducing this model of a 'good teacher', we need to know its strengths and limitations.

One of the outcomes of this personalistic model is that *some* students are selected out in formal and informal processes in the teaching/learning relationship. Tom remembers a situation that occurred outside school time with a history teacher:

> She actually took me to a museum to see how different styles throughout history have changed. And she shouted me a book on Aboriginal dot painting from South Australia and I just sat down. Now I know it's wrong. I copied some of the pictures onto canvas. Then I got my own ideas and that just triggered me off. (Tom: interview transcript)

The strengths of this personalistic model have been peppered throughout this chapter in terms of attachment to schooling via sports teachers, or art/music/drama teachers. It is a model that is in part a response to the authoritarian past where much symbolic and overt violence occurred in schooling for Indigenous students. The centrality of ethical and political issues in terms of pedagogy to Indigenous teacher education students can be found in all the student narratives.

The limitation of this model however, is that the 'practical ideology' of the students at AREP and NORTEP is continually challenged by the instrumental rationality and technical solutions in teacher education. These practices can tend to overwhelm nurturing and critical tendencies in students (Hursh, 1995:108) by making individual overtures between teacher and learner the only dimension of pedagogy worth scrutiny. Since so much of the personalistic model's success depends on embodied traits and attributes, it is particularly vulnerable to homogenising or stereotyping tendencies when applied to Indigenous cultures. That is, there is the potential for the construction of indigenist teaching identities.

We have now returned to the question raised at the start of this book about how students were constructing an Indigenous teaching identity. I have outlined the dominance of the personalistic model in the students' narratives in order to direct discussion away from this towards a more contextualised and dynamic construction of teaching identities. Despite the dominance of the personalistic model, there is much to build on in terms of the students' practical ideology.

Universal/indigenist tension

In Chapter 5 there was a brief discussion about the "complex system of favours and obligations" (Bartra, 1977:430) that tended to develop in AREP. This arose in part because of structural inequalities within the wider institution and resulted in a reliance on the personal goodwill of teaching staff. The more personalised style of teaching that resulted was appreciated by students but it masked the way in which such strategies were often patronising and/or culturalist. Concealing structural inequalities resulted in the increased dependence on working on the relationship between students and staff in teaching relationships. This is where the universal/indigenist tension was negotiated. Student teachers also felt this tension. There were three ways in which this tension for our students will be analysed: in terms of the political order of schools, the politics of Indigenous education and the politics of the curriculum.

The political order of schools

Connell (1985:131) described this order as a series of "patterns of authority and consent, alliance and cooperation, resistance and opposition". The students at NORTEP and AREP were quite often aware of this order, either as a student, an educational worker in schools or during practical experiences in schools. This was the first aspect of schooling that students encountered which revealed the universal/indigenist tension.

Leeanne, a mature woman in her final year at NORTEP, had found early educational experiences fairly difficult because she spoke little English. This meant that language was an important issue for her as a future Indigenous teacher. The understandings that she brought to teaching as a bilingual person provided her with the sort of insights that led her to suggest during one of her field placements that if she could speak in her own language to the Year 2 students they could make connections and learn faster. The teacher told her that she could only do so for 20% of the time! Since it was not the student's class – and despite NORTEP explicitly encouraging home language instruction and despite the fact that the Saskatchewan languages policy encouraged first language instruction – the political order of the school rendered the student powerless:

> And that brought back bad memories for me. I mean, I can't help it. It brought back bad memories. How else was I supposed to deal with it? I asked why but then when I disagreed I was told you didn't come to terms... so what do you do? (Leeanne: interview transcript)

Not coming to terms with the political order of the school is often one of the first forms of resistance that student teachers demonstrate. Despite inclusive pedagogy at AREP and NORTEP, students eventually have to deal with a range of school contexts that are less than inclusive and where the political order of the school is rarely thrown into question. To be able to negotiate this situation is very difficult given the differential power that the student holds and the hegemony of the universalistic approach to curricula where Indigenous curricula has been carved off and reconstituted as an 'add-on'.

There are different responses to this political order in schools that emanate in part from the particular politics of Indigenous education in Saskatchewan and New South Wales. Also, the structure of the schooling system – Band controlled, provincial, private or state – shapes the possibility for negotiating this order.

The politics of Indigenous education

Aboriginal education in NSW is a concern of mainly the State and Catholic education systems and the Aboriginal Education and Consultative Group (AECG). In NSW the AECG gives Indigenous educators a platform for lobbying about the sorts of changes that Leeanne is referring to above. This leads to a second explanation for heightened awareness among Indigenous teacher education students of the relationship between politics and teaching: many students have prior involvement in Band, student or Indigenous educational politics.

Gloria, who earlier in this section was quoted as saying she "wanted to give back to her community", is one of the few AREP students who have termed themselves *Aboriginal* teachers unlike NORTEP students who really emphasise that they will be *native* teachers. In the case of NORTEP students, they are being produced for 'the north' which is majority Indigenous but quite diverse culturally and socio-economically. But even though AREP students focus on systemic schools with diverse populations, they are produced by particular ideological discourses in Indigenous education.

Gloria's educational story exemplifies the political experiences of many of the younger AREP students. Gloria grew up around the area known as the 'Wellington Common' – a contested site for the Wiradjuri nation in central NSW – and attended a school where 40% of the population were Aboriginal (a high number relative to other areas). She has many relatives who have succeeded at AREP and has been actively involved as an Aboriginal student representative in her hometown. Gloria went to an all-Aboriginal pre-school[3] and was one of the first students when it opened. In Year 12 she became "like a junior AEA" (p.4) sitting on Aboriginal and Student Support and Parent Awareness (ASSPA) and Priority Schools Program (PSP) committees for the local primary and highschool (Catholic and Public).

Becoming an Aboriginal teacher is a different process for some of these younger students than it was for the first students attending AREP and NORTEP. This is partly because there has been a different history of involvement in schooling, which has focussed on Aboriginality through representation on formal committees. Gloria has

---

[3] Aboriginal preschools began operating in the late 1970s with Murawina at Redfern and later Mt Druitt.

234

spent a lot of time working at the interface of Aboriginality and schooling, the space provided by national guidelines for Aboriginal people to participate in decision-making processes.

On the one hand these committees and associations agitate and advocate for change. On the other hand there have been some concerns over the degree to which change is constrained through discourses that operate on the principles of binaries and which has been referred to as the 'new racism' in Indigenous adult education (McConaghy, 1997a:251). The logic of binaries is based on the 'two-race' theory and the supposed incompatibility of cultures (*ibid.*). As discussed in Chapter 4, such discourses showed a preference for viewing relations inside schools as a consequence of racialised cultural differences. Students can see that this is sometimes counterproductive but have difficulty articulating an alternative analysis (Hursh, 1995, Hesch, 1995). Why is this so?

McConaghy provides a powerful critique of Indigenous education policy making as articulated by government and Indigenous organisations (1997a). She argued that while the intent of the policies is to represent a diversity of Indigenous peoples in Australia, it actually contains diversity because it relies on the two-race binary. This means it favours activities that shore up racialised understandings and practices where Indigenous students are concerned. In terms of the students at AREP and NORTEP, this means they are being shaped by, and are shaping, particular constructions of Aboriginality.

Through Donna's story it is possible to see how binaries impact on a person's sense of self as well as agency. When this narrative has been explored I will briefly compare and contrast it with a Canadian example.

Donna was a mature woman from the south coast of NSW who had difficulties with early schooling. "I was behind, because I was in a really low class. A lot of Koori kids were in low classes" (Donna: 8, lines 8-9). Donna came from a large family living in very basic accommodation. The roof leaked and she remembered all the fuss to make the beds and have everything looking good for the welfare officers who were coming to inspect their home. This seemed natural since Donna wasn't made to feel any fear about the process by her parents. Since they could 'pass' in the wider community Donna's family chose to protect her from the 'reality' of these 'inspections' so that she might grow up with more opportunities to live and work in the 'white' world. But Donna's Aboriginality did give her access to

AREP. When she started university, Donna initially began welfare studies but changed to teaching after one year. Here she reflects on the impact her studies were having on her sense of identity as an Aboriginal person and she points to some of the reasons for changing her career:

> It was a real challenge for me, because I'm married to a non-Aboriginal person. And it was a real challenge for me, because I started to reflect anger. Really finding out where I actually belonged. I knew I came from a very loving family. You know... but what is it about me being Aboriginal? That was going beyond being proud of who you are... *and* you are Aboriginal. (Donna: interview transcript)

The challenges that Donna was feeling came from her studies where she was learning about Australia's racist history and the role of welfare in removing children from Aboriginal families. Her anger was partly directed at her parents for excluding her from this knowledge. No longer feeling she could do welfare, Donna changed to teaching:

> I thought oh my god, if this is what it's all about. It was like... and that's where I went into a bit of turmoil. The challenges came in place and I started putting the pieces together, and saying *this* is what happened to my parents! And here I am thinking: "What am I doing here studying this course?" (Donna: interview transcript)

The curriculum at the time Donna was studying was based on the race-relations paradigm upon which binaries are produced. In this approach, there are the historical oppressors who are normally 'white' and the oppressed who are normally 'black'. By reading off the cause and effects of relations between races, there are victors and victims. Given that Donna's husband was 'white' and a number of family members – including Donna – looked 'white' it is not surprising that she was confused. For example, did 'passing' make her more fortunate than others? Less Aboriginal? Donna's anger is partially a response to the role of welfare in relation to taking children away and a sense of withdrawal of agency. This latter theme is evident when speaking of the way in which other students reproduce these discourses related to victims and victors:

> I get very frustrated at times when I hear, especially when Aboriginal students get up and say "These white... you know". And they have got to be... In order to be who they are today and to be where they are today, they've got other traits in them; other cultural backgrounds inside them to be here. (Donna: interview transcript)

Despite the language of essentialism which she can't 'escape' because of the ideological hegemony of the race-relations paradigm in Indigenous education, the general logic of Donna's narrative indicates that she wrestles with this tendency in the politics of Indigenous education.

The students at NORTEP also have to deal with the effects of such binaries. Earlier in this chapter, there was a discussion of the way in which binaries of 'good and bad' when associated with 'Indianness' and 'whiteness' created some major personal identity issues for Jessie. Binaries are employed in a process of differentiation, not only as shorthand for the dominant and Other but also in hierarchies of power within Indigenous communities. Thus, binaries help to produce inequalities. In the next section, I will tease out the ways in which the students try to make sense of the relationship between these wider politics and the production of knowledge.

Politics of the curriculum

> Aboriginal students understand each other. You don't have that understanding in the mainstream. I remember I was trying to put Aboriginal perspectives into everything. Other students got sick of it. They just didn't want to know anymore. Whereas here you've got the Aboriginal input through everything, and it is accepted. So that's a big thing. (Nina: interview transcript)

Every student at AREP and NORTEP who took part in this study felt that one of the greatest advantages to their enclave programs was the opportunity to bring in their 'cultural' knowledge without having to constantly justify a different perspective. When students compared and contrasted their experiences with non-enclave programs they commonly revealed a lack of sensitivity to the diversity of students in these classrooms. Lucy-Anne's anecdote, which follows, shows the sort of pedagogical processes that can be exclusionary:

... like you can't tell by looking at me that I'm native and we did this novel called Flash, on this one native guy and it was really controversial that book. I didn't like it at all. We had to make comments and some guy got up and said I don't even know why native people were born. And that's like "who are you to judge us?" (Lucy-Anne: interview transcript)

One of the pedagogical practices that create a sense of not belonging or exclusion is the tendency to focus on or judge others as if they do not exist. Teacher educators in the last chapter talked about the 'crap' that came from mainstream students and how these programs protected students from the sorts of experiences that Nina and Lucy-Anne speak about. In Chapter 7 there was also a discussion of Alison Jones' experience in New Zealand when she separated students based on ethnicity in their feminist studies classes (1998). The Indigenous students got sick of having to "tell their stories of oppression" to the Pakehas. In these types of contexts the studying of Others effectively "removes the focus from the social production of difference to the management of racialised identities" (Singh, 1998:6). Students responding to this colonising demand for narrative (Jones, 1998) often collapse into a defiant talking back (Ellsworth, 1994). In classrooms where there is no consideration of cultural diversity, the culture of the classroom is not conducive to speaking at all. John, one of the AREP students who tried full time study for one year echoes Lucy-Anne's experiences in explaining the dynamics:

You're completely different. Just the atmosphere of the class is completely different to AREP. They are more, I don't know. There is not much talking going on. Some of the kids were just too astute. They were very up themselves... that far. I could not relate to them. Being Aboriginal you know how people could relate. Even if you don't know them, you can relate to them. They are the same culture, the same background. Most of them are the same way that you grew up. And the language itself was a big difference. The language that we use between one another. Most of us can change our language to suit the environments, but when we are in AREP we use both languages. Couldn't do that in full time. (John: interview transcript)

There is a hidden pedagogy and a hidden curriculum operating here that produces particular meanings and forms of consciousness

(Whitty, 1985:32) for these students. A hidden pedagogy "is a tacit set of rules about how competent teaching should proceed" (Hatton, 1994:11). The hidden curriculum on the other hand includes practices such as how 'talk' is used and by whom in classrooms (Grundy, 1994:33).

If we recall and contrast John's experience with Henrietta, that is, being a non-Indigenous northerner in an Indigenous classroom, we can see that there is tension arising from racialised and deracialised discourses. Henrietta was personally rejected because of her 'whiteness'; Lucy-Anne felt bruised by the insensitivity of another student and John remained invisible in a 'mainstream' classroom. We can see the complexities of racialisation in these contexts where a number of other factors were operating to constrain teaching and learning relationships. These included the differing institutional cultures of teaching which are influenced by rooming, differing class sizes and different teaching and learning policies and strategies. It is also important to remember that the teaching staff also noticed these differences.

The reality of the students' lives has provided them with insights and knowledge that creates a more active questioning of pedagogical processes. This difference emerges from material conditions. In addition, linguistic habitus shapes the teaching and learning process. John clearly demonstrates the flexibility of AREP students to shift between dialects and/or registers of English. Students at NORTEP, where interaction is based on the 'talking circle', speak of the interaction in classrooms as supportive and inclusive. This skill is undervalued, as explored in Chapter 8, where Aboriginal English has been discounted as a valid form of communication. However, what John is referring to is more than moving between dialects. A focus on the student's cultural difference is not the issue here. Most importantly, there is a participatory, democratic classroom environment. In addition, it is hard to account for change to the students' own programs if, for example, lecturers are different in different contexts as John discusses later in our interview.

So how can Henrietta's concern about the native studies curriculum be addressed? The Indigenous teacher educators at NORTEP are well aware of the sorts of issues that Henrietta has raised. This was demonstrated in the previous chapter where I discussed Murray's concern for contemporary Indigenous community issues as well as historical traditions and historical race-relations. We can see that people do respond to these contradictions and that programs such as NORTEP and AREP are continually being transformed. Indeed, there was a similar struggle over knowledge in AREP, as I discussed in Chapter 5. Donna's experiences of a curriculum that focussed only on Australia's racist history was self-defeating in the context of her personal social relations. She was married to a non-Indigenous person and raised in a family that used 'passing' as a survival strategy in a racialised society. These are complex issues for AREP and NORTEP staff, but they are vital to understanding the program's success and future direction.

One way in which NORTEP has attempted to change its curriculum is to focus on multicultural perspectives. Multiculturalism in education in Canada has similarly been critiqued for its reliance on static concepts of culture and lack of focus on equitable outcomes (Hesch, 1993; Wotherspoon, 1995). NORTEP student, Brian, argued that although there was a lot of Indigenous content in his education at NORTEP there was room for other perspectives:

> They try to have a focus on a multicultural education like we don't just focus on... like we don't just focus on native issues... We sort of look at the opposite of native issues and plus there are some students here who are non-aboriginal. I think it would be unfair to them if they just had to stick to aboriginal content all the time. (Brian: interview transcript)

Although NORTEP and AREP are separate programs, they are connected to a changing student population and the demands of a culturally diverse society. Government mandates in Australia and Canada in this regard demonstrate the interaction of different levels of the field of Indigenous education with that of wider policies designed to 'manage' national cultural diversity. While there are limitations to a culturalist curriculum, many students speak about being able to bring in their 'own knowledge'. This usually means knowledge that has been defined as 'Indigenous'. It is knowledge that is available to them through extended networks, such as family or Indigenous organisations. As owners of Indigenous knowledge students feel a sense of authority. This is empowering, because it provides a resource that is both accepted as belonging to 'them' and is respected because it 'proves' their aboriginality.

Students are making connections however, between their previous knowledge and institutional knowledge. There is an approach to teaching in the two programs that attempts to foster an integration of a sense of identity or belonging within the constraints of systems that have historically created a sense of being an outsider. This means that it is difficult not to reproduce racialised social relations.

Conclusion: Inside/outside teacher identities

A non-Indigenous colleague and myself once talked of the tension that we felt working both inside/outside Aboriginal education. She was speaking of the moments when you both understand your positioning from the perspective of an insider with cultural knowledge but from the politically vexatious position of an outsider at the same time. This is another way of saying what Reynolds (1999) said at the beginning of this book. The language is inadequate though, because it sets up a kind of dichotomy that doesn't quite express the dimensions of this experience. It is a human experience, but at the same time manifestly different according to context. In the racialised contexts of the AREP and NORTEP the common understanding or 'knowing' about racism and discrimination can make you an insider, while the different ways in which you have known that experience can make you an outsider. This is so for the administrators, teacher educators and students in this study.

Becoming an Indigenous teacher therefore requires a process of cultural construction that is conscious:

> I didn't want to have it that we became more European. I wanted to be able to express myself, and keep my feelings in the way that I felt about being an Aboriginal person. (Margaret: interview transcript)

Confirming identity as part of a tertiary program appears to be a critical part of student success (Archibald and Bowman, 1995:6). There were some problems however among several of the students in relation to how much emphasis should be placed on their aboriginality and how that should be framed within the curriculum. When I asked Sharon at NORTEP about whether there was enough native studies content in the curriculum she replied:

> There's maybe an overdose of it! (Sharon: interview transcript)

241

For other students, there was a much greater identification with this type of culturalist curriculum. Hesch also found that his students at SUNTEP reacted poorly to his course on racism and were much more comfortable with aspects of the curriculum that celebrated a kind of traditional, homogenised culture (Hesch, 1993). As discussed in Chapter 5, students resisted the changing direction of CIACS at UWSM, partly because of the removal of the word rural from the program title, but also because the new curriculum was focussing more on racism and cultural studies rather than on anthropological studies around aboriginality. So there was a similar response to the removal of a culturalist curriculum.

What does this tell us about the pedagogical principles that students have taken on about culture and the curriculum? At first, it appears that students are privileging knowledge about culture, seeing it as something that is 'read off' rather than continually negotiated. However, their 'practical ideology' means they are constantly finding that there are tensions between culture as negotiated and the indigenist model of cultural difference.

Within the students' narratives is the development of a cultural repertoire. It is not a simple process of AREP and NORTEP constructing students' identities. The students are actively engaged in the negotiation of these identities themselves. I would therefore argue that the students are, like my colleague, and myself, at once both inside/outside Indigenous teacher identities. They are becoming/unbecoming *Indigenous* teachers. This is an ongoing process and involves an active selection of ideas, materials and strategies. This is how agency shapes Indigenous education outcomes.

For example, Rita reflected on how her course had given her knowledge about child-rearing practices:

> Maybe why I chose teaching was because I think once you're a mother, you can understand your children a lot more too. Especially in the home environment and so forth. If they are over there playing on their own (for example)... and they're happy, you just let them keep on playing on their own. You just don't disturb them; you don't chastise them and say: "Look here why don't you interact more with these other kids?" You just let the child be happy because the child is there for... his/her own mind all the time... and they are learning. (Rita: interview transcript)

The promise of education is that it will reveal the 'secrets' of success. Rita has connected particular aspects of theories of child development as one of the ways to increase the chance of success for her children. There is a realisation that *social and cultural capital* has much to do with educational success and that it is learned within the family in addition to school.

Similarly, Lucy-Anne, reflecting on her cultural background and its relationship to schooling, provides a contemporary, incisive view of cultural practice. There is no middle class romanticised view of culture based on tradition and persistence (Rowse, 1988) in her concept of Métis culture. Lucy-Anne's cultural knowledge is based on the reality of living in marginalised communities:

> Like, um, we're Métis and like our culture is like jigging and stuff like that eh? We never did any of that in school. I don't know. We learned a lot about the fur traders and, um, the Europeans and the first arrival of the Europeans... (Lucy-Anne: interview transcript)

The process of selecting and connecting knowledge based on professional, cultural and personal understandings continues beyond the teacher education program. This voice of a NORTEP graduate shows that there are processes of selection, inversion and constant innovation:

> My approach to the curriculum was not to only follow what was laid out in the curriculum. I followed it, but the resources I more or less ignored. I figured out where I could find something that was maybe a little bit better than what was in the curriculum. (Friesen and Orr, 1995:20)

There is some difficulty, however, in dealing with relationships in communities. This is a critical issue for many of the students and is definitely a factor in the burn-out of Aboriginal teachers. The difficulty of being a student, let alone neophyte teacher, coupled with the pressure to attend to 'community' problems is sometimes overwhelming. "Some Aboriginal teachers feel they have become part of the problem, as school systems fail to meet the needs of Aboriginal students" (McNinch, 1994:3). This is despite increased retention due in part to a more personalistic pedagogy.

The paths to AREP and NORTEP were shaped by a number of factors. The process of selection by teachers, the 'chain' of relatives who had completed AREP/NORTEP and attachment to schooling were evident in most of the student narratives. Schooling had therefore provided support and a future for the Indigenous teacher students which is not dissimilar to other students studying teaching (Connell, 1985). For all students there was individual benefit either in terms of confidence, future employment, knowledge for its own sake or cultural identity.

In addition, all students articulated a collective identity – either Aboriginal, Indigenous, native or northerner. This was generally expressed as providing a political purpose to their work:

> Well see we're role models. When we have an Aboriginal Cultural Day... we organised for every person that we had helping out – or most people that we had helping out – were Aboriginal people. We had sports activities. We had Aboriginal people doing that. (Debbie: interview transcript)

The students that felt this way were planning to return to specific communities. For some NORTEP students there was the chance to work with elders to revive or maintain languages. Other NORTEP and AREP students expressed a need to leave communities, as there were too many difficulties to attend to when living and working in the same place. Others are less certain about teaching but glad for the cultural capital that they have gained for their families:

> And I've felt that I've grown in a lot of ways. It's made me become more of a responsible person as well. And I'm also passing that on to my children, to be responsible for their own little actions, or whatever too. While they're at home you know? (Rita: interview transcript)

There is a sense that students also develop practices as a community of learners that they value. While Hesch (1993) found his student teachers at SUNTEP were organic intellectuals and would be useful as change-makers, he also found that their knowledge was subverted by the hegemony of individualism and competition that prepared them for the market. In this chapter we examined how the political order of the school also impacted on students' attempts to change practices that they knew were contributing to student failure. At these moments students in these situations are inside/outside an Indigenous teaching identity.

In the next chapter, the conclusion, I want to explore how AREP and NORTEP have addressed some of the inequalities they were set up to confront. To do this there will be an overview of the success of the programs and how they were shaped. Using the insights of students, teacher educators and administrators outlined in this and previous chapters, I will outline the dimensions of issues that have arisen and their negotiation. In addition, I will outline areas of AREP and NORTEP that are on-going and being negotiated. Following this discussion, some implications for policy development and implementation will be considered.

Chapter 10

Conclusion

Review

The purpose of this comparative Australian/Canadian book was to understand how the legacies and continuation of processes of racialisation were negotiated in the context of, and by comparing, two Indigenous teacher education programs. The two case studies – AREP and NORTEP – were produced from historically inequitable social and cultural relations in these two colonialised countries. While the programs resulted from structural inequalities they were also shaped by, and were indeed a consequence of, Indigenous and non-Indigenous agency. To examine the processes of negotiating racialised identities in the two enclave Indigenous teacher education programs, I asked six central questions.

- What are the colonial legacies for Indigenous education in Australia and Canada?
- Why were enclave programs for Indigenous teacher education students in NSW and Saskatchewan created and what have been their experiences to date?
- In what ways do administrators of Indigenous education programs reproduce or contest the racialised spaces within educational institutions?
- What assumptions underlie teaching philosophies in AREP and NORTEP and how are they challenged/reproduced, reframed and/or transformed?
- How do teaching staff and students negotiate racialised identities in each program?
- How do Indigenous students in AREP and NORTEP construct an identity as Indigenous teachers?

The questions were addressed using Bourdieu's framework for a theory of practice. Bourdieu's theory of practice attempts to get beyond the dichotomy of subjective and objective knowledge

(Grenfell and James, 1998:10). The purpose of using this model was to make it possible to speak about a 'third space' (McConaghy, 1997a) which is neither overly structurally deterministic nor reliant on individual agency. It is the 'third space' where the negotiation of cultural identities is enacted or where complementarity is revealed. The social practice in this third space is made up of individual strategy within constraint:

> ... strategy rests on a practical 'feel for the game', allowing any number of possible and original 'moves' within the general 'sense of limits, commonly called the sense of reality' (Bourdieu, cited in Grenfell and James, 1998:19).

Individual strategy is the result of combined practical good sense and commonly accepted practices in a semi-automatic manner (Grenfell and James, 1998:10). In this study, strategy is shaped by the field of Indigenous education, which is in turn shaped by the habitus of administrators, teacher educators and students in this study. The multilevel framework reflected in the questions posed at the start of this book provided a number of ways in which to understand this strategy. In employing this framework to understanding processes of racialisation, the study was seeking to understand better the experiences of all those people working in the AREP and NORTEP.

The questions have been slightly reframed as a result of the study and will be addressed in this conclusion.

How useful has the concept of racialisation been in the analysis of AREP and NORTEP?

This book has shown how the processes of racialisation are changing, complex and contradictory. A number of contradictions are evident when we examine the understandings gained from the multilevel analytical framework of Bourdieu. At the level of individual identity, it was possible to see that racialisation was essential to entry for AREP. While being a 'northerner' was the category used at NORTEP, in practice the formal and informal processes of selection at NORTEP meant that predominately Indigenous students were chosen. The contradiction here is that while it is the student's racialised identity that allows them access to tertiary teacher education in the first place, racialisation shapes educational policy and practices which constrain Indigenous students and their quest for education.

At another level, the meso or institutional level, that is at the level of the university, contradictions also emerge. Racialisation allowed separate space for the Indigenous teacher education programs and allowed different modes of course delivery – and the enclave model – to be developed. Universities also directed financial resources to these programs. But racialisation also contains the development of Indigenous teacher programs at tertiary levels because it leads to the reproduction of cultural stereotypes which, as outlined in earlier chapters, were embedded in curriculum practice and in institutional arrangements. There was some difference in this regard between AREP and NORTEP. The marginal nature of the AREP meant that there was a constant danger of patronisation in the form of advocacy by non-Aboriginal teachers and administrators, which restricted individual and community self-determination. On the other hand, the successful survival and continuation of these programs required support from (non-Indigenous) people across the university.

At the macro level, we can see the continuation of racialisation in the way in which Federal governments – particularly the Australian Federal Government – are tightening funding arrangements for "social justice" areas. Yet, in their most recent budget announcements they have given a boost to Indigenous education (Figure 10.1) funding which is in stark contrast to general funding for public education and universities in Australia. Indeed, block release modes such as AREP are reported to have the best outcomes of all modes of study for Indigenous students in higher education in Australia.

Figure 10.1
Funding for Indigenous Education

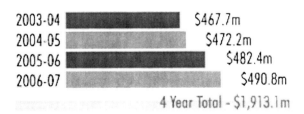

2003-04 $467.7m
2004-05 $472.2m
2005-06 $482.4m
2006-07 $490.8m
4 Year Total - $1,913.1m

Source: http://www.dest.gov.au/at_a_glance.htm#ind (26.08.03)

249

In Canada, programs like NORTEP also experience financial change and more recently constraints, through the devolution of funding. This was occurring at a time of substantial debate about national identity – including the case of Quebec's separation from Canada – and multiculturalism in Canada. Moreover, the position of Indigenous peoples in Canadian society continues to be debated at political, business and social gatherings. These broad debates are really about racialisation in Canada, from the level of national identity through to the level of the neighbourhood and neighbourhood school.

Racialisation has therefore been a useful concept in this study. It has led to a focus on the importance of the way in which the racial difference of Indigenous peoples in Australia and Canada constrained their socio-economic mobility in general, and education outcomes in particular. It has meant a focus on the complexity of, and the contradictions in, individual and institutional dimensions of racialisation. Examples here are the contradictions of Indigenous and non-Indigenous relations in NORTEP and AREP, as well as the contradictions within the Indigenous student body themselves about cultural identity and other matters. Its usefulness can be further demonstrated when the questions that were posed at the start of this conclusion are re-examined. The first of these questions reframes the macro approach and highlights the comparative nature of the study more clearly. It doing so, it assumes a direction for further research.

Has the comparative nature of this study had any explanatory power?

Firstly, at the macro level, the questions concerned with the legacies of colonisation and the reasons for establishing the two Indigenous teacher education programs – AREP and NORTEP – in Australia and Canada were explored. This provided a number of insights into racialised colonial strategies that have historically shaped – in similar but different ways – the field of Indigenous affairs in the two countries. The comparative nature of the study revealed that while there may be similar processes of racialisation that colonialist governments have had in common, the negotiation between State and Indigenous peoples produces different responses to this legacy. This is evident in the different systems of Indigenous racial classification and categorisation in each country and the existence of treaties with Indigenous peoples in Canada but not in Australia. What stands out starkly in both Canada and Australia is the extent to which Indigenous peoples are so disadvantaged when compared to the rest of the population. This was particularly true of Indigenous educational outcomes in both counties and points to the importance of Indigenous teacher education programs in both countries in the first instance.

Therefore, the comparative or cross-cultural nature of this study has been useful in a number of ways. Firstly, we can see that because Australia and Canada are neo-liberal settler societies with political and ideological roots in European colonisation, there are many similarities in government policy. For example, in Chapter 3 I traced the similar welfarist approaches to governance leading to historical policy periods of assimilation, integration and various forms of self-determination. However, the differential manifestations of Indigenous control in Australia and Canada were in part related to the degree to which governments in both countries had acknowledged prior occupation, and partly to the different economic needs of the time. Thus, the creation of the nation state in Canada led to a number of Indigenous Canadian groups being granted treaties. In Australia, Indigenous peoples were removed from their land under the legal lie *terra nullius*. However, not all Indigenous Canadians share treaty rights, so there are structural inequalities between and among groups of Indigenous peoples in Canada which shape their access to education and other institutions.

The second useful comparison, then, is that of intra-Canadian and Australian/Canadian educational rights. We saw how treaty Indians – as part of the original treaties – were able to call for *Indian Control of Indian Education* (National Indian Brotherhood, 1972). Through arguing that treaty obligations had not been met – measured by the failure of provincial education systems to produce equitable outcomes – the beginning of Indigenous control of education began in the early 1970s, with NORTEP created six years later.

In Australia, such rights have not been available for many people even after Mabo, since land rights are based on the ability to prove an uninterrupted occupation of traditional lands. We can see the irony in this condition when one considers the forced removal and resettlement of Aboriginal people in NSW by white governments who now consider this (involuntary) move sufficient to rob them of any claim on their traditional lands (Goodall, 1996). For this, and other reasons, explored in this book Indigenous people living in NSW do not have quite the same rights to determine or control education as in

251

Saskatchewan although they do have strong representation in the Aboriginal Education Consultative Group. The struggle for input into Indigenous student outcomes began in the 1970s, when arguments were couched in terms of inequitable outcomes, and later on when moral and political recognition of cultural difference was more the driving force (NAEC, 1986).

However, Canadian Indigenous peoples also invoke similar moral and political arguments over the *interpretation* of treaty rights. Often, in Australia and Canada these arguments have depended on victim discourses. With a comparative cross-cultural perspective we are able to explain this dependence on victim discourses partly as a consequence of Indigenous people's attempts to capture agency within the constraints of the nation state, and partly because they have been victims of racism.

The significance of this cross-cultural knowledge is that this study has sought to explore the ways in which Indigenous peoples struggle in two different but similar countries to make sense of historical oppression. In this way, it is possible to glimpse moments of agency for change as well as being aware of the constraints to change. One of the ways in which agency was understood was to examine identity politics. For example, one consequence of Canadian treaty rights has been the creation of boundaries within and across the Indigenous population. Racialised taxonomies (emanating from treaty rights) have created notions of 'real' and 'unreal' Indians and consequent unequal access to rights. NORTEP has responded to this through a focus on the 'north' as a way of recognising multiple Indigenous voices that make up the north (as well as the Board of Governors). While the focus on the 'north' was a way to appease government and various community groups when the program was initially set up, it has provided a useful mechanism for uniting disparate voices. However, just as the concept of 'north' provided space for multiple Indigenous voices, there is now pressure to extend this concept to include more *non*-Indigenous students.

When we compare and contrast this situation with that of AREP, it is possible to see how the differing histories produce alternative possibilities for action, opening some doors and closing others. For example, AREP was established to provide access for Indigenous students via a standard course. Unlike the NORTEP brief, which was to provide a standard course but with a concern for cultural maintenance, AREP was seen as an opportunity to increase the number of Indigenous teachers. The idea of cultural maintenance was something that grew out of identity politics in the Aboriginal community in the ensuing period. Cultural maintenance was always a problematic concept in AREP since students were identified collectively as Aboriginal without any formal recognition of identity related to country or region. This was in itself a consequence of earlier policies of Aboriginal dispersal and dispossession. At NORTEP, 'Indian' was most commonly associated with the Cree until recent years in terms of curriculum content. One of the benefits therefore of collective identification is that no single group is privileged. However, a tendency in anthropological subjects to focus on tradition and custom meant that students in AREP were often associating Aboriginality with desert dwelling peoples until contemporary cultural studies were introduced. Unlike NORTEP students, most AREP students were either living in rural towns or highly urbanised spaces. In other words, this racialised discourse of Aboriginality allowed no space for contemporary, professional urban Aboriginals.

These identity politics had the effect of producing a different curriculum – in part a response to student resistance but mainly due to a shift to a cultural studies approach by Indigenous and non-Indigenous academic staff. The new approach focussed on community issues, networks and students' individual histories and representations. Theoretically at least, students were being presented with culture as dynamic rather than reified cultural practices.

This change is also emerging at NORTEP, in part due to a diversified student population. Indian Studies instructors are well aware of the problems associated with a curriculum approved by the SIFC, which only focused on 'Cree as Indian' and argued for Dene to be included in the curriculum. This is why they look at contemporary issues and studies of race in society. But one of the problems for both programs is that a focus on only one aspect of culture – namely 'race' or ethnicity – ignores the 'noise of multidimensionality' (Troyna, 1994). The articulation of issues of racialisation with the social relations of gender, sexuality and class need further consideration. Chapter 9 discussed the gendered, classed and spatial dimensions to students' lives.

Another significant difference between the two programs was the way in which culture as practice had been constructed. At NORTEP, democratic processes of decision-making and student voice permeate all activities. This is a basis from which many students gain a sense of themselves as active participants and constructors of culture. However, because of the hegemony of culturalist approaches, these values and skills were mostly seen as emanating from cultural tradition, although this was being questioned more frequently as the student body was changing. In Chapter 6 there was a discussion of the traditional circle on which the democratic organisation and representation of all parties was based. In Chapter 9, it was possible to see that while democratic processes work in the closed world of NORTEP among predominately Indigenous students, they struggle to operate when Indigenous students are placed in the field with predominately non-Indigenous staff. Future research might focus on whether or not democratic processes occurring at NORTEP are being transferred to the schooling systems now those graduates have been entering the profession for more than two decades.

AREP, on the other hand, does not have a tradition of democratic participation, a situation which has often resulted in student voices being raised in anger. Perhaps this is because AREP, unlike NORTEP, is not based within clearly identified Indigenous communities and the fact that Canada leads Australia in granting Indigenous rights in education and other areas. We can understand this collective struggle in AREP as one of the contradictions of imposing identity politics on students that have the effect of silencing difference and exacerbating tensions. So, while the overt curriculum at AREP is in part challenging culturalist/anthropological traditions, which have been seen as homogenising, the hidden curriculum is also enforcing a non-problematic collective identity. In addition, there has existed minimal opportunity for students to comment on their educational experiences in AREP (other than with a former faculty Dean who met with a group of students each residential over lunch). These tensions can be understood when we look at the comparative viability of the programs.

At NORTEP, band support is becoming critical to the viability of the program. However, there has always been the support and input of a range of identifiable Indigenous and non-Indigenous bodies in shaping the program from its inception. With funding devolution to bands these types of representative structures are critical to the program's future. At AREP, on the other hand, funding is tied directly to the Federal government, which has indicated that given the opportunity, it would cut funding.

There have been a number of institutional forms of managing and supporting AREP. This instability might also reflect the fact that AREP is less grounded in the Indigenous and local community than is NORTEP. In 1999 funding for AREP no longer went through the university's central administration. Goolangullia Aboriginal Education Centre controlled funding of the centre and all of its activities including AREP. To some extent this meant advocacy rested mainly with Goolangullia. Goolangullia in turn depended on various networks to represent their interests. That is, they depended on the lobbying of groups such as the AECG and Aboriginal Higher Education Network. But Goolangullia did not survive either and there were complex reasons for this which need taking up in further research. In part, this occurred because of a radical restructuring across the federated university. The program has returned to the now School of Education and Early Childhood Studies and is coordinated by an Indigenous person. A separate support unit covers student administration and support. It has come full circle.

It seems that larger, identifiable and broad collectives are part of a process of legitimation of Indigenous education programs. The role therefore of Indigenous voice in NSW has been related to pressuring and lobbying and advising, whereas in Saskatchewan, there is control in the sense of having votes on boards or committees represented on NORTEP.

In the period since the establishment of programs such as AREP and NORTEP, we have seen increased networking among Indigenous academics across national boundaries. As a consequence there has been some revision and borrowing of strategy. Sometimes these strategies have been taken out of the context in which they were implemented, thus creating a tendency to further reify the notion of Indigenous beyond national boundaries (Hughes and More, 1993). I hope that this comparative study reveals that while there are some interesting parallels arising from racialisation, these are struggled over and negotiated in different ways producing quite different responses within the two nation States.

Another way in which the comparative nature of this study has enriched understanding of the field of Indigenous education is the extent to which it has revealed the ways in which disciplinary knowledge shapes the field (McConaghy, 1997a). We were also able to see that particular constructions of Indigenous peoples occur across national boundaries. For example, one of the contradictions of colonialism is that supranational collectives of Indigenous peoples have emerged in recent years to form a sort of pan-Indigenous movement that may or may not challenge racialised taxonomies. For example, the World Indigenous Peoples' Conferences on Education provide stimulating opportunities to examine these strategies. But there are contradictions. I refer in particular to the way in which groups of Indigenous peoples – larger and more vocal in number – construct a hierarchy within Indigenous movements, which reflect the homogenising, hierarchical, and racist categories that created objects of them in the first place. Many of the activities of the conferences provide opportunities to share and gather ideas, but as many of my Indigenous colleagues have bemoaned – in Australia and Canada – 'real' Indian often means Navajo and 'real' black often means Maori. An awareness of the contradictions of race-based politics in these instances – including the rejection of simplistic, homogenised Indigenous identities – would provide useful moments from which to analyse and thus enrich understandings of what Indigenous education could look like in a post-colonial world.

The comparative nature of this study has also been useful in examining the institutional arrangements of AREP and NORTEP. NORTEP was a response to Indigenous calls for control over education in Canada and the need for Indigenous teachers to counteract negative experiences of schooling on the part of Indigenous children. Indigenous teachers were considered part of the response to inequitable outcomes and a way to promote cultural understandings and cultural maintenance. Similarly, in Australia, Indigenous teachers were to arrest the embarrassing outcomes for Indigenous students and to provide role models, as well as counteract racist stereotypes. Since these programs were created out of particular racialised understandings of culture – reified, traditional and static – we need to consider what they might look like if we use a model of culture as negotiated. The next question is therefore concerned with the relative methodological and theoretical strengths and weaknesses of the model of *culture as negotiation.*

From the perspective of method and theory, how useful has a model of culture as negotiation been?

As I argued in Chapters 3 and 4 racialisation produces particular tensions that have been predominately understood as cultural dissonance. It seemed important to move beyond fashion and prescription (McConaghy, 1994) in understanding Indigenous education and more specifically Indigenous teacher education. A reliance on cultural dissonance has discursively produced victims and oppressors. Such categories in social life alternatively rob people of agency or fail to account for change. In this study, we saw how teacher educators, students and administrators dealt with – and helped shape – the contradictions of racialisation. It was revealed that models of culture as impediment and culture as resource were limited in their ability to explain change or agency. Therefore, a model of culture was needed that was neither static nor prescriptive.

Developing a model of culture as negotiated was critical to moving the debate forward. This movement has to be from constructions of culture as static to models of culture as dynamic. 'Culture as negotiation' is also a useful method for resisting evangelism in Indigenous educational theorising. This is because it demonstrates that there is 'no quick fix' to living productively with difference nor with resolving entrenched social inequality. The preceding three chapters outlined many instances of the negotiation of culture in the AREP and NORTEP programs.

In this study, the concept of racialisation was used to demonstrate how power operates through the concept of culture. Here the various institutional and policy arrangements could be seen as contributing to particular constructions of culture in Indigenous education. When they provided space for culture, it was often in a way that also constrained other spaces.

The model of culture as negotiation provides an interdisciplinary approach because it involves using multiple levels of analysis. Without the differing levels, it would be impossible to understand the constraints on individuals, and the model of culture as negotiation could collapse into decontexualised accounts of interaction. This criticism of ethnography is founded on the basis of many studies that have 'read off' difference (McConaghy, 1997a; Singh, 1998) as opposed to examining how difference is constructed through negotiation of relations of power. Another problem is that negotiation is only one aspect shaping the lives of people. Once again, it is racialisation that shapes Indigenous and non-Indigenous experiences in the schoolyard, at the bus stop and in the labour market.

A model of culture as negotiation also nods in the direction of the metaphorical 'third' space posited in recent critiques of binaries. It is a useful heuristic device because it enables a way of thinking differently about the tensions in the field of Indigenous education other than collapsing into culturalist explanations. If culture is negotiated in these programs we can learn how tension can lead to productive as well as oppressive consequences. Culture as negotiation is therefore a good model because it shows that the field of Indigenous education is shaped by the habitus of students, teacher educators and administrators.

Indeed the concept of habitus enabled further capturing of this transformative social practice. For example, from habitus an individual can gain cultural and social capital that helps to navigate the field of Indigenous teacher education. Given the historical focus on identity in the field of Indigenous education it is not surprising that the interaction of the habitus of students and teachers and administrators is felt most urgently around such tensions. Often these tensions resulted from identity traps.

In conclusion, the model of culture as negotiation provided a dynamic model of culture to move the debate forward from explanations grounded in 'reading off' cultural difference. The model has explanatory power when examining the differences between Canadian and Australian contexts. This model provided a framework from which to think about the changing dimensions of Indigenous education. That is, it is possible to describe and analyse AREP and NORTEP in ways that move beyond culturalist explanations without denying culture. It then becomes possible to think about future directions in Indigenous teacher education using the framework of culture as negotiation. Before attending to these directions, the main issues arising from 'identity traps' need to be outlined.

How do the participants in this study navigate 'identity traps'?

At the micro-level, I examined the negotiation of racialised identities in the two programs. This revealed areas of tension for administrators, teacher educators and students. In part, this is a consequence of the 'identity traps' that we get into when we try to 'read difference'. The negotiation around, through and out of these traps, provided insights into the dynamics of cultural production. The question above is therefore concerned with returning to the theme of racialisation through the 'identity traps' that the participants in this study encounter. The question points to some important issues for future directions in the area of Indigenous teacher education and Indigenous education in general.

As I have argued in this book, racialisation processes have permeated Indigenous education policy and theory for some time in Australia and Canada. Unpacking the complexities of processes of racialisation as they shape identity is therefore an important task. In the last three chapters of this study, it was revealed how identity politics have created tensions because they are based on racialised understandings of culture. It was possible to see that there were gendered, classed and generational dimensions to identity that at times articulated with racialisation and at other times did not. The final three chapters named the tensions arising from processes of racialisation as they arose within the day-to-day workings of AREP and NORTEP. As Haig-Brown (1995:284) so aptly put it: "By naming tensions, people can begin to address them as issues."

The issues emerge when we examine the basis for these identity traps. Importantly, they are often revealed when we obtain a snapshot of both challenges to, and the reproduction of, the discourse of victim/oppressor that has underscored Indigenous policy making and theorising in education. These include challenges to the way in which the programs are funded; who controls them; how the curriculum is constructed and in whose interests; and how aboriginality and 'whiteness' is constructed.

By drawing on the tensions outlined in the final three chapters of this book, it was possible to see that negotiation was occurring around two key issues. The first of these is that identity in both programs is constructed around the concept of 'race', or culture as race. This leads to all sorts of misrecognition of, or misunderstandings about, identity on the part of students, teaching staff and administrators in the programs. The pathways available to Indigenous students in these situations have been shown to be essentialist or social constructivist. While the former is hegemonic, the social constructivist approach tussles with this tendency.

Non-Indigenous teacher educators also participate in identity politics. This is underscored by a concern about their place in the programs. Should white teachers be there or shouldn't they? If they are there how can they better 'know' the culture of the 'other'? For Indigenous teacher educators there is a struggle over whose Indigenous knowledge to include and how to present it. When we try to answer these questions it becomes easier to see the traps emanating from a focus on racialised identity. Identity traps occur when agents situate tensions in an inability to see or 'read' cultural difference. The fact that we cannot read difference without reifying some true and essential aboriginality or 'whiteness' is concealed.

The second key issue is a consequence of the first but it relates to funding and the issue of Indigenous control. If programs created on the basis of racialised identities are contributing to the ongoing formation of racialised identities, should there be separate Indigenous teacher education programs at all? Indeed, given the fiscal constraints, have they served their purpose? The first key issue about identity is a matter for struggle and negotiation within the programs. It is a task already being undertaken informally and one which will continue. The second key issue and the questions arising are more tied up with policy and it is one that will be considered in the next section.

Future directions

If we listen to the voices of students and their teacher educators, and indeed the administrators in these programs, we have to acknowledge that the two programs provide a different experience from that of full time, mainstream tertiary education. In addition, it is possible to see that Indigenous teacher education students do identify with Indigenous students in schools but not in any uniform way. These programs may therefore provide (for the time being at least) an opportunity to actively engage with and critique educational practices that are designed for Indigenous students. But it is the very diversity of what it means to be Indigenous which should drive these critiques.

Given that racialisation is embedded in the lives of the people in this study, the future of programs like AREP and NORTEP should be assured. They have both been very effective programs that have achieved their aims of increasing the number of Indigenous teachers in Saskatchewan and NSW. They have had to deal with difficult issues related to curriculum, teaching and administration along the way. Yet there are clearly some important issues to consider in terms of future directions. This leads to a number of questions, the answers to which, I think, provide some directions for the future.

Should Indigenous teacher education courses be separate or integrated? Can this experience at AREP and NORTEP be extended beyond those identified as Indigenous without destroying the supportive environment that so many participants have spoken about? How does racialisation relate to indigenisation/Aboriginalisation? What new questions arise about Indigenous teacher identity if these institutional and pedagogical arrangements change? How can teacher educators be more responsive to the specific histories and contexts of students in the two programs?

Separate or integrated?

In this study, it was evident that the AREP and NORTEP provided quite different experiences from mainstream integrated programs. It would be incorrect to conclude that this experience is only different because of the students' 'shared' Indigenous culture. The programs are also different from those provided for mainstream student teachers because of factors such as small group numbers allowing more discussion-based learning. However, the field of Indigenous education, into which all participants have been contained, has created a range of consciousness about racialisation. What has been revealed is a different experience emanating from dimensions of practice that are located in different cultural, geographical and gendered social relations. Aboriginality was thus only one aspect of identity – others are class, region, language – but a very important one.

The focus on a more contextualised learning, in addition to educational processes that are articulated with broad based community needs, is also an important factor in the success of NORTEP in particular. Arguably, these are the important aspects of the programs that have been produced out of the space created by 'separateness'.

The separate nature of the programs in terms of cultural maintenance and identity is also important. Not in any homogenised sense but purely from the point of view of being able to have space to speak about the differing dimensions of that experience. There is a need to be vigilant about homogenising tendencies but in this study we can see that the tensions produced through not attending to student diversity are challenged by agents, namely the students themselves. The principal contradiction will always be there, unresolvable, but once named, there is potential for negotiation.

In summary then, while there is a danger in these programs of reproducing racialised subjects, there are a number of contradictions to consider. They are as follows:

- The programs provide space for rethinking practice related to disadvantage and Indigenous educational disadvantage.
- Students in the programs do not need to 'teach' non-Indigenous students 'about' themselves using victim discourses.
- There is space for examining oppression in multiple ways including but not limited to race and discovering agency.
- The programs provide opportunity in a neo-colonial context which we may wish was gone but patently is not.
- The programs provide a context in which to challenge hegemonic constructions of racialised difference including privilege of the dominant group for students and staff.
- Lastly, there is an opportunity to challenge professional knowledge which, while not without value, nevertheless often reproduces relations of power through educational technologies of assessment, routines, expectations and the sifting and sorting processes of differentiation that exclude racialised difference as a marker of social inequality.

However, there seems little point in keeping the programs 'separate' if the opportunities to explore these dimensions of experience are not included. This is because of the danger in continuing programs that are focussed on identity maintenance alone. Such programs may indeed be more oppressive and limiting for students than sharing their classrooms with non-Indigenous students of a similar class and regional background given the long history of positive relations, as well as negative relations, many have had with each other. After all, they will be working with each other in the long term and Indigenous teachers cannot deal with all the issues on their own.

Indigenous control and the concept of indigenisation

One of the other important elements of separate programs is that they have provided space for Indigenous knowledge and pathways for Indigenous academics. However, indigenisation is a form of racialisation that has many more contradictions to resolve. How, for example, does indigenisation of teaching staff and administration challenge processes of racialisation? This question requires further research.

Also in this book, we found that students in these programs were experiencing quite different pedagogical relationships from those experienced by previous generations. In addition, many had 'white' members in their families. These factors will influence potential student numbers for both programs in the future. It seems to me that Indigenous control is a fundamentally different concept from indigenisation. Simply by increasing the number of Indigenous educators while actively rejecting non-Indigenous educators runs the risk of playing into the hands of 'race-based' politics. This is another contradiction of the racialisation of Indigenous peoples in Saskatchewan and NSW. When everything is collapsed into 'race' there is the danger that other inequalities related to class and gender are concealed. This can only lead to the continued oppression of those who might accept a unitary 'Aboriginal' identity but are not able to take advantages of tertiary education because of other socio-economic factors.

Negotiating Indigenous teaching identities

This study has shown that the production of Indigenous teaching identities is a dynamic process dependent upon understandings that students bring to the programs in terms of habitus in interaction with teacher educators, administrators and other students. While the concept of role model is problematic, students often pointed to a key role model who was prominent in their path to AREP or NORTEP.

We have also seen that an active questioning and searching and construction of what it means or might mean to be an Indigenous teacher is an important dynamic driving further developments of programs like AREP and NORTEP. Implicit here is an ongoing struggle against entrenched racisms within the education sector and in broader society.

This raises new questions about Indigenous teacher identity. If the concept of role model is limiting, then what is the point of having Indigenous teachers? One reason relates to social capital. This study found that many students came to teaching via pathways and networks based on family and community. These are social networks and as more Indigenous teachers are produced then social networks will be expanded. Another reason relates to increased cultural capital resulting from formal tertiary education. Cultural capital is used by students to expose and explore options and to benefit others within families. But another contradiction is that for many students their experiences in AREP and NORTEP led to conflict within their families.

When comparing the successes of programs like AREP and NORTEP we can see a number of important outcomes of these programs. Firstly, they have produced graduates working in many areas. They have also produced pathways for Indigenous academics. They brought to the programs knowledge about 'things that were Indigenous' as well as knowledge of teaching, yet their different experiences within the two programs led them to challenge these very static and homogenising categories.

Conclusion

From this comparative study, we can see that the viability of NORTEP rests in part on its links to the wider community. This is also of critical importance for a program like AREP. Over the next few years the development of more broad-based community support in terms of the curriculum, policy and process, will be critical to both programs. Thus, representativeness means more diversity in terms of staff, advisors and maybe eventually students. Indeed, indigenisation of the workplace may actively militate against broad based community support. This may have in fact been part of the reason that the Goolangullia Aboriginal Education Centre collapsed. The viability of the program I would argue rests upon questioning the policy of indigenisation through a reconstitution of democratic processes, such as those at NORTEP. It is evident that the program can only become stronger and more viable if this were to occur.

It is not surprising that exclusionary practices in higher education institutions have led to policies and practices of indigenisation. But indigenisation is no guarantee of effective programs. Conversely, acknowledging diversity does not necessarily mean that aboriginal programs are not needed. NORTEP is evidence of that. Indeed, the reality of educational contexts in most higher education institutions suggests that there are different dynamics operating in these programs which offer students and staff the opportunity to work through and analyse the legacies of colonial formations. These are the strengths of NORTEP and AREP.

Finally, the title of this book is Negotiating Racialised Identities. Negotiation is a concept that could be seen as agency free of constraint. This was not my intention in this book. Change is not revolutionary in democratic societies such as Australia and Canada; it is usually negotiated, albeit in unequal relations of power. This book has outlined the way in which Indigenous and non-Indigenous people have negotiated a way forward for Indigenous teacher education in Australia and Canada. This is an on-going process and the aim of this book was to provide some informed commentary on past developments and a guide to future directions.

Afterword

Since this book was written there has been some change in the status of the Metis. The Supreme Court decision on the matter of Metis hunting rights in Sault St. Marie, Ontario, was part of the Powley decision. This decision can be found on the Metis National Council web site (http://www.metisnation.ca).

The Canadian Constitution Act of 1982 stated that the "existing Aboriginal rights shall be protected and affirmed". However, the Canadian government holds the position that any rights the Metis might have had were extinguished through the scrip system, set out in the Manitoba Act and subsequently through the Dominion Lands Act. The Metis have always held that the Aboriginal rights continue today, and exist, not as a result of their Indian ancestors but that Metis rights arise from their Metis ancestry as a distinct Aboriginal people. The court upheld this position.

The Supreme Court case set out a determination that Metis rights do exist today, as it relates to the Metis community of Sault St. Marie, Ontario. The Metis Aboriginal rights are held by the Metis community and Steve Powley was recognized as being part of that Metis community. The court also suggests that the Metis may have other rights beyond the right to hunt for food in their traditional territories. It may extend to other areas, such as health and education for example.

Bibliography

500 Nations: Stories of the North American Indian Experience (1995) On compact disc, [CD-Rom]. Available: Microsoft Corporation, [5 November 1999].

Aboriginal Research Institute (1993) *Ethics in Aboriginal Research*, Faculty of Aboriginal and Islander Studies, University of South Australia, May.

Aboriginal Rural Education Program Review Document (1994, unpublished), Prepared by the Macarthur Aboriginal Liaison Unit (MALU), University of Western Sydney Macarthur, Sydney.

Ahenakew, D. (1974) *The Indian and Education*, Monograph No.2, Indian and Northern Education Program, College of Education, University of Saskatchewan, Saskatoon.

Ålund, A. (1991) 'Wrestling with ghosts', *Paradoxes of Multiculturalism*, A. Ålund and C.U. Schierup (eds), Research in Ethnic Relations Series, Aldershot, England, Avebury, pp.89–112.

Anderson, B. (1991) *Imagined Communities*, Verso, New York.

Andrews, R.J. and Hughes, P. (1988) 'Toward a Theoretical Framework for the Development of an Aboriginal Pedagogy', *Aboriginal Pedagogy Project, Curriculum Development Centre*, Department of Employment, Education and Training, Canberra.

Anthias, F. and Yuval-Davis, N. (1993) *Racialized Boundaries: race, nation, gender, colour and class and the anti-racist struggle*, Routledge, London.

Aplin, G., Foster, S.G. and McKernan, M. (1987) *Australians: A Historical Dictionary*, Fairfax, Syme & Weldon Associates, Sydney.

Archibald, J. and Bowman, S.S. (eds) (1995) 'Honouring What They Say: Postsecondary Experiences of First Nations Graduates', *Canadian Journal of Native Education*, Vol.21, No.1, pp.4–9.

Armitage, A. (1995) *Comparing the Policy of Aboriginal Assimilation: Australia, Canada and New Zealand*, UBC Press, Vancouver.

Armstrong, M. (1996) 'Aborigines: problems of race and class', *Class and Class Conflict in Australia*, R. Kuhn and T. O'Lincoln (eds), Longman, Melbourne, pp.58–73.

Aronowitz, S. and Giroux, H. (1993) 'Radical theories of schooling', *Education Still Under Siege*, Oise Press, Ontario, pp.65–109.

Attwood, B. (1989) *The Making of the Aborigines*, Allen and Unwin, Sydney.

Australia's Language: The Australian Language and Literacy Policy (1991) Department of Employment, Education and Training, Australian Government Printer, Canberra.

Australian College of Education (2001) *Teachers in Australian Schools: A Report from the 1999 National Survey, Executive Summary*, Department of Education, Training and Youth Affairs, ACT. Retrieved from WWW 4.10.01. http://www.detya.gov.au/schools/Publications/2001/pd/teachers1999.htm

Bacchi, C.L. (1990), '"Equal" versus "special" treatment', *Same Difference: Feminism and Sexual Difference*, Allen and Unwin, Sydney, pp.108–33.

Barman, J., Hébert, Y. and McCaskill, D. (eds) (1986) *Indian Education in Canada: Volume 1: The Legacy*, University of British Columbia Press, Vancouver.

———. (1987) *Indian Education in Canada: Volume 2: The Challenge*, University of British Columbia Press, Vancouver.

Bartra, R. (1977) 'The problem of the native peoples and indigenist ideology', *Race and Class in Post-colonial Society*, UNESCO, Paris, pp.421–44.

Becker, G. (1957) *The Economics of Discrimination*, University of Chicago Press, Chicago.

Beckett, J. (ed.) (1988) *Past and Present: The Construction of Aboriginality*, Aboriginal Studies Press, Canberra.

Berndt, C. (1994) 'Coloured lenses and social relationships', *Being Whitefella*, D. Graham (ed.), Freemantle Arts Centre Press, Fremantle, pp.151–61.

Bin Sallik, M.A. (1991) *Aboriginal Tertiary Education in Australia: How Well is it Serving the Needs of Aborigines?*, Aboriginal Studies Key Centre, University of South Australia, Underdale.

Bissoondath, N. (1994) *Selling Illusions: The Cult of Multiculturalism in Canada*, Penguin, Canada.

Blainey, G. (1984) *All For Australia*, Methuen, North Ryde.

Blair, D. (ed.) (1989) *The Pocket Macquarie Dictionary*, Jacaranda, Queensland.

Bolaria, Singh B. and Li, P.S. (eds) (1988) *Racial Oppression in Canada*, Garamond Press, Toronto.

Bottomley, G. (1994) 'Post-multiculturalism? The Theory and Practice of Heterogeneity', *Culture and Policy*, Vol.6, No.1, Australian Key Centre for Cultural and Media Policy.
http://www.gu.edu.au/centre/cmp/6_1_Introduction.html

Bourdieu, P. (1990) 'Structures, *habitus*, practices', *The Logic of Practice*, Polity Press, Cambridge, pp.52–65.

Bourdieu, P. and Wacquant, L.J.D. (1992) *An Invitation to Reflexive Sociology*, University of Chicago Press, Chicago.

Bourgeault, R. (1988) 'Race and Class under Mercantalism: Indigenous People in Nineteenth-Century Canada', *Racial Oppression in Canada*, 2nd edn, B. Bolaria, S. Singh and P. Li (eds), Garamond Press, Toronto, pp.41–70.

Bourke, C.J., Burden, J.K. and Moore, S. (1996) *Factors Affecting Performance of Aboriginal and Torres Strait Islander Students at Australian Universities: A Case Study*, Australian Government Publishing Service, Canberra.

Bourke, E., Farrow, R., McConnochie, K. and Tucker, A. (1991) *Career Development in Aboriginal Higher Education*, Evaluations and Investigations Program, Department of Employment, Education and Training, Australian Government Publishing Service, Canberra.

Bowles, S. and Gintis, H. (1976) *Schooling in Capitalist America: Educational Reform and the Contradictions of Economic Life*, New York, Basic Books.

Boyko, J. (1995) *Last Steps to Freedom: The Evolution of Canadian Racism*, Watson and Dwyer, Winnipeg.

Brady, W. (1992, unpublished) 'Beam me up Scotty! Communicating across World Views on Knowledge Principles and Procedures for the Conduct of Aboriginal and Torres Strait Islander Research', Paper presented at the *National Aboriginal and Torres Strait Islander Higher Education Conference*, Hervey Bay, 6–11 December.

Bredo, E. and Feinberg, W. (1979) 'Meaning, power and pedagogy: P. Bourdieu and J-C. Passeron, reproduction in education, society and culture: Essay review', *Journal of Curriculum Studies*, Vol.11, No.4, pp.315–32.

Brennan, F. (1991) *Sharing the Country*, Penguin, Victoria.

Brodie, V. (1993) 'Ordinary White', *The Wailing: A National Black Oral History*, S. Rintoul (ed.), William Heinemann, Melbourne, pp.279–318.

270

Buckley, H. (1993) *From Wooden Ploughs to Welfare: Why Indian Policy Failed in the Prairie Provinces*, McGill-Queen's University Press, Montreal.

Burgmann, V. (1993) *Power and Protest*, Allen and Unwin, Sydney.

Burnaby, B. (1979, unpublished) 'Roles of Languages in Education for Native Children in Ontario', PhD Thesis submitted to the University of Toronto.

Carleton, J. (1994, unpublished) 'Identity and Aboriginality Amongst AEAs in Sydney', Honours Thesis submitted to the University of Sydney.

Carnegie, S. (1991) *Program Review: Northern Teacher Education Program and Northern Professional Access College*, Saskatchewan Education and The NORTEP Council, Saskatchewan.

Castles, S. (1993) 'Racism and Global Change: Issues and Explanations', Background paper prepared for the *United Nations Meeting of Representatives of National Institutions and Organisations Promoting Tolerance and Harmony and Combating Racism and Racial Discrimination*, Sydney, Australia, 19–23 April.

———. (1996) 'The racisms of globalisation', *The teeth are smiling: The persistence of racism in multicultural Australia*, E. Vasta and S. Castles (eds), Allen and Unwin, Sydney, pp.17–45.

Castles, S., Cope, B., Kalantzis, M. and Morrissey, M. (1990) *Mistaken Identity - Multiculturalism and the Demise of Nationalism in Australia*, Pluto Press, Sydney.

Castles, S. and Miller, M.J. (1998) *The Age of Migration: International Population Movements in the Modern World*, Macmillan, Houndsmills.

Centre for Indigenous Australian Cultural Studies (1996, unpublished) 'Indigenous Australian Higher Education at UWS: A Brief History and Review', Centre for Indigenous Cultural Studies, University of Western Sydney.

Chan, J.B.L. (1997) 'Re-examining Police Culture', *Changing Police Culture: Policing in a Multicultural Society*, Cambridge University Press, New York, Melbourne and Cambridge, pp.65–93.

Collins, J. (1991) *Migrant Hands in a Distant Land*, 2nd edn, Pluto Press, Sydney.

———. (1993a) 'Cohesion with Diversity? Immigration and Multiculturalism in Canada and Australia', *School of Finance and Economics Working Paper Series*, No. 28, University of Technology, Sydney.

———. (1993b) 'Ethnic Diversity, "Cultural Capital" and Discrimination in the Australian Labour Market', Paper 2, *Communications and Workplace Conference*, University of Technology, Sydney, 1–4 September.

———. (1996) 'The Economics of Racism or the Racism of Economics', *Economics as a Social Science*, G. Argyrous and F. Stilwell (eds), Pluto Press, Sydney, pp.41–5.

Collins, J. and Castillo, A. (1998) *Cosmopolitan Sydney: Exploring the world in one city*, Pluto Press, Sydney.

Collins, J. and Henry, F. (1994) 'Racism, Ethnicity and Immigration in Canada and Australia', *Immigration and Refugee Policy: Australia and Canada Compared Vol II*, H. Adelman, A. Borowski, M. Burstein and L. Foster (eds), Melbourne University Press, Melbourne, pp.515–48.

Connell, R.W. (1982) *Making the Difference: schools, families and social division*, George Allen and Unwin, Sydney.

———. (1985) *Teachers' Work*, Allen and Unwin, Sydney.

———. (1993) 'Knowledge, Objectivity and Hegemony', *Schools and Social Justice*, Pluto Press, Sydney, pp.30–42.

———. (1996) *Gender and Power*, Polity Press, London.

Connell, W.F. (1993) 'The Setting', *Reshaping Australian Education 1960–1985*, The Australia Council for Educational Research (ACER), Victoria, pp.1–31.

Connolly, P. (1998) '"Dancing to the wrong tune": ethnography, generalization and research on racism in schools', *Researching Racism and Education: Politics, Theory and Practice*, P. Connolly and B. Troyna (eds), Open University Press, Buckingham, pp.122–39.

Coolangatta Statement (1993) World Indigenous Peoples Conference: Education Task Force, Wollongong.

Cope, B. (1993) 'Schooling in the World's Best Muslim Country', *Education Australia*, Issue No. 23, Education Australia, Leichhardt.

Cope, B. and Kalantzis, M. (1997) *Productive Diversity: A New, Australian Model for Work and Management*, Pluto Press, Sydney.

Council for Aboriginal Reconciliation (1993) *Walking Together*, No. 2, Australian Government Publishing Service, Canberra, February.

Cowlishaw, G. (1986) 'Race for Exclusion', *Australian and New Zealand Journal of Sociology*, Vol.22, No.1, pp.3–24.

———. (1988) 'Australian Aboriginal Studies: The Anthropologists' Accounts', *The Cultural Construction of Race*, M. de Lepervance and G. Bottomley (eds), Meglamedia, Sydney, pp.60–79.

Cowlishaw, G. and Morris, B. (eds) (1997) *Race Matters: Indigenous Australians and 'Our' Society*, Aboriginal Studies Press, Canberra.

Dale, R., Esland, G. and MacDonald, M. (eds), *Schooling and Capitalism: A Sociological Reader*, Routledge and Kegan Paul, London.

Daniels, D. (1986) 'The coming crisis in the indigenous rights movement: from colonialism to neo-colonialism to renaissance', *Native Studies Review*, Vol.2, No.2, pp.9–115.

de Lepervanche, M. and Bottomley, G. (1988) *The Cultural Construction of Race*, Meglamedia, Sydney.

Department of Employment, Education, and Training (1989) *National Aboriginal and Torres Strait Islander Education Policy*, Australian Government Publishing Service, Canberra.

Department of Indian Affairs and Northern Development, *1967-68 Annual Report*, Queen's Printer, Ottawa.

———. *1968-69 Annual Report*, Queen's Printer, Ottawa.

———. *1986-87 Annual Report*, Queen's Printer, Ottawa.

Dobbin, M. (1981) *The One-And-A-Half Men*, New Star Books, Vancouver.

Du Charme, M. (1986) 'The Canadian Origins of South African Apartheid', *Currents*, (Summer) No.2.

Eades, D. (1993) 'Aboriginal English', *Pen 93*, Primary English Teaching Association, Newtown, NSW.

Eldridge, J. and Eldridge, L. (1994) *Raymond Williams: Making Connections*, Routledge, London.

Ellsworth, E. (1994) 'Why doesn't this feel empowering? Working Through the Repressive Myths of Critical Pedagogy'(1989) Lynda Stone (ed) *The Education Feminism Reader*, Routledge, New York.

Evans, R. (1975) 'Keeping White the Stain', *Exclusion, Exploitation and Extermination*, R. Evans, K. Saunders and K. Cronin (eds), ANZ Books, Sydney.

Evans, R., Saunders, K. and Cronin, K. (1975) *Exclusion, Exploitation and Extermination*, ANZ Books, Sydney.

Faris, R. (1973) 'Community College Development in Saskatchewan: A Unique Approach', *The Failure of Educational Reform in Canada*, D. Myers (ed.), McLelland & Stewart Ltd., Canada.

Fay, B. (1996) *Contemporary Philosophy of Social Science*, Blackwell, Oxford.

Feagin, J., Vera, H. and Imani, N.O. (1996) *The Agony of Education: Black Students at White Colleges and Universities*, Routledge, New York.

Fine, M., Weis, L., Powell, L.C. and Wong, L.M. (1997) *Off White: Readings on Race, Power, and Society*, Routledge, New York.

Flannagan, T. (1971) *Louis 'David' Riel: Prophet of the New World*, Goodread Biographies, Nova Scotia.

Fleras, A. and Elliott, J.L. (1992) *The 'Nations Within': Aboriginal-State Relations in Canada, the United States, and New Zealand*, Oxford University Press, Toronto.

Fletcher, J.J. (1989a) *Documents in the History of Aboriginal Education in New South Wales*, Fletcher, J.J.: Carlton.

————. (1989b) *Clean, Clad and Courteous: A History of Aboriginal Education in New South Wales*, Fletcher, J.J.: Carlton.

Fowler, B. (1996) 'An introduction to Pierre Bourdieu's understanding', *Theory, Culture and Society*, Vol.13, No.2, pp.1–16.

Frideres, J.S. (1985) 'Native Land Claims', *Ethnicity and Ethnic Relations in Canada*, 2nd edn, R.M. Bienvenue and J.E. Goldstein (eds), Butterworths, Toronto.

————. (1988) *Native Peoples in Canada: Contemporary Conflicts*, 3rd edn, Prentice-Hall, Ontario.

Freire, P. (1972) *Pedagogy of the Oppressed*, Penguin, Harmondsworth.

Friesen, D.W. and Orr, J. (1995) *Voices of Northern Teachers*, McDowell Foundation, Saskatchewan Teachers Federation, Saskatoon.

Garcia, L.M. (1996) 'More black students quit university early', *Sydney Morning Herald*, 28 December.

Gilligan, C. (1977) 'In a different voice: Women's conception of the self and of morality', *Harvard Educational Review*, No. 47, pp.481–517.

————. (1994) 'Woman's Place in Man's Life Cycle', *The Education Feminism Reader*, L. Stone (ed.), Routledge, New York, pp.26–41.

Ginsberg, L. and Keys, P.R. (1995) *New Management in Human Services*, 2nd edn, NASW Press, Washington, DC.

Giroux, H.A. (1988) *Teachers as Intellectuals: Towards a Critical Pedagogy of Learning*, Bergin and Garvey, New York.

————. (1994) 'Travelling Pedagogies', *Disturbing Pleasures: Learning Popular Culture*, Routledge, New York, pp.153–71.

Goodall, H. (1996) *Invasion to Embassy: Land in Aboriginal Politics in New South Wales, 1770-1972*, Allen and Unwin, Sydney.

Goodall, H., Jakubowicz, A., Martin, J., Mitchell, T., Randall, L. and Seneviratne, K. (1990) *Racism, Cultural Pluralism and the Media*, A Report to the Office of Multicultural Affairs, University of Technology, Sydney.

Gordon, M. (1964) 'Assimilation in American Life: The Role of Race, Religion and National Origins', Oxford University Press, New York.

Gore, J. (1993) *The Struggle for Pedagogies*, Routledge, New York.

Goulet, K.N. (1996, unpublished) 'NORTEP: Northern Teacher Education Program, 1976-1996, A Brief Historical Overview', *World Indigenous Peoples Conference, Education*, 16–21 June, Albuquerque, New Mexico, USA.

Grenfell, M. and James, D. (eds) (1998) *Bourdieu and Education: Acts of Practical Theory*, Falmer Press, USA.

Griffiths, M. (1993) 'Self-identity and self-esteem: achieving equality in education', *Oxford Review of Education*, Vol.19, No.3, pp.301–17.

Grundy, S. (1994) 'The curriculum and teaching', *Understanding Teaching: Curriculum and the Social Context of Schooling*, E. Hatton (ed.), Harcourt Brace, Australia, pp.27–38.

Grundy, S. and Hatton, E.J. (1995) 'Teacher Educators' Ideological Discourses',
   Journal of Education for Teaching, Vol.21, No.1, pp.7–24.
Gunew, S. (n.d.) 'Feminism/Theory/Postcolonialism: Agency Without Identity',
   Photocopy.
Gunew, S. and Yeatman, A. (1993) *Feminism and the Politics of Difference,* Allen and
   Unwin, St. Leonards.
Hage, G. (1998) *White Nation: Fantasies of White supremacy in a multicultural society,*
   Pluto Press, Sydney.
Haig-Brown, C. (1988) *Resistance and Renewal: Surviving the Indian Residential
   School,* Tillacum Library, Vancouver.
———. (1995) *Taking Control: Power and Contradiction in First Nations Adult
   Education,* UBC Press, Vancouver.
Hall, S. (1987) 'Minimal Selves', *Identity: The Real Me,* The Institute of Contemporary
   Arts, London, pp.44–6.
———. (1992) 'New ethnicities', in *Race, Culture and Difference,* Open University,
   London, pp.252–9.
———. (1995) 'Negotiating Caribbean Identities', *New Left Review,* No. 209, Jan/Feb,
   p.5.
Hammersley, M. (1992) *What's Wrong With Ethnography?: Methodological
   Explorations,* Routledge, London.
Hammersley, M. and Atkinson, P. (1995) 'Insider Accounts: Listening and Asking
   Questions', *Ethnography: Principles in Practice,* Routledge, London, pp.124–56.
Handley, J. and Kowalchuk, M. (1969) *Indian and* Métis *Education Services in
   Saskatchewan,* Saskatoon Task Force on Indian-Métis Employment, Reference
   Paper 3, Saskatoon, May.
Harris, S. (1990) *Two-Way Aboriginal Schooling: Education and Cultural Survival,*
   Aboriginal Studies Press, Canberra.
Hatton, E. (ed.) (1994) *Understanding Teaching: Curriculum and the Social Context of
   Schooling,* Harcourt Brace, Australia.
Hawkins, F. (1989) *Critical Years in Immigration: Canada and Australia Compared,*
   McGill-Queen's University Press, Kingston and Montreal.
Hawthorn, H.B. (ed.) (1966) *A Survey of Contemporary Indians of Canada,* Vol. 1,
   Indian Affairs Branch, Ottawa.
———. (ed.) (1967) *A Survey of Contemporary Indians of Canada: Economic,
   Political and Educational Needs and Policies,* Vol. 2, Indian Affairs Branch,
   Ottawa.
Hebert, Y.M. (1993) 'The Transformation of Practitioners', *Selected Papers from the
   1988 and 1990 Mokakit Conference,* J. Archibald and S. Selkirk (eds), Mokakit
   Education Research Association, Vancouver.
Heller, A. (1989) 'On understanding social sciences', *Theory and Society,* No.18,
   pp.291–322.
Hesch, R.A. (1993, unpublished) 'Teachers on the Borderlands: The Ideological and
   Cultural Formation of Aboriginal Preservice Teachers', submission for D.Ed. to
   the University of Toronto, Canada.
———. (1995) 'Aboriginal Teachers as Organic Intellectuals', *Anti-Racism, Feminism
   and Critical Approaches to Education,* R. Ng, P. Staton and J. Scane (eds), Ontario
   Institute for Studies in Education, Toronto, pp.99–128.
———. (1996) 'Indigenous Teacher Education in Neo-liberal Settler Societies', Paper
   presented to the *World Indigenous Peoples Conference: Education,* Albuquerque,
   New Mexico, 20 June.

Hornung, R. (1991) *One Nation Under the Gun: Inside the Mohawk Civil War*, Stoddart, Toronto.

House of Representatives Standing Committee on Aboriginal and Torres Strait Islander Affairs (1992) *Mainly Urban. Report of the Inquiry into the needs of urban dwelling Aboriginal and Torres Strait Islander people*, Australian Government Publishing Service, Canberra.

Hughes, P. and More, A. (1993) 'Aboriginal Ways of Learning and Aboriginal Learning Patterns', Paper presented at *World Conference on Indigenous Peoples Education*, Wollongong, Australia, December. Includes Appendix: Learning Styles Identification Scale, Teaching Styles Identification Scale, Behavioural Indicators of Learning Styles.

Human Rights and Equal Opportunity Commission (1991) *Racist Violence: Report of the National Inquiry into Racist Violence in Australia*, Australian Government Publishing Service, Canberra.

Hursh, D. (1995) 'It's More Than Style: Reflective Teachers as Ethical and Political Practitioners', *Critical Discourses on Teacher Development*, J. Smyth (ed.), Cassell, London, pp.101–12.

Indian and Métis Education Policy from Kindergarten to Grade 12 (October 1995), Saskatchewan Education, Training and Employment, Saskatchewan.

Jackson, P. (1989) *Maps of Meaning: An Introduction to Cultural Geography*, Unwin Hyman, Australia.

James, R. (1997) '"Rousseau's Knot" the entanglement of liberal democracy and racism', *Race Matters*, G. Cowlishaw and B. Morris (eds), Aboriginal Studies Press, Canberra, pp.53–76.

Jhappan, C.R. (1992) 'Global Community? Supranational Strategies for Canada's Aboriginal Peoples', *The Journal of Indigenous Studies*, Vol.3, No.1, Gabriel Dumont Institute of Native Studies and Applied Research, Saskatchewan, Canada.

Joe, R. (1990) 'I Lost My Talk', *You Took My Talk: Aboriginal Literacy and Empowerment*, Fourth Report of the Standing Committee on Aboriginal Affairs, Queen's Printer, Canada.

Johnston, E., QC (1991) *Royal Commission into Aboriginal Deaths in Custody: National Report, Overview and Recommendations*, Australian Government Publishing Service, Canberra.

Johnston, K. (1990) 'Dealing with difference', *Education Links*, Issue No.38, Sydney.

Jones, A. (1998, unpublished) 'Pedagogical Desires at the Border: Absolution and Difference in the University Classroom', Paper presented to the *Winds of Change: Women and the Culture of the Universities International Conference*, Sydney, Australia, 13–17 July.

Jordan, D.F. (1984) 'The Social Construction of Identity', *Australian Journal of Education*, Vol.28, No.3, pp.274–90.

Jordan, D. (1985) *Support Systems for Aboriginal Students in Higher Education Institutions*, Vol. 1, Tertiary Education Authority of South Australia.

Jull, D. (1992) 'Indigenous Rights: After the Mabo Case', *Arena*, No. 99/100, pp.61–4, Arena, Melbourne.

Kalantzis, M. (1988) 'The Cultural Deconstruction of Racism: Education and Multiculturalism', *The Cultural Construction of Race*, M. de Lepervance and G. Bottomley (eds), Meglamedia, Sydney, pp.90–98.

———. (1990, unpublished) 'White Man Dreaming: Drawing Australia's Cultural Boundaries: Changes in Commonwealth Immigration and Aboriginal Policies, 1945-1967', PhD Thesis submitted to Macquarie University.

275

————. (1992) 'Competencies, Credentials and Cultures', *Education Australia*, Issue 18, Annandale Printing. Also presented as paper for the joint NSW Ethnic Affairs Commission/Office of Multicultural Affairs Seminar on the Mayer Committee's Proposals, 18 July.

————. (1994) *Cultural Understandings as the Eighth Key Competency*, Final Report to the Queensland Department of Education and the Queensland Vocational Education, Training and Employment Commission, James Cook University, Townsville.

Kalantzis, M., Cope, B., Noble, G. and Poynting, S. (1990) *Cultures of Schooling: Pedagogies for Cultural Difference and Social Access*, Falmer Press, U.K.

Kallen, E. (1990) 'Ethnicity and Human Rights in Canada', *Race and Ethnic Relations in Canada*, P. Li, B. Bolaria and B. Singh (eds), Oxford University Press, Toronto, pp.77–97.

Katz, C. (1992) 'All the World is Staged: Intellectuals and the Projects of Ethnography', *Environment and Planning D: Society and Space*, Vol.10, pp.495–510.

Keeffe, K. (1992) *From the Centre to the City: Aboriginal Education, Culture and Power*, Aboriginal Studies Press, Canberra.

Langton, M. (1981) 'Urbanizing Aborigines: The Social Scientists' Great Deception', *Social Alternatives*, Vol.2, No.2, Diamond Press, Brisbane, Australia, pp.16–22.

Langton, M. (1993) 'The social relationship between Aboriginal and non-Aboriginal', 'Well, I heard it on the radio and I saw it on the television...', Australian Film Commission, Sydney, pp.28–32.

Lechte, J. (1988) 'Ethnocentrism, Racism, Genocide...', *The Cultural Construction of Race*, M. de Lepervance and G. Bottomley (eds), Meglamedia, Sydney, pp.32–45.

Lennon, K. and Whitford, M. (eds) (1994) *Knowing the Difference: Feminist Perspectives in Epistemology*, Routledge, London.

Li, P. (1988) *The Chinese in Canada*, Oxford University Press, Toronto.

Linklater, C. (1973) *Indian Education: The World As It Was, The World As It Is, The World As We Want It To Be*, Monograph No.1, Indian and Northern Education Program, College of Education, University of Saskatchewan, Saskatoon.

Lipka, J. (1990) 'Cross-cultural perceptions of teaching styles', *Kaurna Higher Education Journal*, Issue 1, September, pp.33–42.

LiPuma, E. (1993) 'Culture in a theory of practice', *Bourdieu: Critical Perspectives*, C. Calhoun and M. Postone, (eds), Polity Press, Cambridge, pp.14–34.

Loos, N. and Miller, G. (eds) (1989) *Succeeding Against the Odds: The Townsville Aboriginal and Islander Teacher Education Program*, Allen and Unwin, Sydney.

Lortie, D. (1975) *Schoolteacher: A Sociological Study*, University of Chicago Press, Chicago.

Luck, J. (1998) *Australian indigenous students at University: How do we know them?*, http://www.swin.edu.au/aare/98pap/luc98214.html. Retrieved 18.4.99, 11.13am.

Luke, A., Luke, C. and Mayer, D. (2000) 'Redesigning Teacher Education', *Teaching Education*, Vol.11, No.1, Editorial.

Lynch, H.M. (1990, unpublished), '"Aboriginal" Education Centres in Institutions of Higher Education: A Case Study', Thesis submitted to the Faculty of Education, University of New England, Armidale.

Macarthur Institute of Higher Education (1984) *Aboriginal Rural Education Program: Submission to New South Wales Higher Education Board*, November, 61pp.

Malik, K. (1996) *The Meaning of Race: Race, History and Culture in Western Society*, MacMillan, London.

Malin, M. (1990) 'Invisibility and visibility of the Aboriginal child in an urban classroom', *Australian Journal of Education*, Vol.34, No.3, pp.312–39.

————. (1997) 'Mrs Eyers is no ogre', *Race Matters*, G. Cowlishaw and B. Morris (eds), Aboriginal Studies Press, Canberra, pp.139–60.

Manyarrows, V. (1994) 'Colorism in the Indian Community', *Skin Deep: Women Writing on Color, Culture and Identity*, Crossing Press, California.

Marginson, S. (1993) *Education and Public Policy in Australia*, Cambridge University Press, Australia.

————. (1997a) 'Civics, Citizenship and Difference', *Educating Australia: government, economy and citizen since 1960*, University Cambridge Press, U.K., pp.245–58.

————. (1997b) *Markets in Education*, Allen and Unwin, Sydney.

Markus, A. (1988) 'Australian Governments and the Concept of Race: An Historical Perspective', *The Cultural Construction of Race*, M. de Lepervance and G. Bottomley (eds), Meglamedia, Sydney, pp.46–59.

Martin, J. (1978) *The Migrant Presence: Australian Responses 1947-77*, Allen and Unwin, Sydney.

Massey, D. (1984) 'Introduction: Geography Matters', *Geography Matters: A Reader*, D. Massey and J. Allen (eds), Cambridge University Press, Cambridge, pp.1–11.

Mazurek, K. (1987) 'Multiculturalism, Education and the Ideology of the Meritocracy', *The Political Economy of Canadian Schooling*, T. Wotherspoon (ed.), Methuen, Toronto, pp.141–64.

McConaghy, C. (1994) 'Fashion and Prescription in Representations of Indigenous Education', *Discourse*, Vol.15, No.2, University of Queensland, Australia, pp.81–4.

————. (1997a) *Rethinking Indigenous Adult Education: Culturalism and the Production of Disciplinary Knowledges in a Colonial Context*, PhD Thesis, University of Queensland, December.

———— (1997b) 'Containing diversity: The National Aboriginal and Torres Strait Islander Policy', *A National Approach to Schooling in Australia? Essays on the development of national policies in school education*, B. Lingard and P. Porter (eds), Australian College of Education, Canberra.

McConnochie, K. (1990), *Report on Staff Development Workshop Aboriginal Education Unit*, University of Western Sydney Macarthur, 19–23 February.

McConnochie, K., Pettman, J. and Hollinsworth, D. (1988) *Race and Racism in Australia*, Social Science Press, Wentworth Falls.

McLaren, P. (1994) 'Postmodernism and the Death of Politics', *Politics of Liberation: Paths from Freire*, P. McLaren and C. Lankshear (eds), Routledge, London, pp.193–215.

McLaren, P. and Lankshear, C. (eds) (1994) *Politics of liberation: Paths from Freire*, Routledge, London and New York.

McNinch, J. (1994) *The Recruitment and Retention of Aboriginal Teachers in Saskatchewan Schools*, [On-line] In SSTA Research Centre Report #94-10, Available: http://www.ssta.sk.ca/research/education_equity/94-10.htm [July 15, 1999].

McPherson, J.C. (1991) *MacPherson Report on Tradition and Education: Towards a Vision of our Future*, Department of Indian Affairs and Northern Development (DIAND), Ottawa.

Miles, R. (1982) *Racism and Migrant Labour*, Routledge and Kegan Paul, London.

————. (1993) *Racism after 'race relations'*, Routledge, London.

————. (1994) 'Explaining Racism in Contemporary Europe', *Racism, Modernity and Identity on the Western Front*, A. Rattansi and S. Westwood (eds), Polity Press, Cambridge, pp.189–221.

Miller, G. (1989) 'A reflective analysis of cross-cultural curriculum planning: The development of the Diploma of Teaching (Early Childhood Education)', *Succeeding Against the Odds: The Townsville Aboriginal and Islander Teacher Education Program*, N. Loos and G. Miller (eds), Allen and Unwin, Sydney, pp.117–44.

Mishler, E.G. (1986) *Research Interviewing: Context and Narrative*, Harvard University Press, Massachusetts.

Morgan, S. (1987) *My Place,* Fremantle Arts Centre Press, Fremantle.

Morris, B. (1988) 'The politics of identity: from Aborigines to the first Australian', *The Cultural Construction of Race*, J. Beckett, M. de Lepervance and G. Bottomley (eds) Meglamedia, Sydney, pp.63–86.

Morris, B. and Cowlishaw, G. (1997) 'Introduction: Cultural Racism', *Race Matters: Indigenous Australians and 'Our' Society*, G. Cowlishaw and B. Morris (eds), Aboriginal Studies Press, Canberra, pp.1–10.

Morrison, T. (1993) 'Introduction', *Race-ing Justice, En-gendering Power*, Chatto and Windus, London, pp.vii-xxx.

Morrow, L. (1984) 'Colonisation: Alive and Well in Australia Today', *Women and Labour Conference*, Brisbane.

Muirhead, Justice J.H. (1988) *Interim Report, Royal Commission into Aboriginal Deaths in Custody*, Australian Government Publishing Service, Canberra.

Nakata, M. (1991, unpublished) 'Constituting the Torres Strait Islander: A Foucauldian discourse analysis of the National Aboriginal and Torres Strait Islander Education Policy', B.Ed. (Hons) Thesis presented to James Cook University, Townsville.

———. (1997) 'Who's reading "Misplaced Hopes"?', *Qualitative Studies in Education*, Vol.10, No.4, pp.425–31.

National Aboriginal and Torres Strait Islander Education Policy (1989) Department of Employment, Education and Training, Canberra.

National Aboriginal Education Committee (NAEC) (1986) *Policy Statement on Teacher Education for Aborigines and Torres Strait Islanders*, Australian Government Publishing Service, Canberra.

National Indian Brotherhood (1972) *Indian Control of Indian Education*, National Indian Brotherhood, Ottawa.

National Inquiry into the Separation of Aboriginal and Torres Strait Islander People from their Families (1997) *Bringing Them Home: Report of the National Inquiry into the Separation of Aboriginal and Torres Strait Islander People from their Families*, Human Rights and Equal Opportunity Commission, Sydney.

National Review of Education for Aboriginal and Torres Strait Islander Peoples: Final Report (1995), Department of Employment, Education and Training, Canberra.

Ng, R. (1991) 'Sexism, Racism and Canadian Nationalism', *Race, Class, Gender: Bonds and Barriers*, J. Vorst (ed.), Garamond, Toronto, pp.12–26.

Nicholls, C., Crowley, V. and Watt, R. (1996) 'Theorising Aboriginal Education: Surely it's time to move on?', *Education Australia*, No. 33, Education Australia, Sydney, pp.6–9,

Northern Teacher Education Program and Northern Access Program Information Package (1995) November.

———. (1996) Statistical Data.

Omi, M. and Winant, H. (1993) 'On the theoretical concept of race', *Race Identity and Representation in Education*, C. McCarthy and W. Critchlow (eds), Routledge, New York, pp.3–10.

O'Neil, J.D. and Waldram, J.B. (1989) 'Native Health Research in Canada: Anthropological and Related Approaches', *Native Studies Review*, Vol.5, No.1, p.15.

Parbury, N. (1986) *Survival: A History of Indigenous Life in New South Wales*, Ministry of Indigenous Affairs, New South Wales.

Park, R. (1922) 'Our Racial Frontier on the Pacific', *Survey Graphic*, Issue 9, pp.192–6.

Partington, G. and McCudden, B. (1992) *Ethnicity and Education*, Blackheath, Social Science Press.

Patterson, E.P. (1972) *The Canadian Indian: A History Since 1500*, Collier-MacMillan, Ontario.

———. (1988) 'Native-White Relations', *Social Inequality in Canada: Patterns, Problems, Policies*, J. Curtis, E. Grabb, N. Guppy and S. Gilbert (eds), Prentice-Hall, Ontario, pp.230–4.

Pearson, N. (1993) 'Mabo: addressing a 200-year grievance', in *The Sydney Morning Herald*, 11 November, p.11.

Pettman, J. (1991) 'Racism, Sexism and Sociology', *Intersexions*, G. Bottomley, M. de Lepervanche and J. Martin (eds), Allen and Unwin, Sydney, pp.187–202.

———. (1992) *Living in the Margins*, Allen and Unwin, Sydney.

Petty, B. (1994) 'Try listening to softer voices', *Being Whitefella*, D. Graham (ed.), Fremantle Arts Centre Press, Fremantle, pp.31–7.

Plummer, K. (1983) 'The Doing of Life Histories', *Documents of Life: An Introduction to the Problems and Literature of a Humanistic Method*, Allen and Unwin, London, pp.84–118.

Poynting, S. (1995, unpublished) 'Moving the "Posts": Post-Marxist Concepts of Class and Theories of New Social Movements', PhD Thesis, School of Sociology, University of New South Wales.

Poynting, S. and Noble, G. (1995) 'Racism and the "common sense" of "learning styles"', *Education Links*, Issue No. 51, Sydney.

Prentice, A.L. and Houston, S.E. (1975) *Family, School and Society In Nineteenth Century Canada*, Oxford University Press, Toronto.

Purvis, T. and Hunt, A. (1993) 'Discourse, ideology, discourse, ideology, discourse, ideology...', *British Journal of Sociology*, Vol.44, No.3, September.

Rattansi, A. (1992) 'Changing the subject? Racism, culture and education', *'Race', Culture and Difference*, J. Donald and A. Rattansi (eds), Sage, London, pp.11–48.

Read, P. (1982) *The Stolen Generations: The Removal of Aboriginal Children in NSW 1883 – 1969*, Ministry for Aboriginal Affairs, Sydney.

Read, P. and Edwards, C.I. (1989) *The Lost Children*, Doubleday, Moorebank, NSW, Australia.

Redbird, D. (1980) *We Are Métis: A Métis View of the Development of a Native Canadian People*, Ontario Métis and Non-Status Indian Association, Toronto.

Reeves, F. (1983) *British Racial Discourse*, Cambridge University Press, Cambridge.

Regnier, R., Murphy, K., Smillie, R. and Baldhead, S. (1988) 'Acting and Taking Care of People at the Saskatoon Native Survival School', *Ourschools/Ourselves*, Vol.1, No.1, October, pp.22–44.

Reid, C. (1991, unpublished) 'Girls on the Block: Aboriginality, Schooling and the lives of teenage girls in Redfern', Honours Thesis presented to Macquarie University, Sydney.

———. (1992) 'Sick to Death: The Health of Indigenous People in Canada and Australia', Paper presented at the *Racial Minorities, Medicine and Health Conference*, May, University of Saskatchewan, Saskatoon, Canada.

————. (1993) '2001: A Race Odyssey: Nationalism and the Social Construction of Aboriginality in Australia', Paper presented at the *31st Congress of the International Institute of Sociology*, Sorbonne, Paris, France, 21–25 June. Session on 'Nation States, Communal Conflicts and Citizenship'.

Reid, C. and Holland, W. (1996) 'Aboriginal Rural Education Program: A Case Study in Anti-Racist Strategies', *The Teeth are Smiling: The Persistence of Racism in Multicultural Australia*, E. Vasta and S. Castles (eds), Allen and Unwin, Sydney, pp.112–28.

Reid, C. (1999) 'Whose Self-esteem? Urban Aboriginal students, identity and inequality in education' in *Education Links,* Centre for Popular Education, University of Technology, Sydney.

Reid, J. and Trompf, P. (1991) *The Health of Aboriginal Australia*, Harcourt Brace Jovanovich, Sydney.

Rex, J. (1983) *Race Relations in Sociological Theory*, Routledge and Kegan Paul, London.

Reynolds, H. (1981) *The Other Side of the Frontier*, James Cook University, Townsville.

————. (1987) *The Law of the Land*, Penguin, Ringwood.

Reynolds, H. (1999) *Why Weren't We Told?: A personal search for the truth about our history*, Viking, Ringwood, Victoria.

Richmond, A. (1973) *Migration and Race Relations in an English City*, Oxford University Press, London.

Rintoul, S. (1993) *The Wailing: A National Black Oral History*, William Heinemann Australia, Melbourne.

Rizvi, F. (1987) *Multiculturalism as an educational policy*, Deakin University, Victoria.

Rowse, T. (1988) 'Middle Australia and the noble savage: a political romance', *Past and Present: The Construction of Aboriginality*, J. Beckett (ed.), Aboriginal Studies Press, Canberra, pp.161–79.

————. (1993) *After Mabo: Interpreting indigenous traditions*, Melbourne University Press, Victoria.

Royal Commission on Aboriginal Peoples (1996) *Guide to the Principal Findings and Recommendations of the Final Report of the Royal Commission on Aboriginal Peoples*, Minister of Supply and Services, Ottawa, Canada.

Rust, V.D. (1991) 'Postmodernism and Its Comparative Education Implications', *Comparative Education Review*, November, pp.610–26.

Ryan, W. (1976) *Blaming the Victim*, Vintage Books, New York.

Saskatchewan Indigenous Languages Committee (1991) *On The Critical List: Sociolinguistic Survey of Indigenous Languages in Saskatchewan*, Centre for Second Language Instruction, Saskatoon, Canada.

Saskatchewan Newstart (1972) *Cutback*, Saskatchewan Newstart Inc, Prince Albert, Canada.

Saskatchewan Teachers' Federation (1992) *Indian and Métis Education: Background Paper*, Saskatchewan Teachers' Federation, Saskatoon, April.

Schissel, B. and Wotherspoon, T. (1998) *An Investigation into Indian and Métis Student Life Experience in Saskatchewan Schools*, Research Report to The Minister of Education, Province of Saskatchewan, for the Saskatchewan Indian and Métis Education Research Project, October.

Sennett, R. and Cobb, J. (1972) *The Hidden Injuries of Class*, W. Norton and Co., New York.

Sherwood, J. (ed.) (1982) *Aboriginal Education: Issues and Innovations*, Creative Research, Perth.

She's The First Aboriginal Certificated Teacher: A Credit to Her People (n.d.) photocopy from Department of School Education files.

Sikes, P., Measor, L. and Woods, P. (1985) *Teacher Careers: Crises and Continuities*, Falmer, London.

Singh, M. (1998) 'Globalism, cultural diversity and tertiary education', *Australian Universities' Review*, Vol.41, No.2, pp.12–17.

Slaughter, S. (1991) 'The "Official" Ideology of Higher Education: Ironies and Inconsistencies', *Culture and building the responsive university*, W.G. Tierney (ed.), George Washington University, School of Education and Human Development, Washington DC.

Sleeter, C.E. (1992) *Keepers of the American dream: A study of staff development and multicultural education*, Falmer, London.

Sleeter, C. (1993) 'White Teachers Construct Race', *Race, Identity and Representation in Education*, C. McCarthy and W. Crichlow (eds), Routledge, New York, pp.157–71.

Solomos, J. and Back, L. (1994) 'Conceptualising Racisms: Social Theory, Politics and Research', *Sociology*, Vol.28, No.1, February.

———. (1996) *Racism and Society*, MacMillan, London.

Stasiulis, D.K. (1990) 'Theorizing Connections: Gender, Race, Ethnicity and Class', *Race and Ethnic Relations in Canada*, P.S. Li (ed.), Oxford University Press, Toronto, pp.269–305.

Sykes, R.B. (1986) *Incentive, Achievement and Community*, Sydney University Press, Sydney.

Tajfel, H. (1978) *Differentiation Between Social Groups: Studies in the Social Psychology of Intergroup Relations*, Academic Press, London.

Tatz, C. (1987) *Aborigines in sport*, Australian Society for Sports History, Bedford Park, South Australia.

———. (1996) 'Black diamonds: the Aboriginal and Islander Sports Hall of Fame', Allen and Unwin, St Leonards, NSW.

Taylor, C. (1994) 'The Politics of Recognition', *Multiculturalism: Examining the Politics of Recognition*, A. Gutman (ed.), Princeton University Press, Princeton, pp.25–74.

The Globe and Mail (1992) 'Native Women cling to Charter', 25 May.

Tierney, W.G. (1993) 'Cultural Citizenship and Educational Democracy', *Building Communities of Difference: Higher Education in the twenty-first Century*, OISE Press, Toronto, pp.127–58.

Troyna, B. (1992) 'Multicultural and Anti-Racist Education Policies', *Racism and Education: Structures and Strategies*, D. Gill, B. Mayor and M. Blair (eds), Sage, London.

———. (1993) 'From Deracialisation to Racialisation', *Racism and Education*, Open University Press, Buckingham, pp.21–42.

———. (1994) 'The "Everyday World" of Teachers? Deracialised discourses, the sociology of teachers and the teaching profession', *British Journal of Sociology of Education*, Vol.15, No.3, pp.325–39.

———. (1998) '"The whites of my eyes, nose, ears...": a reflexive account of "whiteness" in race-related research', *Researching Racism in Education: Politics, Theory and Practice*, P. Connolly, and B. Troyna (eds), Open University Press, Buckingham, pp.95–108.

Tucker, W.H. (1994) *The Science and Politics of Racial Research*, University of Illinois Press, Chicago.

Ujimoto, V. (1990) 'Studies of Ethnic Identity and Race Relations', *Race and Ethnic Relations in Canada*, P. Li (ed.), Oxford University Press, Toronto.

van den Berghe, P. (1967) *Race and Racism: A Comparative Perspective*, John Wiley & Sons, New York.

Vasta, E. and Castles, S. (1996) *The teeth are smiling: The persistence of racism in multicultural Australia*, Allen and Unwin, Sydney.

Waldram, J.B. (1989) 'Native People and Health Care in Saskatoon', *Native Studies Review*, Vol.1, No.5, pp.97–113.

Walton, C. (1997) 'Traeger Park School: A Case for Human Rights?', *Indigenous Education: Historical, Moral and Practical Tales*, S. Harris and M. Malin (eds), Northern Territory University Press, Darwin, pp.39–47.

Wammarra Aboriginal Education Centre (1992) *First of Its Kind: N.S.W. Aboriginal Education Policy Implementation Evaluation*, Vol.1, Report, Department of Education, NSW, Sydney.

Ward, M.S. (1986) 'Indian Education: Policy and Politics, 1972-1982', *Canadian Journal of Native Education*, Vol.13, no 2.

Watts, B. (1971) (ed.) *Report of The National Workshop on Aboriginal Education: Priorities for Action and Research*, Department of Education, University of Queensland.

Weaver, S. (1983) 'Australian Aborigine Policy: Aboriginal Pressure Groups or Government Advisory Bodies?', *Oceania*, No.54, pp.1–22, 85–108.

Whatman, S. (1995), 'Promoting Indigenous Participation at Tertiary Institutions: Past Attempts and Future Strategies', *The Aboriginal Child At School: A National Journal for Teachers of Aborigines and Torres Strait Islanders*, Vol.23, No.1, February/March, University of Queensland Printery, Brisbane, pp.36–43.

Whitty, G. (1985) 'The Curriculum as Ideological Practice', *Sociology and School Knowledge: Curriculum Theory, Research and Politics*, Methuen, London.

———. (1994) *Deprofessionalising Teaching?*, Occasional Paper No. 22, The Australian College of Education, Canberra.

Whyte, K. (1983) 'The Development of Curricula/Programs for Indian and Métis People', *Canadian Journal of Native Education*, Vol.9, No.2.

Wildman, S.M. (1996) *Privilege Revealed: How Invisible Preference Undermines America*, New York University Press, New York.

Williams, R. (1988) *Keywords: A Vocabulary of Culture and Society*, Fontana Press, London.

Williamson, A. (1997) 'Misplaced hopes or misplaced meanings? A Rejoinder to Martin Nakata', *Qualitative Studies in Education*, Vol.10, No.4, pp.433–9.

Willis, P. (1981) *Learning to Labour*, Columbia University Press, New York.

Wilson, J. (1973) *Power, Racism and Privilege*, Free Press, New York.

Wotherspoon, T. (1991) 'Indian Control or Controlling Indians?: Barriers to the Occupational and Educational Advancement of Canada's Indigenous Population', *Hitting the Books: The Politics of Educational Retrenchment*, Garamond, Toronto.

———. (1995) 'Multiculturalism and the Management of Race and Ethnic Relations in Canadian Schooling', *Multicultural Education in a Changing Global Economy: Canada and the Netherlands*, T. Wotherspoon and P. Jungbluth (eds), Waxmann Münster, New York, pp.41–60.

———. (1998) *The Sociology of Education in Canada: A Critical Perspective*, Oxford University Press, Ontario.

———. (1999) *Aboriginal/Non-Aboriginal Dimensions of Social Differentiation, Inclusion and Exclusion in Canada*, A discussion paper for the Project on Trends and Social Differentiation Theme, March, Department of Sociology, University of Saskatchewan.

Wotherspoon, T. and Jungbluth, P. (1995) *Multicultural Education in a Changing Global Economy: Canada and the Netherlands*, Waxmann Münster, New York.

Wotherspoon, T. and Satzewich, V. (1993) 'The State and the Contradictions of Indian Administration', *First Nations: Race, Class and Gender Relations*, Nelson, Canada, pp.15–41.

Yeatman, A. (1994) 'Postmodern Epistemological Politics and Social Science', *Knowing the Difference: Feminist Perspectives in Epistemology*, K. Lennon and M. Whitford (eds), Routledge, London, pp.187–202.

York, G. (1990) *The Dispossessed: Life and Death in Native Canada*, Vintage, London.

Young, R.A. (1995) *Colonial Desire: Hybridity in Theory, Culture and Race*, Routledge, London.

Yunupingu, M. (1998) 'Homelands', *Australian Schooldays*, B. Niall and I. Britain (eds), Oxford University Press, Australia, pp.329–33.

Glossary

AECG – Aboriginal Education Consultative Group
AFN – Assembly of First Nations
AREP – Aboriginal Rural Education Program
CIACS – Centre for Indigenous Australian Cultural Studies
DIAND – Department of Indian Affairs and Northern Development
GAEC – Goolangullia Aboriginal Education Centre
ITEP – Indian Teacher Education Program
MALU – Macarthur Aboriginal Liaison Unit
NIB – National Indian Brotherhood
NIC – National Indian Council
NORTEP – Northern Teacher Education Program
SIFC – Saskatchewan Indian Federated College
SUNTEP – Saskatchewan Urban Native Teacher Education Program
TEPS – Teacher Education Programs

LaVergne, TN USA
24 August 2009
155844LV00002B/38/P